Managing Copyright

Emerging Business Models in the Individual and Collective Management of Rights

Managing Copyright

Emerging Business Models in the Individual and Collective Management of Rights

Edited by Rudolf Leška

ALAI ČESKÁ REPUBLIKA

Wolters Kluwer

Published by:
Kluwer Law International B.V.
PO Box 316
2400 AH Alphen aan den Rijn
The Netherlands
E-mail: lrs-sales@wolterskluwer.com
Website: www.wolterskluwer.com/en/solutions/kluwerlawinternational

Sold and distributed by:
Wolters Kluwer Legal & Regulatory U.S.
7201 McKinney Circle
Frederick, MD 21704
United States of America
E-mail: customer.service@wolterskluwer.com

and

Published by:
Wolters Kluwer CZ, U Nákladového nádraží 10, 130 00 Praha 3
E-mail: obchod@wolterskluwer.com
Website: www.wolterskluwer.com

1st edition, 2022, 288 pages

ISBN 978-94-035-0777-4 (Kluwer Law International)
ISBN 978-94-035-0757-6 (e-book, Kluwer Law International)
ISBN 978-80-7676-521-4 (Wolters Kluwer CZ)
ISBN 978-80-7676-522-1 (e-book, Wolters Kluwer CZ)

OBSAH

PART I
INTRODUCTION

WELCOME ADDRESS DELIVERED AT THE OPENING OF THE 2019 ALAI CONGRESS IN PRAGUE

RECONSIDERING THE ROLE OF NATIONAL COLLECTING SOCIETIES

Frank Gotzen*

I am very glad to be back in Prague again.

My first time to come here dates back to 1993, not so long after the end of the communist regime, in a period where you could still walk rather quietly over the Charles bridge without bumping into a mass of tourists. I was happy then to find bed and breakfast at the private home of a colleague of the Charles University. He was a professor in mathematics and very glad to receive a paying guest in his house.

It was amongst other things an occasion for me to discover the real taste of a beer from Plzeň, so different from the various so-called Pilsner beers used as a common denomination for a type of lager beer. And what to say about that marvellous beer from Budvar the taste of which has got nothing in common with the flavourless beverage that is sold in many countries under the German name of Budweiser or Bud. Quite rightly, the Czech brewers invoked unfair competition and trademark arguments in trying to oppose it.

However, in our meeting in Prague now, we are not going to talk on unfair competition rules, nor on trademark law, but we will turn instead to another subject of intellectual property law that is at the very heart and soul of our international association: copyright.

Collective management organisations, especially in the musical field, try to offer as much as possible, both to users as well as to individual authors, a one stop system. Through a worldwide network of reciprocal representation agreements they rely on the local CMO to take care for the protection of their repertoires in another State. This efficient system has been baptized afterwards the "monoterritorial multirepertoire" system. It possessed the huge advantage of offering in each country, at a single address, a worldwide repertoire.

* Prof. Frank Gotzen, Founder and Director Emeritus of the Centre for Intellectual Property Rights, K.U. Leuven, visiting Professor for the Master en Propriedad Intellectual of the Universidad Autónoma de Madrid, member of the Belgian High Council for Intellectual Property, President of the International Copyright Association ALAI.

A WORD FROM THE EDITOR

Rudolf Leška*

It is my pleasure to present to you this collection of papers and reports which encompasses a substantial amount of our current global knowledge in the field of collective management of authors' and related rights. This volume is an output of the 2019 ALAI Congress held in Prague where scholars and practitioners met to discuss outstanding issues related to collective management at the occasion of the 100th anniversary of the establishment of the first Czechoslovak collective management organization. While the full schedule of the congress forms an annex to this book, the individual national reports (summarized in this book by Professor Matanovac Vučković) prepared by the respective national groups of ALAI had to be excluded; you can find them online at the official website of the congress at www.alai2019.org. It was a successful congress, held under the auspices of his excellency, the President of the Czech Republic, with the prominent presence of Mr. Archambeau, the executive director of EU IPO, Mrs. Sylvie Forbin, WIPO Deputy Director General, Mr. Gadi Oron, Director General of CISAC and many other representatives of Czech and foreign governments, collective management organizations, academic institutions and legal practitioners. More than 300 attendees from 44 countries across all continents could visit various Czech landmarks and enjoy a performance of the thoroughly Czech opera Dalibor at the National Theatre, a Pinchas Zukerman concert with the Prague Symphony Orchestra or a very pleasant gala dinner with a musical performance of Czech pieces for a piano trio presented by George Spera (piano), Silke von Lewinski (violin) and Tatsuhiro Ueno (violoncello). To mark the occasion, the Prague 1 post office issued a special stamp on the day of the congress with an image of Prague by Jiří Slíva (which was also used as the congress logo).

As the reader can see, in this book we have taken the liberty to arrange the content somewhat unconventionally. Instead of simply copying the order of the panels presented in Prague, we have decided to start with the opening speeches followed by "full-scale" studies that were written by scholars as a follow-up to the speeches that

---

* Dr. Rudolf Leška is an Attorney-Partner at the copyright boutique firm ŠTAIDL LEŠKA ADVOKÁTI (PRAHA – BRATISLAVA), licensed in Czechia and Slovakia to represent the entertainment industry and advise other clients and the public sector in transactions and litigation concerning the media and copyright. Dr. Leška holds the position of Senior Assistant Professor in copyright and media law at the University of Finance and Administration, Prague (Vysoká škola finanční a správní). He serves as the current President of ALAI Czech Republic.

they presented at the congress. This part is followed by "reports" – brief papers summarizing the contributions of their writers presented at the congress. The book concludes with the general report and summarizing remarks by Professor Paul Torremans.

Unfortunately, not everyone who participated in the panels at the congress is represented in this volume, since the time constraints and the need to focus on other duties have not allowed everyone to prepare a written summary of their thoughts. It is my sincere hope that the strange times of COVID 19 followed by the shameful invasion of the Russian army in Ukraine will soon be over and that ALAI congresses will once again flourish and attract a large number of attendees. My only advice is to take part in these wonderful events if you do not want to miss cutting-edge thinking on copyright.

What a wonderful case, competition law specialists seem to have thought in the early years. What they saw there was a series of undertakings, each of them enjoying a quasi-monopolistic position in their home markets, engaging themselves into a network of market divisions. What a splendid opportunity, they said, for fighting against abuses of dominant positions and for prohibiting agreements which affect free trade and restrict competition.

Following that line of thought, a number of EC interventions ended up in breaking the traditional way of working and favouring a new system of multiterritorial licensing. What we saw in Europe is that in this way repertoires got split up and that the whole idea of a one stop shop was lost. What we also watch is a growing danger for the emergence of a kind of super CMO's, offering mainstream foreign repertoire and putting downward pressure on local author's revenue.

It is time now to reconsider the role of national collecting societies. We should stop viewing them through the glasses of the competition law specialists only. Competition law is too blunt an instrument to be used blindly in our field. Collecting societies, in as far as they group individual authors and artists, are not the normal economic entities competition law uses to deal with. They are undertakings indeed, but they perform not just an economic role but at the same time also a social and a cultural role. There is, in the functioning of a collecting society, a sort of a trade union component that plays a role, as well as a cultural one, as a defender of domestic creation and local culture. In the past the danger of losing sight of these other important elements was very real, at least in Europe.

It is true that, during recent years, the general atmosphere surrounding the functioning of collecting societies showed a tendency to improvement.

We saw this in more recent case law first, where the SACEM decisions of 2013 of the General Court[2] and the OSA judgment of the Court of Justice in case concerning a Czech spa establishment[3] showed a better understanding of the specific role of collecting societies.

Then came the Collective Rights Management Directive.[4] It was set up to harmonize the rules governing the functioning of collective management organisations. The second introductory recital quite rightly starts by declaring that "Collective management organisations enable rightholders to be remunerated for uses which they would not be in a position to control or enforce themselves, including in non-domestic markets". And recital 3 tells us that "Article 167 of the Treaty on the Functioning of the European Union (TFEU) requires the Union to take cultural diversity into account in its action and to contribute to the flowering of the cultures of the Member States, while respecting their national and regional diversity and at the same time bringing the common cultural heritage to the fore. Collective management organisations play,

2 Case T-422/08.

3 Case C-351/12.

4 Directive 2014/26/EU of the European Parliament and of the Council of 26 February 2014 on collective management of copyright and related rights and multi-territorial licensing of rights in musical works for online use in the internal market.

and should continue to play, an important role as promoters of the diversity of cultural expression, both by enabling the smallest and less popular repertoires to access the market and by providing social, cultural and educational services for the benefit of their rightholders and the public".

This same directive also tried to encourage voluntary repertoire aggregation in the field of online music. It was hoped to remedy fragmentation of repertoire by granting to small societies a right to tag on their local repertoire to a larger CMO, capable of monitoring a multiterritorial licensing scheme. In practice it seems however rather difficult to find good examples of smaller societies tagging on their repertoire to a larger society. If this feeling is confirmed, it will be a good reason to re-evaluate the whole system, as is anyway provided in Title V of this directive, with an obligation for the Commission in Article 40 to submit a report on the application of this Directive.

Another proof of a changed state of mind towards the functioning of collective societies can be found in the 2019 Digital Single Market Directive.[5] When it comes to ensuring wider access to content contained in out-of-commerce works much weight is put on the shoulders of collective management organisations. And, more generally, a mechanism of collective licensing with an extended effect, is put forward, that has to be realised through sufficiently representative collective management organisations. These recent texts relate of course to very specific applications, but they certainly show a certain shift in the mind, whereby CMOs start to be considered as allies in the construction of solutions for a new digital single market, rather than as obstacles to it.

Mesdames et Messieurs, le fondateur de notre Association, Victor Hugo, a toujours considéré que la protection des auteurs et des gens de lettres devait dépasser le cadre rhétorique du bel idéal pour améliorer concrètement la condition sociale de l'artiste individuel. Le sujet dont vous allez traiter pendant ces journées vous en donnera l'occasion. Il s'agira pour vous de vous pencher sur un droit d'auteur effectif, qui utilise les ressources de l'action collective.

Il sied donc de remercier les organisateurs de ce congrès, et plus spécialement Rudolf Leška et son équipe, d'avoir choisi le thème de la gestion collective des droits pour aider un droit d'auteur moderne dans son application pratique sur un marché numérique connecté.

C'est avec plaisir que je déclare ouvert ce Congrès de Prague si plein de perspectives.

I am now happy to declare the Prague congress of ALAI open.

5 Directive (EU) 2019/790 of the European Parliament and of the Council of 17 April 2019 on copyright and related rights in the Digital Single Market and amending Directives 96/9/EC and 2001/29/EC.

EU IPO AND THE ENFORCEMENT OF COPYRIGHT

Christian Archambeau*

Thank you for inviting me to address the Association Littéraire et Artistique Internationale on the important issue of copyright protection.

In recent years the EUIPO, as the largest EU agency exclusively devoted to IP rights, has gradually assumed more and more responsibilities in the IP area at the request of the EU institutions. This includes international cooperation activities in IP, and communication, research, and aspects of enforcement for all IP rights, including copyright. Since we are self-financing via the fees paid by businesses for our EU trademark and design registration services, this has allowed the Office to extend its contribution to other areas of IP without drawing upon the general EU budget. Overall, the agency has about 1500 people working on various aspects of IP rights, including the administration of EU trademarks and designs, where we provide 365 days a year service using advanced online tools. Some of these activities, particularly those to copyright, are carries out via the European Observatory on Infringements of IP Rights, which has been taken care of by the Office since 2012. It should be stressed that the Office does not have operational responsibility for enforcement but the research that we carry out is designed to put the issue into context for policymakers. We also promote legal sources, provide databases, communicate the importance of IP rights, and assist the enforcement authorities in various ways, including coordination and the provision of advanced computer tools.

Starting with the economic studies, a key report on the economic contribution of IP intensive industries to the EU economy shows that copyright intensive industries account for 11.8 million jobs in the EU, which is 5.5 % of the total.[1] Copyright in the modern world is an important generator of wealth and, in fact, copyright intensive were found in the contribution study to pay wages that are on average 59 % higher that industries that do not use IP rights at all. Of course, the value of cultural and creative is considerably higher that the narrowly defined copyright intensive numbers in our IP contribution studies. This was highlighted by another report[2], published in July 2019, which examines the EU cultural and creative activities in general as well

* Executive director EUIPO.

1 web/secure/webdav/guest/document_library/observatory/documents/IPContributionStudy/IPR-intensive_industries_and_economicin_EU/WEB_IPR_intensive_Report_2019.pdf

2 https://euipo.europa.eu/tunnel-web/secure/webdav/guest/document_library/observatory/documents/reports/2019_A_Satellite_Account_For_The_European_Union_Creative_Industries/2019_A_Satelite_Account_for_the_European_Union_Creative_Industries.pdf

as those services that are not bought and sold in the marketplace, but which should still be included in the standard measures of economic output.

The aim of the study is to propose the inclusion in economic and statistic measuring of the activities all such services by the creation of so called "satellite accounts". Turning now to the question of how to combat digital infringement of IP rights. This is an important topic and is also, as you are aware, a complex legal area. Online transactions involve a wide range of services including hosting, transmitting or indexing content, and providing internet-based services, sometimes by third parties and often involving several international jurisdictions. As well as legitimate transactions, there is a dark in the internet, with some websites or online marketplaces being used to sell counterfeit goods or as the source of illegal downloads of types of IP protected works. Consequently, new legal questions about the rights and obligations of online intermediaries are being raised all the time.

To make navigation the legal landscape a little easier for all concerned the Office has published a new case law report[3] providing an overview of the latest developments in the EU. In parallel, the Office's collaboration with intermediaries in addressing IP rights infringements has been intensified and this is one of the growing areas of work of the Observatory. An expert group on cooperation with intermediaries has been set up and the Office plans to work more closely with e-commerce platforms. Analysis of digital infringement and covers the analysis of infringing business models, notably facilitated by new technologies, and also the quantification of digital infringement.

Further studies in 2019 that may be relevant include one on the illegal use of television services over the internet or IPTV services[4], and another looking at user traffic to web sites providing copyright infringing content in all 28 Member States[5]. From the preliminary analysis we can say that piracy is declining for music, films and TV, but that there are large variations among the Member States. While enforcement is important, it is equally vital to help consumers distinguish legal offers from illegal ones. The "agorateka" website developed by the Office, which brings together the legal sources in a single portal is one of the answers to this question. More generally, the promotion of culture and preservation of cultural heritage are among the copyright priorities at European level and the EUIPO has been asked to contribute to this directly by creating and managing several databases.

For example, the Office has developed the "Orphan Works Database", which provides information related to orphan works contained in publicly accessible collections, including libraries and audio and video archives in EU Member States. In addition, in the Copyright Directive adopted last April it is foreseen that the EUIPO will establish an online portal 'out of commerce works', to be made available by

---

3 https://euipo.europa.eu/tunnel-web/secure/webdav/guest/document_library/observatory/documents/reports/2019_IPR_Enforcement_Case_Law_Collection/2019_IPR_Enforcement_Case_Law_Collection_en.pdf

4 https://op.europa.eu/en/publication-detail/-/publication/0617f865-1bc6-11ea-8c1f-01aa75ed71a1/language-en

5 https://euipo.europa.eu/ohimportal/en/web/observatory/online-copyright-infringement-in-eu_2021

June 2021. These databases can potentially be valuable resources, but it must be acknowledged that they are only as strong as their content and rely upon many national partners. We know from other research, including a detailed analysis of the behavior and perceptions of EU citizens carried out in 2017[6], that there is a link between piracy and the availability of legal offers. "Agorateka" can only be a small part of the answer to this problem.

More generally, consumers raise their concerns about the difficulties they have to distinguish illegal sources of copyrighted content from legal ones. We will continue to seek help. Notably, the Office has prepared some answers to 'Frequently Asked Questions' on copyright. This is currently the most visited page on the website of the Observatory. In conclusion, I would like to stress that copyright and its protection are important issues at the EU level as the difficult negotiations on the Digital single market directive have shown. The legislature has given us a new framework in which to work. The EUIPO is ready to help implement our new laws. We do not claim to have answers. In fact, we propose a partnership approach to all those who are interested. Our contribution may be, for example, to carry out research, help with coordination, support communication efforts or run pilot schemes that are then rolled by the relevant national or international partners.

We live in a complex world, and we all have to work together to make sense of it, taking advantage of synergies and avoiding duplication of effort. In those areas where our interests meet, we are keen to listen to organizations such as the Association Littéraire et Artistique Internationale, and its members, and find out how best to work together.

6 https://euipo.europa.eu/tunnel-web/secure/webdav/guest/document_library/observatory/documents/IPContributionStudy/2017/european_public_opinion_study_web.pdf

SECTEUR DU DROIT D'AUTEUR ET DES INDUSTRIES DE LA CRÉATION

Sylvie Forbin*

Permettez-moi tout d'abord de vous dire combien je suis heureuse d'être de nouveau parmi vous. Certains se souviendront que j'avais eu le plaisir d'intervenir sur le thème des défis et opportunités du *cloud* pour la gestion du droit d'auteur il y a quelques années à Kyoto en Octobre 2012, je m'exprimais alors dans le cadre d'une autre fonction. Aujourd'hui, j'ai le très grand plaisir de vous adresser ces quelques messages au nom de l'OMPI que j'ai rejoint il y a très exactement trois ans.

Le sujet central de votre rencontre cette année (la gestion des droits dans l'univers numérique) fait partie –vous l'imaginez bien – des priorités des États membres de l'OMPI et de notre organisation. Une question centrale se pose : comment garantir à l'ère numérique que le droit d'auteur, l'infrastructure de gestion et les outils technologiques nécessaires pour documenter efficacement les opérations de perception et de répartition des droits aillent de pair pour permettre aux systèmes de gestion de droits d'être efficaces. Cette question fondamentale est au cœur des préoccupations de l'OMPI.

C'est aujourd'hui une évidence : les industries créatives plus que tout autre secteur économique se développent à une vitesse exponentielle, grâce au numérique, sur un marché extrêmement dynamique et à une échelle mondiale. Pour tirer pleinement parti des avantages économiques de cet environnement global en ligne, les titulaires de droits devraient disposer des outils nécessaires pour négocier, suivre, protéger et concéder sous licence leurs contenus au niveau local, régional et international, et interpréter les rapports d'utilisation des plateformes et services numériques qui utilisent leurs œuvres.

Nous savons tous que certains des acteurs du numérique ont réalisé les investissements nécessaires et acquis la technologie et les compétences requises pour y parvenir. Cependant, la grande majorité des détenteurs de droits ne disposent pas de ces outils et ne peuvent, de ce fait, bénéficier des revenus qui devraient leur revenir. Désarmés face aux géants du numérique, beaucoup de ces auteurs et artistes espèrent trouver dans les sociétés de gestion collective des outils qui leur permettent de distribuer légalement leurs œuvres et de bénéficier de ce marché numérique; ils souhaitent notamment acquérir les compétences nécessaires pour documenter leurs répertoires sur la base des normes et pratiques opérationnelles reconnues leur permettant d'être adéquatement rémunérés pour leur travail créatif.

---

* Vice directrice générale, Organisation Mondiale de la Propriété Intellectuelle.

Je voudrais saluer ici les initiatives lancées par les fédérations internationales telles que la CISAC, l'IFPI, la SCAPR, l'IFFRO, la liste n'est pas exhaustive, pour développer ces outils de connexion et permettre à la gestion collective de relever les défis de l'environnement numérique. Toutefois des efforts restent à faire pour combler les écarts notamment entre les marchés les plus développés et les marchés émergents. A titre d'exemple, pour corroborer ce constat, permettez-moi d'emprunter les chiffres de la CISAC : seules 13% des recettes des sociétés de gestion collective membres de la CISAC proviennent des utilisations numériques; et l'Afrique ne représente toujours que moins d'un pourcent de la totalité des collectes mondiales et représente à ce titre, un potentiel largement sous exploité.

Il est toutefois encourageant de noter que partout dans le monde les collectes ont progressé notamment dans la région Amérique latine et Caraïbes qui a enregistré la plus forte croissance : +22,7 % en 2019 des sociétés membres de la CISAC (source : rapport annuel de la CISAC 2019).

En arrivant à l'OMPI il y a trois ans, mon premier objectif a été de tenter de surmonter le handicap que représente l'absence, dans un trop grand nombre de pays, d'un cadre législatif solide du droit d'auteur et des droits voisins pour protéger et valoriser la créativité. Ce socle juridique constitue la condition préalable et *sine qua non* du bon fonctionnement de la gestion des droits, que l'on parle de gestion individuelle ou de gestion collective. La pertinence et l'efficacité du cadre juridique national repose principalement, en amont, sur l'adhésion la plus large aux traités de l'OMPI et l'adhésion aux normes minimales définies par ces instruments.

Nous nous réjouissons que plusieurs pays aient enfin récemment adhéré à la Convention de Berne ou soient sur le point de le faire, ce qui assure la mise en œuvre du principe du traitement national. Aujourd'hui la très grande majorité des Etats membres de l'OMPI ont accédé à la Convention de Berne. Je ne peux pas m'empêcher à cet égard de saluer rôle fondateur de l'ALAI dans la conception et la naissance de la Convention de Berne.

La progression des Etats membres nous encourage à amplifier nos efforts : Nous avons récemment franchi le cap de la centième adhésion du Traité de l'OMPI sur le droit d'auteur (WCT) et du Traité de l'OMPI sur les interprétations et exécutions et les phonogrammes et les performances de l'OMPI (WPPT), qui compte actuellement 102 parties contractantes.

Le Traité de Beijing sur les interprétations et exécutions audiovisuelles, qui traite des droits de propriété intellectuelle des artistes interprètes ou exécutants sur les interprétations ou exécutions audiovisuelles, comble une lacune importante dans le cadre international du droit d'auteur. Adopté en 2012, le traité accorde aux artistes interprètes ou exécutants des droits économiques pour leurs interprétations ou exécutions fixées ou non fixées (en direct). Le traité confère également aux artistes interprètes des droits moraux. Le Traité de Beijing entrera en vigueur trois mois après que trente parties éligibles auront déposé leurs instruments de ratification ou d'adhésion. À ce stade, 27 États membres ont ratifié et nous espérons atteindre le nombre magique – 30 – d'ici la fin de l'année, ce qui permettrait au traité d'entrer en vigueur.

Mais bien entendu, lorsque les pays ont ratifié les traités, et actualisé leurs législations, il leur faut également mettre en place des règlementations et des systèmes de gestion de droits qui leur permettent de gérer les exploitations au niveau domestique, régional et international de leurs créations et répertoires de façon effective et efficace.

A cet égard, comme le savez, nous avons récemment rassemblé dans un document de référence que nous avons appelé boîte à outils les bonnes pratiques relatives aux organismes de gestion collective. Il s'agit d'un document non normatif qui contient des exemples de lois, de réglementations et de codes de conduite tirés du monde entier. La boîte à outils comprend également des informations provenant des fédérations internationales, notamment la CISAC, l'IFPI, le SCAPR, l'IFFRO et l'AGICOA. Depuis la finalisation de ce document, nous avons constaté que de nombreux organismes de gestion collective ont adopté, sur la base de cet outil, des codes de conduite qui définissent les normes de service pour les membres et les utilisateurs.

Le rôle joué par les organismes de gestion collective et les ayants droit dans la gestion des utilisations transactionnelles et / ou des licences d'utilisation en ligne, revêt un aspect fondamental, mais dépend également de la capacité d'adaptation de ces organismes à développer de nouvelles licences adaptées à l'environnement numérique et aux nouveaux modèles économiques.

Les ayants droit doivent aussi veiller à développer des outils et des accords pour faciliter l'échange transfrontalier de données à l'ère des réseaux numériques. Ceci est fondamental pour obtenir les autorisations nécessaires aux exploitations légales, en permettant d'identifier les œuvres, les interprétations ou exécutions, les enregistrements, les titulaires des droits et les droits qui devront être sécurisés. Pour réaliser ces objectifs, l'existence d'un "*backoffice*" opérationnel et d'une interface en ligne "*user friendly*", sont indispensables.

Les efforts de l'OMPI visent précisément à permettre aux organismes de gestion collective des pays en développement, d'acquérir ces compétences. A cette fin, nous développons et déployons actuellement, sur demande, WIPO Connect, une solution de gestion de droits d'auteur de *backoffice* répondant à ces exigences pour les organismes de gestion collective des pays en développement qui ne peuvent se permettre d'acquérir des solutions IT commerciales. A l'heure actuelle, WIPO Connect se concentre sur le secteur des droits d'auteur de la musique, mais nous nous employons à couvrir à l'avenir les droits voisins et nous espérons pouvoir aussi couvrir d'autres répertoires.

En nous tournant vers l'avenir : L'explosion des industries créatives et les efforts fournis notamment par les pays en développement pour saisir les nouvelles opportunités du numérique ne seront durables que si ces pays parviennent à engranger des résultats rapides et à bénéficier de retours économiques tangibles pour leurs créateurs et leurs industries de la création.

A cet égard, le mandat et la structure intergouvernementale de l'OMPI qui regroupe 177 Etats membres nous permet d'assumer une responsabilité spécifique dans ce domaine et d'accompagner efficacement les pays à atteindre des résultats concrets. Dans la mise en œuvre de cette mission, je tiens à souligner que nous attachons une grande importance aux partenariats noués avec des organisations telles que la CISAC, l'IFRRO, SCAPR, l'IFPI.

Par ailleurs, il est dans l'intérêt de toutes les parties prenantes, de renforcer l'efficacité de la gestion au niveau global pour aboutir à une situation gagnant/gagnant à tous les niveaux de la chaine de valeur. Le droit d'auteur et les organismes de gestion collective garde toute leur pertinence à l'ère du numérique et continuent de démontrer leur capacité d'adaptation à l'évolution technologique.

Les Etats membres, nous le constatons, recherchent, au titre de cette mission d'intérêt public – le soutien à la créativité et aux industries créatives à travers la rémunération des ayants droit-, de plus grandes articulations voire interfaces entre les systèmes qui relèvent aujourd'hui de la propriété d'un gouvernement, d'un organisme de gestion voire de sociétés de droit privé.

Bien entendu, parmi ces données, nos Etats membres reconnaissent la sensibilité des données dites business. Ils reconnaissent également l'importance de respecter les données personnelles mais ils s'interrogent sur l'intérêt de concevoir un système qui réponde à une meilleure fluidité des données générales portant sur les transactions entre ayants droits, intermédiaires et utilisateurs.

Ne pourrait-on définir quelques axes sur lesquels nous pourrions envisager de travailler tous ensemble, notamment concernant la fiabilisation des identifiants, l'amélioration de l'interopérabilité et la facilitation de l'accès à ces outils dans le cadre des nouveaux modèles économiques?

Permettez-moi de conclure en remerciant l'ALAI de cette invitation. L'appui constant de l'ALAI et de ses membres au système multilatéral, à travers notamment votre participation aux sessions du Comité permanent sur le droit d'auteur et les droits voisins (SCCR) ne s'est jamais démenti, et constitue pour l'OMPI une fierté et grande source d'inspiration pour la mise en œuvre de notre mandat et de notre mission. Vous voyez que nous avons beaucoup de chantiers devant nous et je n'ai pas eu le temps d'évoquer avec vous l'importance que se posent certaines parties prenantes sur l'équilibre entre droit exclusif et droit à rémunération dans ce nouvel écosystème numérique, la question de la reconnaissance de droits collectifs dans le domaine de la création qui intéresse beaucoup d'Etats membres et enfin la discussion sur la place des exceptions et limitations dans ce nouvel environnement qui voit exploser les exploitations numériques et transfrontalières.

Je vous remercie de votre attention et je compte, chers membres de l'ALAI sur votre engagement qui nous est si précieux.

COLLECTIVE MANAGEMENT OF RIGHTS IN A TRANSFORMING MARKET

Gadi Oron*

I am delighted to be here today and I would like, first, to express my appreciation for all the people who made this conference possible. In particular, I would like to thank Mr Rudolf Leška, the president of the ALAI group here in the Czech Republic, and his team, who I know have been working tirelessly, for many months, to organise this ALAI event. I am very happy and proud that we, at CISAC, could partner with ALAI this year and be associated with this conference.

CISAC is the international confederation of authors' societies. We bring together 239 authors' societies from 122 countries. These societies collectively represent over 4 million authors who come from different disciplines of the arts. Many of them are music creators – songwriters and composers, but our societies also represent visual artists, film and TV directors and screenwriters, playwrights of dramatic works, and authors of literature.

Our societies' mission is, first and foremost, to generate increased remuneration for their affiliated creators. Royalties' collections by our member societies last year – in 2018 – totalled more than $US 10 billion.

Collection and distribution of royalties is indeed the main task of collective management organisations and the main reason for their establishment, but they serve creators far beyond collecting royalties. Throughout their history, authors' societies have taken a leading role in advocacy and policy making with the goal of enabling creators to be adequately protected and equitably remunerated. This has become an increasingly challenging task, particularly with transformation to the digital world. However, history teaches us that societies have always had to evolve and adjust their operations to match a transforming market. And transformation has always been fuelled – and triggered – by technology.

Today, the world of collective management is changing more rapidly and more decisively than ever, in order to stay successful and relevant in the 21st century but, alongside this theme of transformation, there is an equally strong theme of continuity. This because the core principles and the key functions of collective management remain as vital as they were at the founding of our sector some 200 years ago. If you examine the ecosystem in which societies operate today, you see this mix of change and continuity. This ecosystem is characterised by an inherent imbalance of power between, on one hand, the creators, and, on the other, those powerful commercial

* Director General of CISAC, the International Confederation of Authors and Composers Societies.

entities which are the main users of creative works. This imbalance is, of course, nothing new. It is at least 200 years old. And when one views this in a historical perspective, it easy to identify a remarkable convergence between past and present.

At the heart of the comparison between the present landscape and that of the past, is the place of the "intermediary". Just as today, 200 years ago rightsholders had to keep challenging the power of the intermediaries that attempt to control rights, dictate the terms of access to the cultural marketplace, and retain a disproportionate share of the revenues from the use of creations. So, if you think our sector has a major struggle with digital intermediaries today, let me share with you a quote from the Marquess *Robert de Flers*, a French playwright and one of CISAC's founding fathers. De Flers' exhorted authors around a mission he described as "the elimination of the intermediary".

He says:

"...I am not talking about the honest, active and useful intermediary – there are indeed a few; not many perhaps, but some; but of the parasitical and noxious intermediary who deprives us of the money owed to us, who deforms our works – or allows it to be deformed, who debases them by programming them in theatres where they shouldn't be and translates them in languages that are from no country at all. This intermediary, Gentlemen, I believe we have just been burying. It seems to me one of the most joyful funerals which I might conceivably be invited to attend."

De Flers was speaking on 13th June 1926, the historic day in which CISAC was established. So you might forgive him for being a little euphoric about the impending doom for intermediaries which he perceived as being just around the corner... But this quote also sets today's copyright battles in a fascinating historical context. If you replace the theatre owners of the 1920s with today's larger internet platforms, the 93-year-old quote truly comes to life. The men and women who shaped collective management politics understood the importance of a proportional remuneration as a direct reflection of creators' economic rights. Today we understand the same thing – and we know that the fight for fair remuneration for creators is ultimately a fight for fair treatment by the "intermediaries".

Indeed, the issues that occupied the authors who founded societies, are the same as those that are facing us today. Technologies come and go, politics fluctuate, business models mutate, but the challenges for rightsholders remains essentially the same. Collective management came into being because of a practical need to manage legal rights which the authors cannot manage individually. Creators understood that in negotiations with users, the collective is much stronger than the individual. Societies' role very quickly extended far beyond negotiations and collections of royalties, to the mission of protecting and safeguarding creators' moral and economic interests and to shaping the legislative environment for cultural activity.

Technological change has reinforced this mission.

First, at an operational level, the digital world has created a greater need than ever to manage rights collectively. With the sheer volume of data processing that's involved in rights management today, collective administration is essential, both economically and operationally.

Second, negotiating as a collective to offset the strong position of commercial users is more important today, possibly than ever before. The digital world may have liberated the consumer and revolutionised the way creators can access a global audience, but it has also created dominant giants with enormous negotiating power that are the world's largest users of creative works.

Third, lobbying and influencing decision-making is more important in today's multi-stakeholder world than it ever was. Copyright users have immense political power and influence. The recent debate around the EU Directive on Copyright in the Digital Single Market dramatically demonstrated this. Prominent copyright users took advantage of their influence over mass audience and, while spreading misinformation and using scare tactics, they made significant effort to block the Directive which they considered disadvantageous to their business.

The ecology of the cultural sector is changing at a breath-taking pace. Our market is rapidly becoming more global and increasingly more diverse. This is fuelled by two phenomena: the *first* is that platforms are constantly improving consumer experience and offering a growing selection of repertoire. The *second* is the rapidly changing consumer behaviour and preference.

There are 2 recent examples to demonstrate this:

- YouTube recently reported that among the Top 10 most viewed music videos in 2019 so far, only one is in English. Five out of the Top 10 music videos are in Spanish, two in Korean and two originated in in India.
- Another example of globalisation comes from the audio-visual sector. While the TV market is switching to on-demand streaming and consumers are gradually turning their back on linear TV broadcasts, the dominant online platforms are increasingly involved in the production of original content.

The traditional broadcasters are not sitting on their hands, though. Rather, they react by boosting their own original productions, with some of them reporting up to 100 times more original TV shows. They are also offering catch-up streaming services for their broadcasts.

The consequences of these market developments are substantial structural changes to licensing models. Collective management structures have had to adapt, re-invent and modernise to a global, diverse and fast-paced reality. They have had to become more effective in capturing value. They have had to offer new types of licenses. They have had to develop the capacity to deal with enormous amounts of data in order to monitor and monetise the diversified types of commercial use. And they have had to improve the speed and efficiency of their distribution of royalties to their affiliated rightsholders. The technologies driving change are new; but the phenomenon of societies adapting the system is nothing new. In fact, the very establishment of the collective management system back in the 18th century came in response to a need that previously did not exist.

A bit of history is very instructive here. Collective management was founded by playwrights who realised they could obtain better conditions and better remuneration for their use of their works when they negotiated collectively with theatre owners.

In a hot summer evening on the 3rd July 1777, the famous French playwright Pierre Beaumarchais brought together a group of 22 authors to discuss the poor remuneration paid for their works by the *Théâtre-Français*. In the case of Beaumarchais, the complaint centred on the low remuneration he received from the *Comédie Française* for the use of his play *the Barber of Seville*. The action by this small group of authors eventually led to change. In 1791 France passed the first law on authors' rights. Shortly afterwards, entities that managed the new authors' rights were created. Once established in the world of theatre, the principle of collective management proved essential to other repertoires as well.

The famous story goes that in 1847 the French composer, Ernest Bourget, visited *Les Ambassadeurs,* a café in Paris where live music was being performed. When Bourget heard some of his own compositions being played, he was angry that his permission for their use had not been sought and that he was not being paid, while he, of course, had to pay the establishment for his drink.

With a few other composers, he brought an action against the owner of the café. They asked the court to either forbid the performance of works in the café or to hold that they, the creators of the works, should be paid for these performances.

The court of course found in their favour. The principle was thus established that authors and composers had a performing right in their works. But having the rights was not enough. For these authors, there was the practical problem of monitoring and enforcing their rights. And so the first music authors society was formed – SACEM. Others followed, in Italy, Germany, the UK and the US. The developments in France, however, were especially significant because they took place before the Berne Convention of 1886 was signed.

Since those early days, the history of CMOs has been one of constant changes in the licensing market. Societies have always had to adjust to new forms of exploitation and technologies: from traditional public performance to broadcasting; mechanical reproductions and private copying; cable distribution; satellite transmissions and of course, the internet.

Digital technologies have had a radical impact on the way music, films, books and other creations are accessed. They have created new business models and destroyed or marginalised old ones. Yet, this has not changed the fundamental principles underlying collective administration of rights. Indeed, the market changes have made those principles more relevant than ever.

In the digital world negotiations over creators' remuneration are taking place not just with powerful entities, but with some of the world's largest corporations. Advocacy work has become more complex due to the commercial interests involved. And in the management of rights, CMOs have a dramatically enlarged role, with the capacity to process enormous amounts of data that are simply impossible to conduct individually.

I spoke about the past and the present, so I would like to conclude with some thoughts about the future. The cultural and creative industries are continuing to grow phenomenally. With that comes exponential growth in activities related to the management of rights. Collective Management Organisations are responding proactively to this evolution. They have re-shaped, evolved and transformed to operate in a global landscape where both rightsholders and users have more freedom of choice. They have also pursued unprecedented cross-border collaborations among themselves: from joint ventures in the offering of licenses, through consolidation of back-office activities and cross-border initiatives on data, to one-stop-shop solutions bringing together authors and neighbouring rights owners. These initiatives are taking shape and form in every region of the world, with the overarching goal of simplifying the licensing business, cutting down costs, and serving creators better. There is also a marked increase in competition among traditional non-profit CMOs as well as the entry of new players, some of which are for-profit entities, into the market. The sheer scale of data processing that's involved in collective management today requires substantial investment in technical capabilities. The scene is set for greater competition and greater pressure for societies to improve.

What is for certain is that the future of our sector is digital. The key features of the digital world I have mentioned will, I believe, continue to shape the agenda of CMOs in the future:

- Creators will continue to face an imbalance in bargaining power between them the and the commercial users of their works.
- Societies will continue to see a proliferation of digital uses of content and will face an increasing burden in administering rights and monitoring use.
- Users will continue to demand innovating and cross-border licensing solutions
- And finally – both creators and societies will need to be play a decisive and active role in advocacy, in lobbying and influencing policymaking in order to secure meaningful protection for copyright.

OPENING SPEECH

Rudolf Leška

Dear Colleagues, Friends, Honourable Guests,

In 1926, my predecessor in the office of the president of then-Czechoslovak ALAI Chapter, dr. Jan Löwenbach, welcomed his international guests: members of ALAI who arrived from Warsaw to Prague to celebrate and discuss the new Czechoslovak Copyright Act at a symposium following the Warsaw Congress. The challenges that we face today are new, but the substance remains – securing for creators, artists and the creative industry as a whole just remuneration for their talent, virtuosity, and effort, and not allowing others to reap where they have not sown.

As in 1926, when participants were greeted by the first president of the Czechoslovak Republic, Prof. T. G. Masaryk, and the Minister of Foreign Affairs and later president, Dr. Edvard Beneš, we have gathered here today under the auspices of H.E. Miloš Zeman, President of the Republic, and the Ministry of Culture.

It is impossible to organize congresses like this one without the financial support of generous people and organizations. It is to their credit that the registration fees were not prohibitive. The first among our sponsors is ALAI which substantially contributed to this congress from membership fees from all around the world. Our platinum partner, CISAC, welcomed the congress agenda and helped not only with a significant and most generous contribution but also with organizational support.

Our most crucial Czech partner is the collecting society OAZA which represents sound designers and sound engineers – a newly establishing field in copyright law, as we can observe in the new US law, while OOA-S, the collecting society in the field of visual arts, is our silver partner.

Nevertheless, our thanks go to everyone who contributed either funds or their own time to prepare the congress (other partners include Czech collecting societies INTERGRAM, OSA and DILIA, law firms TYCOVÁ DVOŘÁK, Bird & Bird and ŠTAIDL LEŠKA ADVOKÁTI and the Czech Bar Association) and to everyone who agreed to present their ideas here, especially EU IPO Executive Director Christian Archambeau and WIPO Deputy Director General Sylvie Forbin.

Welcome to Prague!

PART II STUDIES

IS COMPETITION AMONG COLLECTIVES LEADING TO POSITIVE CHANGES IN COLLECTIVE MANAGEMENT?

Daniel Gervais*

In this short contribution, I describe regulatory efforts concerning collective management of copyright and related rights in the European Union and the United States and the role of competition and competition law in that context. I then attempt to draw a few lessons for the future. Let us begin with the US.

The United States

The American Society of Composers, Authors and Publishers (ASCAP) was the first CMO administering the public performance of musical works (hence designation as a Performing Rights Organization or PRO) in the United States. It was created by mostly "serious music" composers/writers and music publishers in 1914. Broadcasters decided to create a competing organization, Broadcast Music, Inc. (BMI) in 1939.

Those two CMOs have been competing in a number of ways. In its first decades of existence, BMI was able to convince authors and publishers to affiliate with them by agreeing to work with less "successful" writers (eg. those who had fewer published works), or those working in genres that ASCAP did not seem too interested in at the time (blues, jazz, rhythm and blues, gospel, and later country, folk, Latin, and even initially rock and roll). BMI also made deals with certain publishers and in some cases offered fixed fees in comparison to ASCAP's two-tier system at the time said to favor more established writers. There was no direct competition on rates paid by users, however. If one of the two organizations had set much lower rates for the use of musical works, its revenue would have been affected in a way that might have made it difficult to attract writers and publishers.

Both CMOs were eventually regulated under US competition (antitrust law). They each negotiated a set of rules with the US Department of Justice (DoJ) that were enshrined in federal court orders known as a "consent decrees." The decrees had no end date—to my knowledge the only consent decrees in the history of

* Milton R. Underwood Chair in Law, Vanderbilt University. Former Deputy Secretary General of the International Confederation of Societies of Authors and Composers (CISAC). Vice-President of Copyright Clearance Center, Inc. and Vice-Chair of the International Federation of Reprographic Rights Organizations (IFRRO).

antitrust law that do not sunset at some point. Each one provided a mechanism for a federal judge in New York (a different judge for each CMO) to set rates for the use of musical works.

The two major PROs were not alone. SESAC (originally the Society of European Stage Authors and Composers) was formed in 1930 to represent, as the name indicates, European stage authors and composers but its focus changed in the 1960s. SESAC started to acquire the right to license writers in other genres, including Bob Dylan and Neil Diamond, and then continued to expand to represent major writers including Rush, Mariah Carey and Adele. SESAC was acquired by the private equity firm Blackstone Group in 2017.

Then recording industry executive Irving Azoff established a new PRO, Global Music Rights, in 2013.

Competition is pervasive in several ways. All those CMOs have nonexclusive rights from their members/affiliates, and major publishers (labels) can also go around them for "low hanging fruit" – deals with large users like Apple, Spotify or Google -, thereby increasing the administrative costs of the CMOs.

As I see things now, with four CMOs competing in the same field, only some of which are subject to consent decrees, it is much less clear that antitrust law constraints are well adapted or indeed required. Recall that, as a point of comparison, there are now only three major "labels" sharing most of the world's sound recording rights and they are not subject to a similar set of constraints.

In 2021, the DoJ ended a long review process of the consent decrees. There were several issues at play, including, to name three main ones, (a) whether fractional licensing is permissible (meaning that a PRO need not license all rights in a work); (b) whether partial withdrawal is permissible (meaning that an author or publisher is able to limit the RPO's ability to grant licenses to certain types of users); and (c) whether the PROs should become more like certain foreign CMOs and license other rights in musical works, such as mechanical rights. As of early 2021, these issues were also the subject of litigation in federal courts. Those courts have thus far taken the position that the consent decrees do not require full work licensing or permit partial withdrawal.

Rates for the digital use not of musical works but of sound recordings in the United States is subject to an entirely different system, entirely outside of antitrust regulation. A Copyright Royalty Board (CRB), part of the United States Copyright Office, sets rates for noninteractive digital uses of sound recordings.

The system was profoundly altered by the 2018 Music Modernization Act (MMA), which created a new Music Licensing Collective (MLC) to administer a "compulsory licensing structure for making and distributing musical works with a blanket licensing system for digital music providers to make and distribute digital phonorecord deliveries (e.g., permanent downloads, limited downloads, or interactive streams)."[1] As the MLC only started its operations in 2021, it is too early to comment on its success but

1 https://www.copyright.gov/music-modernization/115/

its establishment was marred by deals to split so-called black box funds just before the MLC began its work.

The MMA did more than create the MLC and new blanket license, however. It also made two significant changes affecting PROs, namely a partial repeal of a strange provision that directed the judges setting rates under const decrees to disregard the price paid for sound recordings, and the creation of a rotating "wheel" of judges to set rates under such decrees instead of the same judge presiding over the fate of each PRO for years.

We are thus in a wait and see moment with courts, and the new MLC taking its first steps. We shall see whether it will make its parents proud.

The European Union

CMOs have been regulated in myriad ways in EU member States, from special ad hoc committees (France) to a quasi-absence of regulation. The European Commission and Parliament started two decades ago to try to advance Europe-wide rules via courts and legislation. The following is but a quick tour d'horizon.[2]

First on our timeline, the 2002 Simulcasting Decision marked an important step in the early stages of the process. The International Federation of the Phonographic Industry (IFPI) had applied to the Commission for "negative clearance" or, alternatively, for exemption under what was then Article 81(3) of the EU Treaty, in respect of a model reciprocal agreement between record producers' rights administration societies for the licensing of "simulcasting".

The Decision emphasized that within the EEA the Internet was best seen as a single territory, and, therefore, a one-stop shop license should be available for Internet broadcasts. This set the stage for European regulatory efforts. The Decision also mentioned two issues that would become a recurring theme for years to come, namely the need for transparency and "competition", especially on administrative costs.

To quote from the Decision:

"The collecting societies will be able to actually compete and to differentiate themselves in terms of efficiency, quality of service and commercial terms. ... This represents a major evolution from the situation concerning traditional rights licensing where, given the de facto monopoly enjoyed by all collecting societies in their national territories, actual competition between societies does not occur in most relevant markets.[3]

---

2 Much more detailed analysis is contained in Lucie Guibault and Stef van Gompel, Collective Management in the European Union, in D. Gervais (ed), *Collective Management of Copyright and Related Rights*, 3rd edn (Kluwer, 2016).

3 http://eur-lex.europa.eu/LexUriServ/LexUriServ.do?uri=CELEX:32003D0300:EN:HTML, para 119

The Decision was followed, in January 2005, by the Commission's work programme on Collective management[4], which itself followed a Communication on the Management of Copyright and Related Rights in the Internal Market[5], identified three regulatory objectives:

- To ensure the transparency and efficiency of collective management societies;
- To ensure that the control of collective management societies is exercised in such a way that a similar general interest protection level can be guaranteed in all Member States;
- To enhance competitiveness of creative industries, including small ones as well as individual authors and artists, to strengthen innovation and to promote culture and cultural diversity.

This led very quickly to Commission Recommendation of 18 May 2005 on collective cross-border management of copyright and related rights for legitimate online music services. [6] Here is a key point made in that document:

"In the era of online exploitation of musical works, commercial users need a licensing policy that corresponds to the ubiquity of the online environment and which is multi-territorial. It is therefore appropriate to provide for *multi-territorial licensing* in order to enhance greater legal certainty to commercial users in relation to their activity and to *foster the development of legitimate online services*, increasing, in turn, the revenue stream for rightholders."[7]

The Substance of the Recommendation was four-fold:

- Freedom to license;
- Freedom of users to choose;
- Freedom of rights holders to choose "irrespective of the Member State of residence";[8]
- Rationalization and transparency.[9]

There was a quick response from CMOs. ICMP/CIEM[10] and GESAC[11] agreed on harmonized minimum standards in a 'Common Declaration' which distinguished interactive and non-interactive uses. This was followed by the "Cannes Agreement", a deal between 13 CMOs (BIEM members[12]) and five large publishers setting the stage for multi-territorial licensing within the EEA.

A Commission Decision of 4 October 2006 referred to as the "The Cannes Extension Agreement"[13] – made, as the name suggests, in the wake of the Cannes Agreement – noted he following:

4 Commission of the European Communities, Commission Work Programme for 2005 – COM(2005) 15 final.
5 Commission (EC), 'The management of copyright and related rights in the internal market' (Communication), COM (04) 261 final, 16 April 2004
6 Available at http://www.wipo.int/wipolex/en/details.jsp?id=8613
7 Ibid.
8 Ibid, at para 9.
9 Ibid. at para 10 and art 14.
10 Representing music publishers.
11 European group of music CMOs.
12 BIEM represented CMOs administering mechanical rights.
13 https://ec.europa.eu/competition/antitrust/cases/dec_docs/38681/38681_216_1.pdf

"[T]here is currently very little scope for price competition among collecting societies."[14] This may have signaled a shift of the focus from transparency, efficiency competition and freedom of authors and publishers to choose a CMO within the EEA to ways to reduce rates paid by users.

Price competition was on the menu.

Enter the European Parliament.

In a resolution of 13 March 2007 on the above-mentioned Commission Recommendation of 18 October 2005, the Parliament took a broad view of the matter. Ostensibly, its three main concerns were:

- National membership. The Parliament was concerned that letting rights holders shop their online rights would weaken national CMOs, noting that the "existing network of national CRMs plays an important role in providing financial support for the promotion of new and minority European repertoire and whereas this should not be lost"[15];
- The promotion of cultural diversity; and
- The impact on CMO governance of giving large rights holders' too much clout.

The resolution was very critical of the 2005 Recommendation. It criticized the consultation process that had led to the adoption of the Recommendation and indeed sought to limit its ambit and impact, though Parliament did support multi-repertoire licenses for cross-border and online uses and use in mobile telephony and other digital network. The Parliament also called on any future regulation in this area not to undermine the "competitiveness of the underlying creative businesses, the effectiveness of the services provided by CRMs or the competitiveness of user businesses – in particular small rightholders and users[16]" and to "allow only fair and controlled competition, without territorial restrictions, but with the necessary and suitable qualitative criteria for the collective management of copyright and the preservation of the value of the rights."[17]

The heavy guns of antitrust would then reverberate across the continent. Based on a complaint filed by RTL and Music Choice, DG COMP issued a decision on 16 July 2008.[18] It went quite far. It found that membership rules restricted desirable competition between CMOs on the market for the provision of services to right holders and could also affect competition between collecting societies on the market for the licensing of rights to commercial users, which it then determined was prohibited as "infringement by object" under EU rules. It stated that the (acknowledged) territoriality of copyright did not require a national assignment of rights for

14 Ibid, para 28.

15 Ibid, at J.

16 Ibid at para 6.

17 Ibid.

18 Case COMP/C2/38.698 — CISAC. For a more detailed discussion, see Alain Andries and Bruno Julien-Malvy, 'The CISAC decision — creating competition between collecting societies for music rights', (2008) *Competition Policy Newsletter*, online: https://ec.europa.eu/competition/publications/cpn/2008_3_53.pdf.

the purpose of administration abroad on a strictly national basis. Territorial restrictions in contracts between CMOs known as Reciprocal Representation Agreements (RRAs) were found to be a prohibited concerted practice. And this was not (just) a contractual matter: "Even where collecting societies have, in individual cases, dropped the explicit exclusivity, no change in the allocation of territories among the collecting societies could be observed".[19] In other words, actual practice, despite changes to RRAs, effectively led to "national monopolies for the multi-repertoire licensing of public performance rights and has the effect of segmenting the EEA into national markets".[20]

The decision was sent to the General Court for review. The Court disagreed with the Commission on the existence of a "concerted practice relating to the national territorial limitations",[21] and annulled a key part of the 2008 Decision. Commission Decision. The decision can be read as a disagreement over the evidence, with the court giving CMOs the benefit of the doubt.[22]

Hopefully, the brief account contained in the preceding pages is sufficient to demonstrate the concerns that have animated European regulators. There are four major ones:

(a) governance
(b) efficiency/costs
(c) transparency/reports, and
(d) two "single market" issues
   i. multi-territorial licensing (music)
   ii. membership

What would be the next step, after the annulment of DG COMP's decision? The regulatory roller-coaster became a smoother ride with the adoption of Directive on Collective Rights Management adopted on 26 February 2014.[23] In line with the above concerns, it introduced an element of competition by allowing right holders to choose a CMO. It leaves the door open for mandatory collective management; contains general and hardly enforceable admonitions such as the need for CMOs to act in the best collective interests of the rightsholders they represent and use "utmost diligence", notes that noncommercial licenses were desirable, and paves the way for multiterritorial licensing by reducing the number of licenses a user needs to operate a multi-territory. It introduced a system of repertoire aggregation, a delegation of authority to license digital music between CMOs that has not, to date at least, been a resounding

19 Case COMP/C2/38.698 — CISAC, para 206.

20 Ibid.

21 Case T442/08, 12 April 2013, at para 182, online: https://curia.europa.eu/juris/document/document.jsf?text=cisac%2BCOMP%2B&docid=136261&pageIndex=0&doclang=EN&mode=req&dir=&occ=first&part=1&cid=11870367#ctx1

22 See in particular ibid, paras 91-99.

23 Directive 2014/26/EU of the European Parliament and of the Council of 26 February 2014 on collective management of copyright and related rights and multi-territorial licensing of rights in musical works for online use in the internal market, OJ L84/72, 20.3.2014, online https://eur-lex.europa.eu/legal-content/EN/TXT/?uri=CELEX%3A32014L0026

success. Under this system a CMO may request under certain conditions, another CMO to represent its repertoire.[24] Finally, the Directive did not impose a mandatory legal form for CMOs.

This was not to be the end station of the regulatory train. Two 2019 directives, namely the DSM directive[25] and the Online Broadcasting Directive[26] laid down additional rules that are highly relevant.

The DSM contains an entire chapter (2) dedicated to "Measures to facilitate collective licensing" and introduces "collective licensing with an extended effect", a new name for what is often called Extended collective Licensing (ECL) or what I prefer to call extended repertoire.[27] This system, first established under Nordic copyright reforms in the late 1950s and 1960s, allows a CMO which has been able to convince a substantial number of right holders (typically in its territory of operation) to join a particular licensing scheme to obtain by law an extension of its repertoire to all relevant works, except those of right holders who choose to opt out. Put differently, an opt in system becomes opt out.

Despite the considerable academic scholarship questioning the value of this system – some of which is a subset of the scholarship that sees all forms of collective management of authors' rights as a *malum in se* – historically very few right holders have opted out. This of course does not provide conclusive evidence that the system works well, but it is relevant information.

The other 2019 directive (Online Broadcasting Directive) provides that "Member States shall ensure that rightholders may exercise their right to grant or refuse the authorisation for a retransmission only through a collective management organisation."[28] Recital 16 goes a step further:

"This Directive should allow agreements concluded between a CMO and operators of retransmission services for rights that are subject to mandatory collective management under this Directive to be extended to apply to the rights of rightholders who are not represented by that CMO, without those rightholders being allowed to exclude their works or other subject matter from the application of that mechanism."

24 See ibid, para 46.

25 Directive (EU) 2019/790 of the European Parliament and of the Council of 17 April 2019 on copyright and related rights in the Digital Single Market and amending Directives 96/9/EC and 2001/29,OJ L130/92 17.5.2019 (DSM directive)

26 Directive (EU) 2019/789 of the European Parliament and of the Council of 17 April 2019 (Online Broadcasting Directive) laying down rules on the exercise of copyright and related rights applicable to certain online transmissions of broadcasting organisations and retransmissions of television and radio programmes, and amending Council Directive 93/83/EEC, OJ L130/82, 17.5.2019

27 See D. Gervais, Collective Management of Copyright and Related Rights: Theory and Practice in the Digital Age in Collective Management of Copyright and Related Rights, 3rd edn (Kluwer, 2016), ch. 1.

28 See above n. 27, art 4. See also ibid recital 16.

Lessons

At no point in history has there been a wider and more open "store of meanings" of cultural content. Almost all of it is online, much of it free of charge. This in turn may allow authors have access and are influenced by "foreign" cultures in a way that might make "foreignness" itself a very different notion. This can lead to more global or at least non-geographically bounded cultural productions and unbounded collective management to emerge. The question is, should CMOs adapt? Should they compete by jettisoning national or other territorial limitations? This opens up a broader set of questions about the purpose of regulation (here defined in a nutshell as control by public bodies) of CMOs.

There is little doubt that CMOs, like many other types of organizations, need to operate within well-defined and enforceable regulatory bounds. Because they are often unavoidable partners for professional users of copyright material, there may well be a specific case for fairly stringent rules. The hard question is not whether, but rather how: what form should those rules take? I will attempt to draw a few lessons.

First, in the developments of the past few years I see an acknowledgment that the blunt force of competition/antitrust law is simply not optimally adapted to the sophisticated type of rulemaking that is required.

Second, there is little doubt that a number of objectives are widely seen as desirable, namely good governance, efficiency and costs, and real transparency, including publicly available reports (and adequately detailed after available).

Third, as markets and technology stand now,collective management is still required to make copyright work – by which I mean in a nutshell ensuring that professional authors who dedicate their life to producing certain types of literary and artistic material[29] can get a fair return on their investment and craft development.

Easy access to licensing for professional users is desirable, and having fewer CMOs may make that objective easier to achieve. This may in turn imply having fewer CMOs. This is what underpinned two of the EU regulatory objectives, namely allowing authors and other right holders to pick a CMO (this has long been the case in the US), and creating incentives or even obligations for CMOs to cooperate to offer centralized licenses. That being said, the system put in place by the 2014 Directive doesn't quite seem to cut it. Perhaps the more forceful approach of the 2019 Directives will. This is for now an empirical question and theoretical objections remain unconvincing until we can see and analyze actual effects.

The rules on good governance, efficiency and costs, and transparency benefit everyone who deals with a CMO, whether author,other right holder or user. But they are not sufficient. Users need more, namely assurances that dealings with a CMO will not be unduly burdensome and a system to set prices. The former is not unduly

29 I cannot full develop the point here but yere are different types or categories of authors and copyright rules should not be used or applied by them in the same way I explain the differences and their regulatory implications in detail in *Restructuring Copyright*, softcover edition (Edward Elgar, 2019)

difficult. The latter is, as the French say, where *le bât blesse.* Regulators have tried several institutional forms. In theory, I am a fan of specialized boards with lawyers and economists working on the basis of evidence submitted by all sides but I readily acknowledge that in the few countries that use such a system (eg Canada), it has been both burdensome and painfully slow. This strikes me more as a call for structural administrative reform than anything else. There are many precedents that come to mind, including countries that have radically shortened wait times and improved outcomes in their court system or patent offices. Certain stakeholders may well be deliberately pushing the system to its limits precisely to make it not work, and then they can call for its dismantlement. Be that as it may, more comparative and transdisciplinary work is required in this area. There is some work done, for example, by the World Intellectual property Organization but much more is needed, including by bringing the tools of law & economics to bear.[30]

Overall, it seems that competition among CMOs can work on a number of fronts. It already has when it comes to allowing authors and other right holders to choose. Transparency obligations accompanied by audit rules can also shed light on inefficiencies and work hand in hand with good governance rules. I do think, however, that competition in this particular area will be unlikely to work for prices, as a race to the bottom may defeat the whole purpose. This is a strange market but, as I see it, a necessary one. I also accept that this is also an area ripe for more comprehensive, empirical and less ideologically motivated studies.

In sum, these are, as the Chinese curse goes, interesting times for collective management for many reasons, including the regulatory experiments under way in many jurisdictions, Today I only tackled the EU and US, but many more countries are active in this space. All of this should lead to a new, and from my perspective much awaited, wave of understanding in legal and economic scholarship.

---

[30] See D Gervais, The Economics of Copyright Collectives, in P. Menell and B. Depoorter (eds), *Research Handbook On The Economics Of Intellectual Property Law,*(E Elgar, 2019), 489-507.

THE CONTRIBUTIONS AND LIMITATIONS OF COMPETITION LAW TO REGULATE COLLECTIVE RIGHTS MANAGEMENT IN THE EU

Josef Drexl*

1 Introduction

Over the past several decades, competition law developed as a cornerstone of the legal framework for collective rights management in the European Union. EU competition law has particular merits. It provides a uniform set of directly applicable EU rules that are enforced by both national and EU institutions and courts. The law provides severe sanctioning power in form of fines and even structural remedies. Moreover, it applies uniformly – i.e. without discrimination – to all sectors of the economy. Unlike sector-specific regulatory bodies, competition authorities are therefore much less likely to be captured by the interests of the regulated undertakings.

Yet competition law also has its inbuilt limitations. Due to the economics of collective rights management, CMOs traditionally hold natural monopolies in the Member States. Beyond merger control law, EU competition law does not provide any remedies against the emergence of such monopolies. It only prohibits certain conduct of CMOs that can be categorised as an abuse under Article 102 TFEU. Moreover, it cannot build on considerations and goals that fall outside the classical framework for competition law analysis, although this framework certainly allows for flexible application, taking into account the specificities of the products and markets concerned.

Hence, the adoption and implementation of the CMO Directive[1] was a considerable and necessary step toward a more targeted and still competition-oriented regulatory system.[2] Today, the question remains whether there is any need to use competition law as a tool to control the activities of collective rights management organisations (CMOs) in the EU.

---

* Prof. Dr., LL.M. (UC Berkeley); Director of the Max Planck Institute for Innovation and Competition in Munich; Honorary Professor of the University of Munich.

1 Directive 2014/26/EU of the European Parliament and of the Council of 26 February 2014 on collective management of copyright and related rights and multi-territorial licensing of rights in musical works for online use in the internal market [2014] OJ EU L84/72.

2 The principle of undistorted competition is mentioned at the Directive in its Recital 1. One of the goals of the Directive is to enhance competition among the CMOs of different Member States for rightholders.

Especially in the light of institutional shortcomings of the CMO Directive 2014/26/EU, this article will answer this question in the affirmative. In sum, it will be argued that sectoral regulation of the CMOs should not replace competition law. A functioning system of collective rights management is in need of even three parallel enforcement systems – administrative law enforcement and private enforcement of the rules of the CMO Directive, on the one hand, and competition law enforcement, on the other hand. The analysis will focus on the collective management of exclusive rights, such as in the field of music, and it will not specifically address collective management of statutory remuneration rights.

2 The economics of collective rights management

The justification for state control of CMOs arises from the economics of collective rights management[3]. The fact that national CMOs in the EU hold natural monopolies – even where the law has traditionally refrained from providing for a legal monopoly –, can be explained by strong network effects that characterize the markets in which CMOs are active.

2.1 The relevance of direct network effects

First, markets for collective rights management services are characterised by strong *direct* network effects. Direct network effects describe a market situation where the benefit for an individual customer of buying a product increases with the total number of customers buying the same product. As a consequence, markets characterised by direct network effects are prone to turn into a natural monopoly when one competitor has grown so much that customers can no longer afford to shop elsewhere. Hence, in markets with strong direct network effects, firms will compete *for* the market. Every competitor is interested in controlling the future monopoly, while the losing competitors will have to leave the market.

Strong network effects are present in the market for collective rights management services due to the high fixed costs of setting up and running a CMO while the marginal costs of managing the rights for an additional work are relatively small. Accordingly, a CMO can realise considerable economies of scale by increasing the

[3] See also Josef Drexl, Sylvie Nérisson, Felix Trumpke and Reto M. Hilty, 'Comments of the Max Planck Institute for Intellectual Property and Competition Law for a Directive of the European Parliament and of the Council on Collective Management of Copyright and Related Rights in Musical Works for Online Uses in the Internal Market' 44 International Review of Intellectual Property Law & Competition Law 322, paras 5–9 (2013).

number of works it represents. Since rightholders will seek to increase their income, they can be expected to migrate to the larger and, thus, more cost-efficient CMO.

However, in the EU Member States, national CMOs did not typically emerge from 'competition for the market'. Rather, the first CMO established in a market for the administration of a specific category of works (or related rights) typically attained the status of the only CMO in that market from the very beginning. This confirms that said network effects create high market entry barriers that insulate any incumbent against potential competition.

Neither competition law nor sector-specific regulation should attempt to prevent the emergence of such natural monopolies. Otherwise, regulation would endanger said efficiencies that serve the interests of the rightholders. To guarantee such efficiencies, smaller Member States, such as Austria, even provide for a legal monopoly to prevent inefficient rights fragmentation[4]. In contrast, Germany refrained from implementing such approach when the first Act on Collective Rights Management was adopted in 1965.[5] The legislature was on the one hand concerned that a legal monopoly would not be compliant with the fundamental constitutional right of professional freedom, including the freedom to conduct a business[6], but it was equally expecting that the market forces would anyhow lead to the emergence of monopolized markets.

Yet natural monopolies present a case for regulation, since the incumbent can also abuse its strong market position to the detriment of its customers. Indeed, since they do not feel any competitive pressure, monopolistic CMOs may tend to become inefficient administrators. This explains why the CMO Directive provides for transparency requirements regarding the administrative costs as an incentive for CMOs not to waste resources.[7] Even more, the Directive provides that the management fees do not exceed the justified and documented costs[8]. It thereby safeguards the role of CMOs as trustees of the interests of rightholders.[9] By doing so, it indirectly even strengthens the direct network effects that lead to the natural monopoly.

---

4 See Sec. 7 Austrian Law on Collecting Societes (Verwertungsgesellschaftengesetz) of 2016, [2016] Bundesgesetzblatt Part I No. 27. Section 7(2) even provides that, in case of an application of more than one entity, the monopoly shall be granted to the entity with higher likelihood that it will manage the rights duly and effectively. Thereby, it even provides that among entities that already act as CMOs, preference should be given to the entity with the larger economic significance. The conformity of this provisions with EU law, to the extent that it would exclude any cross-border grant of a licence by a CMO established in another Member State for Austrian territory, is highly questionable. Sections 3(2) and 54 of the Law only provide for an exception for the case of multi-territorial licensing of online rights in works for music.

5 Law on the Management of Copyright and Related Rights (Gesetz über die Wahrnehmung von Urheberrechten und verwandten Schutzrechten) of 9 September 1965, [1965] Bundesgesetzblatt Part I, p. 1294.

6 See comments to the Bill of the Federal Government: Entwurf eines Gesetzes über Verwertungsgesellschaften auf dem Gebiet des Urheberrechts of 23 February 1962, Bundestagsdrucksache 4/273, p. 11.

7 Art. 12(1) Directive 2014/26/EU.

8 Art. 12(2) Directive 2014/26/EU.

9 Cf. the definition of CMOs in Art. 3(a) Directive 2014/26/EU. Ibid., para. 6.

2.2 The relevance of indirect network effects – CMOs as platforms in two-sided markets?

Yet CMOs are not only active in one market. They need to collect the income on behalf of the rightholders from others, namely, the users of works and related rights to whom CMOs grant licences. Therefore, competition law enforcers have identified CMOs as undertakings that are at least active in two markets, namely, on the one hand, the market for services provided to the rightholders (the market for collective rights management services) and a market for services provided to users (the licensing market), on the other hand.[10] Users also have an interest in a functioning system of collective licensing through CMOs, which offer a one-stop shop for rights clearing.

In this regard, CMOs appear as intermediaries that, equal to the platform operators in the modern digital economy, serve different customer groups. To analyse the competitive implications that come with such intermediaries or 'platforms', modern economics nowadays relies on the concept of multi-sided markets.[11] In this regard, it is important to understand the *indirect* network effects linked with such platforms. Indirect network effects characterize a market situation where a firm serves different customer groups, and where the attractiveness of the platform for one customer group on one side of the market supports the attractiveness of the platform for the other customer group on the other side of the market.

Such indirect network effects can also be observed in the field of collective rights management. To attract a growing number of rightholders, CMOs must generate income that turns into payments for the rightholders. Conversely, CMOs will only generate sufficient amounts of income to be attractive for rightholders, if they are able to offer a licence to commercial users for a sufficiently attractive repertoire. Thus, attractiveness of the CMO for one customer group on one side of the market sustains the attractiveness for customer group on the other side of the market. This also means that once a CMO is established in a given market as the only (incumbent) operator, market entry for potential competitors will be extremely difficult since a new CMO would have to convince a critical mass of both rightholders and users to accept its offers.

In competition law analysis, the concept of multi-sided markets plays a critical role for defining the relevant market. More concretely, it responds to the question of whether one should distinguish between separate markets or whether it would be more appropriate to assume a single platform market. As regards collective rights management, competition law enforcers still seem to follow the traditional approach of distinguishing different markets. This is not only so because the case law developed

10 See, for instance, Commission Decision of 8 October 2002, Case COMP/C2/38.014–IFPI 'Simulcasting' [2003] OJ EU L107/51, para. 32 (adding a third market, namely, the one for services provided to other CMOs of other countries in the framework of reciprocal representation agreements).

11 On the economic theory of multi-sided markets, see Jean-Charles Rochet and Jean Tirole, *'Platform Competition in Two-Sided Markets'*, vol. 1, Journal of the European Economics Association, p. 990 (2003).

before the economic theory on multi-sided markets emerged.[12] One may also argue that, in the case of CMOs,to take into account the high entry barriers resulting from the indirect network effects, it is not necessary to assume a single platform. Furthermore, the concept of platform markets can explain why especially digital platform operators only charges a price for the service to costumers on one side of the market while they provide a digital service 'for free' to customers on the other side of the market. In this regard, collective rights management is very different. CMOs act as a particular kind of licensing intermediaries. The price that users pay for taking the licence, will be distributed as collective income to the rightholders. CMOs are remunerated by the administrative charge that they deduce and hold back from the income.

2.3 Different competitive situation in the different markets

There is another reason why it is better to distinguish between separate markets for collective rights management services, on the one hand, and for licensing the use of work or related rights, on the other. The reason is that the structure of these markets is very different.

In this regard, the above observation of CMOs holding a natural monopoly needs more precision. Indeed, one should not assume that where a CMO is the only representing the rights for a given category of works or related rights in a country this CMO holds a natural monopoly. In competition law analysis, this conclusion will only be justifiable if customers do not have access to any viable alternative offer. To decide whether there are competitors in the market, competition lawyers typically ask whether customers would switch to the offers of other firms the firm under consideration increases its price to a certain degree (concept of 'demand-side substitutability').[13]

It is not necessary to explain this exercise of market definition any further. It suffices to point out that that, as regards the concept of the situation of rightholders joining a CMO is very different from a user requesting a license from a CMO. The reason is that in the international and European context, rightholders may well be able to choose between different CMOs. While especially individual authors prefer to mandate their rights for the entire world to a single CMO, they are not 'forced' to mandate 'their' national CMO. While there are certainly cultural and linguistic constraints,[14] rightholders especially in the field of music that is popular internationally may often join CMOs abroad. In particular, Latin American song writers may prefer to join a US Amcrican or a European CMO (especially the Spanish one) to their home CMO.

12 For instance, the market definition in the IFPI Simulcasting case (2002) (n. 11) occurred shortly before the cutting-edge publication of Rochet and Tirole in 2003 (n. 12).

13 See Commission Notice on the definition of the relevant market for the purposes of Community competition law [1997] OJ C273/5, paras 15–19.

14 Linguistic constraints of course exist in the field of writings.

These rightholders may be able to increase income by joining the CMO of the largest market, they can increase income since licensing for the use in this larger market, they can avoid the deduction of a second fee, which would necessarily be imposed if the income were collected thorugh the traditional system of reciprocal representation agreements. Other rightholders simply go abroad because the national CMO is less efficient. To promote competition among CMOs from different Member States in the EU was also among the major objectives to get the CMO Directive adopted in 2014.[15]

In contrast, the situation for users is very different. While the CMO Directive seeks to promote direct cross-border licensing through CMOs established in the EU without the traditional use of reciprocal representation agreements[16], the very different repertoires are typically not substitutable. Competition for rightholders would only within the framework of the traditional reciprocal represenation agreements to the extent that the CMO of origin – the one a rightholder has mandated with the management of the world rights – enters into competition with a local CMO, which based on a reciprocal representation agreement can only grant a licence for its given territory. However, originator companies general refrain from such direct cross-border licensing even in areas where cross-border monitoring of the use of works seems possible. This has caused the European Commission to act against CMOs in the EU alleging a concerted refusal of these CMOs to grant such cross-border licences and online use as well as with regard to satellite broadcasts and cable retransmission.[17] Ultimately, however, the Commission did not manage to prove such concerted practice in appeal proceedings before the General Court.[18]

In sum, competition law holds more potential for promoting competition among CMOs for rightholders, while it can hardly enhance competition among CMOs in the interest of users.[19]

15 See also Drexl et al. (n. 3) para. 9.

16 Several years earlier, this goal was the very motivation for the Commission adopting Recommendation 2005/737/EC of 18 May 2005 on collective cross-border management of copyright and related rights for legitimate online music services [2005] OJ L276/54 (the date of the Recommendation was later corrected to 18 October 2005). Its purpose was to incite rightholders to withdraw their rights from the traditional system of reciprocal representation agreement and negotiate with individual CMOs to enable direct multi-territorial licensing of the online rights regarding the repertoire of the individual rightholders. Of course, this possibility was only available for larger music publishers and not individual authors. The latter remained in the traditional system.

17 Commission Decision of 16 July 2008, Case COMP/C2/38.698–CISAC, C(2008) 3435 final.

18 T-442/08 CISAC v Commission ECLI:EU:T:2013:188.

19 Yet, the decision of the Commission in the IFPI Simulcasting case shows that some price competition in the interest of users can be guaranteed in a system of multi-territorial licensing of online rights that builds on reciprocal representation agreements by allowing users to choose among participating CMOs of different countries when seeking such licence. See Commission (n. 7).

3 The competition law framework for collective rights management

One may indeed wonder whether competition law is capable of catering for the particular needs of a functioning system of collective rights management. Such worries stem from the focus of competition law on safeguarding competition in the market, while collective rights management relies on cooperation, centralization and even monopoly to achieve its copyright goals. However, the following analysis can show that competition law is sufficiently sensitive to enable and optimize a system of collective rights management even from a copyright perspective by protecting the legitimate interests of both rightholders and users against the classical risk of abuse exercised by dominant undertakings.

3.1 CMOs are not considered as illegal price cartels

In the light of traditional competition law, CMOs may at first glance appear as associations of competing undertakings (the rightholders) that collude on price. CMOs indeed replace individual licensing by centralized licensing, and thereby charge uniform royalty rates to licensees.

Yet competition law enforcers have found a way to avoid categorizing centralized licensing as an illegal price cartel. First and foremost, they understood that collective rights management helps to solve a market failure of excessive transaction costs that would otherwise prevent the emergence of a functioning licensing market. Such market failure is especially immenent in the case of mass uses of works, such as regards the communication to the public of works. For this reason, in the common law jurisdictions, most CMOs in the field of music still today operate as entities only for the licensing of the public performance rights, while the rightholders retained the reproduction (so-called 'mechanical') right. This solves the problem that a songwriter would not be able to individually license the use of the copyright in her works for music to each and every user who intends to perform these works publicly. Conversely, such users do not only seek a licence from one rightholder at a given moment. Rather, they seek flexibility as regards the use of anybody's music at any time. Accordingly, they depend on access to large portfolios of works and prefer to enter into a single licensing agreement that would cover all of the existing and even future works that they wish to perform. The solution lies in centralized licensing saving transaction costs for both rightholders and users. To allow collective rights management is thus a condition for functioning markets for the rights of public performance. In today's world of online use of works, this system necessarily has to include the reproduction right for such online use as well.

However, in the competition law framework, it is not that easy to overcome the argument that centralized licensing equates with a price cartel. In particular, under US antitrust law, horizontal price fixing is traditionally considered a per se case of anti-competitive behaviour which cannot be justified by any means. Still, the US Supreme Court in the seminal BMI v. CBS judgment, solved the problem by noting that the blanket licence offered by CMOs constitutes a 'different product' as compared to the licence that an individual rightholder could grant.[20] The Court explained this by the fact that the blanket licence allows for immediate use of the covered works, i.e. without the need for additional individual negotiations for future works, and unrestricted flexibility of the licensees to choose the music they would want to perform.[21] Accordingly, the Court was also able to distinguish CMOs from a mere centralised sales agent who would only grand a licence which is identical to the one the individual rightholder would grant.[22] This line of arguments allowed the Supreme Court to review the business model of CMOs under the antitrust rule of reason, which allowed to make US antitrust law the major basis for controlling the activities through the means of consent decrees of the Federal Courts.

While per se prohibitions are not part of the toolbox of EU competition law, it is equally clear that hard-core restrictions such as horizontal price fixing constitute a clear case of a restriction by object in the sense of Article 101(1) TFEU that hardly ever will have a chance to meet the requirements for an exemption under Article 101(3) TFEU. Still, European competition law practice has adopted an approach that is very similar to the one of the US Supreme Court in BMI v. CBS. In the IFPI Simulcasting case in particular the Commission held on the one hand that the new model reciprocal representation agreement for multi-territorial licensing for the online use of related rights in music restricted price competition among the participating CMOs. Although the new model allowed commercial user to choose which CMO would grant the license, this CMO's freedom to choose the royalty rate was considerably limited by the calculation of the global royalty right as an aggregation of the national royalty rates proportional to the volume music would be accessed from the individual countries.[23] Accordingly, irrespective of which CMO the licensee chooses, the multi-territorial licence will remain the 'same product'[24], leaving very little price competition, namely, as regards potential discounts granted by the chosen CMO as regards the use in its own national territory. On the other hand, however, the Commission granted an exemption under Article 101(3) TEFU. Most importantly, it was able to do so, by categorizing the both multi-repertoire and multi-territorial licence as a 'new product'[25] that users would not be offered without this agreement. The

20 Broadcast Music, Inc. v. CBS, Inc., 441 U.S. 1, 21–22 (1979).

21 Ibid., 22.

22 Ibid. A similar issue appears in the context of centralized licensing of football matches through football federations. Also in this regard, EU competition law takes into account the specificities of the sporting sector. On the requirements to escape the cartel prohibition under Art. 101(1) TFEU see Commission Decision of 19 April 2001, Case 35.576–UEFA broadcasting regulations, [2001] OJ L171/12.

23 European Commission (n. 11), paras 67–70.

24 Ibid., para. 67.

25 Ibid., paras 62 (even mentioned in the context of applying Art. 101(1) TFEU) and 88 (in the context of Art. 101(2) TFEU).

categorization as a new product that users would prefer to the traditional territorially restricted licences allowed the Commission to confirm the first requirement of the promotion of technical and economic progress under Article 101(3) TFEU.[26] In addition, the Commission showed considerable sensitivity for the system of collective rights management in the EU by accepting that abovementioned calculation of the global royalty rate based on an aggregation of the national rates fulfilled the third requirement of indispensability under Art. 101(3) TFEU.[27] The Commission indeed recognized that individual CMOs would otherwise not join the system out of fear that the licensing rate for their countries would be brought below the national rate. Here, the Commission seems to note the particular situation of CMOs of smaller Member States that are often not able to work as efficiently as those of larger Member States. By supporting them, the Commission also showed particular sensitivity for cultural diversity, which depends on the existence of local CMOs in all Members State.

3.2 The function of CMOs to protect rightholders against big exploiters

There is another aspect of the practice of EU competition law which shows particular recognition of the functions of CMOs beyond protecting competition. Already in the early BRT v SABAM judgment the CJEU confirmed that CMOs can claim the transfer of rights to the extent that this is necessary to fulfil their task to protect rightholders against big exploiters.[28] In this regard, the Court seemed to respond to a situation of unequal distribution of bargaining power at a time when individual rightholders were confronted with major exploiters and distributors[29], including public broadcasting organizations that even held legal monopolies in many Member States. Whether the liberalisation of the media markets and the advent of online distributions, which has fundamentally changed situation, now argues for giving up this function could certainly be debated.[30] However, the role of individual platforms for distributing music online, including sharing platforms such as YouTube, as major intermediaries for reaching consumers, may indeed argue otherwise.

Yet European law does not provide any privileged treatment to CMOs. In particular, in the GVL case, the CJEU refused to recognize CMOs as undertakings that

26 Ibid., paras 84–88.

27 Ibid., para. 113.

28 Case 127/73 BRT v SABAM ECLI:EU:C:1974:25, paras 9–10.

29 Ibid, para. 9.

30 Indeed, the Commission has meanwhile argued that there is less need for protecting rightholders against big exploiters in the context of online exploitation in particular when it argued against the legality of a prohibition imposed on rightholders to withdraw online rights from a CMO unless they mandate another CMO with the management of their rights. See Commission Decision of 12 August 2002, Case COMP/C2/37.219 Banghalter & Homem Christo v SACEM, SG(2002)231176 (only available in French).

provide 'services of a general economic interest' in the sense of Article 106(2) TFEU.[31] In this context it is important to note that the CJEU considered the mere fact that Germany has only introduced a special regime of sector-specific regulation without conferring the task of collective rights management to any specific entity as an insufficient basis for the application privileged competition law treatment of CMOs pursuant to Article 106(2) TFEU.[32]

The finding in GVL continues to be relevant despite the entry into force and the transplantation of the CMO Directive. Irrespective of how the question of whether Member States may still create a legal monopoly explicitly confirms that its rules are without prejudice to the application of competition law.[33]

3.3 Control of dominance to protect rightholders

Over the years European competition law mostly developed as an instrument to protect rightholders against the dominant position of CMOs. The principles developed through competition law practice now migrated to the CMO Directive.

In the abovementioned GVL case, the CJEU considered it as an abuse in the sense of today's Article 102 TFEU, if a dominant CMO refuses the management of rights only because of the nationality of the rightholder.[34] In the case at hand, such refusal was particularly harmful to foreign performing artists who had to rely on directly mandating the GVL, the German CMO for related rights, with the management of rights under German law, because corresponding rights did not necessarily exist under the national rules of their home countries. Hence, lack of harmonisation[35] and, consequently, also lack of reciprocal representation agreements among CMOs of different Members States[36] made it indispensable that rightholders of other Member States to be accepted by GVL as a condition to collect revenue from the exploitation of their

[31] Case 7/82 GVL v Commission ECLI:EU:C:1983:52, paras 29–32.

[32] Ibid., para. 31.

[33] See the example of Austria, where the legal monopoly was maintained when the country imlemented the Directive. See n. 5 above. Prior to the adoption of the Directive, the CJEU confirmed the compliance of such monopoly with the principle of free movement of services under Art. 56 TFEU. See Case C-351/12 OSA ECLI:EU:C:110 paras 67--79. On this case, see also Josef Drexl, 'Collective Management of Copyrights and the EU Principle of Free Movement of Services after the OSA Judgment – In Favour of a More Balanced Approach' in Kai Purnhagen and Peter Rott (eds.), *Varieties of European Law and Regulation – Liber Amicorum for Hans Micklitz* (Springer 2014) 459.

[34] Case 7/82 GVL v Commission ECLI:EU:C:1983:52 paras 46–57.

[35] The right at hand, namely, the right to equitable remuneration for secondary exploitation of the performances is today harmonised under Art. 8(2) Directive 2006/115/EC of the European Parliament and of the Council of 12 December 2006 on rental right and lending right and on certain rights related to copyright in the field of intellectual property (codified version), [2006] OJ C376/28.

[36] Harmonisation does not guarantee a comprehensive network of reciprocial representation agreements among the CMOs of all Member States. Even today (November 2021), GVL has not concluded such agreements with CMOs in Bulgaria, Hungary and Slovakia. See list of partner CMOs at: <https://gvl.de/gvl/internationales-internationale-repraesentationsvereinbarungen> accessed 7 November 2021.

rights.[37] The CMO Directive today reaches a similar result by vesting rightholders with a right to mandate the CMO of their choice with the management of their rights in Germany.[38] This right exists without restriction as regards the nationality or the country of residence of the rightholder. It therefore also applies to rightsholders from outside the EU.

EU competition case law has also developed limitations regarding the scope of transfer of rights and the freedom to withdraw rights.

In the very early GEMA I decision, the European Commission looked at different aspects of the scope of the transfer of rights and answered the question of whether CMOs may force rightholders to transfer rights for the whole world, for all uses and, finally, for all existing and future works.[39] The Commission considered the first two requirements as abusive, while it allowed the transfer of rights for all existing and even future works.

The Commission was especially critical on the obligation of rightholders to entrust GEMA with the rights for the whole world. Indeed, this would have prevented rightholders from entering into contracts with different national CMOs that would manage the rightholder's rights directly in the different markets. In addition, GEMA had required the transfer of rights even for countries in which it did not directly manage the rights and, maybe, could not even guarantee that royalties would be collected for the rightholder due to the absence of reciprocal representation agreements.[40]

Moreover, in GEMA I, the Commission considered the mandatory transfer of rights for all types of uses an abuse of market dominance.[41] According to the Commission, the holder of right in musical works should be able to freely choice, for instance, to entrust the broadcasting rights to one CMO and the rights for use of the music in films to another CMO. Such a rule also seems to make sense in the light of the later BRT v SABAM judgment of the CJEU.[42] Indeed, in BRT v SABAM, the CJEU tended to consider the mandatory transfer of all copyrights without distinction between the different types of uses an "unfair condition",[43] but finally left it to the referring court to assess the individual case.[44] Indeed, CMOs grant licences only for particular uses and often to specialised users. Likewise, broadcasting companies are in need of licences for broadcasting music and not for film production. And the film producers are not in need of the broadcasting rights in order to use the music for the film production. Hence, there is no reason why the CMO would need all these rights to grant the licensees the market requires.

37 Case 7/82 GVL v Commission ECLI:EU:C:1983:52 para 54 (pointing out that the rightholder would otherwise not be able to collect revenue from Germany).

38 Art. 5(2) Directive 2014/26/EU.

39 Decision 71/224/EEC of the Commission of 2 June 1971, Case IV/26.760–GEMA, [1971] OJ 134/15 (only German, French, Italian and Dutch version available).

40 Ibid., at II.C.2.a) (p. 22).

41 Ibid.

42 Case 127/73 BRT v SABAM ECLI:EU:C:1974:25.

43 Ibid., para. 12.

44 Ibid., para. 13.

This may also explain why in GEMA I the Commission was more generous with regard to the transfer of rights for all works, including future works. This allows CMOs to build up attractive repertoires in competition with other national CMOs that they may then license for mass use in particular.[45] The creation of larger repertoires also serves the interest of the right-holders, who will benefit from the increased economic value of this repertoire.

In GEMA I, the Commission was extremely critical of restrictions that made it more difficult for rightholders to terminate their relationship with GEMA and join another CMO.[46] In particular, the Commission considered the transfer of rights for a fixed period of six years excessive. In this regard, the Commission did not accept GEMA's argument that such a long period was required in order to be able to fulfil its own obligations under its long-term licensing agreements with users, since GEMA could adequately deal with the loss of works under the clauses of the licensing contracts with the users. In particular, the Commission criticised that the termination of membership would have had no influence on the transfer of the rights for a period of six years even with regard to future works, since the users could hardly expect under their licensing agreements with GEMA that they would have access to any future works at the time of the conclusion of the contract.

The question of whether a CMO should be authorised to license a right to users after the rightholder has withdrawn the right was also a major issue in the BRT v SABAM judgment of the CJEU. In this case, the CMO claimed extended use for five more years after the withdrawal of the right-holder from the CMO. Applying a proportionality test, the Court held that especially a compulsory assignment of rights "for an extended period after the member's withdrawal" can be considered an abuse,[47] but still left it to the referring national court to decide the case.

In 2002, in the Banghalter & Homem Christo case,[48] the Commission considered it an abuse that the French CMO SACEM only allowed a withdrawing of the rights under the condition that the rights would be mandated to another CMO. The Commission alluded to technological changes that had occurred that drastically reduced transaction costs for right- holders, enabling them to create systems of direct licensing to users, while individual management was not conceivable before.[49] In general, it considered the enlarged freedom of right-holders to withdraw rights a welcome additional factor of more competitive pressure on dominant CMOs.[50] Despite this liberalisation, the Commission still seems to follow the approach in BRT v SABAM by confirming the function of CMOs to protect rightholders against big exploiters while balancing this function with interest of rightholders to make use of their freedom to

45 European Commission (n. 36) at II.C.2.a) (pp. 22–23).

46 Ibid., at II.C.2.c) (p. 24).

47 Case 127/73 BRT v SABAM ECLI:EU:C:1974:25, para. 12.

48 European Commission (n. 33).

49 Ibid., 11.

50 Ibid., 10.

benefit from competition by migrating to other CMOs or licensing their rights directly to users by applying a proportionality test.

The rules of the CMO Directive seem to follow this approach by creating more legal certainty as to how the line should be drawn between the interests of the individual rightholder to make use of competition and the function of the CMO to manage rights effectively. On the one hand, it introduces an obligation of CMOs to accept rightholders, whereby the latter have rather broad choice in defining the scope of the mandate, namely, as regards the 'rights, categories of rights or types of works and other subject-matter of their choice, for the territories of their choice, irrespective of the Member State of nationality, residence or establishment of either the collective management organisation or the rightholder'.[51] And it confirms the right of rightholders to withdraw their rights by serving a notice not exceeding six months, whereby the CMO can at best claim that the withdrawal take effect only at the end of the financial year.[52]

3.4 Control of dominance to protect users

As pointed out further above, users may be more in need of protection of competition law since the portfolios of works and rights of CMOs located in different Member States will rarely constitute viable substitutes for users. Commercial users, such as broadcasters, online platforms, etc., typically seek access to the use of works contained in the portfolios of CMOs located in very different countries.

Despite the fact that users seem more exposed to the anti-competitive risks of abuse of market dominance by CMOs, the European Commission in particular has so far largely refrained from exercising control over the licensing practices of CMOs.[53] The reason is that control mostly regards the tariffs set by CMOs as a basis for the royalty rates they charge. Under the rules of Article 102 TFEU, this would require the Commission to make a judgment of whether the licensing practices of CMOs constitute an exploitative abuse and, more specifically, a case of excessive pricing in the sense of Article 102(a) TFEU. Since competition agencies are generally hesitant to act as price regulators, the overall inactivity of the Commission in this field should not surprise anybody.

Yet cases relating to the control of licensing rates have very much contributed to the emergence of a case law of the CJEU on the control of excessive pricing.[54] The relevant judgments so far were triggered by referrals from national courts. This case

51 Art. 5(2) Directive 2014/26/EU.

52 Art. 5(4) Directive 2014/26/EU.

53 It was only in the GEMA I case (n. 43) at II.C.5. (p. 25), that the Commission undertook to also enforce the law against discriminatory royalty rights to the extent that GEMA inposed higher royalty rates on imported music discs.

54 See in more detail than here Josef Drexl, *Copyright, Competition and Development*, Study of the Max Planck Institute for Intellectual Property and Competition Law on behalf of WIPO (2013) 247–251, available at: <www.wipo.int//export/sites/www/ip-competition/en/studies/copyright_competition_development.pdf> accessed 7 November 2021.

law started with judgments on two referrals from French courts. In both the Tournier and the Lucazeau case, the CJEU relied on a comparison with the royalty rates in other countries as a test to identify the excessiveness of royalty rates.[55] Hence, the Court refrained from relying on the profit rate analysis which builds on a comparison of the price with the costs of producing the product. Indeed, this seems justified, and even required, since for copyrighted works the cost of production do not seem to be a very good benchmark for assessing the value of the work. Even more, a cost assessment cannot be implemented in practice where the product is a licence for an extremely large portfolio of existing and future (hence, still unknown) works.

In later decisions, the CJEU further developed the Tournier and Lucazeau approach. In the Kanal 5 case, the CJEU went deeper as regards the tariff structure of the Swedish CMO STIM that calculated the royalty rates differently for public and private TV stations.[56] In the Latvian AKKA/LAA case, the CJEU clarified sub-issues on how to apply the comparison test of Tournier and Lucazeau. *Inter alia*, the Court clarified that for judging on the excessiveness of the royalty rate one has to look at the overall amount charged by the CMO, including the amounts later paid to the rightholders.[57]

In sum, this case law shows that EU competition law does not accept a function of collective rights management in the form of maximizing income for rightholders. In short: EU law does not come with a right of rightholders nor CMOs to charge monopoly prices. This conclusion is not in conflict with European copyright legislation. It was in the framework of applying the principle of free movement of services where the CJEU has also held that copyright protection can be considered as a mandatory requirement that can restrict free movement of services (cross-border satellite broadcasts of football matches in the case at hand), but that copyright law does not come with a right to generate the 'highest possible remuneration'.[58]

In several other Member States, national competition agencies have equally made very important experience in using competition law as a regime to control the royalty rates of CMOs. This is especially the case in Ireland and Spain. In Ireland, the legal situation was rather peculiar prior to the entry into force of the European Regulation 1/2003 for the enforcement of EU competition law.[59] Under the former Irish Competition Act of 1991, CMOs were required to notify their tariffs to the Irish Competition Authority and ask for clearance. Yet, apart from acting against discriminatory royalty rates, the Authority very much refrained from more intensive control of the

55 Case C-395/87 Tournier ECLI:EU:C:319; Joined Case C-110/88, 241/88 and 242/88 Lucazeau ECLI:EU:C:1989:326.

56 Case C-52/07 Kanal 5 ECLI:EU:C:2008:703.

57 Case C-177/16 AKKA/LAA ECLI:EU:C:2017:689 (a case, which first initiated by the Latvian competition authority).

58 Joined Cases C-403/08 and C-429/08 Football Association Premier League and Murphy ECLI:EU:C:2011:631, para. 108 (referring to the wording of EU copyright directives that only provide for a right to 'reasonable' remuneration).

59 Council Regulation (EC) No 1/2003 of 16 December 2002 on the implementation of the rules on competition laid down in Articles 81 and 82 of the Treaty, [2003] OJ L1/1.

royalty rates.[60] More experience was gathered in the Spanish competition system where the former Competition Commission several times had to deal with especially discriminatory royalty schemes and did not hesitate to impose fines on the Spanish CMO SGAE.[61]

While the CMO Directive puts more emphasis on the rights of rightholders and on enhancing competition in the market of collective rights management services, it does not entirely neglect the protection of users against unjustified royalty rights. In Article 16(2)(2), the Directive explicitly states that '[t]ariffs for exclusive rights and rights to remuneration shall be reasonable in relation to, inter alia, the economic value of the use of the rights in trade'. Without doubt, existing competition case law can serve a guidance for the interpretation of the standard of reasonableness. Case law from the Member States so far seems to concentrate more on the reasonableness of the concrete conditions of licensing than the reasonableness of the royalty rates.[62]

3.5 Limitations of competition law

The major conclusion from the foregoing analysis is that competition law has worked as framework legislation that has largely helped to develop appropriate principles of regulation of the collective rights management in Europe that could be used as building blocks for the later CMO Directive.

However, the analysis also shows particular limitations of competition law. One major shortcoming is the reactive character of EU competition law. While both Articles – Arts 101 and 102 TFEU – provide for a legally binding prohibition that directly applicable to CMOs, especially Art. 102 TFEU is too general to serve as the only legal framework for effective regulation of CMOs. In particular, to become effective, it requires enforcement action not least by the competition authorities. Such enforcement remains largely reactive to complaints and therefore takes a long time to develop. Where cases are referred from the national level to the CJEU, the case law has resulted in certain tests and standards, without necessarily drawing clear lines of what is considered a competition law violation and what is considered legal.

More importantly, competition law demonstrates particular institutional weaknesses, which have increased even more with the entry into force of Regulation 1/2003.

60 See in more detail Drexl (n. 58) 251–252.

61 See in more detail Drexl (n. 58) 252–253.

62 See German Federal Supreme Court (*Bundesgerichtshof*) of 9 September 2021, Case I ZR 113/18 – Deutsche Digitale Bibliothek II (pointing out that restrictions on the use of rights – namely, obligations on the licensee to prevent framing – can be reasonable if they pursue the goal of preventing third parties from copyright infringements). The case at hand only incited Court to refer questions on the interpretation of Art. 3(1) InfoSoc Directive 2001/29/EC to the CJEU concerning the requirements under which framing can be considered a communication to the public, while not referring any questions as to the interpretation of Article 16(2)(1) CMO Directive. See the judgment of the CJEU on the referral case: Case C-392/19 VG Bild-Kunst v Stiftung Preußischer Kulturbesitz ECLI:EU:C:2021.

This Regulation made the exemption of Article 101(3) TFEU directly applicable.[63] Under this new regime CMOs are no longer required to notify new types of reciprocal representation agreements prior to their implementation as was the case at the time of IFPI Simulcasting. Quite on the contrary, CMOs are now required to self-assess the conformity of their conduct with Article 101(3) TFEU without being able to request guidance from the competition authorities.

Regulation 1/2003 also pushes aside national competition law as a basis for control of restrictive agreements, since it prevents national competition law from prohibiting an agreement among undertakings or decisions of associations of undertakings that are illegal under EU competition law.[64] This resulted in complete autonomous harmonisation of national competition law with EU competition law in the field of Article 101 TFEU as regards both substantive and procedural law. For instance, this was the reason why Ireland gave up its pre-notification system for the tariffs set by CMOs on the occasion of the entry into force of Regulation 1/2003.

Of course, the reform under Regulation 1/2003 applies to all sectors of the economy. However, while there are reasons for reforming the system, the downsides of the reform particularly affect the markets related to collective rights management. This is so because, despite the fact that collective rights management has produced considerable competition law practice, the Commission has neither adopted any block exemption regulations applicable in the framework of Article 101(3) TFEU nor guidelines that would address collective rights management. The latter is also true for the Guidance Paper on the application of Article 102 TFEU. It does not provide any insights on how to apply the provision to the operation of CMOs as dominant undertakings.[65] The obvious reason is that this Guidance Paper is limited to cases of exclusionary abuse, while potential abuses of the dominant position of CMOs vis-à-vis both rightholders and licensees have to be framed as cases on exploitative abuse.

Moreover, competition law also has shortcomings as regards substantive law. To win cases, competition law enforcers have to be able to argue and prove cases in the light of the concepts of competition law. The reason why the Commission lost the CISAC case before the General Court is to be explained by the problems to argue and prove the presence of a concerted practice as a competition law concept.[66]

4 Need for competition law in the future

The preceding analysis raises the question whether competition law is still needed as a system for control of the conduct of CMOs after the entry into force and

63 Art. 1(2) Regulation 1/2003.

64 Art. 3(2), 1st sentence, Regulation 1/2003.

65 See Communication from the Commission – Guidance on the Commission's enforcement priorities in applying Article 82 of the EC Treaty to abusive exclusionary conduct by dominant undertakings, [2009] OJ C45/7.

66 See text at n. 18 and n. 21 above.

implementation of the CMO Directive. This part answers this question in the affirmative and explains it predominantly with institutional shortcomings of the alternative enforcement mechanisms available in the EU.

4.1 Competition law as one of three available control mechanisms

In this regard, it is important to note that there are three mechanisms of control of CMOs that make use of different parts of the law and different institutions. Competition law is just one of of these control mechanisms. The other two are administrative enforcement and private enforcement of the rules of the CMO Directive.[67] Administrative enforcement relies on enforcement through administrative sector-specific regulatory bodies that need to be set up by the Member States. Competition law is enforced through the competition law authorities and the competent courts. Private enforcement relies on actions initiated by individuals – in particular rightholders or users – before the competent private law courts.

The CMO Directive puts its focus on administrative enforcement, and only safeguards the availability of remedies under competition law and private law enforcement of the Directive in Recital 56 by stating that the Directive is 'without prejudice to the application of rules on competition, and any other relevant law in other areas including … private international law relating to the conflict of laws and the jurisdiction of courts'.

The three control mechanisms do not only differ with regard to the competent institutions. They also differ with regard to the applicable national law.

In a cross-border context, the applicable competition law is traditionally identified according to the so-called effects doctrine. The European legislature explicitly enacted it in the conflict rules concerning private competition law claims. Article 6(3)(a) Rom II Regulation provides for the application of the law of the country 'where the market is, or is likely to be, affected'.[68] In the field of private enforcement of competition law, jurisdiction of the courts in the EU is assessed under the rules of the Brussels I Regulation[69]. Since jurisdiction and applicable law do not necessarily coincide, a competent court may have to apply the competition law of another country (including third countries) pursuant to Article 6(3)(a) Rom II Regulation. As regards administrative enforcement of competition law, the effects doctrine governs both the applicable law and the identification of the competent competition authority.

67 See Art. 36(1) Directive 2014/26/EU.

68 Regulation (EC) No 864/2007 of the European Parliament and of the Council of 11 July 2007 on the law applicable to non-contractual obligations (Rom II), [2007] OJ L199/44.

69 Regulation (EU) No 1215/2012 of the European Parliament and of the Council of 12 December 2012 on jurisdiction and the recognition and enforcement of judgments in civil and commercial matters, [2012] OJ L351/1.

In the field of administrative enforcement of the CMO Directive, the applicable principles are very different. Its Article 36(1) concentrates administrative control of a CMO in the hands of the competent authority designated by the law of the Member State where the CMO is established (so-called country of origin principle). This provision also provides that this authority will exclusively apply its own national law to guarantee compliance of the CMO with the rules of the Directive. These rules fundamentally depart from the competition law approach especially with regard to the control of the CMOs vis-à-vis users, since in a case of cross-border licensing Article 36(1) CMO Directive disconnects both the competent authority and applicable law from the affected market.

As regards private enforcement of the rules of the CMO Directive, its Article 36 does apply. Rather the general rules of the Brussels I Regulation to identify the courts with international jurisdiction and the rules an applicable law including those of the EU Rome I and Rome II Regulations apply. The problem here is that the law applicable to issues of collective rights management is highly uncertain and hardly explored. In particular many issues that arise in the context of private law claims of especially rightholders and users raise issues of characterization. Most recently however the International Law Association based on the work of a group of researchers from different jurisdictions has adopted the so-called Kyoto Guidelines on conflict of laws in intellectual property,[70] which include specific rules on the law applicable to collective rights management.[71]

4.2 Application to different fields of enforcement

Based on on these introductory remarks, it is possible to identify the need of competition law with regard to different field of competition law application.

As regards the protection of rightholders, the additional benefit of competition law is rather limited. Administrative control exercised by the authority in the Member State where the CMO is established is adequate to ensure the respect of the relevant rules of the CMO Directive applicable to the protection of rightholders. Moreover, the rules of CMO Directive explicitly formulate individual rights that the Members States shall ensure.[72] As regards the enforcement of these 'rights' Articles 33 through 34 CMO Directive require Member States to guarantee the creation of CMO-internal

70 International Law Association, 'Guidelines on Intellectual Property and Private International Law ("Kyoto Guidelines")' 12 Journal of Intellectual Property, Information Technology and E-Commerce Law 3 (2021).

71 Guideline 27. See comments by Josef Drexl in Marie-Elodie Ancel et al., 'International Law Association's Guidelines on Intellectual Property and Private International Law ("Kyoto Guidelines"): Applicable Law' 12 Journal of Intellectual Property, Information Technology and E-Commerce Law 44, paras 80–115 (2021).

72 See in particular Art. 5(1) Directive 2014/26/EU introducing the following paragraphs that equally use the terminology according to which the Members shall ensure rights of the righholders.

complaint procedures and the availability of alternative dispute resolution procedures to rightholders. Most importantly, Article 35(2) CMO confirms that righholders as a particular group of parties have a right 'to assert and defend their rights by bringing an action before a court'. In sum, this shows that – in compliance also with the general principle of full effectiveness of European law – Member States have to ensure a system of private enforcement of the rules of the Directive based on individual rights of the righholders. In the international context, rightholders from abroad will typically bring action against a CMO before the courts of the Member State where the CMO is established pursuant to Article 4(1) Brussels I Regulation.[73] As regards the applicable law, Guideline 27(1)(b) Kyoto Guidelines recommends applying the law of the state where the CMO has its actual seat of administration to questions regarding the relationship between the CMO and rightholders. This choice-of-law rule has the particular advantage of allowing the CMO to design its rules of organisation and operation against the backdrop of a single law with regard to all rightholders the CMO represents. This rule thereby also guarantees that the same national rules apply irrespective of whether the rights of rightholders are enforced by the local administrative authority or private law courts.[74] Competition law enforcement will not contribute much beyond such administrative and private enforcement. Most importantly, the possibility to complain to competition authorities adds a second layer of administrative enforcement especially in the case where the sector-specific regulatory authority is not able, or unwilling, to enforce the law effectively.

In contrast, competition law can be expected to still play a major role as regards control of the licensing practices of CMOs. The reason is that concentrating administrative enforcement in the hands of the authority of the Member State where the CMO is established, pursuant to Article 36(1) CMO Directive, does not guarantee effective enforcement of the rules of Article 16 on licensing[75] where licences are granted for other Member States.

This is especially the case as regards identifying the appropriate royalty rate, for which Article 16(2)(2) provides that the tariffs set by CMO shall be ‚reasonable', the main criterion of which being the 'economic value of the use of the rights in trade'. With this latter standard, the Directive obviously refers to the market conditions in the Member State for which the licence is granted. Assessing the economic value of the use according to the circumstances in the Member State for which the licence is

[73] Likewise special jurisdiction for contractual matters pursuant to Art. 7(1)(a) Brussels I Regulation should lead to jurisdiction of the Court in the Member State where the CMO is established, since based on a contract with a foreign rightholder the CMO will have to perform its obligation in that Member State.

[74] See also Drexl (n. 75) para. 84.

[75] This has already been criticized by Drexl (n. 36) 480-481 (regarding the Commission's view prior to the adoption of the CMO Directive that the same result was to be derived from Art. 16 Services Directive 2006/123/EC of the Parliament and the Council of 12 December 2006 on services in the internal market, [2006] OJ L376/36. In OSA, the CJEU rejected this view of the Commission; see Case C-351/12 OSA ECLI:EU:C:110 paras 64–66 (arguing that Art. 17 No. 11 Services Directive provides for an exception from the application of Art. 16 to the services provided by CMOs).

granted is to be taken from the provisions of the law of the Member State where the CMO is established. Yet it should be equally clear that this authority in the country of establishment will be less well equipped – and maybe even less willing – to engage in a sound assessment of the economic circumstances in – potentially – multiple foreign markets than the respective authorities in the Member States for which the licence is granted. This suboptimal institutional choice contained in Article 36(1) CMO Directive as regards control of the licensing practices pays tribute to the internal market goal of liberalizing the operation of CMOs in cross-border cases by avoiding multiplication of control through various authorities in the Member States.

The risk of institutional failure of centralized administrative control of cross-border licensing practices of CMOs is however remedied by a different institutional choice made for both private enforcement and competition law enforcement. As regards private enforcement, Guideline 27(2) Kyoto Guidelines recommends applying the law of the state for which protection is sought to all aspects of the relationship between the CMO and users who seek a licence, including the principles applicable to the calculation fo the royalty fees.[76] This choice-of-law rule indeed seeks to guarantee a level playing field for all CMOs to compete in the state for which the licence is granted irrespectice of where the CMOs are established. However, this level playing field also need to be guaranteed institutionally. Article 35(1) CMO Directive provides for an obligation of the Member States to ensure that disputes between CMOs and users can be brought to private law courts or other independent bodies. Yet the CMO Directive does not contain any rules on international jurisdiction of such courts and bodies. This latter question remains a matter of the application of the Brussels I Regulation. In this regard, in the Austro-Mechana case, the CJEU has already decided that such disputes on the appropriateness of remuneration where European copyright law provides for a right to 'fair compensation' can be brought to the courts of the Member States where the use of the copyright and the related rights took place according to special jurisdiction provision of Article 7(2) Brussels I Regulation on delicts.[77] The logic of this holding lies in the fact that remuneration is indeed required by the law as a compensation for the harm inflicted on the rightholder by the unauthorized use of the copyright or related right.[78] It is equally clear that courts and bodies in the country where the use takes place are much better placed to assess the 'harm' in economic terms. Accordingly, in the framework of private enforement, users have access to the courts and bodies in the Member State for which the licence is granted to assess the economic value criteria of Article 16(2)(2) CMO Directive in the light of the economic circumstances that characterize the market conditions in that state. Beyond such cases relating to statutory remuneration rights, the courts and bodies of the country of the use of rights should also be considered to have jurisdiction where the conflict relates to the licensing of exclusive rights. In this regard, Article 7(2) Brussels I Regulation

76 Guideline 27(2)(e) Kyoto Guidelines. See also Drexl (n. 75) para. 111.
77 Case C-572/14 Austro-Mechana ECLI:EU:C:2016:286.
78 Ibid., paras 43–44.

may not be as obviously applicable. Yet also in this case courts have to assess the value of the use based on a statutory standard (Article 16(2)(2) CMO Directive), albeit for the purpose of controlling the tariffs for the licensing of exclusive rights. This makes Article 7(2) Brussels I Regulation a better legal basis for allocating jurisdiction than Article 7(1) Brussels I Regulation on special jurisdiction for contractual matters. In this regard, it should also be noted that in Austro-Mechana the CJEU has denied the application of Article 7(1) on contractual matters in the context of remuneration rights with the argument that application Article 7(1) requires a contractual obligation that the party has freely assumed.[79] This is exactly not the case where the dispute relates to the application of a statutory standard for such contractual obligation. It follows that Article 7(2) Brussels I Regulation provides for the much better suited legal basis for jurisdiction in cases relating to the appropriateness of royalty rates also in the case where CMO license exclusive rights to users.

Competition law allocates jurisdiction and identifies the applicable law very much along the lines for private enforcement. Based on the effects doctrine the competition law of the state for which the licence is granted will govern the control of licensing practices vis-à-vis licensees for the very purpose of guaranteeing a level playing field for all CMOs active in the market of that state. This law will be enforced by the competition authorities and agencies of this country. Hence, competition law also provides a control framework that can fill the gap created by an institutional failure of the centralization of administrative enforcement in the country of the CMO's establishment. In comparison to private enforcement, competition law enforcement regarding the relationship between CMOs and users may additionally be important also in the future, because it can provide further practice informing the sector-specific authorities as well as the private law courts and independent bodies when interpreting and assessing the economic value of the use of rights in the sense of Article 16(2)(2) CMO Directive.

Finally, it has to be stressed that competition law is not limited to the control of unilateral conduct of CMOs as regards their relationship to rightsholders and users. Competition law will particularly be needed also in the future as regards the control of reciprocal representation agreements under Article 101 TFEU and the control of mergers and other forms of concentrations involving CMOs.

4.3 Additional insights from merger control law

As regards merger control law, recent EU practice shows that concentrations involving CMOs require again close consideration of the effects on the two markets regarding services to users, on the one hand, and services provided to rightholders, on the other hand.

A good example is provided by the decision of the European Commission to clear the joint venture for the establishment of the Zeta platform for multi-territorial

[79] Ibid., para. 35.

licensing of online use of works for music between PRS for Music from the UK, STIM from Sweden and GEMA from Germany.[80] The clearance decision contains important statements with regard to both the licensing market and the market for collective rights management services to rightholders.

As regards the licensing market, the Commission argued that the mere fact that the repertoires of the individual CMOs were to be aggregated for the purpose of multi-territorial licensing would not increase the market power as compared to the one of the individual CMOs. This is a confirmation of the earlier consideration that the repertoires of different CMOs should not be considered as competing substitutes. Because of the character of the individual repertoires as complements their aggregation is much more likely to lead to lower royalty rates by making licensing more efficient than to raising royalty rates.[81] The even more remarkable statement in the decision however is the secondary finding that the tariffs set by Zeta will be subject to the control exercised by the sector-specific administrative authorities of the UK and Germany, from where Zeta was planned to operate.[82] In this regard, the Commission may seem overly optimistic as regards the effectiveness of such control. Against the backdrop of the preceding analysis, the Commission's statement should not be understood in the sense that competition law oversight of the tariffs set in the framework will per se not be needed in the future.

In the light of the preceding analysis, it is remarkable that the Commission was more concerned about negative effects of the joint venture on the position of rightholders than users. With regard to the market for services provided to rightholders, the Commission made the establishment of the joint venture dependent on several commitments. Among the rightholders Zeta was planned to represent were also third-party rightholders such as other CMOs that would mandate Zeta with the multi-territorial licensing of their repertoires[83] as well as so-called 'option 3 publishers' who, following the Commission's Recommendation of 2005[84], withdrew their mechanical rights regarding the Anglo-American repertoire from the European system of collective rights management to license them directly to users[85]. With regard to the latter, Zeta presents an attempt to bring these publishers back into the system of collective rights management of the repertoires of multiple rightholders, whereby cooperation with the British PRS for Music was important since it used to function as a licensing hub for the public performance rights in European jurisdictions concerning the repertoires of

[80] Commission Decision of 16 June 2015, Case M.6800 – PRSfM/STIM/GEMA/JV, C(2015) 4061 final.

[81] Ibid., para. 261.

[82] Ibid., para. 267.

[83] Note that Art. 30(1) CMO Directive obliges a CMO that is already granting multi-territorial licences to accept another CMO's request to also license its repertoire on the condition that this latter CMO is not itself engaging in multi-territorial licensing of its own repertoire.

[84] Commission Recommendation (n. 17).

[85] For a critique on the emerging consequences for users see Morten Huviid, Simone Schroff and John Street, 'Regulating Collective Management Organisations by Competition – An Incomplete Answer to the Licensing Problem?' 7 Journal of Intellectual Property, Information Technology & Electronic Commerce 256, paras 25-28 (2016).

CMOs of other Anglo-American CMOs. The commitments made by the parties of the Zeta joint venture apply both to other CMOs and the option 3 publishers and pursue the goal of ensuring that other providers of multi-territorial licensing services to enter the market. For that purpose, the commitments provide in particular for portability of data so to allow other CMOs and option 3 publishers to migrate more easily to other multi-territorial licensing plartforms.

In sum, these commitments show again that intervention of competition law may still be more needed in the market for services provided to rightholders to keep markets contestable and reap the potential gains of market entry by new competitors.

5 Conclusion

The analysis shows that over many decades European competition law has developed considerable case law in the field of collective rights management. It thereby demonstrated considerable sensitivity for the particularities of the markets involved as well as the need for protection of both rightholders and users that are exposed to the market dominant position of CMOs in the Member States. This case law obviously influenced the EU legislature when it adopted the CMO Directive of 2014 as a competition-informed piece of sector-specific regulation.

However, with the implementation of the CMO Directive the need of competition law control of the activity of CMOs in the EU has not disappeared. While the CMO Directive puts a particular focus on the rights of rightholders, its rules on the protection of users concerning the licensing practices of CMOs, including their tariffs, suffer from particular institutional shortcomings consisting in the concentration of sector-specific administrative control in the Member State of the CMO's establishment. The Directive makes this institutional choice on purpose, namely, to promote cross-border competition among CMO's by enhancing cross-border licensing. Part of this system is the typical approach of internal market regulation to concentrate administrative control in the country of origin of the regulated party. Yet the problem remains the guarantee of effective enforcement of the licensing rules of Article 16 CMO Directive. At least, private enforcement of this rule – despite some legal uncertainties regarding jurisdiction and the rules on applicable law – can help to mitigate the consequences of institutional failure linked to the concentration of administrative enforcement in the state of the establishment of the CMO. It is also here where competition law enforcement guaranteeing the application of the law of the country of the affected market enforced by competition authorities and courts in that country will still be needed. As regards the control of the tariffs of CMOs, competition law practice will continue to be important to provide guidance inspiration for sector-specific authorities and courts when they have to apply the 'economic value' criterion of Article 16(2)(2) CMO Directive.

Moreover, the control of competition law as regards the control of reciprocal representation agreements and mergers cases involving CMOs. Recent merger control law shows that the focus there has to be put on keeping the market open for new entrants that may compete with better services to rightholders. The real challenge that European law is still struggling with in the field of collective rights management of rights in music is to guide the development towards a more integrated system of multi-territorial licensing for online rights that provides non-discriminatory access of all rightholders to the market against the backdrop of a highly complex international licensing system and strong vested interests[86]. In this context, the Zeta merger case of the European Commission provides just additional evidence that competition law can at best fulfil a moderator and enabling function. The Commission's Zeta decision thereby follows the tradition of the IFPI Simulcasting case concerning a new type of reciprocal representation agreements enabling multi-territorial licensing for the digital age.

This once new type later failed not because EU competition law would not accept it, but because large institutional rightholders did not want to support. Therefore, competition law, given its limited tools, should not be blamed for such past – and maybe even future – failures.

86 It has not been the specific purpose of the preceding analysis to comprehensively evaluate the EU policy, including both competition law and the CMO Directive, on multi-territorial licensing of online rights. See, for further reading, Emanuela Arezzo, 'Competition and Intellectual Property Protection in the Market for the Provision of Multi-Territorial Licensing of Online Rights in Musical Works – Light and Shadows of the New European Directive 2014/26/EU' 46 International Review of Intellectual Property and Competition Law 535 (2015).

COMPETITION AND COLLECTIVE MANAGEMENT OF COPYRIGHT IN THE 2019 EU COPYRIGHT DIRECTIVES: AN OVERVIEW

Sylvie Nérisson*

Since competition is everywhere (cf. the objective of further harmonisation in the first recital of DSM Directive), and since professors Drexl and Gervais cover in this book the hard core of competition, this overview seeks to find out what the EU legislator has done with the tool that the 2014 Collective Management Directive (2014/26) had finally regulated: what about collective copyright management in the 2019 package directives (2019/790 Digital Single Market Directive and 2019/789 Revised SatCab Directive or "SatCab 2")?

The ambition to update the 2001 Infosoc Directive, perhaps to fill in its gaps, certainly to codify or repair what recent CJEU case law had been able to raise (Soulier Doke, C-301/15) or open up (VOB, *C-174/15*), combined with the revision of the 1993 Cable and Satellite Retransmission Directive, has inevitably led to disappointment. But the evolution concerning collective management is clear: Directive 2001/29 devoted only two recitals to it, blowing both hot and cold, the 18th one reinforcing existing extended collective licences schemes (the very ones that are the subject of a general clause in Article 12 of DSM Directive), and the 17th one exhorting CMOs to "a higher level of rationalisation and transparency with regard to compliance with competition rules." The 2019 directives reflect this ambivalent approach of the EU towards these simultaneously sacred and untouchable cows, between the carrot of blessing and the stick of constant suspicion.

The recitals of the SatCab 2 Directive contain an argumentation that could have led one to believe that the EU would intervene very broadly in contractual practice by extending the scope of compulsory collective management of exclusive rights beyond what has been in force since 1993: Recitals 1, 3 and 4 describe the difficulties of the licensing market, and Recital 14 refers to the benefits of compulsory collective management for cable operators. However, the compulsory collective management provided for in Article 4 of SatCab 2 directive leaves room for individual management as soon as the operator owns the rights to the broadcasts it retransmits.[1]

* Lecturer (maître de conferences) University of Bordeaux, IRDAP.

1 See Article 5, and on this directive in general: G. Vercken and V. Tabary, "L'autre directive", *Légipresse* n° 372, p. 343, June 2019.

The DSM Directive, too, presents in its preliminary recitals elements that could lead one to believe in the full integration of collective management into European copyright law: further harmonisation of copyright law serves the development of a system "ensuring that competition in the internal market is not distorted" (rec. 1), "provid[ing] a high level of protection for rightholders, facilitat[ing] the clearance of rights and creat[ing] a framework in which the exploitation of works or other protected subject-matter can take place", and the objective "to avoid fragmentation of the internal market" and to respect and promote cultural diversity while highlighting Europe's common cultural heritage (rec. 2). These objectives have justified past interventions in relation to collective management.

However, aficionados of the regulation of collective management remain disappointed. Although collective management appears several times in these two directives, it remains a tool that seems to combine all the defects proscribed by competition law,[2] but a tool that is still used on an *ad hoc* basis as a last resort (the last avatar of the passion for compulsory collective management before 2019 was the management of the remuneration due to performers after extension of the term of their protection, see Directive 2011/77). Let us therefore see the traces of this attraction-repulsion, in other words of this ambivalence of the European legislator towards collective management in the 2019 package.

The seduction of collective management lies in its massive licences, so it is used to allow cultural heritage institutions to digitise and disseminate the works in their collections that are no longer commercially exploited. Nevertheless, it is used in a sector where nothing can be expected from the market since the market has given up on the exploitation of these objects. And it is being used 7 years after the attempt to allow such massive digitisation through the Orphan Works Directive.

In this bold series of provisions designed to increase the supply available online through the interplay of collective management, Article 8 (probably also designed to address the publishers' habit of acquiring rights for astronomical periods of time, or to discourage such publishers from purchasing rights for unreasonable durations), it is to be welcomed that, exceptionally, collective management is not provided for as a residual, but rather as a last resort before an exception or limitation that can only be provided for in the absence of a CMO representing the relevant right holders (see Art. 8 par. 3), and that the open nature of the licences proposed by the CMOs is finally mentioned in a directive: they are non-exclusive licences (art. 8 par. 1).

Thus, without forgetting the search for a market without distortion of competition, it is notable that without expressly providing for a customer allocation clause such as was systematically excluded by the European Commission when CISAC presented it with model agreements at the beginning of the 21st century (*contra* the *OSA* C-351/12 and *CISAC* T 442-08 judgments of the CJEU), Article 8 par. 6 of the DSM directive

[2] Cf. the summary by J. Drexl, "Collective rights management (CMOs)", "CMOs as a necessary evil", pp. 211 et seq. in *Copyright, Competition and Development*, 2013, https://www.wipo.int/export/sites/www/ip-competition/en/studies/copyright_competition_development.pdf.

restricts the freedom of those seeking a licence. This is probably because the purpose of this geographical distribution is not to arbitrarily divide up a market between competitors, but rather to specify the connection to be made in order to verify the CMO's representativeness criterion, and to encourage fruitful collaboration and not competition between CMOs on these repertoires. This intervention in a field generally left in the blind spot of the EU legislator (and in the principles of the founding treaties) is undoubtedly explained, above all, by the low economic stakes of the exploitation of these works that no one imagines monetising. Having said that, it was probably the same consideration that led the French legislator to set up articles L. 134-1 et seq. of the French intellectual property code, thinking that no one would challenge a system that made works lost in the shelves of the National library visible and profitable for digital exploitation without either the publisher or the author having to do much except not oppose the system. This was forgetting the authors, who are not satisfied with "benefiting from the legitimate use of their works" rec. 45 *in fine*.

The general clause of Article 12 will reassure Member States who only had Recital 18 of Directive 2001/29 to ensure the conformity with EU law of their regimes for the extension of the repertoires over which CMOs can grant licences. Once again, one can see a restrained passion, a reasonable love of the EU for collective management, since this rich article 12 contains a second paragraph which reads more like a (at least) 3-step test, than an unreserved recognition of the relevance of extending to an entire sector the terms of a contract negotiated by the bulk of the interested parties, an extension always tempered by the possibility of opting out of the general licence par. 3 c).

One cannot reproach a legislator for being restrained, reasonable and ambivalent; the search for a balance requires these reservations. However, one may also be disappointed to see collective management promoted as a tool for exploitation (to enable operators to rebroadcast programmes, to enable libraries to distribute their collections, the extension of the licence is considered as "providing total legal certainty for users", rec. 45 DSM), but totally absent from the parts devoted to the remuneration of the author and performers.

While setting out framework principles for extended collective licenses and intervening in the remuneration of authors, one might have hoped for the recognition and framework of a provision on the relationship between the fairness of remuneration and the tariffs issued by the CMOs. However, this may have been a step into the minefield of the nature of the author's remuneration (the fruits of ownership, or remuneration for an authorization or a work) and the representativeness of these organisations, which are often organisations of rights holders rather than of authors or holders of related rights, and which include not only the heirs of authors but also their assignees, who also become holders of related rights.

This is the latest illustration of the false confidence that the 2019 package has given to collective management: when, in Article 16, the DSM Directive defuses what the HP v. Reprobel case law had provoked in its judgment of 12 November 2015 (C-572/13), without saying a word about collective management (recital 60 lifts the veil), whereas that is precisely what this article aims to do (the benefit of royalties to compensate for an exception or limitation, managed by a CMO bringing together authors – referred to in the 2001 Directive as rightholders suffering the harm of the compensated exception – and publishers (transferees of rights) impaired by the exception, but not mentioned in the InfoSoc Directive as rightholders. It is this relationship between author and publisher, a symbiotic relationship (especially in the field of music and the written word), that the repeated prohibition of discrimination among the rightholders represented in the CMO[3] anchors within the CMO. It is to be hoped that the CMOs will be able to pacify this relationship.

We will conclude with the impression that collective management, like its encounter with competition law, remains in the blind spot of the European legislator's intervention, but that this is no doubt to be welcomed, particularly in view of the contractual genius of market operators – the vicissitudes of the neighbouring right of press publishers, which after litigation before competition authorities seems to be moving towards voluntary collective management, will probably provide an example of this – but also of the sectoral approach adopted by the legislator in the field of copyright, which leads to a fragmentation that it would be mistaken to try to fix with a systemic recourse to collective management.

[3] See Art. 8(3)(b) and 12(3)(b).

ARGENTINIAN EXPERIENCE WITH COMPETITION AND TARIFF SETTING

Delia Lipszyc*

I shall divide my work into four parts: a bit of history, the collective management paradigms applicable in the case; the Argentine experience and a brief conclusion.

History

The first CMO in the Latin American region was founded in Argentina, more than a century ago, by authors of dramatic works, and it developed in a similar way to collective management in France, where it began with the SACD.[1] That first Argentine entity was the Society of Dramatic Authors, established on September 11, 1910 and it held its first meeting in January 1911 in the city of Buenos Aires.

Internal disagreement led to the creation, in the late 1920s, of the *Círculo Argentino de Autores* (Argentine Circle of Authors).

But experience showed that the entire sector was weakened by the duplication of societies, so several steps were taken towards unity until December 17, 1934, when the current General Society of Authors of Argentina (ARGENTORES) of Reciprocal Protection (*Sociedad General de Autores de la Argentina –ARGENTORES– de Protección Recíproca*), was created as a civil and mutual association.

On the other hand, in 1936 the authors and composers of musical works incorporated SADAIC, the Argentine Society of Authors and Composers of Music, civil, cultural and mutual entity (*Sociedad Argentina de Autores y Compositores de Música, entidad civil, cultural).*

Founded as one-of-a-kind societies, they were both ultimately vested with the official legal representation of authors (SADAIC in 1967 and ARGENTORES in 1973),[2] that is, the legal recognition that they had been in practice representing authors since their foundation.[3]

---

* Professor at the Law School of the University of Buenos Aires. President of ALAI-Argentina. The English translation of this text was revised by Pablo Wegbrait.

1 *Société des Auteurs et Compositeurs Dramatiques.*

2 By laws number 17,648 and 20,115.

3 The collective management of the rights of directors of cinematographic and audiovisual works has been carried out since 2009 by DAC (an acronym for Argentine Association of Cinematographic and Audiovisual Authors and Directors). Executive Order 124/09 recognized to DAC the representation of cinematographic directors and authors of audiovisual works in general (Argentine and foreign) and their beneficiaries, to receive and manage fees paid pursuant to law 11,723 for any type of

Among the powers recognized to both societies are granting authorizations for the use of the works they manage; entering into contracts for the use of repertoires; setting minimum tariffs or striking deals with different categories of users; collecting and distributing the amounts accrued for the use of the works and instituting the necessary legal actions.

Paradigms of Collective Management

I shall only refer to the five paradigms that are most related to what was discussed in the judicial case that I shall present in the following chapter:

(a) *Collective management activity includes at least two basic aspects: collection and distribution.*

(b) *One society for each category of managed right. When several collective management societies operate in one country, the condition is that each kind of rights of works of the same category should not be managed by more than one entity* (Argentina, Austria, Chile, France, Mexico, Switzerland, etc.).

In this regard, Mihály Ficsor has pointed out that, in relation to certain categories of rights, many of the fundamental advantages of collective management can only be achieved through one single organization (the convenience and legal certainty of the granting of user licenses, the possibility to authorize the use of the entire world repertoire in one single license, the considerable reduction of administrative expenses, etc.) so it seems appropriate to avoid parallel organizations and create a single one for each category of rights.[4]

The theory and practice of collective management, backed by certain historical experiences, shows that competition between CMOs managing the same kind of rights, far from improving the conditions of their use, is detrimental to the sectors concerned because:

- It is inconvenient for users if, as usual, they wish to access works available in the market. If management of works of the same class is divided between two or more entities, they will be subject to several claims and they will have to pay several overlapping fees, which can determine the involvement of the government authority in some way not desired by local authors (as it happened, for example, in Brazil);
- It harms the authors, because competition often leads to a "rate war", resulting in a considerable decrease in revenue and creating conditions for non-compliant users to avoid payment through different subterfuges: confronting one society against the other, forcing them to sue legally arguing that the claimant's repertoire has not been used, forcing them to prove which works were actually used, and so on.

exploitation, use, making available interactively or communication to the public, in any form, of their works fixated in recordings or other audiovisual media.

Other CMOs deals with the rights of performers (AADI), producers of phonograms (CAPIF), performers in audiovisual works (SAGAI), authors of visual works (SAVA) and authors and publishers for reprographic rights (CADRA).

4 Ficsor, M., *Collective administration of copyright and related rights*, Geneva, WIPO, 1991, §243, p. 73).

A collective management strategy subject to the need to overcome such everyday inconveniences is impracticable and not only does it neutralize the advantages that it entails but it also discredits CMOs and weakens copyright itself.

Uniform rates according to the use and the user

Even if CMOs have the power to establish compensation schemes, as in Argentina, where both societies (SADAIC and ARGENTORES) are legally vested with the power to set tariffs (Executive Order No. 5146 of 1969, regulation of law 17.648, art 3.b, and Executive Order No. 461 of 1973, regulating the law 20,115, art. 2.b, respectively), it is preferred for tariffs to result from agreements, because of the obvious benefits for all interested parties to have a relationship between authors 'and users' representatives that develops in a manner satisfactory for all parties, which is usually reached only after long and protracted discussions.

The tariffs are agreed (or fixed by the CMO) on different bases[5] according to the kind of use. They vary by country – and even within it at different times – although some rules can be considered traditional (because they are observed internationally.

The free use of works does not prevent the authors of the works from being entitled to compensation, except in the specific cases in which the law establishes limitations of the right of public representation or execution that allows free and non-compensated use[6] (usually it is noted that the organizers can not claim to be exempt from the payment of consumption of electric energy by relying on the absence of a lucrative purpose or the beneficial or cultural purposes of the act).

The rates are a minimum. They are a starting point, not a cap.

In the CMOs that manage rights of representation of dramatic and dramatic-musical works the general tariffs usually are a *minimum*.

Individual authors may condition the use of works to the payment of higher compensation, but they cannot accept a lower one. The "minimum tariffs" function as starting points (they guarantee minimum compensation that cannot be reduced, similar to the situation in Labor Law with the rates established in collective bargaining agreements applicable to workers belonging to a certain branch of industry).

(c) *The social / cultural activities.*

The role of the CMO is not limited to the administration of Copyright. They carry out important welfare activities (social protection programs of their members)[7]

5 Compensation may be proportional to the one resulting by the exploitation of the works (it could either be a flat fee or result from a percentage). Although, in principle, percentage remuneration is considered the most fair because it is the only one that allows the author to participate in the economic success of the work.

6 In Spanish, "utilización libre y gratuita", which may be translated as "free and non-compensated use" because in English free may mean "non-compensated" and also "free" (in the sense of "freedom"). However, in Spanish "libre" means "free" as in "freedom" and "gratuita" means free in the sense of "non-compensated".

7 They usually include the granting of ordinary and extraordinary pensions in favor of the authors; pensions in favor of certain heirs of the author; assistance in case of disease, maternity and special needs; supply of medical assistance services for members and their primary family members; funeral subsidies; collective insurance; etc.

and cultural activities (aimed at improving the technical and artistic abilities of their members).[8]

The Argentine Experience

In April 1995, *Transeuropa Video Entertainment San Luis, S.A.* secured from the North American literary agency ICM the rights for the performance in Argentina of the play "*El beso de la mujer araña – El musical*" ("The Kiss of the Spider Woman – The Musical"), an adaptation to musical comedy of the well-known play by the Argentine writer Manuel Puig.

Before the premiere at a frontline theater in the city of Buenos Aires (the Lola Membrives Theater), the lawyer of Transeuropa (the theater company) warned ARGENTORES to refrain from collecting royalties in that case due to the contract signed with the American literary agency ICM, considering the intent of the authors represented by it and also taking into account that ICM requested that ARGENTORES should be excluded from all participation arguing that it had delayed remitting royalties in previous opportunities. ICM also relied on the Economic Deregulation Act passed in 1991 that had left without effect the monopolistic powers of ARGENTORES and SADAIC, according to the opinion of the Undersecretary of Economy issued as a result of the request by an association of Cinematographic Producers, whose secretary was Transeuropa's lawyer.

Subsequently, the latter filed a lawsuit against ARGENTORES with the purpose of stating that the CMO lacked the power to set tariffs, collect royalties and control amounts resulting from ticket sales.

In the same judicial proceedings, Transeuropa obtained an injunction ordering ARGENTORES to refrain from collecting royalties in the performances that would take place at the Lola Membrives Theater.

This forced ARGENTORES to institute a claim for royalty collection against Transeuropa and against the owner of the theater where the play would be represented.

Both proceedings (the declaratory action instituted by Transeuropa and the action for royalty collection instituted by ARGENTORES) were heard simultaneously by the same court.

Different interlocutory judgments throughout these proceedings lifted the prohibition to control the show and ordered an attachment of 15% of the amounts collected (that is, the fee claimed by ARGENTORES for the public performance of a musical

8 Through the organization of courses for musical, dramatic-musical, dramatic or literary training; stimulating creative activity; protecting the cultural heritage they manage, through the collection and publication of the works and their promotion and dissemination; ensuring the defense of the national intellectual and artistic tradition; encouraging the legislative and scholarly progress of Copyright and its dissemination and defense in Argentina and abroad; establishing or acquiring libraries linked to the branches of art belonging to the works they manage, establishing collections of musical and dramatic works, etc., catalogues of musical repertoires, treatises, publications and other related creations; etc.

comedy) as well as the designation of a controller in the ticket office of the theater, a fine against the theater for delay in delivering a portion of the amounts subject to attachment and the filing in the court record of the collection report.

Representations of the work ended on December 10, 1995, earlier than expected.

ARGENTORES managed to file with the court several reports from official bodies about the CMO's social importance issued by the Ministry of Culture, the *Fondo Nacional de las Artes* (National Fund for the Arts), the Ministry of Justice and the Copyright Office, as well as entities linked to the sector: the Latin American branches of the CISAC, the representatives of foreign authors in the country, SADAIC, and the *Asociación de Empresas Teatrales* (Association of Theater Companies).

The most complex task was the one carried out before the *Dirección Nacional de Desregulación Económica* (National Department of Economic Deregulation) of the Ministry of Economy which, in the other proceedings, had already expressed a position contrary to the interests of authors' societies through a senior official.

With great effort to overcome prejudice from officials, ARGENTORES was able to demonstrate that it was not included within the parameters laid down by the Economic Deregulation Act and that its function was socially useful and necessary, which ultimately led the Ministry of Economy, Public Works and Services to adopt Resolution No. 618/97.[9] Among the reasons for the Resolution it is stated that "*the regulations of authors' societies and their powers are linked to cultural aspects and are clearly different from the objectives and scope of Executive Order No. 2284/91 for Economic Deregulation, which does not mention either copyright or authors, nor artistic works, nor entities in charge of the management of said interests*."

The first instance judge upheld the right of ARGENTORES to collect royalties and its monopolistic powers, ordering payment to the CMO of the royalties claimed.[10]

Both parties appealed, but when the Court of Appeals was ready to hand down a judgment, the court convened a hearing in which they reached a settlement.

Before giving an account of the content of the settlement, it must be said that from the outset, numerous attempts for an agreement took place, which were initiated even before Transeuropa instituted the declaratory action. Attempts were renewed at the entity's headquarters, in the court of first Instance – at the judge's request – and, in some cases, with the participation of the court-appointed supervisor.

At the Court of Appeals, the representatives of the companies sued by ARGENTORES and their lawyers met again with executives of the entity.

The advantages of the agreement finally reached were, among others, that:

- The validity of the powers of ARGENTORES to set tariffs and to control income was reaffirmed,

9 An exception from the application of the provisions of Executive Order No. 2284/91 for Economic Deregulation is provided for authors' rights contemplated under Law No. 17.648 and the Decree-Law 20,115/73, which recognized the Argentine Society of Authors and Composers of Music (SADAIC) and the General Society of Authors of Argentina (ARGENTORES), respectively.

10 Regarding the declaratory action initiated by Transeuropa, the judge considered that it was not necessary to hand down a judgment because, at that time, the performances had already ceased.

- Manuel Puig's heirs who, at all times had supported Argentores, were satisfied. Without this support the entity's actions would have appeared contrary to the will of the author's heirs, and without ARGENTORES the heirs would have charged ICM several times less than the amounts resulting from applying the minimum 15% tariff.

Conclusion

The guiding principles of collective management outlined above reveal that they can hardly be perceived as adjusted to the rules of competition if it is not first considered that CMOs do not compete with each other and what is the meaning of their existence for the validity and effectiveness of copyright.

That is why we see how often the decisions of national antitrust offices are contrary to collective management in general and to monopolistic CMOs in particular, as well as to uniform tariffs, which are ultimately overturned by the courts, indicating that CMOs do not involve an abuse of a dominant position.[11]

A good example of the above in Latin America is, among others, a recent case involving SADAIC.[12]

In my opinion, when addressing the issue it is useful to remember the *SACEM / discotheques* case, a conflict that began in 1978 and for ten years caused great controversy around collective management in France, and that Jean-Loup Tournier described as "unprecedented judicial war" describing it and analyzing with great mastery and knowledge of collective management in the article published in the RIDA in 1989.[13]

History repeats itself.

11 In this regard, it is worth noting the analysis of the question of the dominant position of CMOs by Thierry Desurmont in "The SACEM and competion law", *RIDA*, no. 140, April 1989, ps. 117-179.

12 In August 2019, Division III of the Federal Chamber of Civil and Commercial dismissed the fine imposed by the Ministry of Commerce based on alleged abuse of a monopolistic position in setting the rates that hotels must pay to the Argentine Society of Authors and Composers of Music (SADAIC). The fine originated in a complaint filed in 2009 by the Federation of Hotels of the Republic of Argentina (FEHGRA), in which SADAIC was accused of alleged abuse of a dominant position in setting the rates for communication to the public of musical works in hotel rooms, substantially through televisions made available to guests. In the judicial decision, the Court said, among other things, that the rates set by SADAIC were reasonable as reported by the accounting experts who had participated in the administrative procedure. It was also noted that it had not been demonstrated that SADAIC's tariffs affected the general economic interest of consumers nor the hotels' financial situation. (Source: www.sadaic.org.ar).

13 Tournier, Jean Loup – "The SACEM/Discotheques conflict an unprecedented legal war", *RIDA*, n° 140, April 1989, ps. 3-17.

GEOBLOCKING IN EU COPYRIGHT LAW

Tatiana Eleni Synodinou*

EU copyright law has attempted to resolve the antithesis between the ideal of the single market and the concept of copyright territoriality through a modest approach, which is based on the axiom of safeguarding copyright territoriality and of the accompanying geoblocking practices. The aim of this article is to critically analyse the EU's steps towards the circumvention of the principle of territoriality and of geoblocking and to demonstrate that, as the efforts to create a digital single market are intensified, a strict EU geoblocking policy in relation to services offering access to copyright-protected works cannot be retained. The article is divided into three parts. Part one is dedicated to the consequences of the principle of territoriality on European copyright law (II). Part two is dedicated to the steps, both jurisprudential and legislative, which have been taken to move away from the principle of copyright territoriality at the European level (III). Part three is dedicated to the recently adopted Geoblocking Regulation 2018/302, while possible ways to move forward are also analysed (IV).[1]

1 Introduction

Walls, fences, barricades and boundaries are always and everywhere to be found. They were there in the past and they are there now.[2] From the mythic wall of biblical Jericho, which was constructed as many as 12,000 years ago, to erecting a fence in order to indicate one's ownership, walls and boundaries have been linked both to exclusion and seclusion: to keep some people in and others out.

Similarly, copyright – the most sacrosanct of all properties[3] – has always been defined by boundaries and borders. The entire construction of copyright is built on the power of the copyright holder to exclude. At the same time, copyright laws, based on the principle of copyright territoriality, are conceived as geographically defined

* Associate Professor, Law Department, University of Cyprus.

1 This study was first published in GRUR International, vol. 69, issue 2, February 2020, pages 136–150, under the titl: "Geoblocking in EU Copyright Law: Challenges and Perspectives". The study is freely available on line at: https://academic.oup.com/grurint/article/69/2/136/5717989?login=true.

2 Ed Williams and Anna Johnson, 'Walls and Fences: Perspectives from Universities and Museums' 50(3) Journal of the Southwest 227-241 (2008).

3 Jane Ginsburg, "Une chose publique?' The author's domain and the public domain in early British, French and US copyright law' in Paul Torremans (ed), *Copyright Law: A Handbook of Contemporary Research* (Edward Elgar 2007) 145.

rights. Being born from the specific socio-economic, cultural and legal idiosyncrasy of certain enlightened states in the 18th century, copyright law has always had a pronounced territorial identity. Even though the commercialisation of copyright-protected works beyond national borders created the need for extraterritorial, international principles with a universal dimension,[4] the strong link of national copyright laws with the territorial bodies from which they derive has remained.

On the basis of the foregoing, controlling access to copyright-protected content via geoblocking appears to fit well into a mainstream conception of copyright law. Geoblocking is a technological protection measure which *de facto* restores the principle of copyright territoriality in the potentially borderless internet by restricting access to copyright-protected content on the basis of the user's geographical location. In this context, geoblocking complements copyright law. Geoblocking safeguards the copyright owner's contractual power/freedom[5] to geographically divide, by contract, the markets for the work, to fix different prices for different territories and to maximise the profits deriving from the exploitation of the work. In this context, geoblocking makes territorial licensing agreements effective by limiting access to copyright works to a national public or a linguistically homogenous audience located in a given territory.[6] In order to ensure that licensees comply with their licences, licensees are required to apply geoblocking measures to block access to copyright-protected content from territories which are not covered by their allocated licence.

For internet actors, geoblocking often appears to be the only means to tackle the legal uncertainty caused by the lack of uniform copyright law within the EU. However, even if compliance with different national copyright laws does not require geoblocking, internet actors may still choose to partition markets in order to protect their different interests, such as localised versions of content, maximisation of revenues through staggered content release, and exclusive licensing to local content providers.[7]

Conversely, EU law is based on the principle of the abolition of national markets and their replacement by a single market where prices tend to converge for the benefit

4 Alexander Peukert, 'Territoriality and Extraterritoriality in Intellectual Property Law' in Günther Handl, Joachim Zekoll and Peer Zumbansen (eds), *Beyond Territoriality: Transnational Legal Authority in an Age of Globalization* (Brill Academic Publishing 2012) 189-228 <https://ssrn.com/abstract=1592263> accessed 3 September 2019.

5 Multi-Territory Licensing of Audiovisual Works in the European Union, Multi-Territory Licensing of Audiovisual Works in the European Union Final Report Prepared for the European Commission, DG Information Society and Media, October 2010, available at <http://www.keanet.eu/docs/mtl%20%20exec%20summ%20en.pdf> accessed 3 September 2019.

6 Giuseppe Mazziotti, 'Is Geo-Blocking a Real Cause for Concern in Europe' (*Cadmus*, EUI Department of Law Research Paper No 2015/43, 1) <https://cadmus.eui.eu/handle/1814/38084>; Tambiama André Madiega, 'Digital Single Market and geo-blocking' (*European Parliamentary Research Service Blog*, 13 May 2015) <http://epthinktank.eu/2015/05/13/digital-single-market-and-geo-blocking/> accessed 3 September 2019).

7 Marketa Trimble, 'Copyright and Geoblocking: The Consequences of Eliminating Geoblocking' 25 Boston University Journal of Science and Technology Law (2019) <https://ssrn.com/abstract=3330876> accessed 3 September 2019).

of consumers. Business models based on the fragmentation and separation of markets are inherently at odds with the enhanced economic integration of a single market, the aim of which is to abolish national markets.[8]

The collision between geoblocking and EU law necessarily impacts on the development of EU copyright law. Geoblocking, as an expression of the principle of territoriality, loses its main justification in the case of a unitary copyright. Conversely, EU copyright law cannot evolve into a unitary law, but can only continue along the patchworked path of harmonisation, as long as the combination of territoriality and geoblocking persists.

The aim of this article is to critically overview the dominant territorial licensing and geoblocking practices of copyright protected works, whose fundamental justification is the sacrosanct copyright territoriality principle. The article will inquire on the effects of territoriality on EU copyright law and on the steps which have been taken at an EU level towards an overcoming of this principle. The analysis will be based on a juxtaposition of the jurisprudential and the legislative steps for the overcoming of territorial licensing and of geoblocking practices. The main thesis of this article is that competition law alone cannot provide an answer to the legal challenges linked to cross-border access to copyright-protected content in a constantly developing digital environment and that legislative intervention in the field of copyright law will be needed. As the efforts to create a digital single market are intensified, a strict EU geoblocking policy in relation to services offering access to copyright-protected works cannot be retained. In this context, the forthcoming evaluation of the Geoblocking Regulation 2018/302 is an opportunity to explore alternative ways to deal with the question, such as introducing the obligation for an EU trader to legitimately and passively distribute copyright-protected content in response to a consumer's request, provided that the latter pays the legitimate additional cost of the licensing in her/his country.

The article is divided into three parts. Part one is dedicated to the consequences of the principle of territoriality on European copyright law (II). Part two is dedicated to the steps, both jurisprudential and legislative, which have been taken to move away from the principle of copyright territoriality at European level (III). Part three is dedicated to the Geoblocking Regulation 2018/302, while possible ways to move forward are also analysed (IV).

8 Communication of the European Commission on Creative Content Online in the Single Market, COM(2007) 836 final, 3 January 2008, 5.

2 Territotiality in EU Copyright Law: a Retrospective

2.1 The Foundations of the Principle of Territoriality and its Consequences on European Copyright Law

Geoblocking is an expression of the well-established principle of copyright territoriality. According to this principle, copyright law applies to and is enforceable only in the territory of those Member States that grant it.

Copyright territoriality is an expression of national sovereignty. It enables nation states to adjust their IP policies and subsequently their national IP laws to match their particular national needs.[9] Generally speaking, 'the territoriality principle holds that a state has no competence to prescribe legal rules to govern activities that occur outside its national borders'.[10] The principle is enshrined in the rule of national treatment established in Art. 5(2) of the Berne Convention[11] and it has been confirmed within the EU by the Court of Justice of the European Union (CJEU).[12]

---

9 Annette Kur and Thomas Dreier, *European Intellectual Property Law: Text, Cases and Materials* (Edward Elgar 2013) 13.

10 Peter Goldsetin and P Bernt Hugenholtz, *International Copyright – Principles, Law and Practice* (Oxford University Press 2013) 97.

11 P Bernt Hugenholtz and others, 'The Recasting of Copyright & Related Rights for the Knowledge Economy' (2006) Amsterdam Law School Research Paper No 2012-44, 23 <https://ssrn.com/abstract=2018238>.

12 See: Judgment of 14 July 2005,Case C-192/04 *Lagardère Active Broadcast v Société pour la perception de la rémunération équitable (SPRE) and Gesellschaft zur Verwertung von Leistungsschutzrechten mbH (GVL)* EU:C:2005:475, para 46 ('... the principle of the territoriality of those rights, which is recognised in international law and also in the EC Treaty. Those rights are therefore of a territorial nature and, moreover, domestic law can only penalise conduct engaged in within national territory.'); Judgment of 27 February 2014, Case C-351/12 *OSA – Ochranný svaz autorský pro práva k dílům hudebním o. s. v Léčebné lázně Mariánské Lázně a. s.* EU:C:2014:110, para 76 ('The observations submitted to the Court have not shown, as regards a communication such as that at issue in the main proceedings, that – as European Union Law stands at present – there is another method allowing the same level of copyright protection as the territory-based protection and thus territory-based supervision of those rights, a method of which legislation such as that at issue in the main proceedings forms a part'); Judgment of 16 June 2011, Case C462/09 *Stichting de Thuiskopie* EU:C:2011:397, para 36 ('It follows from the foregoing that, if a Member State has introduced an exception for private copying into its national law and if the final users who, on a private basis, reproduce a protected work reside on its territory, that Member State must ensure, in accordance with its territorial competence, the effective recovery of the fair compensation for the harm suffered by the authors on the territory of that State'). See further art 3(3) and annex, Directive 2000/31/EC of the European Parliament and of the Council of 8 June 2000 on certain legal aspects of information society services, in particular electronic commerce, in the Internal Market ('Directive on electronic commerce') [2000] OJ L 178/1 (the country of origin rule under the electronic commerce Directive does not apply to intellectual property rights). For the sources of the principle of territoriality, see: Peukert (n 3).

Consequently, there is no uniform EU copyright law, but there are 27 individual national copyright laws which apply respectively within the territory of each Member State.[13] National copyright laws are independent and might present significant differences. As a result, the same work can be protected in one Member State, but not in another. Its author or rightholder might be a different person, depending on which Member State's law applies and divergent copyright exceptions apply within the territory of the EU.

The principle of territoriality appears to be an obstacle to the free movement of goods and services in the internal market, since its direct effect is the segmentation of the EU Market into 27 national markets.[14] As Jane Ginsburg has noted, although authors and their works in a digital environment are no longer territorially tethered in all circumstances, 'regimes must still derive their authority from territorial sovereigns'.[15] Indeed, rightholders can diversify the terms of offer for services giving access to copyright-protected content depending on the 'territory' (the location) of the user. This result is contrary to the EU's aim of abolishing restrictions on trade in goods and cultural products among EU Member States. Territorial licensing for content protected by copyright on a country-by-country basis in the EU 'leads to extensive market fragmentation'.[16]

EU copyright law was born with this inherent antinomy: despite being designed as substantially territorial in nature (in an age of privileges expressly limited to a specific territory under the control of the sovereign),[17] it then had to accommodate the needs and aims of the internal market.

The CJEU attempted to overcome this conflict of aims at an early stage by establishing the legal fiction that EU law could regulate the 'exercise' of national Member State copyrights in order to establish and maintain the internal market.[18] On the other hand, EU law could not prejudice the national Member State's laws on property ownership and on the 'existence' (the essence) of the copyright itself. The application of national measures that obstruct the free movement of goods or services is permitted only if it is necessary for safeguarding the 'specific subject matter' – the essence – of copyright,[19] which has been broadly perceived as covering the exclusive

13 P Bernt Hugenholtz, 'Copyright Territoriality in the European Union, Note' European Parliament, Directorate General for Internal Policies Policy Department C: Citizens' Rights And Constitutional Affairs Legal Affairs 2010, 6.

14 Tatiana Synodinou, 'EU Portability Regulation: In-depth Analysis of the Proposal' (Study prepared for the JURI Committee of the EU Parliament, 2016) .<http://www.europarl.europa.eu/thinktank/en /document.html?reference=IPOL_IDA(2016)571369>.

15 Jane C Ginsburg, 'Cyberian Captivity of Copyright: Territoriality and Author's Rights in a Networked World' 15 (2) Santa Clara Computer & High Tech Journal 349-350 (347) (1999).

16 Jacklyn Hoffman, 'Crossing Borders in the Digital Market: A Proposal to End Copyright Territoriality and Geo-Blocking in the European Union' 49 Washington International Law Review 143, 144 (2016).

17 Lydia Lundstedt, 'Territoriality in Intellectual Property Law' (thesis, Stockholm University 2016) 73-74.

18 Valérie Laure Benabou, *Droits d'auteur, droits voisins et droit communautaire* (Bruylant 1997) 41-44.

19 Mireille van Eechoud and others, *Harmonizing European Copyright Law: The Challenges of Better Lawmaking* (Kluwer Law International 2009) 3.

right of exploitation of the work,[20] but also moral rights.[21] In the context of justifying exceptions to free trade, intellectual property rights are cleared as long as they do not create 'artificial barriers to trade', while at the same time the competence of the Member States to define intellectual property rights is preserved.[22] Action can be taken only against the resulting effects of the intellectual property rights, such as they have been defined by the Member States, if these effects are in breach of the EC Treaty provisions. So, a competition law decision will not query the existence of copyright, but it will evaluate, under the specific circumstances of each individual case, whether an exclusive right has been exercised in such a way that there is infringement of competition law.[23]

Neither the CJEU or the EU legislator attacked the principle of copyright territoriality as such, immediately. The legitimacy of business models which rely on exclusive rights to exploit a copyright-protected work in a specific territory was upheld as early as 1982 in the *Coditel II* case,[24] from which it can be deduced that EU law tolerates territorial fragmentation in certain industries. Even though there is some damage to market integration, the Court of Justice referred to the specific nature of the cinematographic industry (e.g. dubbing and subtitling, and the system of financing) and held that exclusive licences need not necessarily restrict competition.

---

[20] See Judgment of 21 June 2012, Case C5/11 *Donner* EU:C:2012:370, para 36 ('The application of provisions such as those at issue in the main proceedings may be considered necessary to protect the specific subject-matter of the copyright, which confers inter alia the exclusive right of exploitation. The restriction on the free movement of goods resulting therefrom is accordingly justified and proportionate to the objective pursued, in circumstances such as those of the main proceedings where the accused intentionally, or at the very least knowingly, engaged in operations giving rise to the distribution of protected works to the public on the territory of a Member State in which the copyright enjoyed full protection, thereby infringing on the exclusive right of the copyright proprietor').

[21] Judgment of 20 October 1993, Joined cases C-92/92 and C-326/92 *Phil Collins v Imtrat Handelsgesellschaft mbH and Patricia Im- und Export Verwaltungsgesellschaft mbH and Leif Emanuel Kraul v EMI Electrola GmbH* EU:C:1993:847, para 20 ('The specific subject-matter of those rights, as governed by national legislation, is to ensure the protection of the moral and economic rights of their holders. The protection of moral rights enables authors and performers, in particular, to object to any distortion, mutilation or other modification of a work which would be prejudicial to their honour or reputation. Copyright and related rights are also economic in nature, in that they confer the right to exploit commercially the marketing of the protected work, particularly in the form of licences granted in return for payment of royalties (see the judgment in Joined Cases 55/80 and 57/80 *Musik-Vertrieb membran v GEMA* [1981] ECR 147, paragraph 12).'

[22] LLD Claes Granmar, 'Intellectual Property Rights and the Single Market' in Jan Rosén (ed), *European Intellectual Property Law* (Edward Elgar 2016) 38.

[23] Michel M Walter and Silke von Lewinski (eds), *European Copyright Law, A Commentary* (Oxford University Press 2010) paras 3.0.5, 3. 0.6, 3.0.7.

[24] Judgment of 6 October 1982 *Coditel SA, Compagnie générale pour la diffusion de la télévision, and others v Ciné-Vog Films SA and others (Coditel II)* EU:C:1982:334, para 15.

2.2 The Principle of Exhaustion – Offline and Online

The response of EU law to the problem of the partitioning of EU territory into different markets defined by divergent national copyright laws has been industry-based and grounded on the classic but unclear dichotomy between the sale of goods and the provision of services.

For the distribution of tangible goods, the doctrine of exhaustion of the distribution right enables the free movement within the internal market of a tangible good subject to copyright protection (an original work or copy) after its first sale or other transfer of ownership by the rights holder or with his consent in the territory of a Member State.[25]

There are various justifications for the exhaustion principle. Exhaustion reconciles the buyer's right of physical ownership with intellectual property protection,[26] it enhances freedom of trade and the availability of cultural assets, and it prevents the partitioning of the EU market[27] by, at the same time, safeguarding a remuneration for the first sale which is considered to be 'fair profit' for the copyright holder.[28]

However, even though there might be reasonable arguments in favour of applying equal treatment to the resale of works sold in tangible and intangible formats,[29] no similar principle has been affirmed for intangible goods.[30] On the contrary, a teleological understanding of the InfoSoc Directive, interpreted in light of Art. 6 of the WIPO Copyright Treaty[31] and of one of the Agreed Statements to the WIPO Copyright

---

25 Article 4 para 2 of Directive 2001/29 (the Infosoc Directive) establishes the rule of Community-wide exhaustion of the distribution right. According to this rule, the right is exhausted within the territory of the Community and the European Economic Area if the first sale or other transfer of ownership of an original work or of a copy of it is made by the rightholder or with his consent.

26 Sam Ricketson and Jane C Ginsburg, *International Copyright and Neighbouring Rights, The Berne Convention and Beyond* vol I (Oxford University Press 2006) para 11.43; Poorna Mysoor, 'Exhaustion, Non-exhaustion and Implied Licence' 49 IIC 656 (2018); Andreas Wiebe, 'The economic perspective: exhaustion in the digital age' in Lionel Bently, Uma Suthersanen and Paul Torremans (eds), *Global Copyright, Three Hundred Years Since the Statute of Anne, from 1709 to Cyberspace* (Edward Elgar 2010) 322.

27 Benedetta Ubertazzi, 'The Principle of Free Movement of Goods: Community Exhaustion and Parallel Imports' in Irini Stamatoudi and Paul Torremans (eds), *EU Copyright Law, A Commentary* (Edward Elgar 2014) 39.

28 André Lucas, 'International exhaustion' in Bently, Suthersanen and Torremans (n 25) 306.

29 Peter Mezei, 'Digital first sale doctrine ante portas: Exhaustion in the online environment' JIPITEC 2015, (23) 27.

30 Recital 28 of the Information Society Directive (Directive 2001/29) states that copyright protection under this Directive includes the exclusive right to control distribution of the work incorporated in a tangible article. Recital 29 of the same Directive appears to exclude such a possibility. See also art 1(2) of the Rental and Lending Directive (2006/115) (the rental and lending rights are not exhausted by any sale or other act of distribution of originals and copies of copyright works) and Recital 43 of the Database Directive 96/9 (the right of re-utilisation of a database is not exhausted by the online transmission of the database).

31 According to this provision, '(1) Authors of literary and artistic works shall enjoy the exclusive right of authorizing the making available to the public of the original and copies of their works through sale or other transfer of ownership. (2) Nothing in this Treaty shall affect the freedom of Contracting Parties to determine the conditions, if any, under which the exhaustion of the right in paragraph

Treaty,[32] may on the face of it lead to the assumption that the right of distribution and its exhaustion concern only a work or its tangible copies.[33]

The CJEU's *Used Soft* ruling[34] initiated a broader discussion about the extension of the principle of exhaustion to digitally-supplied intangible goods, where new hybrid economic models of 'distribution' of works on digital networks blur the borderlines of the fundamental dichotomy between goods and services.[35] [36] In that case, the CJEU confirmed the existence of digital exhaustion under the Software Directive by stressing the specific internal market rationale of exhaustion in the EU context, which is that of avoiding the partitioning of markets, and thus limiting any restrictions on the distribution of protected works to what is necessary to safeguard the specific subject matter of the intellectual property concerned.[37] The *Used Soft* findings were, however, established as a *lex specialis* which applies only to software. The restricted scope of application of the *Used Soft* ruling was confirmed in the *Ranks* case (C-166/15),[38] where the CJEU ruled out exhaustion in the case of backup and other non-original copies, even if the original support was damaged or destroyed.[39]

Furthermore, the unidimensional approach of *Used Soft* disregards the fact that certain copyright-protected works are themselves 'hybrid' and complex, in the sense that they combine various creative elements. In this context, the CJEU held in the *Nintendo* case[40] that video games constitute complex subject matter, comprising not

---

(1) applies after the first sale or other transfer of ownership of the original or a copy of the work with the authorization of the author.'

32 As it is stated: 'As used in these articles, the expressions "copies" and "original and copies," being subject to the right of distribution and the right of rental under the said Articles, refer exclusively to fixed copies that can be put into circulation as tangible objects' <https://www.wipo.int/treaties/en/text.jsp?file_id=295456> accessed 3 September 2019.

33 Eleonora Rosati, 'Online copyright exhaustion in a post-Allposters world' [2015] 10(9) JIPLP 673-681 <SSRN: https://ssrn.com/abstract=2613608> accessed 3 September 2019.

34 Judgment of 3 July 2012, Case C-128/11 *UsedSoft GmbH v Oracle International Corp* EU:C:2012:407.

35 When a work is commercially offered to users for downloading, there is a hybrid form of distribution where basic elements of a contract of sale and of a provision of services are present. See: Agnès Lucas-Schloetter, 'La revente d'occasion de fichiers numériques contenant des oeuvres protégées par le droit d'auteur' in Carine Bernault and others, 'Mélanges en l'honneur du professeur André Lucas' Lexis Nexis 2014, 580.

36 Digital works are now offered both as a service, usually from a platform where files are centrally hosted, or as a product, with a full transfer of the file similar to a sale, the latter representing a hybrid that is functionally closer to a distribution than to a form of communication/making available. See: Caterina Sganga, 'Waiting for Tom Kabinet, a.k.a. Why EU copyright needs digital exhaustion, and how the CJEU can help with this – Part 1' (*Kluwer Copyright Blog*, 15 April 2019) <http://copyrightblog.kluweriplaw.com/2019/04/15/waiting-for-tom-kabinet-a-k-a-why-eu-copyright-needs-digital-exhaustion-and-how-the-cjeu-can-help-with-this-part-1/> accessed 3 September 2019.

37 Eleonora Rosati, *Copyright and the Court of Justice of the European Union* (Oxford University Press 2019) 122.

38 Judgment of the Court of 12 October 2016, Case C-166/15 *Ranks and Vasiļevičs* EU:C:2016:762.

39 Sganga (n 35).

40 Judgment of 23 January 2014, Case C-355/12 *Nintendo Co Ltd v PC Box Srl* EU:C:2014:25.

only a computer program but also graphic and sound elements. In relation to the possible application of the principle of exhaustion, will the software part of the video game prevail and lead to exhaustion or not?

Applying different rules in relation to the exhaustion of the distribution right to complex works consisting of computer programs and other copyright-protected elements (music, audiovisual works, etc.) raises uncertainties in relation to their digital dissemination, which necessarily impacts on new business models. Additionally, a clear distinction between goods and services solely on the basis of their tangibility might prove ambiguous, since permanent control over a copy also exists in certain forms of digital 'distribution'.[41]

The *Tom Kabinet* case[42] was expected to shed some light on the question of admissibility of digital exhaustion under Art. 4(2) of Directive 2001/29. The Advocate General, in his Opinion which was delivered on 10 September 2019, excludes the application of the distribution right to the supply of e-books by downloading online for permanent use, since such a use is covered by the right of communication to the public. Furthermore, as is highlighted in the Opinion, the supply of e-books by downloading online also implies creation of a copy of that file on the receiving computer, which will either be authorised by the holder of the exclusive right of reproduction or will come under an exception to that exclusive right.[43] The CJEU followed the Advocate's General Opinion and held the provision of ebooks is an act of communication to the public and, therefore, there is no digital exhaustion under the InfoSoc Directive.[44]

In any case, it is doubtful whether the judgment itself can offer a stable and concise legal framework covering the broader issue of digital exhaustion.[45] Such a legal framework would presuppose a shift of focus away from the concept of 'intangible copies' and towards the actual use[46] and the establishment of a fair remuneration for the rightholders, such as giving the copyright owner a fee commensurate with the intensity of the usage rather than an exclusive right.[47]

41 Andreas Wiebe, 'The Principle of Exhaustion in European Copyright Law and the Distinction Between Digital Goods and Digital Services' GRUR Int 2009, 114, 115.

42 Request for a preliminary ruling from the Rechtbank Den Haag (Netherlands) lodged on 16 April 2018, Case C-263/18 *Nederlands Uitgeversverbond, Groep Algemene Uitgevers v Tom Kabinet Internet BV, Tom Kabinet Holding BV, Tom Kabinet Uitgeverij BV*.

43 Opinion of the Advocate General Szpunar, delivered on 10 September 2019, Case C263/18 *Nederlands Uitgeversverbond,Groep Algemene Uitgevers v Tom Kabinet Internet BV, Tom Kabinet Holding BV, Tom Kabinet Uitgeverij BV*.

44 Judgement of the Court (Grand Chamber), 19 December 2019, EU:C:2019:1111.

45 Peter Mezei, *Copyright Exhaustion. Law and Policy in the United States and the European Union* (Cambridge University Press 2018) paras 182, 191, 195.

46 Ole-Andreas Rognstad, 'Legally Flawed but Politically Sound? Digital Exhaustion of Copyright in Europe after UsedSoft' Oslo Law Review 1/2014, 1. <https://www.idunn.no/oslo_law_review/2014/01/legally_flawed_but_politically_sound_digital_exhaustion_of> accessed 3 September 2019.

47 Wiebe (n 25) 326-327.

3 The Steps Towards an Overcoming of the Principle of Territoriality

Apart from certain sporadic interventions in specific fields (namely the official establishment of the exhaustion of the right of distribution in the Software,[48] the Database[49] and the Information Society Directive[50] and the adoption of the 'country of origin' principle in the 'SatCab' Directives),[51] the EU legislator has traditionally been reluctant to deal in a structured way with the side-effects of copyright territoriality for the EU market.

On the other hand, by applying classic competition law principles, the CJEU has proved to be much more efficient as regards the prohibition of mechanisms aiming to impose absolute territorial exclusivity in the EU market for copyright-protected works.

3.1 Geoblocking and Competition Law

3.1.1 The CJEU's Murphy Decision

The steppingstone for stronger EU scrutiny of territorial licensing restrictions in the audiovisual sector was the CJEU's seminal ruling in the joined cases C-403/08 and C-429/08 (the '*Murphy* Ruling').[52]

The CJEU was called on to answer, among other things, whether the territorial restrictions included in the licensing agreements between the FAPL (the holder of 'broadcasting rights' over football matches in the UK) and the broadcasters of football matches constitute a legitimate practice, which is justified by the specific subject matter of intellectual property, entitling them to commercially exploit works or, conversely, constitute absolute territorial exclusivity which unlawfully fragments the single European market.

48 Article 4 para 2 of the Directive 2009/24/EC of 23 April 2009 on the legal protection of computer programs (Codified version).

49 Article 5(c) of Directive 96/9/EC of 11 March 1996 on the legal protection of databases.

50 Article 4 para 2 of Directive 2001/29/EC of the European Parliament and of the Council of 22 May 2001 on the harmonisation of certain aspects of copyright and related rights in the information society.

51 Article 1(2)(b) of Directive 93/83/EEC of 27 September 1993 on the coordination of certain rules concerning copyright and rights related to copyright applicable to satellite broadcasting and cable retransmission and art 3 of Directive (EU) 2019/789 of the European Parliament and of the Council of 17 April 2019 laying down rules on the exercise of copyright and related rights applicable to certain online transmissions of broadcasting organisations and retransmissions of television and radio programmes, and amending Council Directive 93/83/EEC.

52 Case C-403/08 *Football Association Premier League Ltd and Others v QC Leisure and Others* and judgment of 4 October 2011, Case C-429/08 *Karen Murphy v Media Protection Services Ltd.*

The CJEU held that whilst the FAPL could still grant rights on a territorial basis, the relevant provisions in the FAPL's broadcasting licence agreements prohibiting the supply of decoding devices outside the contracted territory (in this case Greece) artificially made that territorial exclusivity 'absolute,' and therefore infringed Art. 101 TFEU. For the CJEU, this cannot be justified in light of the objective of protecting intellectual property rights.

The CJEU did not reverse *Coditel I*[53] and *Coditel II*'s[54] finding that the rules of the Treaty cannot in principle constitute an obstacle to the geographical limits, which the parties to a contract of assignment of intellectual property rights have agreed. However, the Court distinguished the present case by means of *Coditel I*,[55] by emphasising that, contrary to *Coditel I*'s factual basis, in *Murphy* the communication to the public was made on the basis of an authorisation granted by the rightholders, which can take account of the actual and potential audience in the other Member States.[56] The CJEU points out that derogations from the principle of free movement can be allowed only to the extent to which they are justified by the public interest purpose of safeguarding rights which constitute the specific subject matter of the intellectual property concerned.[57]

In the CJEU's view, the specific subject matter of intellectual property rights is guaranteed when the rightholders receive an 'appropriate remuneration'[58] which can be calculated on the basis of the actual and potential audience in the other Member States.[59]

Murphy was initially perceived as an earthquake which could cause the territorial licensing of copyright to collapse. The prerequisite of an 'appropriate remuneration' for rightholders, instead of the highest possible remuneration, is market-based/economically-oriented[60] and on the face of it appears to be technologically neutral. It could, in principle, also neutralise restrictions aimed at guaranteeing territorial exclusivity in relation to other types of communication, such as online streaming.

An immediate effect has been that contractual territorial restrictions imposed by rightholders on broadcasters should be revisited, since agreements aimed at partitioning national markets must be regarded, in principle, as agreements whose object is to restrict competition.[61]

53 Judgment of 18 March 1980, Case C-62/79 *SA Compagnie générale pour la diffusion de la télévision, Coditel, and others v Ciné Vog Films and others* EU:C:1980:84, para 16.

54 See para 136 *Murphy*, with reference to the judgment of 6 October 1982, Case C-262/81 *Coditel SA, Compagnie générale pour la diffusion de la télévision, and others v Ciné-Vog Films SA and others* EU:C:1982:334, para 15.

55 See *Murphy*, para 118, with reference to *Coditel I*, para 16.

56 *Murphy*, para 118.

57 *Murphy*, para 94.

58 *Murphy*, para 108.

59 *Murphy*, paras 112, 113.

60 Thomas Riis and Jens Schovsbo, 'The borderless online user: carving up the market for on line streaming services' in Paul Torremans (ed), *Research Handbook on Copyright Law* (2nd ed, Edward Elgar 2017) 307, 309.

61 *Murphy*, paras 139, 143.

However, they may still be legitimate if other circumstances falling within their economic and legal context can justify the finding that such agreements are not liable to impair competition.[62]

It should be borne in mind that in *Coditel II*, the Court mentioned that 'the characteristics of the cinematographic industry and of its markets, […] especially those relating to dubbing and subtitling for the benefit of different language groups, to the possibilities of television broadcasts, and to the system of financing cinematographic production in Europe serve to show that an exclusive exhibition licence is not, in itself, such as to prevent, restrict or distort competition'.[63]

In the view of the CJEU, in the present case the FAPL did not put forward any circumstance falling within the economic and legal context of such clauses that would justify the finding that these clauses are not liable to impair competition.[64]

This finding cannot be affected by the fact that the foreign decoding device was used for commercial purposes, although it was restricted to private use. A subscription for private use through a domestic decoding device could also be used for commercial purposes, and there is no higher risk for such abuse in the case of foreign decoding devices (the risk that certain persons will use foreign decoding devices in disregard of the purpose for which their use is restricted is comparable to the risk which arises when decoding devices are used in purely internal situations).[65]

Furthermore, the screening of match transmissions by the Greek broadcaster in UK pubs (as opposed to private residences) involved a communication to a new public which was not considered by the rightholders when they authorised the broadcasting of their works.[66] The authorisation granted for broadcasting sports content via satellite does not cover the subsequent communication by the subscribers (public houses) to a new public in the context of a profit-making activity.[67]

Even though the broadcasting of the football matches themselves is not a copyright infringement, given that sports events are not protected by copyright, the inclusion in the broadcast of copyright-protected works, such as logos and anthems, could enable the FAPL to claim copyright infringement based on the unauthorised communication of these works to a new public.[68]

On the other hand, provided that communications within a private circle are not covered by the right of communication to the public, contractual clauses between rightholders and broadcasters cannot impose absolute territorial exclusivity in relation to private authorised screening of the works.

62 *Murphy*, para 140.
63 *Coditel II*, para 16
64 *Murphy*, para 143.
65 *Murphy*, para131.
66 *Murphy*, para 199.
67 *Murphy*, para 204.
68 Miguel Poiares Maduro, Giorgio Monti and Gonçalo Coelho, 'The Geo-Blocking Proposal: Internal Market, Competition Law and Regulatory Aspects' (January 2017) Study for the European Parliament upon the request of the Committee on Internal Market and Consumer Protection, 21, with reference to the case *Football Association Premier League Ltd Ltd v Luxton* [2014] EWHC 253 (Ch).

Overall, *Murphy* could be read as prohibiting restrictions on 'passive sales',[69] thus of sales made by a licensee in response to unsolicited orders from outside the allocated sales territory of the licensee, since its practical result has been that clauses which prohibit a licensee from selling decoding devices in response to unsolicited requests from individual consumers who are located outside the licensee's exclusive territory constitute a violation of competition law.[70]

That said, national licences continue to be permitted within the EU, but it is necessary to redesign the drafting of provisions restricting the capacity of broadcasters to respond to passive requests for access to the service from other EU Member States.[71]

The *Murphy* judgment has been a starting point for further consideration of the hot topic of territorial restrictions and geoblocking in relation to the transmission of copyright-protected audiovisual content.

In fact, a crucial question is whether the *Murphy* precedent, which has restricted the granting of absolute territorial protection in respect of sports broadcasting, could also apply to movie licensing for personal use via satellite broadcasting and online streaming.

Murphy's findings might be limited by the fact that the case concerned the broadcasting of sports events which, as held by the CJEU, do not constitute copyright-protected works. It is therefore doubtful whether it could directly cover films and other audiovisual content protected by copyright.[72] Murphy's findings were also limited by the fact that the use of the decoding devices was made in the context of a satellite transmission, i.e. a specific type of transmission for which the EU legislator has adopted the country of origin principle for the clearance of copyright.

3.1.2 The Sky Case

The next significant step in the scrutiny of territorial restrictions and geoblocking (as a means to effectively comply with contractual restrictions) was made in the EU

69 According to the EU Commission's set of guidelines providing assistance to firms on how to assess the compatibility with art 101 TFEU of vertical agreements falling outside the scope of the Regulation's safe harbour, '"passive" sales mean responding to unsolicited requests from individual customers including delivery of goods or services to such customers. General advertising or promotion that reaches customers in other distributors' (exclusive) territories or customer groups but which is a reasonable way to reach customers outside those territories or customer groups, for instance to reach customers in one's own territory, are passive sales. General advertising or promotion is considered a reasonable way to reach such customers if it would be attractive for the buyer to undertake these investments also if they would not reach customers in other distributors' (exclusive) territories or customer groups'. See: COMMISSION NOTICE Guidelines on Vertical Restraints, Brussels, SEC(2010) 411.

70 Riis and Schovsbo (n 591) 304.

71 To the extent that satellite broadcasters choose to respond to such passive requests, an appropriate price adjustment mechanism is permissible. See: Jenine Hulsmann, 'Exclusive Territorial Licensing of Content Rights After the EU Premier League Judgments', 26(3) Antitrust 36 n 1 (2012).

72 Ubertazzi (n 26) 44.

Commission's investigations of the *Sky* decisions and the Judgment of the General Court of December 2018 in Case T873/16 (*Canal*+ Ruling).

Specifically, in 2014[73] and 2015[74] the Commission initiated proceedings pursuant to Art. 2(1) of Commission Regulation (EC) No. 773/2004[75] against several major Hollywood studios regarding the anti-competitive effect of contractual clauses contained in the licensing agreements between the film studios and Sky, whereby the studios granted Sky exclusive pay- TV and subscription video-on-demand rights with regard to certain films in the United Kingdom and Ireland.

Sky's exclusive licence was accompanied by clauses that prohibit Sky UK from making its retail pay-TV services available via internet and/or satellite transmission, in response to unsolicited requests from consumers located inside the European Economic Area ('EEA') but outside the United Kingdom and Ireland, and by clauses that require the relevant studio to ensure that in their licensing agreements with broadcasters (located in the EEA) other than Sky UK, that these broadcasters are prohibited from responding to unsolicited requests from consumers residing or located in the United Kingdom and Ireland.

In the Statement of Objections and the Supplementary Statement of Objections, the Commission reached the preliminary conclusion that the Contested Clauses are liable to impair competition[76] and to have an anti-competitive object because they are designed to prohibit or limit cross-border passive sales of retail pay-TV services and to grant absolute territorial exclusivity to Sky UK and other broadcasters. Specifically, the contested clauses restrict Sky UK's ability to accept unsolicited requests for its pay-TV services from consumers located abroad, i.e. from consumers located in Member States where Sky UK is not actively promoting or advertising its services ('passive sales'). Furthermore, there were no circumstances falling within the economic and legal context of the Contested Clauses, including the nature of the services affected and the conditions of the functioning and structure of the markets in question, that would justify the finding that the clauses are not liable to impair competition and therefore do not have an anti-competitive object.[77]

[73] On 13 September 2014 the Commission initiated proceedings pursuant to art 2(1) of Commission Regulation (EC) No 773/2004 against, *inter alia*, Paramount Pictures International Limited (formerly Viacom Global (Netherlands) B.V.), Viacom Inc. (together 'Paramount Pictures'), Universal Studios International B.V., CPT Holdings, Inc., Warner Bros. International Television Distribution Inc., British Sky Broadcasting Limited (to date 'Sky UK Limited') and British Sky Broadcasting Group Plc. (to date 'Sky Limited').

[74] On 23 July 2015, the Commission initiated proceedings pursuant to art 2(1) of Commission Regulation (EC) No 773/2004 against, *inter alia*, Comcast Corporation, Colgems Productions Limited, Sony Corporation, The Walt Disney Company, The Walt Disney Company Limited and Time Warner, Inc.

[75] Commission Regulation (EC) No 773/2004 of 7 April 2004 relating to the conduct of proceedings by the Commission pursuant to arts 81 and 82 of the EC Treaty.

[76] Article 101 of the Treaty on the Functioning of the European Union.

[77] See: European Commission – Press release, Antitrust: Commission sends Statement of Objections on crossborder provision of pay-TV services available in UK and Ireland Brussels, 23 July 2015 <http://europa.eu/rapid/press-release_IP-15-5432_en.htm>.

Two decisions have been adopted within the framework of the pay-TV (Sky UK) investigation: the decision of 26 July 2016, making the commitments offered by Paramount Pictures binding;[78] and the decision of 7 March 2019 making the commitments offered by Disney, NBC Universal, Sony Pictures, Warner Bros and Sky binding.[79]

The Commission's decision making the commitments offered by Paramount (in April 2016) binding,[80] in response to the Commission's competition concerns, was appealed by the French pay-TV broadcaster Canal+.

The General Court, in its ruling of 12 December 2018 in the *Canal+* case,[81] maintained the Commission's decision. In brief, the General Court held that the contested contractual clauses were restrictions of competition in terms of their object, and that the commitments made legally binding under the Commission's decision do not affect the granting of exclusive territorial licences as such,[82] but their aim is to put an end to absolute territorial exclusivity intended to eliminate all competition between broadcasters. Clauses under which the holder is required to prohibit all its contracting partners in the EEA market from making passive sales to geographic markets situated outside the Member State in respect of which it grants them an exclusive licence, confer a contractually specified absolute territorial exclusivity and thereby infringe Art.

78 The Decision makes legally binding the commitments offered by Paramount Pictures International Limited (formerly Viacom Global (Netherlands) B.V.) and Viacom Inc. (hereinafter jointly referred to as 'Paramount') under art 9 of Council Regulation (EC) No 1/2003 ('Regulation (EC) No 1/2003') in a proceeding under art 101 of the Treaty on the Functioning of the European Union ('the Treaty') and art 53 of the EEA Agreement.
This Decision concerns the film licensing agreements Paramount has entered into with Sky UK Limited (formerly British Sky Broadcasting Limited) and Sky Plc. (formerly British Sky Broadcasting Group Plc.) (hereinafter jointly referred to as 'Sky'). See: Summary of Commission Decision of 26 July 2016 relating to a proceeding under art 101 of the Treaty on the Functioning of the European Union and art 53 of the EEA Agreement (Case AT.40023 *Crossborder access to pay-TV*) (notified under document C(2016) 4740 final) [2016] OJ C 437/5-7.

79 The Decision makes legally binding the commitments offered by Universal Studios International B.V., Universal Studios Limited and Comcast Corporation (together 'NBC Universal'), CPT Holdings Inc., Colgems Productions Limited and Sony Corporation (together 'Sony Pictures'), Warner Bros. International Television Distribution Inc. and Warner Media LLC (together 'Warner Bros.'), The Walt Disney Company, The Walt Disney Company Limited (together 'Disney') and Sky UK Limited and Sky Limited (together 'Sky') under art 9 of Council Regulation (EC) No 1/2003 ('Regulation 1/2003') in a proceeding under art 101 of the Treaty on the Functioning of the European Union ('the Treaty') and art 53 of the EEA Agreement. This Decision concerns the film licensing agreements that NBC Universal, Sony Pictures, Warner Bros. and Disney have each entered into with Sky. NBC Universal, Sony Pictures, Warner Bros. and Disney are hereinafter referred to as 'the Studios'. See: Summary of Commission Decision of 7 March 2019 relating to a proceeding under art 101 of the Treaty on the Functioning of the European Union and art 53 of the EEA Agreement (Case AT.40023 *Crossborder access to pay-TV*) (notified under document C(2019) 1772) C/2019/1772 [2019] OJ C 132/8-11.

80 In October 2018, Disney also offered commitments to the European Commission in response to the Pay-TV investigation. The remaining studios and Sky UK proposed commitments in December 2018, just after the decision of the General Court in the case *Groupe Canal+ v European Commission*.

81 Judgment of 12 December 2018, Case T873/16 *Groupe Canal+ SA v European Commission* EU:T:2018:904.

82 *Groupe Canal+* (n 80) para 44.

101(1).[83] Following *Murphy*,[84] it was further found that where a licence agreement is intended to prohibit or limit the cross-border provision of broadcasting services, it is deemed to have the purpose of restricting competition, unless other circumstances falling within its economic and legal context justify the finding that such an agreement is not liable to impair competition.

As a result, geoblocking clauses may not be covered under Art. 101(3) TFEU on the basis that they promote production and cultural diversity within the EU, since they go beyond what is necessary for the production and distribution of audiovisual works protected by copyright.[85]

Accordingly, geoblocking clauses are not necessary to ensure the protection of copyright, since the subject matter of copyright is not to guarantee rightholders the opportunity to demand the highest possible remuneration, but only an appropriate remuneration, namely a remuneration which corresponds to the number of views.

In any case, a broadcaster seeking to passively distribute films outside the licensed contractual territory will have to clear copyrights. So, rightholders could negotiate licensing fees that would also include the potential audience in Member States not covered by the licence.

Even though the *Canal+* judgment used rather broad language in relation to geoblocking clauses, it is uncertain whether the judgment itself is a sound basis for advocating its general application to all geoblocking clauses related to audiovisual content.

Firstly, as noted by Thomas Riis and Jens Schovsbo, not all restrictions on passive sales are prohibited, but only contractual agreements which seek to eliminate all competition, and thus imply 'absolute territorial protection'.[86]

The decisive test for assessing whether or not limitations in agreements which prevent users from subscribing to or accessing online services in EU countries other than their own violate competition, is whether or not such limitations are necessary for the rightholders to receive fair compensation.[87] Accordingly, for limitations on

83 *Groupe Canal+* (n 80) para 45.

84 *Groupe Canal+* (n 80) para 48: 'In that context, where a licence agreement is designed to prohibit or limit the cross-border provision of broadcasting services, it is deemed to have as its object the restriction of competition, unless other circumstances falling within its economic and legal context justify the finding that such an agreement is not liable to impair competition (judgment of 4 October 2011, *Football Association Premier League and Others*, C403/08 and C429/08, EU:C:2011:631, paragraph 140).'

85 *Groupe Canal+* (n 80) para 67: 'In any event, it must be stated that the considerations set out in paragraphs 53 to 57 above preclude the application of Article 101(3) TFEU, since the relevant clauses impose restrictions that go beyond what is necessary for the production and distribution of audiovisual works that require protection of intellectual property rights and thus do not satisfy at least one of the cumulative conditions laid down in Article 101(3) TFEU, namely the condition that the agreement in question does not impose on the undertakings concerned restrictions which are not indispensable for the protection of those rights (see, to that effect, judgment of 4 October 2011, *Football Association Premier League and Others*, C403/08 and C429/08, EU:C:2011:631, paragraph 145)'.

86 Riis and Schovsbo (n 59) 309 (with reference to judgment of 8 June 1982, Case 258/*78 L.C. Nungesser KG and Kurt Eisele v Commission of the European Communities* EU:C:1982:211).

87 Riis and Schovsbo (n 59) 309.

passive sales (such as was the case in *Murphy*), the competition authorities and the courts should be expected to be somewhat restrictive in their evaluation.[88] Additionally, the application of the legal construction of 'passive sales' in the audiovisual sector might not be as straightforward as it first appears. Indeed, the territorial exclusivity enjoyed by distributors might be considered as relative in the sense that the distributor's exclusivity relates only to a specific mode of exploitation (exploitation in cinemas, DVD and VoD, movie channels, pay-TV, SVoD, general channels) and it is most often temporary.[89]

Secondly, unilateral geoblocking is still possible, since it does not raise competition concerns.

Thirdly, cross-border passive sales infringe copyright, unless they are also covered by a licence.[90] In this context, the judgment has the potential to create incentives for distributors to seek EU-wide licences and to develop business models in order to address passive sales outside the licence territory.[91]

Fourthly, where the risk of copyright infringement inevitably impedes distributors attempting to engage in any cross-border competition in non-licensed territories, a requirement to use geoblocking appears incapable of producing restrictive effects on competition.[92] The question is whether competition between broadcasters would otherwise have occurred, had it not been for the geo-blocking clause [93] and whether the latter restricts competition beyond the restrictions resulting from copyright protection.

Last but not least, it should be noted that the *Canal+* judgment has been appealed by *Canal+* before the CJEU. In its judgment the CJEU annulled the decision of the General Court because the latter failed properly take to account the impact of the commitments on the contractual rights of third parties and for violation of the principle of proportionality. Even though the commitments did not directly apply to Canal+ they have automatically implied that Paramount would not be able to honour certain contractual obligations with Canal+. At the same time, it is noteworthy that the CJEU

88 Riis and Schovsbo (n 59).

89 Pierre Sirinelli and Sarah Dormont, Rapport sur les ventes passives, Mission du CSPLA sur les ventes passives, June 2019, 33 <https://www.culture.gouv.fr/Sites-thematiques/Propriete-litteraire-et-artistique/Conseil-superieur-de-la-propriete-litteraire-et-artistique/Travaux/Missions/Mission-du-CSPLA-sur-les-ventes-passives> accessed 3 September 2019

90 The *Canal+* judgment (T-873/16), and the end of the Pay-TV Case (or the illusion of precedent) <https://chillingcompetition.com/2019/01/23/the-canal-judgment-t-873-16-and-the-end-of-the-pay-TV-case-or-the-illusion-of-precedent/>.

91 Yves Botteman and Camille Keres, 'A Holiday Reading: Pay-TV Case (Finally) Moves Forward' (*Antitrust and Competition Blog*, 21 December 2018) <https://www.steptoeantitrustblog.com/2018/12/holiday-reading-pay-TV-case-finally-moves-forward/> accessed 3 September 2019.

92 Juha Vesala, 'Geoblocking Requirements in Online Distribution of Copyright-Protected Content: Implications of Copyright Issues on Application of EU Antitrust Law' 25 (3) Michigan State International Law Review 606 (2017).

93 Ciaran Fitzerald Morgan, 'The legality of geo-blocking: could Sky's recent commitments in the "Pay-TV" case impact European sports broadcasting?' (*LawInSport*, 1 August 2019) <https://www.lawinsport.com/content/articles/competition-law/item/the-legality-of-geo-blocking-could-sky-s-recent-commitments-in-the-pay-TV-case-impact-european-sports-broadcasting?category_id=125> accessed 3 September 2019.

affirmed that the General Court did not commit an error of law by relying on Murphy, having regard both to the objectives that the licence agreements seek to achieve and to the economic and legal context in which they are included, they have as their object the restriction of competition within the meaning of Article 101 (1) TFEU.[94]

3.2 The Legislative Initiatives for Less Copyright Territoriality

As with case law, legislative initiatives have also addressed the issue of territorial licensing practices.

One particular way to adapt EU copyright law to a cross-border context has been to address the uncertainty regarding the application of copyright law by designating one law to be applicable to specific cross-border communications of copyright-protected works.[95] In this context, the country of origin principle was established in the Satellite and Cable Directive.[96] According to this principle, a satellite broadcaster must clear rights only in the country where the satellite transmission is initiated in order to provide broadcasting services in all countries where the broadcast is received. Consequently, the satellite broadcaster must acquire a licence from the copyright holders only for the EU country which is at the 'origin' of the transmission.

While a possible extension of the 'country of origin' principle to online communications[97] has been discussed and supported by various stakeholders[98] and scholars,[99] this policy option has been only partially and minimally integrated into the new SatCab Directive on broadcasters' online services and retransmissions of radio and TV programmes, which was adopted by the Council of the European Union on 17 April

---

[94] Judgment of 9 December 2020, Case C-132/19 P *Groupe Canal+ v Commission* (Appeal Case before the General Court T-873/16), ECLI:EU:C:2020:1007.

[95] Tambiama Madiega, EU copyright reform: Revisiting the principle of territoriality (*European Parliament*, Briefing September 2015) <http://www.europarl.europa.eu/RegData/etudes/BRIE/2015/568348/EPRS_BRI%282015%29568348_EN.pdf> accessed 3 September 2019.

[96] Article 1(2)(b) of the Directive 93/83/EEC of 27 September 1993 on the coordination of certain rules concerning copyright and rights related to copyright applicable to satellite broadcasting and cable retransmission. According to the 'country of origin' rule, a satellite transmission is deemed to occur only in the EU country where the satellite transmission is carried out (ie, where the programme signals are fed into an uninterrupted transmission chain leading to the satellite and down to earth).

[97] Under this scenario, a service provider would only have to obtain a license from the Member State where the copyright work occurs (country of origin) in order to make available the copyrighted work in the EU. See Madiega (n 94).

[98] See, for example, European Broadcasting Union Copyright White Paper: Modern copyright for digital media Legal analysis and EBU proposals (2010).

[99] PB Hugenholtz, 'Copyright without Frontiers: is there a Future for the Satellite and Cable Directive? in Schriftenreihe des Instituts für Europäisches Medienrecht (EMR), *Die Zukunft der Fernsehrichtlinie – The Future of the 'Television without Frontiers' Directive* vol 29 (Nomos 2005); P B Hugenholtz, SatCab Revisited: The Past, Present and Future of the Satellite and Cable Directive, IRIS (15 August 2012). IRIS Plus 2009-8, 7-19; Amsterdam Law School Research Paper No 2012-42; Institute for Information Law Research Paper No 2012-36 <https://ssrn.com/abstract=2129782>.

2019.[100] Indeed, the country of origin principle has been established in the new Sat-Cab Directive only for certain types of programmes[101] and only for ancillary online services.[102] The rule does not apply to broadcasts of sports events and works and of other protected subject matter included in them.[103]

The country of origin principle was also established, although in a different context, in the Audiovisual Media Services Directive, which was recently revised.[104] The principle applies to national rules concerning the content of television broadcasting and other 'audiovisual media services' within the coordinated field. However, copyright lies outside the fields coordinated by the Directive.[105] The Audiovisual Media Services Directive addresses territoriality by allowing Member States to prevent pay-TV providers from acquiring territorially exclusive rights over the broadcasting of 'events which are regarded by that Member State as being of major importance for society'.[106] However, this provision, which was not subject to revision, has no obvious ramifications for the film industry and its financing.[107]

A similar approach has also been followed in the Portability Regulation 2017/1128,[108] which guarantees the portability of existing subscriptions giving access to copyright-protected works (such as films, sports events, e-books, video games and music). One of the biggest innovations of the Regulation lies in the legal fiction introduced

100 Directive (EU) 2019/789 of the European Parliament and of the Council of 17 April 2019 laying down rules on the exercise of copyright and related rights applicable to certain online transmissions of broadcasting organisations and retransmissions of television and radio programmes, and amending Council Directive 93/83/EEC.

101 The programmes that are covered by the principle are: (a) radio programmes, and (b)television programmes which are: (i) news and current affairs programmes or (ii) fully financed own productions of the broadcasting organisation in an ancillary online service by or under the control and responsibility of a broadcasting organisation.

102 The ancillary services covered by the legislation include simulcasting, catch-up services and other services that complement the main broadcast, such as previews.

103 Article 3 of Directive 2019/789.

104 Directive (EU) 2018/1808 of the European Parliament and of the Council of 14 November 2018 amending Directive 2010/13/EU on the coordination of certain provisions laid down by law, regulation or administrative action in Member States concerning the provision of audiovisual media services (Audiovisual Media Services Directive) in view of changing market realities PE/33/2018/REV/1 [2003] OJ L 303/69-92.

105 Nevertheless, the rules of the Directive may have an indirect impact on copyright law, as the European Court of Justice has on several occasions interpreted copyright notions in light of the Audiovisual Media Services Directive and its predecessor, the Television without Frontiers Directive. See: Research for CULT Committee – Film Financing and the Digital Single Market: its Future, the Role of Territoriality and New Models of Financing, European Parliament, Policy Department for Structural and Cohesion Policies.
Directorate-General for Internal Policies, PE 629.186 – January 2019 with reference to: European Commission Guidelines on Vertical Restraints, [2010] OJ C 130/1, 52; Joined cases C-403/08 & C-429/08 *Football Association Premiere League et al. v QC Leisure et al. & Murphy v Media Protection Services Ltd* 2011 E.C.R.I-09083, 9083.

106 Article 14(1) of the revised Directive.

107 Research for CULT Committee (n 106).

108 Regulation (EU) 2017/1128 on cross-border portability of online content services in the internal market of 14 June 2017.

in its Art. 4. According to this provision, which follows the same line of reasoning as the 'country or origin' principle of the SatCab Directive, the provision of an online content service to, as well as access to and use of this service by, a subscriber, in accordance with Art. 3(1), shall be deemed to occur solely in the Member State of residence. Consequently, the act of communication to the public and of receipt of the service shall be deemed to occur solely in the Member State of the subscriber's residence and not in the place where it physically occurs (the Member State where the consumer is 'temporarily' present). In the case of technological limitations (mainly geoblocking), the service provider has an obligation to enable access to and use of the online content service. This, in practice, means that the service providers must monitor and confirm the subscriber's temporary location in other Member States, and that they must 'disable' their geoblocking measures. If the service provider does not apply geoblocking but restricts access to and use of the online content service to a particular territory (Member State) only contractually, this contractual obligation shall be unenforceable.[109]

Even though the Portability Regulation is a first step towards removing the effects of geoblocking measures, it only affects a very small proportion of the EU's population, namely travellers, short-term migrants and tourists, representing about 2.5 million EU citizens by 2020.[110]

Online distribution of copyright-protected content is also regulated by the Directive in terms of certain aspects concerning contracts for the supply of digital content and digital services (the 'Digital Content Directive').[111] The Directive establishes rules governing contracts for the supply of digital content (such as digital films, music, e-books, applications, etc.), and also covers the provision of digital services (such as social media platforms, on-line games, pay-per-view access to films, cloud computing, etc.).[112] However, the Directive does not deal with the question of geoblocking and does not interfere with EU copyright law legislation.[113]

109 Tatiana Synodinou, 'EU Portability Regulation: In-depth Analysis of the Proposal, Study prepared for the JURI Committee of the EU Parliament' (*EP Directorate General for Internal Policies*, August 2016) <http://www.europarl.europa.eu/RegData/etudes/IDAN/2016/571369/IPOL_IDA(2016)571369_EN.pdf>.

110 Maria José Schmidt-Kessen, 'EU Digital Single Market Strategy, Digital Content and Geo-Blocking: Costs And Benefits Of Partitioning EU's Internal Market' Copenhagen Business School Law Research Paper Series No 19-05 <https://ssrn.com/abstract=3311110> accessed 3 September 2019.

111 Directive (EU) 2019/770 of the European Parliament and of the Council of 20 May 2019 on certain aspects concerning contracts for the supply of digital content and digital services [2019] OJ L 136/1-27.

112 European Parliament, 'Legislative Train – Contracts for Supply of Digital Content and Digital Services to Consumers' <http://www.europarl.europa.eu/legislative-train/theme-connected-digital-single-market/file-jd-digital-content-and-digital-services>.

113 Article 3(8) states explicitly that 'This Directive shall be without prejudice to Union and national law on copyright and related rights, including Directive 2001/29/EC of the European Parliament and of the Council. This provision is complemented by analogous references in two recitals. Specifically, recital 20 states that 'This Directive is also without prejudice to the distribution right applicable to these goods under copyright law'. Furthermore, recital 36 provides that the Directive 'should also be

Attempts have also been made to promote the crossborder licensing of music.[114] The EU legislator has chosen a system that could be defined as a 'European Licensing Passport' in the Collective Management Directive 2014/26/EU,[115] one of the core objectives of which is to facilitate the multi-territorial licensing by CMOs of authors' rights in musical works for the provision of online services. Collecting societies wishing to license online rights for musical works on a multi-territory basis must comply with conditions governing efficient data handling, invoicing capabilities and transparency.[116] However, this is also a non-ambitious approach which maintains the intact territorial nature of copyright as a matter of principle.[117]

Specific EU legislative interventions facilitating the cross-border circulation of copyright-protected works having a specific status or specific cross-border uses have also taken place in relation to orphan works, out of commerce works, uses for the benefit of the blind and visually impaired, and teaching uses. Specifically, Art. 4 of the Orphan Works Directive[118] provides for the mutual recognition of orphan work status all over the EU. Articles 3 and 4 of the Regulation (EU) 2017/1563,[119] which has transposed in the EU the legal provisions of the Marrakesh Treaty,[120] enables the export of accessible format copies of works or other subject matter to third countries and the import such copies from third countries which are parties to the Marrakesh Treaty. More recently, Art. 5 para. 3 of the Directive 2019/790 on copyright and related rights in the Digital Single Market[121] establishes the country of origin principle for cross-border teaching activities through secure electronic environments, by stating that the use shall be deemed to occur solely in the Member State where the educational establishment is established. Under a similar line of reasoning, Directive2019/790 provides for uses of out of commerce works under the exception of Art. 9, in that they shall be deemed to occur solely in the Member State where the cultural heritage institution undertaking that use is established.

without prejudice to Union and national law on copyright and related rights, including the portability of online content services'.

114 See: Commission Recommendation of 18 May 2005 on collective cross-border management of copyright and related rights for legitimate online music services [2005] OJ L 276/54-57.

115 Directive 2014/26/EU of the European Parliament and of the Council of 26 February 2014 on collective management of copyright and related rights and multi-territorial licensing of rights in musical works for online use in the internal market [2014] OJ L 84/72-98.

116 Benjamin Farrand, *Networks of Power in Digital Copyright Law and Policy: Political Salience Expertise and the Legislative Process* (Routledge 2014) 49.

117 Hugenholtz (n 12) 16.

118 Directive 2012/28/EU of the European Parliament and of the Council of 25 October 2012 on certain permitted uses of orphan works [2012] OJ L 299/5-12.

119 Regulation (EU) 2017/1563 of the European Parliament and of the Council of 13 September 2017 on the cross-border exchange between the Union and third countries of accessible format copies of certain works and other subject matter protected by copyright and related rights for the benefit of persons who are blind, visually impaired or otherwise print-disabled [2017] OJ L 242/1-5.

120 Marrakesh Treaty to Facilitate Access to Published Works for Persons who are Blind, Visually Impaired, or otherwise Print Disabled [2018] OJ L 48/3-11.

121 Directive (EU) 2019/790 on copyright and related rights in the Digital Single Market [2019] OJ L 130/92-125.

Overall, the EU legislator has adopted a piecemeal and primarily reserved approach to the issue. This is also confirmed by the recently adopted Directive on copyright in the Digital Single Market[122] which does not deal with the question of geoblocking.

4 The Geoblocking Regulation: a Failure or an Opportunity?

4.1 The Need for New Solutions in Light of the EU's Evolution

The inconsistency and timidity of the EU legislator in tackling the sensitive issue of geoblocking in relation to copyright-protected works has been solemnly affirmed in the recently adopted Geoblocking Regulation.[123]

The Regulation aims to abolish the obstacle of 'geoblocking', that occurs where traders operating in one Member State block or limit access to their online interfaces, such as websites and apps, for customers from other Member States wishing to engage in cross-border transactions.[124] Specifically, the Geoblocking Regulation aims to further clarify the scope of application of Art. 20 of Directive 2006/123/EC[125] by defining certain situations in which different treatment based on nationality, place of residence or place of establishment cannot be justified under that provision.[126]

The Regulation, in line with the material scope of the Services Directive,[127] introduces a distinction between services, the main feature of which is the provision of access to and use of copyright-protected works and audiovisual services.

[122] ibid.

[123] Regulation (EU) 2018/302 of the European Parliament and of the Council of 28 February 2018 on addressing unjustified geo-blocking and other forms of discrimination based on customers' nationality, place of residence or place of establishment within the internal market and amending Regulations (EC) No 2006/2004 and (EU) 2017/2394 and Directive 2009/22/EC.

[124] Recital 1 of the Regulation (EU) 2018/302.

[125] Directive 2006/123/EC of the European Parliament and of the Council of 12 December 2006 on services in the internal market [2006] OJ L 376/36-68. According to this provision: '1. Member States shall ensure that the recipient is not made subject to discriminatory requirements based on his nationality or place of residence. 2. Member States shall ensure that the general conditions of access to a service, which are made available to the public at large by the provider, do not contain discriminatory provisions relating to the nationality or place of residence of the recipient, but without precluding the possibility of providing for differences in the conditions of access where those differences are directly justified by objective criteria'.

[126] Recital 4 of the Regulation (EU) 2018/302.

[127] See art 2(2)(g) of the Directive 2006/123/EC of the European Parliament and of the Council of 12 December 2006 on services in the internal market [2006] OJ L 376/36-68.

Audiovisual services, including services whose main purpose is the provision of access to broadcasts of sports events, and which are provided on the basis of exclusive territorial licences, are explicitly excluded from the scope of this Regulation.[128]

In relation to services whose main feature is the provision of access to and use of other copyright-protected content (such as e-books, music, games and software), the Regulation has adopted a mitigated approach. Recital 8 states that they are in principle covered by the scope of the Regulation, subject however to the specific exclusion and the subsequent evaluation of that exclusion for which this Regulation provides. These exclusions are found in Arts. 1 and 4(1)(b) of the Regulation. According to Art. 1(5), the Regulation shall not affect the rules applicable in the field of copyright and neighbouring rights, notably the rules provided for in Directive 2001/29.

Non-audiovisual electronically supplied services, whose main feature is the access and use of copyright-protected works, are covered by certain provisions of the Regulation, but not by the non-discrimination obligation laid down in Art. 4 (i.e. the prohibition of different conditions on the basis of nationality, place of residence and place of establishment).

Specifically, Art. 3 of the Regulation, which bans the blocking of access to websites and re-routing without the customer's prior consent, and Art. 5, which prohibits discrimination in the area of electronic payment means on the basis of 'nationality', apply also to non-audiovisual electronically supplied services, whose main feature is the access and use of copyright-protected works. This means that a trader providing these services cannot prevent its clients from accessing different versions of its website, marketplace or app store, or cannot re-route them, without their explicit consent, on the basis of criteria based on the customer's nationality, residence or establishment (including indirect criteria such as their IP address or the customer's payment details).[129] Moreover, where these services are provided on a cross-border basis, regardless of their exclusion from Art. 4 of the Regulation, the trader is prevented from discriminating against the electronic payment means on the basis of 'nationality', e.g. because a credit or debit card of an accepted category or brand is issued in another Member State or because a direct debit or credit transfer is performed through a bank from another Member State (provided the currency used is accepted by the trader).[130]

Nonetheless, the practical effect of the application of these articles is minimal, since they do not make lawful the provision of access to copyright-protected content to consumers located in non-licensed territories. So, even though the user will be able to access a foreign provider's website, this will be mainly for information purposes (such as for price-comparison purposes), since a cross-border transaction will be lawfully made only if the service provider has cleared copyright for the territory

[128] See art 3(1)(5) and Recital 8 of the Regulation (EU) 2018/302.

[129] EU Commission, Questions & Answers on the Geo-blocking Regulation in the context of e-commerce, 2018.

[130] EU Commission, Questions & Answers on the Geo-blocking Regulation in the context of e-commerce, 2018.

of the user. The same applies to the non-discrimination rule in relation to electronic payment means.

More importantly, Art. 4, which prohibits the application of different general conditions of access to the service on the basis of a customer's nationality, residence or establishment – including the option of denying access to the service – does not apply to the provision of copyright-protected content services.

Furthermore, the service provider will in any case have to comply with national laws, including territorial copyright laws, which prevent the trader from providing the services to certain customers or to customers in certain territories.[131]

As regards non-unilateral geoblocking, Art. 6 goes one step further than competition law and establishes an absolute prohibition on agreements preventing traders from responding to unsolicited customer requests. These provisions shall be automatically deemed null and void, regardless of the trader's market position.[132] However, this does not apply to copyright content services.

Overall, the Geoblocking Regulation has a very limited effect on the cross-border provision of copyright content services in the EU. However, the door has been left open for a possible review of the non-application of Arts. 4 and 6 to copyright content services, following an initial evaluation of the Regulation on March 2020.[133]

Such an extension, if decided on, would prohibit the use of both unilateral and non-unilateral geoblocking measures provided that the service provider (trader or distributor) has acquired a licence that covers the territory where the user is located. In this respect, the Regulation would move one step further away from EU competition law.

However, a trader would probably be reluctant to respond to demands emanating from individual consumers in various EU Member States or to attempt to clear copyright in 27 different jurisdictions, even if he is free to do so. In this context, the extension of the Geoblocking Regulation alone to include copyright content services is only one piece of a bigger puzzle. The completion of a true digital single market requires that more radical solutions be adopted in the field of copyright clearance: solutions which will either keep, but significantly limit, the principle of territoriality (such as the introduction of a country of origin principle with adjustments to make it fit for online communications) or which abolish it by replacing the territorial copyright laws of Member States by a unified copyright law[134] in the form of an EU Copyright Code which would enable pan-European licensing.

---

131 According to art 4, para 5 of the Geoblocking Regulation, 'The prohibition set out in paragraph 1 shall not apply in so far as a specific provision laid down in Union law, or in the laws of Member States in accordance with Union law, prevents the trader from selling the goods or providing the services to certain customers or to customers in certain territories'.

132 Lars Kjølbye, Elisabetta Righini and Peter Citron, 'EU Adopts Ban On Unjustified Geo-Blocking' (*Kluwer Copyright Blog*, 19 March 2018) <http://copyrightblog.kluweriplaw.com/2018/03/19/eu-adopts-ban-unjustified-geo-blocking/> accessed 3 September 2019.

133 Article 9 of the Regulation (EU) 2018/302.

134 See P Bernt Hugenholtz, 'Harmonisation or Unification of European Union Copyright Law' 38 Monash U. L. Rev. 4 (2012).

Even though these options appear understandable, and even indisputable, from the perspective of the EU's four freedoms, there are no simple answers to the existential dilemmas of EU copyright law.

Copyright territoriality is not restricted only to its economic dimension, and thus to the rightholder's power to license the work in 27 parallel markets, but is a component of the complex identity of copyright law which, unlike other branches of intellectual property, has always been a fascinating and unique amalgam of property and culture.

The business models of production and distribution of copyright-protected cultural goods are tailored to the same idiosyncrasies as those behind national copyright law cultures.

Having divergent copyright ownership, moral rights and contract law rules might mean that in one Member State, the investor or the distributor has sole control over the fate of the work, while in others he does not. In other words, the essence and the exercise of copyright act as communicating vessels.

Furthermore, the unification of laws, like any globalisation process, brings with it an economic pattern of major multinational players who aim to sell the same products globally. In this context, a side-effect of pan-European licensing and of abolishing the territoriality principle within the EU might be less investment in local and culturally more differential content. This would impact negatively on the preservation of cultural and linguistic diversity and heritage.[135] In this context, it has been argued that territorial restrictions could be acceptable, and even desirable as they are 'supporting cultural creations targeted at national audiences and having no (or little) international appeal'.[136]

On the other hand, laws are also subject to the principle of evolution. European copyright law shares the same destiny. Either it will promote the ideal of union or it will stay inactive and leave to national copyright laws the competence to build their own pluralist answers to technological and societal changes.

At a time of challenges and ordeals for the EU, such as Brexit, EU law needs to depart from the dominant economic formation of the integration process and to make the establishment of an EU market for culture a primary objective. In this context, copyright territoriality and the geoblocking mechanism should be seriously reconsidered.

While geoblocking is often seen as a fortress which preserves and protects the richness and uniqueness of national cultures, like every wall, it carries with it the danger of seclusion. In this sense, claims for cross-border access to cultures should not be seen as opportunist or populist pleas, but as a vehicle for the discovery of bridges, common values and objectives which bring Europeans together.

The time has come for more advanced, bolder, compromises. This presupposes a new, workable balance between copyright law principles, competition law rules and fundamental rights.

135 Communication from the Commission on a Digital Single Market Strategy for Europe, COM(2015)192 final, 6 May 2015, part 3, para 1.2.

136 Giuseppe Mazziotti, 'Is Geo-Blocking a Real Cause for Concern in Europe?' (2016) EUI Department of Law Research Paper No 2015/43 <https://papers.ssrn.com/sol3/papers.cfm?abstract_id=2728675> accessed 3 September 2019.

Competition law alone cannot provide an answer to the legal challenges linked to cross-border access to copyright-protected content in a constantly developing digital environment. In this context, legislative intervention in the field of copyright law will be needed.

Competition law has, however, an important message to give. With or without copyright territoriality, rightholders need to be adequately protected and should receive an 'appropriate remuneration' for the use made of their works. This means that in every scenario (adoption of the 'country of origin' principle or of an EU unified copyright title), the rightholder will not be denied his exclusive rights for the whole EU territory by being paid for the transmission in just one country. The option demonstrated both by the *Murphy* and *Canal+* judgments is that a service provider should be encouraged to seek multi-territorial or pan-European licences, and that in this case, the copyright holder can negotiate an amount that considers the potential audience both in the Member State for which the exclusive licence is granted and any other Member State in which the programmes covered by the distribution are also received. Such an option is now facilitated by technology, since the technology necessary for receiving works covered by the rights in question, both online and via (encrypted) satellite transmission, enables the actual and potential audience to be determined. In this context, broadcasters will compete only if they are willing to adapt their business models to embrace this opportunity.[137] However, the cost involved in acquiring a licence is often the main obstacle to the pan-European or multi-territorial provision of digital services providing access to copyright-protected works.[138]

4.2 Some de lege ferenda Thoughts: Compulsory License as a Means for an Effective Overcoming of Geoblocking in the EU?

Additionally, and even more radically, a true digital single market would require not only that an EU trader should not be precluded from responding to individual passive sales requests submitted by consumers located anywhere in the EU, but that an EU consumer should also have the right to access copyright-protected works all over Europe under the same general terms.

This would mean in practice that the EU trader should be obliged to provide the service, at the consumer's request. The consumer would then have to pay the legitimate additional licensing cost in her/his country. This right would be based on

137 Simonetta Vezzoso, 'Geo-blocking of Audio-visual Services in the EU: Gone with the Wind?' (*Competition Policy International*, 13 January 2019) < https://www.competitionpolicyinternational.com /geo-blocking-of-audio-visual-services-in-the-eu-gone-with-the-wind/> accessed 3 September 2019.

138 European Commission, Preliminary Report on the E-commerce Sector Inquiry, SWD (2016) 312 final, Table C. 6, 227.

the fundamental EU axiom of the free movement of goods and services, but also on a claim emanating from the EU citizen to have access to the cultures of EU Member States. Even though the EU has no competence to rule on cultural matters, in light of the growing significance of human rights in the EU legal order, the EU's fundamental economic freedoms could be interpreted in a way favouring cross-border access to cultural goods.[139]

Such a model would imply a mechanism of compulsory licensing, collective management with possibilities of cross-border licensing, and probably a system of mediation with the consumer.

Compulsory licensing of copyright-protected works in the EU results from the application of competition law principles, when the exercise of copyright in certain circumstances has an adverse effect on consumer welfare or is an abuse of a dominant position.[140] In this context, assets protected by intellectual property and which are critical to accessing a network, have been in certain exceptional cases[141] treated as 'essential facilities' under competition law.[142]

Mechanisms of compulsory licensing provided by copyright legislation are not unknown, even though they remain marginal. In this context, at the international level, Art. 13 of the Berne Convention enables Members of the Union to limit the right of recording of musical works if the recording of the musical work and words has already been authorised by the author, on the condition that this limitation shall not be prejudicial to the rights of these authors to obtain equitable remuneration, which, in the absence of agreement, shall be fixed by the competent authority. As noted by Ricketson and Ginsburg, 'this is normally taken to mean that the conditions and the reservations which are imposed will take the form of

139 In this context, the CJEU in the case *Commission v Spain* found that Spain violated the freedom of movement of EU citizens when applied different conditions for the visit to museums for Spanish and other EU citizens. Even though a pan European right of trans border access to culture has not been explicitly affirmed in this decision, an implicit link of the freedom of receive services and of the freedom movement with the access to cultural goods has been recognised. See judgment of 15 March 1994, Case C-45/93.

140 For a general overview, see Valentine Korah, *Intellectual Property Rights and the EC Competition Rules* (Hart Publishing 2006); Jarrod Tudor, 'Compulsory Licensing in the European Union', 4 (2) Geo. Mason J. Int'l Com. Law 222- 258; Hanna Stakheyeva, 'Intellectual Property and Competition Law: Understanding the Interplay' in Ashish Bharadwaj, Vishwas H Devaiah, and Indranath Gupta (eds), *Multi-dimensional Approaches Towards New Technology* (Springer 2018) 3-19.

141 See judgment of 6 April 1995, Joined cases C-241/91 P and C-242/91 *Radio Telefis Eireann (RTE) and Independent Television Publications Ltd (ITP) v Commission of the European Communities* EU:C:1995:98; Case C-418/01 *IMS Health GmbH & Co. OHG v NDC Health GmbH & Co. KG* EU:C:2004:257; Case T-201/04 *Microsoft Corp. v Commission of the European Communities* EU:T:2007:289.

142 Jeffrey Church and Roger Ware, 'Network Industries, Intellectual Property Rights and Competition Policy', in Robert D Anderson and Nancy T Gallini (eds), *Competition Policy and Intellectual Property Rights In the Knowledge-Based Economy* (University of Calgary Press 1998) 227, 230-239. See also Mauro Squitieri, 'Refusals to License Under European Union Competition Law After Microsoft' 11 (1) Journal of International Business and Law (2012) <http://scholarlycommons.law.hofstra.edu /jibl/vol11/iss1/4> accessed 3 September 2019.

compulsory licenses'.[143] Similarly, Art. 11bis(2) of the Berne Convention provides for the possibility of compulsory licences for the broadcasting right and of the rights of retransmission, wire diffusion and public communication by means of loudspeakers for all categories of works. Furthermore, both the Berne[144] and Universal[145] Conventions contain special exceptions applicable only to developing countries, allowing a system of compulsory licences to reproduce or translate works for the purpose of teaching, scholarship or research.

Additionally, compulsory licensing in the field of copyright law could be facilitated by the existence of established collective management organisations in the EU Member States, which would provide for a more effective application of a compulsory licensing instrument, compared to patent law.[146]

In the case of a compulsory licence, the copyright owner must permit the use required of his work, though he retains the right to negotiate the terms of such use. If the parties cannot agree, the terms are settled by an administrator, a judge[147] or an arbitrator. In this context, a key element of such a mechanism is the calculation of an appropriate 'fair' remuneration of the rightholder for mandatory licensing in the consumer's country. Once again, the lessons of competition law would be useful, such as taking some inspiration from the FRAND patent law licensing model (licensing on fair, reasonable and non-discriminatory" terms) for non-exclusive licences granted by patent holders who participate in standards-setting arrangements

The origin of FRAND commitments lies in a series of U.S. antitrust enforcement actions in the early to mid-20th century, which sought to break up cartel arrangements among groups of competitors that tended to restrict access to markets and otherwise distort competition.[148] FRAND-based methodology and the notion of access on FRAND terms is also part of EU competition law. As noted by Heim and Nikolic, 'the concept of "fair, reasonable and non-discriminatory" access is used by competition authorities as a "good faith" notion, applied as a competition law remedy to ensure the supply of a particular product or the access to specific infrastructure, while 'from a theoretical perspective, it could be argued that Art. 102 TFEU already embraces a FRAND-based notion; it eschews excessive prices, while promoting access and non-discrimination obligations, as required under the "special responsibility"

143 Ricketson and Ginsburg (n 25) 815. However, mechanical recording licenses exist in few Berne countries, but not to the EU Member States, since the Directive 2001/29 does not leave room to the Member States for such a general statutory license. See Paul Goldstein and P Bernt Hugenholtz, *International Copyright: Principles, Law, and Practice* (Oxford University Press 2019) 378.

144 See Appendix to the Berne Convention 'Special Provisions Regarding Developing Countries'.

145 Article Vbis of the Universal Copyright Convention.

146 Matthias Leistner, 'The Requirements for Compulsory Dependency Licenses: Learning from the Transformative Use Doctrine in Copyright Law' in Reto M Hilty and Kung-Chung Liu (eds), *Compulsory Licensing: Practical Experiences and Ways Forward* (Springer 2015) 232.

147 Guide to the Rome Convention and to the Phonograms Convention, WIPO 1981, 17.

148 Jorge L Contreras and Anne Layne-Farrar, 'Non-discrimination and FRAND commitments' in Jorge L Contreras (ed), *The Cambridge Handbook of Technical Standardization Law, Competition, Antitrust, and Patents* (Cambridge University Press 2017).

of dominant firms'.[149] When FRAND licensing terms are defined, there should be a single set of terms based on what a truly willing licensor and a truly willing licensee would have agreed in the particular circumstances.[150]

Even if FRAND commitments and compulsory licences are legal constructs which differ in various ways, FRAND commitments are made voluntarily by participants, whereas compulsory licences are imposed by governmental action against the will of the intellectual property holder[151] – these forms of licences share the objective of producing a fair and reasonable licence for intellectual property.[152]

Certainly, the patent FRAND licensing model cannot find direct application in copyright law. However, the line of reasoning of its licensing principles (namely the commitment to license on 'fair, reasonable and non-discriminatory' terms) could be used for the development of a similar licensing philosophy in the area of compulsory copyright licensing. Indeed, in the absence of a set of licensing principles, both the licensing conditions and the calculation of the rightholder's remuneration would be left entirely to negotiation between the parties. This could hamper the mechanism's effectiveness, while the risk of unjustified discrimination between EU traders would also be present.

Specifically, as regards licensing on FRAND terms, the non-discriminatory aspect has historically been seen as a crucial prerequisite of every intellectual property compulsory licensing mechanism. As early as 1866, in *Re Mallet's Patent*,[153] where the first intellectual property compulsory licence in the UK was granted, the Judicial Committee recommended a term extension of four years of a patent for the fire-proofing of buildings upon the condition of granting licences to all persons who may be desirous of having them upon the same terms and, by doing so, it ensured that the terms of an existing licence shall be available to all.[154] Under a compulsory copyright licensing mechanism for the online transmission of copyright-protected works upon unsolicited requests from consumers located in other EU Member States, the non-discriminatory principle would require that licensors treat each individual licensee in a similar manner. While there might be differences in price or other licensing terms,[155] those differences must be justified. The underlying licensing condition included in a licensing agreement must be the same for 'similarly situated' licensees.[156]

---

149 Mathew Heim and Igor Nikolic, 'A FRAND Regime for Dominant Digital Platforms' JIPITEC 10 (1) 2019 https://www.jipitec.eu/issues/jipitec-10-1-2019/4883/> accessed 3 September 2019.

150 Lionel Bently and others, *Intellectual Property Law* (5th edn, Oxford University Press 2018) 679.

151 JL Contreras, 'A Brief History of FRAND: Analyzing Current Debates in Standard Setting and Antitrust Through a Historical Lens' 80 Antitrust Law Journal 39, 45 (2015).

152 Srividhya Ragavan, Brendan Murphy and Raj Davé, 'FRAND v. Compulsory Licensing: The Lesser of the Two Evils' 14 Duke L. & Tech. Rev. 83 (2016) <https://scholarship.law.tamu.edu/facscholar/725> accessed 3 September 2019.

153 In Re Mallet's Patent (1866) 4 Moo PC (NS) 175, 179; 116 ER 282, 284.

154 David J Brennan, 'The First Compulsory Licensing of Patents and Copyright' (2017) 17 Legal History 1-45 <https://ssrn.com/abstract=3012345> assessed 3 September 2019.

155 Contreras and Layne-Farrar (n 147) 186-208.

156 Dennis W Carlton and Allan L Shampine, 'An Economic Interpretation of FRAND' 9 Journal of Competition Law & Economics 546 (2013).

Licensing on 'fair and reasonable terms' mainly refers to the licensing rates, but it can also be perceived more broadly as excluding anti-competitive behaviour which would be considered unlawful if imposed by a dominant firm in its relative market, such as requiring licensees to buy licences for products they do not want, in order to get a licence for the products they do want, or imposing 'exclusive dealing' arrangements, i.e. restrictive conditions on the licensees' dealings with the licensor's competitors.[157]

The concept of 'fair and reasonable licensing' shares some common characteristics with the copyright law notion of 'equitable remuneration', at least as regards the objective of calculating a fair price. While it might, on the face of it, appear unconventional to assimilate principles which have been developed for the licensing of patents in the field of copyright law, such an inspiration of patent law compulsory licensing is supported by the history of Art. 13 of the Berne Convention. In this context, it should be borne in mind that the proposal for an 'equitable remuneration' in Art. 13 of the Berne Convention comes originally from a German proposal, which was based on the system of compulsory licences under German patent law.[158] Based on this, Ricketson and Ginsburg propose to interpret the concept of 'equitable remuneration' as set out in Art. 13, with reference to the criteria set by a German court decision for the licensing of patents, in the sense that the licence fee should grant reasonable compensation to the patentee, but it should also enable the licensee to sustain the operation of his business.[159]

As regards the definition of 'equitable remuneration', European copyright law focuses on the 'economic value of the use'.[160] At the same time, a flexible approach is adopted, which takes into account a variety of factors and makes the calculation of the equitable remuneration a careful balancing exercise. In this context, it was held in the *SENA* case, that:

'Article 8(2) of Directive 92/100 does not preclude a model for calculating what constitutes equitable remuneration for performing artists and phonogram producers that operates by reference to variable and fixed factors, such as the number of hours of phonograms broadcast, the viewing and listening densities achieved by the radio and television broadcasters represented by the broadcast organisation, the tariffs fixed by agreement in the field of performance rights and broadcast rights in respect of musical works protected by copyright, the tariffs set by the public broadcast organisations in the Member States bordering on the Member State concerned, and the amounts paid by commercial stations, provided that that model is such as to enable a proper balance

157 Organisation for Economic Co-operation and Development, Directorate for Financial and Enterprise Affairs Competition Committee, Licensing of IP Rights and Competition Law (*OECD*, 29 April 2019) 21 <https://one.oecd.org/document/DAF/COMP(2019)3/en/pdf> accessed 3 September 2019.

158 Ricketson and Ginsburg (n 25) 816.

159 Ricketson and Ginsburg (n 25) 816, with reference to the decision of the German Patent Court in the: Case No 3 Li 1/90 (EU), 7 June 1991.

160 Silke von Lewinski, 'Rental and Lending Rights Directive' in Michel Walter and Silke von Lewinski, European Copyright law, A commentary (Oxford University Press 2010) 324.

to be achieved between the interests of performing artists and producers in obtaining remuneration for the broadcast of a particular phonogram, and the interests of third parties in being able to broadcast the phonogram on terms that are reasonable, and that it does not contravene any principle of Community law'.[161]

It is noteworthy that the requirement of 'reasonable terms' and the need to safeguard the compatibility of the licensing terms with EU law principles reflect the idea of a 'fair and reasonable' licensing, both as regards the prohibition of anti-competitive behaviour and the determination of a reasonable price. It could be argued that, by analogy to patent law, in order to address the problem of royalty stacking,[162] which arises when the implementers must pay royalties to multiple owners, the hypothetical negotiation also needs to reflect the presence of copyright and related rights held by others that apply to the same 'product'.

Lastly, the whole mechanism should be accompanied by out-of-court dispute settlement tools. Out-of-court dispute settlement procedures, such as mediation between the user of copyright-protected works and rightholders, have already been recognised in European copyright law, such as when implementing Art. 6(4) of the Information Society Directive,[163] and more recently as a way to enable users to dispute the disabling of access to, or the removal of, works or other subject matter uploaded to platforms by them, in the context of Art. 17 of the Directive on Copyright in the Digital Single Market.[164]

161 Judgment of 6 February 2003, Case C-245/00 *Stichting ter Exploitatie van Naburige Rechten (SENA) and Nederlandse Omroep Stichting (NOS)* EU:C:2003:68, para 46.

162 'Royalty stalking' occurs when cumulative royalty rates cannot be kept at reasonable levels when there are several licensors of essential patents on the same standard. Each licensor is expected to seek a too high a royalty rate, ignoring the fact that stacking high royalties would hamper the demand for standard compliant products. See: Yann Ménière (author) and Nikolaus Thumm (ed), 'Fair, Reasonable and Non-Discriminatory (FRAND) Licensing Terms, Research Analysis of a Controversial Concept' (European Commission, 2015) 14 <http://publications.jrc.ec.europa.eu/repository/bitstream/JRC96258/jrc96258.pdf> accessed 3 September 2019.

163 According to this provision, '… in the absence of voluntary measures taken by rightholders, including agreements between rightholders and other parties concerned, Member States shall take appropriate measures to ensure that rightholders make available to the beneficiary of an exception or limitation provided for in national law in accordance with Article 5(2)(a), (2)(c), (2)(d), (2)(e), (3)(a), (3)(b) or (3)(e) the means of benefiting from that exception or limitation, to the extent necessary to benefit from that exception or limitation and where that beneficiary has legal access to the protected work or subject-matter concerned'. The Directive does not specify the kind of measure to be taken. In this context, some Member States have introduced a system of mediation or similar alternative dispute resolution systems. See Walter and von Lewinski (n 22) 1072.

164 Specifically, para 9 of art 17 states that 'Member States shall also ensure that out-of-court redress mechanisms are available for the settlement of disputes. Such mechanisms shall enable disputes to be settled impartially and shall not deprive the user of the legal protection afforded by national law, without prejudice to the rights of users to have recourse to efficient judicial remedies.

5 Conclusion

Overall, the EU policy on copyright law and geoblocking has attempted to resolve the antithesis between the ideal of the single market and the concept of copyright territoriality through a modest and careful approach, which is based on the axiom of safeguarding copyright territoriality, and of the accompanying geoblocking practices. As the efforts to create a digital single market are intensified, it appears that a strict EU geoblocking policy in relation to services offering access to copyright-protected works cannot be retained. In this context, the article demonstrated that mechanisms for 'circumvention' of the principle of territoriality will have to be devised. As proposed, those mechanisms must be based on a balanced approach and on the principle of safeguarding an appropriate, fair remuneration for rightholders, which would be calculated on the basis of clear criteria. In this context, the forthcoming evaluation of the Geoblocking Regulation is an opportunity for exploring alternative ways to deal with the question, such as introducing the obligation for an EU trader to legitimately passively distribute copyright-protected content in response to a consumer's request, provided that the latter pays the legitimate additional cost of the licensing in her/his country. This new 'user right' would have a hybrid justification and would be based on the fundamental EU axiom of the free movement of goods and services, but also on a claim emanating from the EU citizen to have access to the cultures of EU Member States.

DIGITAL CONTENT PORTABILITY AND ITS RELATION TO CONFORMITY WITH THE CONTRACT

Pavel Koukal*

Introduction

Cross-border issues related to the use of the digital content by consumers have been covered by several pieces of EU legislation in recent years. The availability of digital goods or services in the on-line environment is of a complex nature[1] and can be viewed from different perspectives, each of which concerns various stages of making digital assets available to the consumer audience.

Differences in the laws of the EU Member States regarding national consumer protection and contract law are seen as the main obstacle which prevents consumers from enjoying the full benefits of cross-border e-commerce with digital assets and also as a serious barrier for business operators who must adapt their services to different legal conditions set by the national legislations[2] in the field of contracts, consumer or copyright protection.[3]

---

* Associate professor, Masaryk University, Faculty of Law, pavel.koukal@law.muni.cz. The author would like to express his gratitude to prof. Markéta Trimble from the William S. Boyd School of Law, UNLV (USA) for the substantive comments on the working versions of this paper. Certain parts of this paper were previously published in Koukal, P (2018), p. 814-820. Due to postponement of the publication of this book from the date of the conference, this text is almost literal reprint of a text that the author has meanwhile published in the Masaryk University Journal of Law and Technology [Koukal (2021), p. 53-79].

1 Trimble, M (2012), p. 624 ff.; Hoffman, J (2016), p. 148 ff.; Helberger, N et al. (2013), p. 42-45; Staudenmayer, D (2016), p. 2721, 2722; Spindler, G (2016) Digitale Wirtschaft – analoges Recht: Braucht das BGB ein Update?, p. 805 ff.; Spindler, G (2016) Verträge über digitale Inhalte – Anwendungsbereich und Ansätze Vorschlag der EU-Kommission zu einer Richtlinie über Verträge zur Bereitstellung digitaler Inhalte, p. 147 ff., 219 ff.; Loos, M B M (2011), p. 45-48; Bach, I (2019), p. 1705 ff.; Carvalho, J M (2019), p. 194 ff.; Spindler, G, Sein, K (2019), p. 415 ff.; Synodinou, T E (2020), Geoblocking in EU Copyright Law: Challenges and Perspectives, p. 136 ff.; Oprysk, L, Sein, K (2020), p. 594 ff.

2 Communication from the Commission to the European Parliament, the Council, the European Economic and Social Committee and the Committee of the Regions. A Digital Single Market Strategy for Europe from 6.5.2016, COM (2015) 192 final, p. 5; Arnerstål, S (2015), p. 882; Helberger, N et al. (2013), p. 42.

3 Loos, M B M et al. (2011), p. 14, 39, 102; Lehman, M In De Franceschi, A (2016), p. 115; Schulze, R In De Franceschi, A (2016), p. 131; Oprysk, L, Sein, K (2020), p. 597.

From the legal perspective, we can see several phases where EU law interferes with the process of making digital content available to users (consumers). At the beginning of the regulatory chain, we find the legal regulation of rights, which apply to digital content. In the middle of the distribution chain, we find the legal regulation of the (i) intermediaries;[4] (ii) collecting societies;[5] (iii) rights to access the digital content of libraries, universities, and research institutions;[6] or (iv) legislation on audio-visual media suppliers.[7] Last but not least, it is necessary to set forth rules for (v) consumer protection in the digital market,[8] and in this regard to focus on the (vi) aspects of the cross-border availability of the digital content.[9]

The aim of this paper is to analyse possible convergences and divergences of two legislative acts: the Portability Regulation [Regulation (EU) No. 2017/1128] and the Digital Content Directive [Directive (EU) No. 2019/770]. The Digital Content Directive expressly states: "*It should also be without prejudice to Union and national law on copyright and related rights, including the portability of online content services*" (Recital 36 Digital Content Directive). This provision means that the Directive does not change any provisions in the Portability Regulation. However, we must ask what the relationship is between these two pieces of legislation when they regulate similar subject matter.

We will focus especially on the rights of consumers who use digital content in other EU Member States. Nevertheless, we will also address the relationship between cross-border portability and the system of possible unitary rights and try to argue that the use of geo-blocking practices is not primarily a question of the existence of unitary rights,[10] but a question of the contractual limits imposed on the practices of digital content providers.

---

4 Art. 17 Directive (EU) 2019/790 of the European Parliament and of the Council of 17 April 2019 on copyright and related rights in the Digital Single Market and amending Directives 96/9/EC and 2001/29/EC.

5 Directive 2014/26/EU of the European Parliament and of the Council of 26 February 2014 on collective management of copyright and related rights and multi-territorial licencing of rights in musical works for online use in the internal market.

6 Art. 3 – 7 Directive 2019/790/EU.

7 Directive (EU) 2019/789 of the European Parliament and of the Council of 17 April 2019 laying down rules on the exercise of copyright and related rights applicable to certain online transmissions of broadcasting organisations and retransmissions of television and radio programmes, and amending Council Directive 93/83/EEC; Directive (EU) 2018/1808 of the European Parliament and of the Council of 14 November 2018 amending Directive 2010/13/EU on the coordination of certain provisions laid down by law, regulation or administrative action in Member States concerning the provision of audiovisual media services (Audiovisual Media Services Directive) in view of changing market realities.

8 Directive (EU) 2019/770 of the European Parliament and of the Council of 20 May 2019 on certain aspects concerning contracts for the supply of digital content and digital services.

9 Regulation (EU) 2017/1128 of the European Parliament and of the Council of 14 June 2017 on cross-border portability of online content services in the internal market. See also Hoffman, J (2016), p. 145; Mazziotti, G (2016), p. 365 ff.; Trimble, M (2016), p. 45 ff; Engles, S; Spindler, G (2016) Die Modernisierung des europäischen Urheberrechts Der Vorschlag zur Portabilitäts-VO und die Planungen der EU-Kommission, p. 73 ff.; Nordemann, J B (2018), p. 179 ff.;

10 Hoffmann, J (2016), p. 168 ff.

With the Digital Content Directive, the EU is responding to the needs of the digital economy in the area of private law. The directive pursues a viable and a technology-oriented approach; it covers all types of digital content or services, harmonizes contractual aspects of B-2-C obligations where the consumer's counter performance is based on monetary payments or on providing personal data.[11] Moreover, the directive intends to regulate consumer rights in case the digital content or service is not in conformity with the contract and stipulates consumer rights and remedies. The Digital Content Directive is strongly inspired[12] by the provisions of the Commission's proposal for a Regulation on a Common European Sales Law (hereinafter"CESL")[13] which was intended to constitute an optional instrument that would actually create a parallel contract-law regime to coexist alongside national contract-law provisions.[14]

The Portability Regulation removes barriers to cross-border portability and prohibits the implementation of geo-blocking[15] measures within the EU Digital Single Market. This should enable the digital content consumers who subscribed to content services in the Member State of their permanent residence to receive a service or a download of pre-paid content, in a country, which they are temporarily visiting.

11 According to Art. 3 (1) Digital Content Directive this directive shall also apply where the trader supplies or undertakes to supply digital content or a digital service to the consumer, and the consumer provides or undertakes to provide personal data to the trader. Thus, the directive also comprises a new business model called "performance against data." However, the data must be classified as a consideration, which means that the trader is not processing data to fulfill his/her contractual or legal obligations. See also Carvalho, J M (2019), p. 197; Bach, I (2019), p. 1706; Spindler, G, Sein, K. (2019), p. 418; Lehmann, M In De Franceschi, A (2016), p. 117.

12 COM (2015) 634 final, p. 2; Lehmann, M In De Franceschi, A (2016), p. 113; Spindler, G, Sein, K. (2019), p. 415.

13 In October 2011, the European Commission issued a proposal for the Common European Sales Law (CESL) which was intended to give traders the choice to sell their products to customers in another Member State on the basis of a single set of contract law rules that would stand as an alternative to the national contract law of each Member State. The CESL project [also called the "Blue-Button Project"; Schulte-Nölke, H (2011), p. 89] was intended to be an autonomous set of private-law rules parallel to the national laws of EU Member States. Thus it should not represent the European private law in the sense of choice-of-law rules such as the Rome I or Rome II Regulation, but an optional instrument suitable for both B2C and B2B relationships that could be chosen by contracting parties as a set of directly applicable legal rules regulating the specific contractual relationships. CESL should be applied as a "twenty-eighth legal order" which complement the laws of the EU Member States, but only if the contracting parties explicitly made a choice of this legal instrument (opt-in principle). During the discussions in the Council and the European Parliament, the European Commission finally decided to withdraw the CESL proposal on the grounds that a new proposal would cover only the e-commerce aspects in the Digital Single Market. The reasons for the withdrawal of the CESL proposal were substantial. In particular, the United Kingdom expressed strong reservations regarding the inconsistency of the proposal with the common-law. See also An Optional Common European Sales Law: Advantages and Problems Advice to the UK Government, The Law Commission and The Scottish Law Commission [online]; Lehmann, M In De Franceschi, A (2016), p. 113; Schulze, R In De Franceschi, A (2016), p. 128.

14 Beale, H (2013), p. 22 ff; Twigg-Flesner, Ch (2013), p. 45 ff.; Schulze, R (2012), p. 85 ff.; Pongelli, G (2013), p. 11 ff., 17.

15 SWD (2015) 270 final, p. 3, 6, 55; Hoffman, J (2016), p. 164.

Further, the Portability Regulation targets the illegal use[16] of copyrighted content which has been partially supported by the use of geo-blocking practices.

Both legislative acts regulate similar issues related to consumers' expectations that they will be able to effectively use digital content without technological, functional or cross-border restrictions. The question of cross-border portability is the key subject matter of Art. 3 (1) Portability Regulation, and might also be seen as an "accessibility" issue and therefore be subsumed under the concept of "conformity of the digital content with the contract" within Art. 8 (1) (b) Digital Content Directive.

It is obvious that the Digital Content Directive regulates a considerably wider range of legal relations. The reason for this is that it applies to all contracts with digital content and is targeted not only at cross-border relations, but also at situations in which digital content is supplied by the content provider to the consumer within the territory of a state. Although the directive does not aim to regulate any intellectual property issues [Art. 3 (9) Digital Content Directive], the directive will have a direct impact on copyright licences. This is because digital content is generally supplied based on licence contracts.[17]

Compared with the wide range of consumer issues prescribed by the Digital Content Directive, the Portability Regulation creates new consumer (subscriber) rights for when a consumer uses digital services in a Member State of their "temporarily presence" [Art. 2 (4), Art. 4 Portability Regulation].[18] Whereas the Digital Content Directive applies for domestic transactions as well as for cross-border transactions, the Portability Regulation is applicable only in the case of cross-border delivery of on-line digital goods or services. On the other hand, the Portability Regulation lays down rules which are directly applicable not only to the service providers, but simultaneously to copyright holders. This is because geo-blocking practices are primarily asserted by a copyright or by the related rights holders.[19]

The key question that this paper aims to answer is whether a consumer will be entitled to pursue claims arising from the non-conformity of digital content with the contract, as provided by Art. 8 and 14 of the Digital Content Directive, in the event that he or she is not allowed to access digital services in states other than the Member State of his or her residence due to the application of geo-blocking measures by digital content providers. If the answer to this question is yes, we will then focus on

[16] COM (2015) 626 final, p. 4, 11.

[17] Many service providers of digital content use contractual terms in which the user receives a limited licence to use the digital content. If you subscribe to Spotify, Netflix, iTunes or Google-Play, you enter into a licence agreement, not a purchase agreement. The content providers keep the intellectual property rights and provide the consumer a limited, non-exclusive, revocable licence to make personal, non-commercial use of the digital content. See Arnerstål, S (2015), p. 752; Loos, M B M et al. (2011), p. 14; Oprysk, L, Sein, K (2020), p. 595 ff. The impact of the Digital Content Directive on licence contracts will consist in definition of digital content, its integration into the consumer's digital environment, but especially in the regulation of the rights the consumer have if the digital content is not in conformity with the licence contract.

[18] Engles, S; Nordemann, J B (2018), p. 193.

[19] COM (2015) 627 final, p. 2, 4; Recitals 10 and 29 Portability Regulation.

the hierarchy of remedies provided to the consumer in the event the digital content does not conform to the contract (Art. 14 Digital Content Directive), as well as on issues related to the quality of content transmitted to the subscriber under Art. 3 of the Portability Regulation. When analysing the Portability Regulation we will also discuss whether the European Commission should propose uniform copyright protection under Art. 118 TFEU rather than ensuring cross-border portability. However, we will defend the thesis that ensuring cross-border portability by Art. 3 (1) of the Portability Regulation and also by the prohibition of geo-blocking via provisions of the Regulation 2018/302/EU[20] is the appropriate legislative tool to enable the subscriber to enjoy the cross-border use of the digital content.[21]

The Material Scope of the Digital Content Directive

After the CESL proposal was withdrawn,[22] the Commission decided to abandon the comprehensive "optional instrument approach".[23] The proposal for the Digital Content Directive was presented by the Commission in December 2015 and was submitted according to Art. 114 TFEU. The Commission's aim was to adopt a fully harmonizing directive (Recital 6, Art. 4 Digital Content Directive) instead of the comprehensive regulation. Thus the Digital Content Directive represents targeted[24] legislation which harmonizes mandatory consumer contract-law rules.

Although the Consumer Rights Directive[25] has fully harmonized certain rules for the online supply of digital content (especially pre-contractual information and the

20 Regulation (EU) 2018/302 of the European Parliament and of the Council of 28 February 2018 on addressing unjustified geo-blocking and other forms of discrimination based on customers' nationality, place of residence or place of establishment within the internal market and amending Regulations (EC) No 2006/2004 and (EU) 2017/2394 and Directive 2009/22/EC

21 Differently see Hoffmann, J (2016), p. 169 ff.

22 The CESL proposal has never received approval by the Council (see fn. No. 243). On 16. 12. 2014, the Commission officially placed the CESL on the list of proposals intended to be modified or withdrawn. Later, on 9. 12. 2015, the Commission presented a modified text that would harmonize contract rules for the supply of digital content and the online sales of goods. See Communication from the Commission to the European Parliament, the Council, the European Economic and Social Committee and the Committee of the Regions. Commission Work Programme 2015. A New Start, from 16. 12. 2014, COM (2014) 910 final; Communication from the Commission to the European Parliament, the Council, the European Economic and Social Committee. Digital contracts for Europe – Unleashing the potential of e-commerce from 9. 12. 2015, COM/2015/0633 final; See also Clive, E (2015).

23 Impact Assessment: Proposals for Directives of the European Parliament and of the Council (1) on certain aspects concerning contracts for the supply of digital content and (2) on certain aspects concerning contracts for the online and other distance sales of goods from 17.12.2015. SWD (2015) 274 final/2, p. 52.

24 Beale, H (2016). p. 8; Lehmann, M In De Franceschi, A (2016), p. 115; Schulze, R In De Franceschi, A (2016), p. 135; Spindler, G, Sein, K. (2019), p. 415.

25 Art. 5, Art. 9 and Art. 14 Directive 2011/83/EU of the European Parliament and of the Council of 25 October 2011 on consumer rights, amending Council Directive 93/13/EEC and Directive 1999/44/

rules related to the right of withdrawal),[26] there were almost no specific EU rules to protect consumers if the digital content does not fulfil the requirements of functionality, interoperability, or accessibility.[27]

The Digital Content Directive has a broad scope, which is be applied on different types of contracts concerning digital supply.[28] This is one of the important distinctions[29] from the Contracts for the Sale Directive,[30] which covers just the contract of sales [Art. 1, Art. 2 (a) Contracts for the Sale Directive]. The Digital Content Directive also does not differentiate between the categories of digital content or digital services (Recital 19 Digital Content Directive), because such differentiation in the field of rapidly evolving technologies would probably lead to discrimination between suppliers. Therefore, all kinds of data, copyrighted works (films, music, photos, computer games), as well as all possible forms of digital content provided by consumers (blogs, discussion forums, text-based collaboration formats etc.) are covered by the material scope of the directive,[31] no matter if they are available on-line or if the digital content is contained on CDs or DVDs.[32]

EC of the European Parliament and of the Council and repealing Council Directive 85/577/EEC and Directive 97/7/EC of the European Parliament and of the Council.

26 Art. 6 and 9 Consumer Rights Directive; See also Beale, H (2016), p. 6; Carvalho, J M (2019), p. 194.

27 For digital content, there were just minimum requirements regulated by the Unfair Contract Terms Directive [Art. 3, 4 (2) Council Directive 93/13/EEC of 5 April 1993 on unfair terms in consumer contracts]. Another standard was set by the Consumer Sales and Guarantees Directive (Art. 2 and 3 Directive 1999/44/EC of the European Parliament and of the Council of 25 May 1999 on certain aspects of the sale of consumer goods and associated guarantees), but just with regard to "tangible movable items" [Art. 1 (2) b) Directive 1999/44/EC] such as CDs or DVDs.

28 Spindler, G, Sein, K (2019), p. 415.

29 Zoll, F (2016), p. 251; Spindler, G (2016) Verträge über digitale Inhalte, p. 147.

30 Directive (EU) 2019/771 of the European Parliament and of the Council of 20 May 2019 on certain aspects concerning contracts for the sale of goods, amending Regulation (EU) 2017/2394 and Directive 2009/22/EC, and repealing Directive 1999/44/EC. Directive 2019/771/EU and Directive 2019/770/EU should complement each other. While Directive 2019/770/EU (Digital Content Directive) lays down rules on certain requirements concerning contracts for the supply of digital content or digital services, the Directive 2019/771/EU (Contracts for the Sale Directive) lays down rules on certain requirements concerning contracts for the sale of goods. Accordingly, Directive 2019/770/EU applies to the supply of digital content or digital services, including digital content supplied on a tangible medium, such as DVDs, CDs, USB sticks and memory cards, as well as to the tangible medium itself, provided that the tangible medium serves exclusively as a carrier of the digital content. In contrast, the Directive 2019/771/EU should apply to contracts for the sale of goods, including goods with digital elements which require digital content or a digital service in order to perform their functions [Recital 13, Art. 3 (3) Contracts for the Sale Directive].

31 However, the Directive does not apply to digital content, which is embedded in goods in such a way that it operates as an integral part of the goods and its functions are subordinated to the main objective of the goods (Recital 21 Digital Content Directive). Thus, toys which contain music or even audio-visual clips will fall outside the scope of the Digital Content Directive, even though they contain digital content. Goods with incorporated digital content fall under Article 3 (3) Contracts for the Sale Directive.

32 According to Recital 20 and Art. 3 (3) of the Digital Content Directive it is irrelevant whether the supply of digital content is carried on data carriers such as CDs or DVDs or through the downloading or streaming accessible via Internet. This is an important clarification, as the data carriers will not fall

In a similarly broad manner, the EU regulates types of contracts with regard to counter performance. The directive treats contracts in which a consumer provides personal data as contracts for consideration [Recital 24, Art. 3 (1) Digital Content Directive]. Although the consumer receives digital content from the supplier "for free", if he or she gives access to his or her personal or other data, the contracts will fall under the material scope of the directive.[33]

Finally, the directive is not intended to have any effect on copyright issues [Recital 36, Art. 3 (9) Digital Content Directive], especially on the distribution right applicable to digital goods under the copyright law (Recital 20 Digital Content Directive). Thus, all questions concerning digital rights management systems, as well as the effects of the principle of exhaustion, are omitted. The consumer therefore cannot argue that the limitations on further use of the digital content (such as the re-sale or lending of e-books) are not in conformity with the contract since the consumer, upon receiving the digital content, is not entitled to further distribution of the copyrighted content due to the copyright limitations, which are still applicable.[34]

The Digital Content Directive also has no direct application on relations between consumers and copyright holders.[35] It only regulates the legal responsibilities of digital content providers who, as legal entities, are usually different from subjects that are the original or derivative owners of the copyright. With regard to the on-line dissemination of copyrighted works uploaded to the Internet by third parties, the Digital Content Directive stipulates that "where a restriction resulting from a violation of any right of a third party, in particular intellectual property rights, prevents or limits the use of the digital content or digital service in accordance with Articles 7 and 8, Member States shall ensure that the consumer is entitled to the remedies for lack of conformity provided for in Article 14, unless national law provides for the nullity or

under the Contracts for the Sale Directive, including provisions on conformity with contract, rules on the burden of proof etc.

33 On the other hand, the directive does not apply if the data collected from the consumer are necessary for the "performance of the contract" or "for meeting legal requirements" [Art. 3 (1), Recital 25 Digital Content Directive]. The Directive is applicable only to that extent where the personal data are actively required by the provider and does not cover situations where the digital content is provided for free and data collected from the consumer are used only for security or registration purposes. Moreover, automatically generated personal data such as IP addresses or data collected and transmitted by means of cookies, without the consumer actively supplying it, also do not fall under the material scope of the directive. However, Member States may, on an optional basis, provide that the Directive also applies to such cases (Recital 25 Digital Content Directive). Similarly, situations in which the consumer is exposed to advertisements in order to gain access to digital content do not fall under the material scope of the directive. For criticism on the exclusion of cookie-based services like Google Analytics see Spindler, G (2016). Verträge über digitale Inhalte, p. 149; Beale, H (2016) Scope of application and general approach of the new rules for contracts in the digital environment, p. 13.

34 Critical remarks on this approach are by expressed by Beale. Beale, H (2016), Scope of application and general approach of the new rules for contracts in the digital environment, p. 27. Oprysk and Sein conclude that specific contractual arrangements that prohibit, for example, backups or file sharing outside the user's family, may be contrary to reasonable consumer expectations within the meaning of Art. 8 (1) (b) Digital Content Directive. Oprysk, L, Sein, K (2020), p. 620.

35 Spindler, G (2016), Verträge über digitale Inhalte, p. 149.

rescission of the contract for the supply of the digital content or digital service in such cases“. After the implementation of the Digital Content Directive into the national legislation of the EU Member States, the intermediaries, who request payments for the use of digital content or who require personal data from the consumer, will have to provide a legal guarantee to the consumer that the digital content is in conformity with the contract, especially that it does not conflict with the intellectual property rights of third parties ("third party rights" or "legal non-conformity").[36]

The Digital Content Directive uses positive [Art. 3 (1 – 3), (6)] and negative definitions [Art. 3 (4), (5), (10)] for the determination of its material scope. In this regard, Art. 3 (7) of the Digital Content Directive stipulates: "If any provision of this Directive conflicts with a provision of another Union act governing a specific sector or subject matter, the provision of that other Union act shall take precedence over this Directive". In relation to portability, the Directive then specifically provides that: "It should also be without prejudice to Union and national law on copyright and related rights, including the portability of online content services" (Recital 36 Digital Content Directive).

If we focus on the relation between the "conformity with the contract" and the "portability matters", it seems necessary to analyse whether Art. 3 (7) of the Digital Content Directive sets the rule on the negative scope of the directive, and therefore all the issues regulated by the special legislation are excluded from the scope of the Digital Content Directive, or whether this provision contains only a specialty rule. The specialty rule would mean that the Portability Regulation would be applied only to the extent to which it regulates the "specific sector or subject matter", such as the availability of digital content in the Member State of the temporary presence of the consumer, but other issues, such as remedies concerned with the non-availability of digital content, would fall under the scope of the national laws transposing the provisions of the Digital Content Directive.

Portability of Digital Content as a Consumer-Law Issue

From the perspective of consumer protection, which is more stressed by the Digital Content Directive[37] than by the Portability Regulation,[38] we should return to the question of what the relation between these two pieces of EU legislation is.

36 Oprysk, L, Sein, K (2020), p. 598. See also Recital 54 Digital Content Directive.

37 Consumer law and copyright law deal with digital content from opposing positions. While consumer law focuses on the ownership of the purchased items or the right to use them under reasonable expectations of the consumer, copyright law considers digital content from the owners' perspective and especially highlights that ownership of a physical copy of a work does not grant any ownership in the copyright itself. Helberger N et al. (2013), p. 46; Loos, M B M (2011), p. 30, 31; Oprysk, L, Sein, K (2020), p. 597.

38 Engles, S; Nordemann, J B (2018), p. 179.

Portability and geo-blocking are two different sides of the same coin.[39] While portability is positively characterized as the ability "to play, listen, and watch digital content on different kinds of devices, to lock-in or lock-out situations that are the result of product bundling or interoperability issues, social exclusion, and geographical impediment because of region coding and restrictive licencing practices",[40] the notion of geo-blocking is primarily negative,[41] as it is used by copyright holders or digital content providers to block foreign IP addresses[42] in order to prevent consumers from having cross-border access to digital content services.[43]

Portability reflects consumers' natural expectations that the digital content, which covers many kinds of "intangible assets", will be available across borders and ubiquitous. If consumers complain[44] about territorial restrictions on the broadcasting of copyrighted works or sporting events applied by the suppliers, we can remark that consumers are merely applying their "common sense". They see no relevant reason for the lack of availability of digital content in the Digital Single Market[45] (or even in the global market), even though they know nothing about the theoretical aspects of intangible assets. The consumers argue that if the EU developed a Single Market in the sphere of physical goods or services, similarly they should have on-line access to the digital content throughout the EU. The digital content should be lawfully accessible not only in the Member State of the consumer's permanent residence, but also when travelling to another EU Member State.[46] Moreover, the natural characteristics of intangible assets (as well as the expectations of consumers) are highlighted by the fact that the Internet has been developed as a medium available and accessible without physical boundaries.[47]

In the past, with the exception of films and sporting events,[48] providers in EU countries did not generally impose territorial restrictions on digital content. Even

---

39 SWD (2015) 270 final, see fn. 235.

40 Helberger, N et al. (2013), p. 40. Similarly Synodinou, T E (2020), Geoblocking in EU Copyright Law: Challenges and Perspectives, p. 144; Engles, S; Nordemann, J B (2018), p. 182.

41 However, geo-blocking may also have a positive role in the digital environment. While Hoffmann points to the negative aspects of geo-blocking, such as language discrimination, consumer frustration or the obstacles to create a Digital Single Market [Hoffmann, J (2016), p. 145], Trimble on the other hand argues that geo-blocking also plays important roles in the Internet legal landscape. Geo-blocking serves as a tool for delimiting jurisdiction and enforcing decisions within territorial boundaries; it serves the purposes of enhancing security and partitioning markets, and also enables compliance with territorially-defined laws (such as privacy and personal data protection). See Trimble, M (2016), p. 47-50.

42 Other methods of controlling the Internet users' geographical location may also be used, such as global positioning system (GPS). Trimble, M (2012), p. 605. For simplicity, in this paper we will only use geo-location based on the IP address.

43 SWD (2015) 270 final, p. 39, 58; Trimble, M (2016), p. 46; Hoffmann, J (2016), p. 145.

44 SWD (2015) 270 final, p. 54 ff.

45 SWD (2015) 270 final, p. 3, 6. However, for opposite views concerning the defence of geo-blocking activities based on the protection of investment of film producers and cultural differences among EU Member States see Mazzotti, G (2016), p. 369 ff.

46 SWD (2015) 270 final, p. 6; Engles, S, Nordemann, J B (2018), p. 184.

47 Trimble, M (2012), p. 570; Trimble, M (2016), p. 147.

48 SWD (2015) 270 final, p. 8-10, 39.

though there could have been cultural and economic (i.e. protecting the investments of film producers) reasons for the territorial division of markets,[49] most digital assets (i.e. musical works, computer programs or e-books) were provided without border restrictions. From the consumers perspective it was hardly justifiable[50] that audio-visual producers or broadcasting organizations so strongly insisted on a territorial-based dissemination of digital assets. If we compare how copyrighted works have quite recently been provided around the EU with a federal state such as Germany, we could say that it was unlikely that a broadcaster provided a territorially-limited licence to a German citizen solely for Free State Bavaria. The end-users in Germany were allowed to watch a Bayern Munich football match in Dresden because the geo-blocking restrictions have not been applied. Thus, the arguments based on the economic models[51] of film distribution among EU Member States were not convincing, since the dissemination model could hardly prevail over the basic principles of the EU single market such as free movement of goods and services [Art. 26 (2), Art. 56 TFEU] and over consumer protection [Art. 12, Art. 114 (3), Art. 169 TFEU]. Even though the problem of the territorial scope of copyright protection could probably be efficiently solved by the adoption of the EU-wide Copyright Regulation (adopted under Art. 118 TFEU, which would create unitary EU copyright protection),[52] the real effects of the Portability Regulation showed that the accessibility has not been question of the unitary rights but about the removal of territorial barriers in the sphere of contract law.[53] The problem is that under the regime of unitary rights, we may still find examples in which licences are granted not across the entire territory of the EU, but in several states only. For example, Council Regulation No. 2017/1001 of 14 June 2017 on the European Union trade mark expressly enables the trademark owner to grant a licence for the "whole or part of the EU".[54] Although it is hard to presume that the example on the territorial limits of broadcasting in Germany would actually happen, it may still be possible under the EU Copyright Regulation to

49 Mazzotti, G (2016), p. 373-375. Another reason for the application of the geo-location techniques are provided by Trimble. She explains that geolocation reflects the territorial based legal regulations not just in the area of IP, but also with respect to the personal data protection. Moreover, it enables the supplier to provide the tailored content, included differential pricing, localizing advertising, and Internet searching. Trimble, M (2012), p. 586, 589.

50 Cross-border portability has been considered to be a modern distribution tool not only by consumers, but also by the audio-visual industry. In 2013, several members of the audio-visual industry have adopted the joint statement at the Licences for Europe forum where they confirmed that they were prepared to work on cross-border portability in the EU. See Licences for Europe – Structured Stakeholder Dialogue 2013, WG 1 Audio-visual Subgroup, Joint Statement on Cross-border Portability of lawfully-acquired Audio-visual Content [online].

51 Mazzotti, G (2016), p. 371. See also SWD (2015) 270 final, Annex 4.

52 Hoffmann, J (2016), p. 166 ff.; Mazzotti, G (2016), p. 375.

53 Peifer, K, N In De Franceschi, A (2016), p. 166.

54 The same rule applies also to the Community Designs [Art. 32 (1) Council Regulation (EC) No 6/2002 of 12 December 2001 on Community designs] and on the future European Patent with the unitary effect [Art. 3 (2) Regulation (EU) No 1257/2012 of the European Parliament and of the Council of 17 December 2012 implementing enhanced cooperation in the area of the creation of unitary patent protection].

provide licences on a territorial basis, unless such a possibility is expressly forbidden by the legislation.

The Portability Regulation is usually analysed in terms of copyright protection,[55] underlying the principle of territoriality. However, portability is not primarily a question of the territoriality of the copyright but a question of the licencing policy of copyright holders.[56] Consistent with the holdings of the CJEU in the Premiere League decision,[57] the Portability Regulation does not tackle the territoriality of copyright protection[58] but the discriminatory geo-blocking practices applied by copyright owners or digital service providers. The obligation stipulated by Art. 3 (1) of the Portability Regulation that enables a subscriber who is temporarily present in a Member State to access and use the online content service makes the contract law in EU Member States "cross-border and consumer friendly".[59] Portability as a limit on the contractual freedom of copyright holders might be seen as a more efficient way to fulfil consumer expectations, since even under the regime of EU unitary copyright, digital content may still be distributed on a territorial basis.[60] It is for this reason that digital content providers may grant licence for a part of the territory and use the consumer's IP address as an identifier to control for the territorial scope of the licence. Although it has been indicated by some authors that geo-blocking

55 Hoffmann, J (2016), p. 145, 149 ff.; Mazotti, G (2016), p. 367,368; Engles, S; Nordemann, J B (2018), p. 180 ff.

56 Arnerstål, S (2015), p. 752; Synodinou, T E (2020), EU Internet Law: Regulation and Enforcement, p. 38.

57 Judgment of the Court (Grand Chamber) of 4 October 2011 Football Association Premier League Ltd and Others v QC Leisure and Others (C-403/08) and Karen Murphy v Media Protection Services Ltd (C-429/08).

58 As has been described above, copyrighted works such as musical works, software and e-books have been distributed on an EU-wide basis and the end user licence agreements granted to consumers the right to use the copyrighted content in all EU Member States even though 28 different copyright regulations still existed.

59 SWD (2015) 274 final/2, p. 18.

60 Digital content provider activities would probably be analysed also from EU competition law perspectives. Mazzoti points out the competition law issues when focusing on the CJEU in the Premiere League case. In this regard he remarks that restrictions to competition in the field of providing services might be justified by objective criteria. Therefore the creation of barriers to cross-border accessibility of services can be justified for example by supporting cultural creations targeted at national audiences [Mazotti, G (2016), p. 373]. Even though the EU competition law applies different criteria for assessing service provider activities than the consumer law does, the author of this paper is of the opinion that both fields of EU law converge in the regulation of portability issues. If the EU Commission declares that geo-blocking activities are unfair, that they conflict with consumer expectations and that they create serious obstacles to creating a Digital Single Market (Recital 4 Portability Regulation; SWD (2015) 270 final, p. 3), then the limitations on the licencing policy might be set by the competition law as well. For example, the Commission Regulation (EU) No 316/2014 of 21 March 2014 on the application of Article 101(3) of the Treaty on the Functioning of the European Union to categories of technology transfer agreements sets limits on the licencing policy of the owners of essential patents, while they are forced to apply the FRAND licences (fair, reasonable and non-discriminatory) on a non-exclusive basis. The main rationale of the Portability Regulation is the same, since it imposes limits on the licencing policy of copyright owners and the providers of digital content.

practices reflect the territorial character of copyright protection,[61] when we consider consumer protection and the related contractual issues, they seem to be caused more by the licencing policy of the digital content providers than they are by the traditional principles of copyright.

Portability as a Subcategory of Conformity with the Contract

The central role of European consumer law is to function as corrective justice[62] and to protect the weaker party.[63] Contractual dealings between consumers and suppliers must respect the legitimate interests of both parties and must reflect a fair balance between their legitimate interests. When assessing the fairness of consumer transactions, it is important to compare them with the principle of "reasonable expectation". If a product or service does not meet the reasonable expectations of the consumer, such as the availability of a product in the required time and place, then the contract can no longer be assumed to reflect the consumer's free will to commit to the transaction.[64] In the event that a consumer cannot utilize a product in a way that corresponds to his or her reasonable expectations, we can find grounds under which the consumer can contest the conformity with the contract.[65]

There are two basic approaches to defining the concept of conformity: a subjective approach based on contractual agreements and an objective approach based on legally established conformity criteria.[66] A third possibility would be a mixed approach which uses both criteria as applied, for example, in the Consumer Sales and Guarantees Directive, as well as in the Contracts for the Sale Directive.[67] Art. 7 of the Digital Content Directive gives priority to the subjective approach but it also introduces the objective criteria in Art. 8.

As a general rule, the criteria used to assess conformity are the contractual stipulations which are "clearly and comprehensively" contained in the contract [Art. 12 (4) and (5) Digital Content Directive], or the conditions which are deemed to represent an integral part of the contract, such as pre-contractual information [Art. 7 (b) Digital Content Directive].

In the absence of explicit contractual provisions, or if the clauses are ambiguous Art. 8 (1) of the Digital Content Directive stipulates that the digital content or digital service shall be fit "for the purposes for which digital content or digital services of

61 Hoffmann, J (2016), p. 151.
62 Micklitz, H W (1999), p. 167 ff.
63 Cherednychenko, O (2007).
64 Helberger, N, Hugenholtz, P B (2007), p. 1082.
65 Helberger, N et al. (2013), p. 45.
66 Staudenmayer, D (2016), p. 2722; Spindler, G (2016), Verträge über digitale Inhalte, p. 152.
67 COM (2015) 634 final, p. 12; SWD (2015) 274 final/2, p. 46.

the same type would normally be used, taking into account, where applicable, any existing Union and national law, technical standards or, in the absence of such technical standards, applicable sector-specific industry codes of conduct". The objective test of conformity with the contract is then linked to other criteria such as "technical standards" or "applicable sector-specific industry codes of conduct" [Art. 8 (1) (a) Digital Content Directive].

Although the Digital Content Directive may be criticized for its lack of such norms and codes[68] or for its emphasis on a supplier's ability to craft overly comprehensive contractual provisions to exclude the application of the objective test, in terms of portability requirements the Directive seems to be satisfactory. We may consider the Portability Regulation as a sui generis form of such regulatory treatment.

In practice we can identify three main conformity problems: (1) accessibility, functionality and compatibility issues, (2) insufficient quality, and (3) deficiencies, errors or other safety and security issues.[69] These challenges can be caused by matters such as lack of connectivity, the application of DRM mechanisms which create obstacles for the transfer of digital content from one device to another, incompatibility of formats and standards,[70] or even the abuse of the copyright protection when prohibiting the consumer from making private copies of lawfully acquired software or film.[71]

Portability[72] matters are primarily concerned with "accessibility requirements" [Art. 8 (1) (b) of the Digital Content Directive]. Geo-blocking practices are usually connected to the use of an Internet Protocol address to identify a consumer's location. When this happens, the consumer is hindered from accessing digital content/service or is re-routed to a local website with different products or pricing.[73] Although such practices could be in conformity with the licence conditions of the major digital content providers, they generate frustration for a great deal of consumers[74] who cannot use their subscription services or the content they have previously purchased in other countries.

From the perspective of accessibility, both the Portability Regulation and Digital Content Directive aim at facilitating access to digital content and they seem to be complementary. Although the Digital Content Directive does not explicitly mention the cross-border portability of digital content, it is obvious that the reasonable expectations of consumers on the accessibility of digital content in other EU Member states are supported by the Portability Regulation and the Digital Content Directive as well.

---

68 Spindler, G (2016), Verträge über digitale Inhalte, p. 153; Mak, C (2016), p. 16; Beale, H (2016), Scope of application and general approach of the new rules for contracts in the digital environment, p. 21. Art. 8 (1) was strongly influenced by Art. IV. A. – 2:302 DCFR and Articles 99 and 100 CESL.

69 Loos, M B M et al. (2011), p. 108.

70 Ibid, p. 109-113.

71 Helberger, N, Hugenholtz, P B (2007), p. 1093, 1095. Similarly see Oprysk, L, Sein, K (2020), p. 601 ff.

72 "'Portable' means a feature of an online content service whereby subscribers can effectively access and use the online content service in their Member State of residence without being limited to a specific location" [Art. 2 (6) Portability Regulation].

73 Hoffmann, J (2016), p. 145.

74 SWD (2015) 270 final, p. 16.

For these reasons, a consumer's inability to access the digital content which was provided in their home Member State while he or she is temporarily located in another Member State is to be considered a breach of "conformity with the contract" according to the objective criteria test regulated by Art. 8 (1) of the Digital of the Content Directive.

We may conclude that the Portability Regulation should be considered as a special piece of legislation in terms of Art. 3 (7) of the Digital Content Directive. Thus, it only regulates specific issues related to the accessibility of digital content, however, areas such as burden of proof, consumer claims, rights of third parties, and remedy for the failure to supply are covered by the Digital Content Directive. Respectively, these consumer law issues will be regulated by provisions which will be adopted after the implementation of the directive into the national legal orders of the EU Member States.

In the following part of this paper we will focus on selected details of this special kind of non-conformity with the contracts. We will analyse whether the unenforceability provision adopted by the Portability Regulation is consistent with traditional terms which are used by legislators in the EU Member States for to express the invalidity of contracts. Next we will concentrate on the hierarchy of remedies which the consumer may pursue if the performance is not in conformity with the contract. Finally, we will make a few remarks on the quality requirements of digital content provided by a service provider in a Member State that a consumer visits temporarily.

Specific Issues Related to the Breach of Cross-Border Portability

When analysing specific relations between the Portability Regulation and the Digital Content Directive, we should first consider the differences in the terminology and the scope of both legislative acts. While the Digital Content Directive uses the terms "consumer"[75] and "trader",[76] the Portability Regulation deals with the consumer as a "subscriber"[77] and it indirectly defines the "provider of the online content service"[78] as the person providing audio-visual media services or other online

75 "'Consumer' means any natural person who, in relation to contracts covered by this Directive, is acting for purposes which are outside that person's trade, business, craft, or profession" [Art. 2 (6) Digital Content Directive].

76 "'Trader' means any natural or legal person, irrespective of whether privately or publicly owned, that is acting, including through any other person acting in that natural or legal person's name or on that person's behalf, for purposes relating to that person's trade, business, craft, or profession, in relation to contracts covered by this Directive" [Art. 2 (5) Digital Content Directive].

77 "'Subscriber' means any consumer who, on the basis of a contract for the provision of an online content service with a provider whether against payment of money or without such payment, is entitled to access and use such service in the Member State of residence" [Art. 2 (1) Portability Regulation].

78 "'Online content service' means a service as defined in Articles 56 and 57 TFEU that a provider lawfully provides to subscribers in their Member State of residence on agreed terms and online, which is portable and which is: (i) an audiovisual media service as defined in point (a) of Article 1

services with protected subject matter, such as copyrighted works or broadcasting. The material and personal scope of the Digital Content Directive is broader because it also relates to the supply of offline digital assets such as the distribution of CDs or DVDs. The Portability Regulation is applicable only to online content services [Art. 1 (1) Portability Regulation].

Unlike the Digital Content Directive, the Portability Regulation concerns also those instances where digital content is provided for free and the provider requests personal data from the consumer only for the purposes of processing "for the purpose of supplying the digital content or digital service in accordance with this Directive or for allowing the trader to comply with legal requirements to which the trader is subject" [Art. 3 (1) Digital Content Directive].

Another difference between the legislative acts can be found in the presence of the cross-border element. While the Portability Regulation is applicable only in situations when the consumer uses the digital content in another Member State [Art. 2 (4), Art. 3 (1) Portability Regulation], the Digital Content Directive regulates both the cross-border and the domestic relations which exist between the supplier of the digital content and the consumer.[79]

Further on in this paper we will explore situations in which digital content is provided (i) online, (ii) in exchange for money and (iii) in a Member State of the EU which is different from the state of the consumer's permanent residence. In these instances, both legislative acts would be applicable.[80]

Portability and Unenforceability

As has been explained above, both pieces of EU legislation overlap on the issue of accessibility to digital content or services. The Digital Content Directive subsumes accessibility under conformity with the contract [Art. 8 (1) (b) Digital Content Directive] and the Portability Regulation uses accessibility to define portability [Art.

of Directive 2010/13/EU, or (ii) a service the main feature of which is the provision of access to, and the use of, works, other protected subject matter or transmissions of broadcasting organisations, whether in a linear or an on-demand manner" [Art. 2 (5) Portability Regulation].

79 COM (2015) 634 final, p. 10.

80 According to Art. 4 (3) TEU, and Art. 288 (3) TFEU, as well as the settled case-law of the CJEU, the courts of the Member States, are required to interpret national provisions in such a way as to achieve the objectives set by directives [so-called indirect effect of directives; see judgments of the CJEU in Von Colson and Kamann v Land Nordrhein-Westfalen (C-14/83), Marleasing v. Comercial Internacional de Alimentación (C-106/89), Kolpinghuis Nijmegen (C-80/86)]. The national courts are, in principle, required to adopt such an interpretation in cases falling within the period after the transposition period of the directive has expired. However, such an interpretation is possible also before the expiry of the transposition period, but it is not the public authority's responsibility, and its admissibility depends on national law. Before the expiry of the transposition period the Member States courts are only required to refrain as far as possible from interpreting national law, which could seriously endanger the achievement of the objective pursued by the directive [CJEU in Konstantinos Adeneler and Others v Ellinikos Organismos Galaktos (ELOG), C-212/04, para. 123].

2 (6) Portability Regulation]. We have also come to the conclusion that if an online content service, which is normally available to a subscriber in the Member State of his or her permanent residence, but can not be accessed in other EU Member States, it not only contravenes with Art. 3 (1) of the Portability Regulation, which entitles the consumer to have online access to digital content in other Member States, but also breaches the conformity with the contract.

Since the Portability Regulation requires providers to enable the cross-border portability of online content services [Art. 3 (1) Portability Regulation] and any contractual provision which does not comply with this requirement is unenforceable [Art. 7 (1) Portability Regulation], such legislative construction strongly affects the contractual law of EU Member States and brings new problems related to the fact that the EU Regulation declares certain categories of contractual provisions unenforceable.

If we examine other EU regulations we can see that the European legislator usually uses the term "null and void"[81] contract. This is based on the fact that almost all legal systems subsume provisions which breach mandatory legal rules under traditional categories of nullity (invalidity).[82] Such provisions are automatically deemed invalid, as if they never existed. If material loss or immaterial damage arises in relation to the invalidity of a contract, the entitled person may claim damages for loss[83] or request the return of the performance supplied under the contract.[84]

On the other hand, the term unenforceability has a different meaning in the majority of EU legal systems. Such unenforceable contractual provisions are not automatically invalid from the beginning, but they may not be enforced if the impaired party raises an objection of avoidance or relative nullity.[85] Only if such notice is addressed to the other contractual party, then the agreement is null from the beginning.

"Unenforceability" also refers to situations in which the contractual provision itself is valid, but it cannot be enforced.[86] Provisions which are valid but may not be

81 See for example Art. 7 (4) Regulation (EU) No. 492/2011 of the European Parliament and of the Council of 5 April 2011 on freedom of movement for workers within the Union; Art. 18 Regulation (EC) No. 392/2009 of the European Parliament and of the Council of 23 April 2009 on the liability of carriers of passengers by sea in the event of accidents. Similarly, Art. 101 (1) TFEU prohibits agreements between undertakings which have as their object or effect the prevention, restriction or distortion of competition within the common market and declares such prohibited agreements to be "automatically void" [Art. 101 (2) TFEU].

82 DCFR II.-7:302; Bar, von Ch, Clive, E, Schulte-Nölke, H (2009), p. 544 ff.

83 DCFR II.-7:304.

84 DCFR II.-7:303.

85 DCFR II. – 7:209; DCFR II. – 7:212. Most European legal systems stipulate that contracts violating mandatory legal rules are void. On the other hand, legal orders differ in the kinds of nullity and its effect. Belgian, Slovenian, Austrian, Czech and Slovak law distinguish between "absolute" and "relative nullity". Absolutely null and void contracts violate mandatory rules that aim at the protection of public interests. The nullity exists ipso jure which means that it is not necessary to invoke the invalidity before the court and the court should declare the voidance of the contract ex officio. In other EU Member States the situation is similar. Thus for example in France even "absolute nullity" must be claimed before the court and the judge may choose to raise the nullity. Bar, von Ch, Clive, E, Schulte-Nölke, H (2009), p. 570.

86 Bar, von Ch, Clive, E, Schulte-Nölke, H (2009), p. 3699. Similarly Engles, S; Nordemann, J B (2018), p. 195.

enforced by the creditor are called "natural obligations"[87] in civil law jurisdictions. In fact, they represent merely a moral claim.[88]

The term unenforceability contained in Art. 7 (1) of the Portability Regulation, even though it presumably means an absolute nullity of respective contractual provisions,[89] would probably cause problems of interpretation by national courts either due to the inconsistency with traditional concepts of invalidity known in the majority of the civil law jurisdictions, or due to inconsistency with the legal terms used in primary and secondary EU legislation for defining effects resulting from the breach of mandatory legal provisions.

It would be more consistent[90] with the traditional concept of voidance and also with the terminology used in other EU regulations if Art. 7 (1) of the Portability Regulation contained the term "void" or "null and void". Such a solution would be more explicit and presumably lead to a more consistent application of the Portability Regulation by the courts in the EU Member States.

Portability as a Serious Breach of the Contract

If we address portability from the perspective of conformity with the contract, we see that the primary function here consists not in the nullity or the unenforceability of the contractual provision, but in the remedies (Art. 13 and 14 Digital Content Directive) that a consumer may request if the performance does not comply with the subjective or objective standards laid down by Art. 7 and 8 of the Digital Content Directive. The Digital Content Directive explicitly stipulates that the supplier shall be liable to the consumer for lack of conformity [Art. 14 Digital Content Directive].

---

87 Bar, von Ch, Clive, E, Schulte-Nölke, H (2009), p. 3990-3994; Snyder, D V (1996), p. 424 ff.

88 Bar, von Ch, Clive, E, Schulte-Nölke, H (2009), p. 3699.

89 This may be deduced from the rationale of Recital 25 and Art. 7 (1) of the Portability Regulation. In the impact assessment [SWD (2015) 270 final, p. 45] it is declared that the restriction of the freedom to conduct a business (Art. 16 and 17 European Charter of Fundamental Rights) would be justified in light of the cross-border portability of online content services for European consumers. From this perspective, we can assume the obligation to enable cross-border portability [Art. 3 (1) Portability Regulation] and the parallel declaration that any contractual provisions which breach this obligation is unenforceable [Art. 7 (1) Portability Regulation], represent a breach of the mandatory legal rules. For this reason the violation of Art. 3 (1) of the Portability Regulation would constitute the absolute nullity (voidance) of any contractual provision which would not comply with these legal requirements. However, *Engles* and *Nordemann* conclude that the term unenforceability does not affect the validity of the provisions which contravene with Art. 3 (1) Portability Regulation and only makes them legally unenforceable. Engles, S; Nordemann, J B (2018), p. 195.

90 Inconsistency with the standard contract law terminology could have been precluded if the European Commission had used theoretical contributions which were formulated by European private-law projects. The differences between different concepts of nullity and unenforceability are clearly explained by the Draft Common Frame of Reference formulated by the Study Group on a European Civil Code and Acquis Group.

The remedies referred to in Art. 14 of the Digital Content Directive correspond to the content and structure of consumer claims with rights conferred by Art. 3 (2) of the Consumer Sales and Guarantees Directive, but they are specially modified to the digital content. Thus, a hierarchy of remedies[91] is guaranteed at two levels. The basic remedy is that the consumer is entitled to have the digital content brought into conformity with the contract free of charge [Art. 12 (1) (3) Digital Content Directive]. At the second level, the consumer is entitled to terminate the contract, request a price reduction,[92] or claim damages.

Criticisms of the hierarchy of remedies emerge when we compare the Digital Content Directive with the Consumer Sales and Guarantees Directive; it becomes evident that terminating a contract for the supply of digital content is effectively less harmful than terminating a contract for physical goods.[93] In this respect it is argued that a consumer's option to immediately terminate a contract upon the breach of the conformity would enhance his or her negotiating position.[94]

Such criticism makes sense especially when we pay attention to portability issues. On the one hand, we can argue that if a supplier uses geo-blocking practices and the digital content is not available in another EU Member State, it is logical to remedy the situation by ensuring cross-border portability, since Art. 3 (1) of the Portability Regulation requires that the provider of an online content service will enable a consumer to access the online content service. On the other hand, we may ask why the consumer should be required to notify the provider in order to restore their access. However, it is possible that a provider might not be able to remove the geo-blocking mechanisms within a reasonable time frame [Art. 14 (3) Digital Content Directive]. Moreover, the supplier of the digital content might not be willing to bring the digital content into conformity with the contract because it is clear from the circumstances [Art. 12 (3) (e) Digital Content Directive] that geo-blocking is a commonly used practice.

We believe that in the sphere of the portability of the digital content a consumer should not first be forced to request that the provider enable cross-border portability, and only as a secondary claim be entitled to choose between terminating the contract and reducing the price. The Digital Content Directive contains a rule that in specific cases in which non-conformity with the contract is of a serious nature [Art. 14 (4) (d) Digital Content Directive] the consumer should be entitled to pursue a price reduction or termination of the contract as a first course remedy.

A similar remedy was anticipated by the CESL when Art. 87 CESL regulated that the non-performance of an obligation by one party is fundamental if "(a) it substantially deprives the other party of what that party was entitled to expect under the

[91] Zoll, F (2016), p. 253.

[92] The Digital Content Directive refers only to the reduction of a monetary price since the reduction of personal data would hardly be possible [Art. 14 (4) Digital Content Directive]. Spindler, G (2016). Verträge über digitale Inhalte – Haftung, Gewährleistung und Portabilität Vorschlag der EU-Kommission zu einer Richtlinie über Verträge zur Bereitstellung digitaler Inhalte, p. 221.

[93] Zoll, F (2016), p. 253.

[94] Mak, C (2016), p. 24.

contract, unless at the time of conclusion of the contract the nonperforming party did not foresee and could not be expected to have foreseen that result; or (b) it is of such a nature as to make it clear that the non-performing party's future performance cannot be relied on". In such a case, Art. 114 (1) of the CESL enabled the buyer to terminate the contract if the seller's non-performance under the contract was fundamental under the terms of Article 87 of the CESL. Furthermore, Art. 114 (2) of the CESL provided that in a "contract for the supply of digital content between a trader and a consumer, where there is a non-performance because the goods do not conform to the contract, the consumer may terminate the contract unless the lack of conformity is insignificant".

We can conclude that the portability requirements represent an important legal duty imposed on the provider of the digital content and the consumer should be automatically entitled to terminate the contract if the provider does not allow him or her access to digital content in the country of his or her temporary residence.

Portability and Quality

Although the Portability Regulation allows a consumer access to online content services in a Member State of his temporarily presence [Art. 3 (1)], which should lead to the restoration of cross-border accessibility of digital content, the Portability Regulation reduces the quality requirements applied to such services available abroad [Recital 22, Art. 3 (3) Portability Regulation]. Although the provider is required to inform the consumer of the quality of the services accessible in other Member States [Art. 3 (4) Portability Regulation], the EU has chosen not to set legal requirements with regard to the quality of the service delivered in the other EU Member States [Art. 3 (3) Portability Regulation]. Thus, service providers would not be obliged to adapt the technical infrastructure necessary to ensure the same quality of their online services available in foreign countries.[95] The Portability Regulation Impact Assessment explains that "if service providers see a need to adapt the technical infrastructure, it might lead to more substantial costs, e.g. the cost of upgrading the Internet connection of the origin server [...] Such costs would be substantial if providers of AV content services decide to invest in CDN in order to ensure quality of their service also when accessed in other MS".[96]

From a consumer law perspective, such an approach is very surprising since the Digital Content Directive, when defining the objective requirements of conformity with the contract, relies on the "standards, open technical specifications, good practices and codes of conduct" [Recital 50; Art. 8 (1) (a) Digital Content Directive].

If the quality of cross-border online content services is not covered by the Portability Regulation and especially if such quality is reflected only if the provider expressly acknowledges[97] in the licence or service contract that he or she will enable the

95 SWD (2015) 270 final, p. 32, 59; Engles, S; Nordemann, J B (2018), p. 187.

96 SWD (2015) 270 final, p. 42.

97 COM (2015) 627 final, p. 8.

same quality of accessibility of the digital content in another Member State [Art. 3 (3) Portability Regulation], then the contractual position of the consumer is obviously very weak. Actually such a permissible reduction of quality may lead to circumventing the prohibition of geo-blocking practices. From the perspective of conformity with the contract, we see that even though there might be existing "technical standards" which are applied internationally (or in certain fields of online content services),[98] it would not be possible to apply them since the Portability Regulation, as a particular piece of EU legislation [Recital 36; Art. 3 (7) Digital Content Directive], excludes provider liability for the quality of the online content services in cross-border situations.

These risks have probably been precluded by Art. 3 (1) Portability Regulation which aimed to enhance the quality of online services provided abroad. The provider of an online content service provided against payment of money shall enable the accessibility to digital content in the same manner as in the Member State of residence "including by providing access to the same content, on the same range and number of devices, for the same number of users and with the same range of functionalities". Furthermore, the provider shall neither "take any action to reduce the quality of delivery of the online content service" [Art. 3 (3) Portability Regulation] nor "impose any additional charges on the subscriber for the access to and the use of the online content service" [Art. 3 (2) Portability Regulation].

Conclusions

When we analyse the relation between the Digital Content Directive and the Portability Regulation we see that both legislative acts address the issue of access to digital content from different perspectives. The Portability Regulation focuses on the cross-border portability of digital content in other EU Member States [Art. 3 (1) Portability Regulation), while the Digital Content Directive specifies the consumer rights related to the distribution of digital content and subsumes the accessibility of the digital content under the notion of the "conformity of the digital content with the contract" [Art. 8 (1) Digital Content Directive).

We have argued that even though both pieces of EU legislation use different legal terminology and in some aspects have different scopes of application, they can be complementary in the question of cross-border portability of digital content provided to consumers for monetary counter performance. This means that the Portability Regulation will be applied in respect to the cross-border accessibility of digital content, but other issues, such as remedies concerned with the non-availability of the digital content, will fall under the scope of the Digital Content Directive, respectively under national regulations, which will be issued to transpose the directive into national law.

[98] Loos, M B M et al. (2011), p. 47, 48.

Furthermore, we have deduced that the Portability Regulation contains the mandatory legal provisions which limit the contractual freedom of the copyright holders and service providers. The dissemination model of digital assets must respect the basic principles of the EU single market such as free movement of goods and services [Art. 26 (2), Art. 56 TFEU] and the protection of the consumer [Art. 12, Art. 114 (3), Art. 169 TFEU]. Such legal requirements could not be solved by the adoption of the EU Copyright Regulation (adopted under Art. 118 TFEU, which would create a unitary EU copyright protection). Therefore, the EU legislator have correctly focused on removing territorial barriers in the sphere of contract law. Under the regime of unitary rights, we may still find examples in which licences are granted not for the entire territorial scope of protection, but for several states only. The cross-border accessibility of digital content is thus not primarily a question of the territoriality of the copyright but a question of copyright holders' and service providers' licencing policies.[99]

---

[99] References:

An Optional Common European Sales Law: Advantages and Problems Advice to the UK Government, The Law Commission and The Scottish Law Commission. at: <http://www.lawcom.gov.uk/app/uploads/2015/03/Common_European_Sales_Law_Summary.pdf>

Arnerstål, S (2015). Licensing digital content in a sale of goods context. GRUR Int., Volume 64, Issue 9

Bach, I (2019) Neue Richtlinien zum Verbrauchsgüterkauf und zu Verbraucherverträgen über digitale Inhalte. Neue Juristische Wochenschrift. Volume 72, Issue 24.

Bar, von Ch, Clive, E, Schulte-Nölke, H (2009) Principles, Definitions and Model Rules of European Private Law Draft Common Frame of Reference (DCFR). at: <https://www.ccbe.eu/fileadmin/speciality_distribution/public/documents/EUROPEAN_PRIVATE_LAW/EN_EPL_20100107_Principles__definitions_and_model_rules_of_European_private_law_-_Draft_Common_Frame_of_Reference__DCFR_.pdf>

Bar, von Ch, Swann, S (2010) Principles of European Law. Study Group on a European Civil Code. Unjustified Enrichment. Munich: Sellier.

Beale, H (2013) The CESL Proposal: An Overview. Juridica International. Volume 20, Issue 1.

Beale, H (2016) Scope of application and general approach of the new rules for contracts in the digital environment. Workshop of JURI-Committee of the European Parliament. at: <http://www.epgencms.europarl.europa.eu/cmsdata/upload/4a1651c4-0db0-4142-9580-89b47010ae9f/pe_536.493_print.pdf>

Beale, H (2016) The future of European contract law in the light of the European Commission's proposals for Directives on digital content and online sales. DP. Revista de Internet, Derecho y Política. Issue 23.

Craig, P, de Burca G. (eds.) (1999). The Evolution of EU Law, Oxford: Oxford University Press.

Carvalho, J M (2019) Sale of Goods and Supply of Digital Content and Digital Services – Overview of Directives 2019/770 and 2019/771, Journal of European Consumer and Market Law, Volume 8, Issue 5.

Clive, E (2015). Proposal for a Common European Sales Law withdrawn. at: <https://www.unisob.na.it/universita/facolta/giurisprudenza/age/proposal_cesl_withdrawn.pdf>

Communication from the Commission to the European Parliament, the Council, the European Economic and Social Committee and the Committee of the Regions. A Digital Single Market Strategy for Europe from 6.5.2016, COM (2015) 192 final. at: <https://eur-lex.europa.eu/legal-content/EN/TXT/?uri=CELEX%3A52015DC0192>

Communication from the Commission to the European Parliament, the Council, the European Economic and Social Committee and the Committee of the Regions Towards a modern, more European copyright framework from 9.12.2015, COM (2015) 626 final. at: <https://ec.europa.eu/transparency/regdoc/rep/1/2015/EN/1-2015-626-EN-F1-1.PDF>

Communication from the Commission to the European Parliament, the Council, the European Economic and Social Committee and the Committee of the Regions. Commission Work Programme 2015. A New Start, from 16. 12. 2014, COM (2014) 910 final. at: <https://eur-lex.europa.eu/legal-content/EN/ALL/?uri=COM:2014:910:FIN>

Communication from the Commission to the European Parliament, the Council, the European Economic and Social Committee. Digital contracts for Europe – Unleashing the potential of e-commerce from 9.12.2015, COM/2015/0633 final. at: <https://eur-lex.europa.eu/legal-content/en/TXT/?uri=CELEX%3A52015DC0633>

De Franceschi, A (2016) European Contract Law and the Digital Single Market: The Implications of Digital Revolution. Mortsel: Intersentia.

Engles, S; Nordemann, J B (2018) The Portability Regulation (Regulation (EU) 2017/1128): A Commentary on the Scope and Application. Journal of Intellectual Property, Information Technology and Electronic Commerce, Volume 9, Issue 2.

Helberger, N et al. (2013) Digital Content Contracts for Consumers. Journal of Consumer Policy. Volume 36, Issue 1.

Helberger, N, Hugenholtz, P B (2007), No place like home for making a copy: private copying in European copyright law and consumer law, Berkeley Technology Law Journal, Volume 22, Issue 3

Hoffman, J (2016) Crossing Borders in the Digital Market: A Proposal to End Copyright Territoriality and Geo-Blocking in the European Union. George Washington International Law Review, Volume 49, Issue 3.

Impact Assessment: Proposal for a Regulation of the European Parliament and of the Council to ensure the cross-border portability of online content services in the internal market from 9.12.2015. SWD (2015) 270 final. at: <https://ec.europa.eu/transparency/regdoc/rep/1/2015/EN/1-2015-627-EN-F1-1.PDF>

Impact Assessment: Proposals for Directives of the European Parliament and of the Council (1) on certain aspects concerning contracts for the supply of digital content and (2) on certain aspects concerning contracts for the online and other distance sales of goods from 17.12.2015. SWD(2015) 274 final/2. at: <https://eur-lex.europa.eu/LexUriServ/LexUriServ.do?uri=SWD:2015:0274:FIN:EN:PDF>

Koukal, P (2018) Consumer Protection and the Portability Regulation. In Staníčková, M (eds.) Proceedings of the 4th International Conference on European Integration. Ostrava: VŠB – Technical University of Ostrava.

Koukal, P (2021) Digital Content Portability and Its Relation to Conformity with the Contract. Masaryk UJL & Tech. Volume 15, Issue 1.

Licences for Europe – Structured Stakeholder Dialogue 2013, WG 1 Audio-visual Subgroup, Joint Statement on Cross-border Portability of lawfully-acquired Audio-visual Content. at <https://ec.europa.eu/licences-for-europe-dialogue/sites/licences-for-europe-dialogue/files/1-AV-portability.pdf>

Loewenheim, U (2010) Handbuch des Urheberrechts. 2nd ed. Verlag C.H.Beck, München

Loos, M B M et al. (2011). Analysis of the applicable legal frameworks and suggestions for the contours of a model system of consumer protection in relation to digital content contracts. at: <https://op.europa.eu/en/publication-detail/-/publication/4fee0cc7-5f4d-46c5-897b-48844f07f027>

Mak, C (2016) The new proposal for harmonised rules on certain aspects concerning contracts for the supply of digital. <http://www.europarl.europa.eu/supporting-analyses>

Mazziotti, G (2016) Is Geo-blocking a Real Cause for Concern in Europe?'(2016). EIPR. Volume 38, Issue 6.

Micklitz, H W (1999) Principles of Social Justice in European Private Law. Yearbook of European Law. Volume 19, Issue 1.

Cherednychenko, O (2007) Fundamental Rights, Contract Law and the Protection of the Weaker Party: A Comparative Analysis of the Constitutionalisation of Contract Law. Sellier, München.

Oprysk, L, Sein, K (2020) Limitations in End-User Licensing Agreements: Is There a Lack of Conformity Under the New Digital Content Directive? IIC – International Review of Intellectual Property and Competition Law, Volume 51, Issue 5.

Pongelli, G (2013) The Proposal for a Regulation on a Common European Sales Law (CESL) and its Gradual Evolution. Comparative Law Review. Volume 4, Issue 1.

Proposal for a Directive of the European Parliament and of the Council on certain aspects concerning contracts for the online and other distance sales of goods from 9.12.2015, COM(2015) 635 final. at: <https://ec.europa.eu/transparency/regdoc/rep/1/2015/EN/1-2015-635-EN-F1-1.PDF>

Proposal for a Regulation of the European Parliament and of the Council on addressing geo-blocking and other forms of discrimination based on customers' nationality, place of residence or place of establishment within the internal market and amending Regulation (EC) No 2006/2004 and Directive 2009/22/EC from 25.5.2016, COM (2016) 289. at: <https://ec.europa.eu/transparency/regdoc/rep/1/2016/EN/1-2016-289-EN-F1-1.PDF>

Proposal for a Regulation of the European Parliament and of the Council on ensuring the cross-border portability of online content services in the internal market from 9.12.2015, COM (2015) 627 final. at: <https://ec.europa.eu/transparency/regdoc/rep/1/2015/EN/1-2015-627-EN-F1-1.PDF>

Proposal for a Regulation of the European Parliament and of the Council on a Common European Sales Law, COM (2011) 635 final. at: <https://eur-lex.europa.eu/legal-content/EN/ALL/?uri=CELEX:52011PC0635>

Rafel, R M (2016) The Directive Proposals on Online Sales and Supply of Digital Content (Part I): will the new rules attain their objective of reducing legal complexity. IDP: Revista de Internet, Derecho y Politica. Issue 23.

Ramalho, A (2014) Conceptualising the European Union's Competence in Copyright – What Can the EU Do? International Review of Intellectual Property and Competition Law. Volume 45, Issue 2.

Schulze, R, Schulte-Nölke H (eds.) (2011) European Private Law – Current Status and Perspectives. München: Sellier.

Schulze, R (2012) Common European Sales Law (CESL) – Commentary. Baden-Baden, München, Oxford: C.H. Beck, Hart, Nomos.

Snyder, D V (1996) The Case of Natural Obligations. Lousiana Law Review. Volume 56, Issue 2.

Spindler, G (2016). Die Modernisierung des europäischen Urheberrechts Der Vorschlag zur Portabilitäts-VO und die Planungen der EU-Kommission. Computer und Recht, Volume 32, Issue 2.

Spindler, G (2016) Digitale Wirtschaft – analoges Recht: Braucht das BGB ein Update? Juristenzeitung. Volume 71, Issue 17

Spindler, G (2016) Verträge über digitale Inhalte – Anwendungsbereich und Ansätze Vorschlag der EU-Kommission zu einer Richtlinie über Verträge zur Bereitstellung digitaler Inhalte. Multimedia und Recht, Volume 19, Issues 3,4.

Spindler, G (2016) Verträge über digitale Inhalte – Haftung, Gewährleistung und Portabilität Vorschlag der EU-Kommission zu einer Richtlinie über Verträge zur Bereitstellung digitaler Inhalte, Multimedia und Recht, Volume 20, Issue 4.

Spindler, G, Sein, K (2019) Die endgültige Richtlinie über Verträge über digitale Inhalte und Dienstleistungen. MMR – Zeitschrift für IT-Recht und Recht der Digitalisierung. Volume 22, Issue 7.

Staudenmayer, D (2016) Verträge über digitalen Inhalt Der Richtlinienvorschlag der Europäischen Kommission. Neue Juristische Wochenschrift. Volume 69, Issue 37.

Synodinou, T E (2020) Geoblocking in EU Copyright Law: Challenges and Perspectives. GRUR International. Volume 69, Issue 2.

Synodinou, T E (2020). EU Internet Law: Regulation and Enforcement. Cham: Springer Nature Switzerland AG.

Thomas, J. et al. Statement of the European Law Institute On the European Commission's proposed Directive on the Supply of Digital Content to Consumers COM (2015) 634 final. at: <http://www.europeanlawinstitute.eu/home/news-contd/article/the-eli-publishes-its-statement-on-the-european-commissions-proposed-directive-on-the-supply-of-dig/?tx_ttnews%5BbackPid%5D=180991&cHash=c0009025cff265addbd4819c8110e410 >

Trimble M (2012) The Future of Cybertravel: Legal Implications of the Evasion of Geolocation. Fordham Intellectual Property Media & Entertainment Law Journal. Volume 22, Issue 3.

Trimble, M (2016) The role of geoblocking in the Internet legal landscape. IDP: Revista de Internet, Derecho y Politica. Issue 23.

Twigg-Flesner, Ch (2013) The Europeanisation of Contract Law. Current controversies in law. 2nd ed. London (UK), New York (USA): Routledge.

VOLUNTARY, MANDATORY AND EXTENDED COLLECTIVE MANAGEMENT IN THE LIGHT OF INTERNATIONAL AND EU NORMS

Mihály Ficsor*

Introductory Remarks

In this paper, certain basic structural aspects of collective management are reviewed. The main focus is the discussion of the mandatory and extended collective management systems (in connection with the latter, also the presumption-based systems). Nevertheless, before this, it seems justified to also refer briefly to voluntary collective management. It is discussed in which cases and under what conditions these various management forms may be applied.

Voluntary Collective Management

In the triangle of voluntary, mandatory and extended (as well as presumption-based) collective management, the discussion present voluntary collective management seems to be the easiest. It follows from the freedom of association that rightholders may establish a society or other organization in order to join their forces to exercise their rights efficiently. This basic principle is duly expressed in Article 5 the EU Directive on collective management (Directive 2014/26/EU; hereinafter: the CM Directive); in particular in these provisions:

"2. Rightholders shall have the right to authorise a collective management organisation of their choice to manage the rights, categories of rights or types of works and other subject-matter of their choice, for the territories of their choice, irrespective of the Member State of nationality, residence or establishment of either the collective management organisation or the rightholder. Unless the collective management organisation has objectively justified reasons to refuse management, it shall be obliged to manage such rights, categories of rights or types of works and other subject-matter, provided that their management falls within the scope of its activity [...].

* Member of the Hungarian Copyright Council, former Assistant Director General of the World Intellectual Property Organization (WIPO).

"4. Rightholders shall have the right to terminate the authorisation to manage rights, categories of rights or types of works and other subject-matter granted by them to a collective management organisation or to withdraw from a collective management organisation any of the rights, categories of rights or types of works and other subject-matter of their choice, as determined pursuant to paragraph 2, for the territories of their choice, upon serving reasonable notice not exceeding six months. The collective management organisation may decide that such termination or withdrawal is to take effect only at the end of the financial year [...].

"7. In cases where a rightholder authorises a collective management organisation to manage his rights, he shall give consent specifically for each right or category of rights or type of works and other subject-matter which he authorises the collective management organisation to manage. Any such consent shall be evidenced in documentary form."

There are three issues which should be mentioned in this context. First, whether it should be allowed to establish a collective management organization (CMO) freely without any authorization/accreditation by a competent authority. To this question, a negative answer is justified; the governments, in order to duly fulfill the obligations of their countries under the international treaties and to guarantee adequate exercise of the rights of the interested rightholders, should make it sure that only organizations suitable for appropriate, lawful management of copyright function in their territories (and also that they may function without any inappropriate obstacles).

The second issue is whether it is justified to authorize/accredit only one CMO to manage a certain right in a given country. Concerning this issue, the phenomenon of "natural monopolies" should be taken into account. Such a monopoly exists – and it not only should be accepted as a reality but it also should be supported – where, with the appearance of more than one actor in the field of a given activity, efficiency goes down, costs go up, and revenues go down.[1] In the field of collective management, there are such situations, and where they exist, it seems obvious that the right legislative solution, in the interests of the rightholders – but also in the interests of lawful users – is limiting in this way the number of CMOs (as it has been confirmed by the CJEU in its *OSA* judgment).[2]

The third issue is whether, despite the general principle that rightholders should be free to join a CMO, it may be justified to prescribe collective management of rights where they have not joined an organization. This issue – which means the questions of the applicability of mandatory and extended (or presumption-based) collective management – is discussed below.

---

1 Natural monopoly is a category of monopolies recognized in economic science:
„In the case of natural monopolies, trying to increase competition by encouraging new entrants into the market creates a potential loss of efficiency.
„It may be more efficient to allow only one [organization] to supply to the market because allowing competition would mean a wasteful duplication of resources."
(*See* economicsonline.co.uk/Business_economy/Natural_economics.html)
Natural monopoly: a situation in which one [organization] is able to supply the whole market for a product or service more cheaply than two or more [organizations] could.
(*See* dictionary.cambridge.org/dictionary/english/natural-monopoly).

2 Case C-351/12.

Mandatory Collective Management as a Limitation of Exclusive Rights

The Berne Convention contains two provisions – namely Article 11*bis*(2) and Article 13(1)[3] – under which it is a matter for legislation in the countries of the Berne Union to determine/impose *conditions* under which certain exclusive rights may be exercised.

Article 11*bis*(2) reads as follows:

"It shall be a matter for legislation in the countries of the Union *to determine the conditions under which the rights mentioned in the preceding paragraph*[4] *may be exercised*, but these conditions shall apply only in the countries where they have been prescribed. They shall not in any circumstances be prejudicial to the moral rights of the author, nor to his right to obtain equitable remuneration which, in the absence of agreement, shall be fixed by competent authority." [Emphasis added.]

Article 13(1) provides in a similar way:

"Each country of the Union may *impose* for itself reservations and *conditions on the exclusive right granted to the author* of a musical work and to the author of any words, the recording of which together with the musical work has already been authorized by the latter, to authorize the sound recording of that musical work, together with such words, if any; but all such reservations and conditions shall apply only in the countries which have imposed them and shall not, in any circumstances, be prejudicial to the rights of these authors to obtain equitable remuneration which, in the absence of agreement, shall be fixed by competent authority." [Emphasis added.]

These provisions are regarded as a legal basis for the application of *compulsory licenses*. This is deduced from the way in which the minimum requirement is described for the applicability of such conditions; namely that determining/imposing conditions must not, under any circumstances, be prejudicial to the right to obtain an equitable remuneration. This does not mean, however, that non-voluntary licenses are the only possible "*conditions*" mentioned in those provisions. *Also other conditions* of the exercise of the exclusive rights concerned *may be applied*, and it seems to be clear that mandatory collective management of rights is such a *condition* too, since, it means – referring to the questions above – that:

---

[3] Equally relevant for the TRIPS Agreement and the WCT; *see* Article 9.1 of the TRIPS Agreement and Article 1(4) of the WCT.

[4] Under the "preceding paragraph – paragraph (1) of the same Article: "[a]uthors of literary and artistic works shall enjoy the exclusive right of authorizing: (i) the broadcasting of their works or the communication thereof to the public by any other means of wireless diffusion of signs, sounds or images; (ii) any communication to the public by wire or by rebroadcasting of the broadcast of the work, when this communication is made by an organization other than the original one; (iii) the public communication by loudspeaker or any other analogous instrument transmitting, by signs, sounds or images, the broadcast of the work."

- although the owners of these rights are in the position to do something (namely, to enjoy the exclusive right of authorizing the acts in question), it is provided that *they can only do so in a certain way*;
- although they own such exclusive rights, it is provided that *they can only exploit those rights in a certain manner*; and
- although they are granted such rights, it is provided that *they can only exercise those rights through a certain system* (namely, through collective management).

The freedom to "determine/impose conditions" is allowed in the Convention in an exhaustive way. Therefore, on the basis of the *a contrario* principle, it may be deduced that, in general, the scope of applicability of mandatory collective management of *exclusive rights* is the same as in the case of compulsory licenses.

The analysis above has been made on the basis of the Berne Convention. However, the question of applicability of mandatory collective management also emerges concerning those provisions of the treaties on copyright, such as the TRIPS Agreement and the WIPO Copyright Treaty (WCT), which – in addition to the above-mentioned provisions of the Berne Convention to be applied by reference[5] – provide for further rights or, at least, adapt or clarify the application of the rights already provided, as well as concerning the relevant provisions of the treaties on related rights, in particular the WIPO Performances and Phonograms Treaty (WPPT) and the Beijing Treaty on Audiovisual Performances (BTAP). From this viewpoint, in particular, the following provisions of those other treaties should be taken into account:

- both the TRIPS Agreement and the WCT provide for a further exclusive right of authors; namely, the exclusive right of rental at least for computer programs (which, of course, is hardly relevant for collective management) and audiovisual works (with certain grandfathering limitations);[6]
- the WCT also contains provisions on the exclusive right of distribution[7] (as regards the right of first distribution, with usual exhaustion with the first sale) and on a generally applicable exclusive right of communication to the public (going beyond the scope of the right of communication to the public under the Berne Convention for certain – although from the viewpoint of the right the most relevant – categories of works) including the exclusive right of interactive making available to the public;[8]
- the WPPT and the BTAP also provide for certain exclusive rights, such as the rights of reproduction,[9] distribution (the same way as the WCT),[10] rental[11] and (interactive) making available to the public as a stand-alone right.[12]

5 *See* Article 9.1 of the TRIPS Agreement and Article 1(4) of the WCT.
6 See Article 11 of the TRIPS Agreement and Article 7of the WCT.
7 See Article 6 of the WCT.
8 See Article 8 of the WCT.
9 See Articles 7 and 11of the WPPT and Article 7 of the BTAP.
10 See Articles 8 and 12 of the WPPT and Article 8 of the BTAP.
11 See Articles 9 and 13 of the WPPT and Article 9 of the BTAP.
12 See Articles 10 and 14 of the WPPT and Article 10 of the BTAP.

In these treaties, there are no provisions similar to Article 11*bis*(2) and 13(1) of the Berne Convention allowing both compulsory licenses and mandatory collective management to be applied as *conditions* of the exercise of the exclusive rights concerned. However, this does not mean that, for these rights, no such limitations may be applied. As it has been outlined above, mandatory collective management is a limitation. Therefore, the provisions of the above-mentioned treaties on limitations – Article 13 of TRIPS Agreement, Article 10(2) of the WCT, Article 16 of the WPPT, and Article 13 of the BTAP – may be applied to these exclusive rights.

These provisions provide for the three-step test (for the first time included in the Berne Convention where, under Article 9(2), it was only applicable to exceptions to and limitations of the right of reproduction). The three cumulative conditions ("steps") are that an exception or limitation may only be applied

- in a certain special case,
- provided that it does not conflict with a normal exploitation of the work/performance/phonogram, and
- further provided that it does not conflict with a normal exploitation of the legitimate interests of the rightholders.

While in the Berne Convention, the three-step test under Article 9(2) only allows the inclusion of exceptions or limitations not specifically permitted in the Convention (provided that the three cumulative conditions are fulfilled) concerning the exclusive right of reproduction, under the other above-mentioned provisions on the three-step test, it is allowed to provide exceptions to or limitations of all Berne-plus exclusive rights.[13] Under these provisions, mandatory collective management may also be applied to the exercise of the exclusive rights mentioned – as a limitation thereof – if the three cumulative conditions of the test are fulfilled.

At the same time, it should also be noted that Article 13 of the TRIPS Agreement as well as Article 10 of the WCT, Article 16(2) of the WPPT and Article 13(2) of the BTAP extend the control of the three-step test also to the specifically provided exceptions and limitations. This also applies to the above-mentioned limitations explicitly allowed in the Berne Convention, of which the limitations under Article 11*bis*(2) of the Convention are particularly relevant.

In the case of broadcasting, the prescription of mandatory collective management concerning certain categories of works – such as in particular audiovisual works – would conflict with a normal exploitation of the works and would unreasonably prejudice the legitimate interests of the rightholders. Therefore, under Article 13 of

[13] It is to be noted that Article 13 of the TRIPS Agreement and Article 10(1) of the WCT are also applicable to all rights to be protected under those treaties; that is, also to the exclusive rights provided in the Berne Convention to be complied with under Article 9.1 of the TRIPS Agreement and Article 1(4) of the WCT. This does not mean that new exceptions to or limitations of the rights other than the right of reproduction might be introduced under them, but it does mean that the exceptions and limitations specifically permitted under the Berne Convention may only be applied if, in addition to the specific conditions provided in the relevant provisions of the Convention, they also correspond to the three-step test (in those cases, obviously, to the second and third conditions).

the TRIPS Agreement and Article 10(1) of the WCT – which, as mentioned above, do apply also to the exceptions and limitations specifically permitted under the Berne Convention[14] – such a limitation (since it would conflict with the second and third conditions of the three-step test) is not allowed.[15]

In accordance with this, in those national laws where (compulsory license and/or) mandatory collective management is provided concerning the right of broadcasting, normally it is not applied to audiovisual works and usually only apply to non-dramatic musical works. This is for example, expressly stated in the copyright laws of certain countries; such as in the laws of Croatia, Hungary and Poland.

The exclusive right of cable retransmission is another matter. In the stage of the transmission of broadcast programs by the cable networks, it would be practically impossible to obtain authorization from the rightholders separately for this simultaneous secondary use. Therefore, for cable retransmission, compulsory licensing or mandatory collective management is necessary for the exercise of the rights concerned (and, in this case, also the rights in audiovisual works).

Mandatory Collective Management of Rights to Remuneration

Above, the questions of applicability of mandatory collective management of *exclusive rights* have been analyzed. However, in those cases where not an exclusive right is involved – and therefore the latitude of the rightholders is limited due to the very nature of the rights – obviously, not the same considerations apply. It is submitted that mandatory collective management is permissible also in cases:

- where a right is not provided as an exclusive right of authorization but rather as a mere right to remuneration (as in the case of the resale right (*droit de* suite) under Article 14*ter* of the Convention or the so-called "Article 12 rights" of performers and producers of phonograms);
- where the restriction of an exclusive right to a mere right to remuneration is allowed (as under Article 9(2) concerning the right of reproduction); and
- where what is concerned is a "residual right;" that is, a right to remuneration which "survives" the transfer of certain exclusive rights, like what is provided in Article 5 of the Rental, Lending and Related Rights Directive (Directive 2016/115/EC) concerning the exclusive rental right of authors and performers or to which Article 12(3) of the BTAP refers in case of the exclusive rights of performers for their performances embodied in audiovisual fixations.

---

14 *See* the preceding footnote.

15 In fact, at certain diplomatic conferences to revise the Berne Convention proposals were presented to exclude the applicability of Article 11*bis*(2) to audiovisual works (practically for such reasons although without reference to the three-step test), but they were not adopted; see Mihály Ficsor: Guide to Copyright and Related Rights Treaties Administered by WIPO, WIPO publication No. 891 (E), 2003, pp. 78-79.

EU Directives on Mandatory Collective Management

Various directives of the EU include provisions on mandatory collective management. They are reviewed below. As it can be seen, all of them are in accordance with the international treaties:

The *Rental, Lending and Related Rights Directive* on the „unwaivable right to remuneration" for rental in favor of authors and performers provides as follows: Article 4(3): „The administration of this right [...] may be entrusted to collecting societies representing authors or performers." Article 4(4): "Member States may regulate whether and to what extent administration by collecting societies of the right to obtain an equitable remuneration may be imposed..." *This is in accordance with the international norms*, since it does not concern the exercise of exclusive rights itself directly; it is a „residual" right to remuneration.

Article 9(1) of the *Satellite and Cable Directive* (Directive 93/83/EEC) reads as follows: "Member States shall ensure that the right of copyright owners and holders of related rights to grant or refuse authorization to a cable operator for a cable retransmission may be exercised only through a collecting society." *This is in accordance with the international norms*, due to Article 11*bis*(2) of the Berne Convention discussed above.

Article 6(2) of the *Resale Right Directive* (Directive 2001/84/EC) contains this provision: "Member States may provide for compulsory or optional collective management of the royalty provided for under Article 1" (the right of resale (droit de suite)). *This is in accordance with the international norms,* since both the Directive and the underlining provision of the Berne Convention (Article 14*ter*) only provides for a right to remuneration.

The *Terms Directive* (Directive 2006/116/EC), in its Article 3, provides in this way: „2b. Where a contract on transfer or assignment gives the performer a right to claim a non-recurring remuneration, the performer shall have the right to obtain an annual supplementary remuneration from the phonogram producer... The right to obtain such annual supplementary remuneration may not be waived by the performer..." „2d. Member States shall ensure that the right to obtain an annual supplementary remuneration as referred to in paragraph 2b is administered by collecting societies." This is in accordance with the international norms, because it is a right to an unwaivable remuneration which does not limit the application of an exclusive right.

Article 4(1) of the *Satellite and Cable Directive II* (Directive (EU)2019/789) includes this provision: "Member States shall ensure that rightholders may exercise their right to grant or refuse the authorisation for a retransmission only through a collective management organisation." This is in accordance with the international norms in view of Article 11bis(2) of the Berne Convention and the three-step test.

Extended (and Presumption-based) Collective Management from the Viewpoint of the International Treaties

One of the most important advantages of a fully developed collective management systems is that CMOs may grant blanket licenses to users for *quasi* the entire world repertoire of works and objects of related rights as regards a given right of a given category of owners of rights. However, even where the system of reciprocal representation agreements is fairly developed (such as in the case of musical "performing rights"), the repertoire in respect of which a CMO grants blanket licenses never covers entirely the world repertoire (since, in certain countries, there are no appropriate partner organizations to conclude reciprocal representation agreements, or because certain authors do not trust a CMO with the exercise of their rights).

There are two basic legal techniques to ensure the operation of blanket licensing. The first one is the *presumption-based* system which usually involves three elements. First, until the contrary is proved, it is presumed that the license granted by the CMO covers all works in the given category for which the rights concerned applies (that is, the lawfulness of authorizing the use of works not being covered by the repertoire of a given organization is recognized either by statutory law or by case law). Second, the organization guarantees that individual rightholders will not claim remuneration from the users to whom blanket licenses are granted, and that, if they still try to do so, such claims will be settled by the organization; and that any users will be indemnified for any prejudice and expense caused to them as a result of justified claims by individual owners of rights. Third, the organization also guarantees that it treats the owners of rights who have not delegated their rights to it without discrimination against them in favor of those authors who have delegated the exercise of their rights to the CMO. Since the presumption may be rebutted, it cannot be said that such a system is in conflict with the provisions on exclusive rights. Nevertheless, now it is ever more frequent that the presumption-based systems are replaced by extended collective management schemes.[16]

This other legal technique – extended collective management – in view of its well-regulated nature, with due guarantees to those righholders who have not joined a CMO, seems to be more advantageous for the holders of exclusive rights. The essence of such a system is that, if there is a CMO authorized to manage a certain right with a sufficiently representative repertoire in the given field, the effect of the licenses

[16] In fact, even in certain copyright laws where, in principle, the concept of presumption is used, it is rather an extended collective management system. For example, Article 157(5) of the Croatian Copyright Law reads as follows:

a) *It shall be presumed* that the collective management organisation[...] has powers of attorney for collective management of rights for which it is authorised for all domestic and foreign holders of such rights, *except for that rightholder who has notified the collective management organisation explicitly in writing not to manage his rights*. [Emphasis added.]

granted by the CMO is extended by the law also to the rights of those rightholders who have not entrusted the organization with the management of their rights.

In addition to the obvious basic criterion that only a CMO that is well established and functions in accordance with the requirements of good governance may be allowed to operate such a system, there are five basic conditions to be fulfilled in order that extended collective management do not have the effect of eroding an exclusive right:

- First, there should be a situation where the effect of collective management only needs to be extended to authorize the use of works of non-mandating rightholders, because, for the effective exercise of the right concerned collective management is indispensable or at least highly necessary; thus, it may be presumed that those rightholders are also ready to make use of this form of exercising the right. For example, this is clearly the case as regards the management of the right of public performance in musical works.
- Second, the concept of "extension" should be applicable in the sense that, because there is a sufficiently representative CMO,[17] the effect of the licenses granted by it may just be extended to those rightholders who, although they need the collective system for benefitting from their rights, still have not joined the organization.
- Third, in particular in the case of exclusive rights, there should be special provisions for the protection of the interests of those owners of rights who have not joined the organization and who do not wish to participate in the collective system. Those rightholders should have the option of freely choosing between either claiming remuneration or "opting out" (declaring that they do not want to be represented by the organization). In the latter case, they are supposed to take care of the exercise of their rights individually. As regards "opting out" from the collective system, a reasonable deadline should be allowed to determine by the CMO in order that it may exclude the works from its repertoire. However, the procedure of "opting out" should be simple and effective. The rightholders should be able to "opt out" by a declaration with all their present and future works and the validity of opting out should not be subject to the fulfillment of burdensome conditions which would make it a *de facto* formality.[18] It is also a requirement that the rightholders who have not authorized explicitly (directly or – through reciprocal representation agreements – indirectly) the CMO to manage their rights be adequately informed about the possibility of opting out and the way it may take place.[19]

[17] Being sufficiently representative normally means three criteria: (i) the CMO should represent a substantial part of the rightholders concerned; (ii) this should be the case for both domestic and foreign rightholders; and (iii) where one organization has to be chosen from among two or various candidate organizations, the one should be chosen which the most corresponds to the conditions mentioned under (i) and (ii).

[18] As discussed below in this article, the CJEU, in its *Soulier and Joke* judgment, found such a condition of an "opt-out" system of the French legislation in power at that time for extended collective management having been introduced to facilitate licensing the use of out-of-commerce works.

[19] As also discussed below, it is the CJEU judgment mentioned in the preceding footnote which has drawn attention to the requirement, which is particularly important where a previously unknown new extended collective management system is introduced (such as in the given case).

- Fourth – although this is a general requirement for any forms of collective management, it is particularly important in the case of extended (as well as mandatory) collective management – due efforts, a kind of "diligent search", should be made to identify and/or to locate the unknown and/or non-locatable rightholders.
- Fifth, the rightholders who have not authorized explicitly the CMO should enjoy equal treatment concerning the terms of the licenses with those who have authorized the CMO.

If these conditions are met, an extended collective management system is not only in accordance with the international treaties, but its benefits derived from its enabling nature also becomes evident. The status of "orphan works" is a good example for this.

Article 2 of the EU Orphan Works Directive (Directive 2012/28/EU) defines "orphan work" as a work (or a phonogram) in the case of which none of the rightholders is identified or, even if one is or more are identified, none is located despite a diligent search for the rightholders carried out in accordance with Article 3 of the Directive. Where there is extended collective management, the non-member rightholders are also covered; thus also those for whose identification and/or location "diligent search" is to be made. This is an obligation of a CMO which may only qualify the work "orphan" – and consider the amount due to the unknown and/or non-locatable rightholder "non-distributable" – if the "diligent search" (for which the well-developed database systems of CMOs are suitable) has not been successful. That is, the CMOs cannot use simply the concept of "unclaimed amounts"; they must not wait for the rightholders to "claim" what is due to them; they are obligated to try to identify and locate them, and to transfer their remuneration if they are found.

Recital (24) of the Directive recognizes the role of collective management and, in particular extended collective management in this respect:

"This Directive is without prejudice to the arrangements in the Member States concerning the management of rights such as extended collective licences, legal presumptions of representation or transfer, collective management or similar arrangements or a combination of them, including for mass digitisation."

Where the above-mentioned requirements are not fulfilled, the extended collective management system may become similar to mandatory collective management and get in conflict with the international treaties.

There are certain academic views that opting-out may be considered as a condition of exercising a right[20] and, therefore, it may conflict with the prohibition of formalities applied as conditions of enjoinment and exercise of copyright and related rights.[21] This may be truly the case if the provisions on "opt-out" do not correspond

20 *See*, for example, Thomas Riis – Jens Schovbo: "*Extended Collective Licenses and the Nordic Experience – It's a Hybrid but is It a Volvo or a Lemon*?, at https://papers.ssrn.com/sol3/papers.cfm?abstract_id=1535230, p. 13 („In order to prohibit the use of the work, the rightholder must 'opt out' of the ECL and therefore the exercise of copyright as an exclusive right can be said to be subject to a formal prerequisite. It is not quite clear whether such a formal prerequisite required by law is prohibited by Article 5 of the Berne Convention.")

21 *See* Article 5(2) of the Berne Convention, Article 20 of the WPPT and Article of the 17 BTAP.

to the requirements outlined above. As discussed below, the CJEU did find certain specific aspects of the French legislation on extended collective management[22] that, according to the Court, did not fulfill the requirements and had created conflicts with the principle of formality free-protection. Nevertheless, in legal literature, the dominant academic opinion (which the author of this article does share[23]), is that the need for opting out in order to exclude a repertoire from the extended effect of the licenses granted by a CMO is not a formality to be fulfilled as a condition of enjoyment and exercise of copyright and related rights; at least, certainly not where the system is in accordance with five criteria outlined above.[24]

From this viewpoint, the first criterion – that collective management should be indispensable or at least highly necessary for effective exercise of the right concerned – is of a key importance. It is what may create a well-founded basis for the presumption that rightholders not represented by a CMO – since they cannot normally exploit their rights in other way – tacitly consent to this form of exercising their rights. Jane Ginsburg, who is also of the view that "opting out" needed for excluding repertoires (about which it may be rightly presumed such a tacit consent of rightholders) is not a formality, points out the parallel with presumptions of transfer of rights in the case of which the need for a rebuttal, rightly enough, is not considered a formality either.[25]

22 As discussed below, these were the lack of due information available to non-members of a CMO and the burdensome need to prove that there is no print license in force.

23 *See* Mihály Ficsor: "*Collective Rights Management from the Viewpoint of International Treaties with Special Attention to the EU Acquis*" in Gervais, Third Edition, Chapter 2, title 5.4 "Why Extended Collective Management Does not Involve Any Formality" (hereinafter: Ficsor in Gervais, Third Edition), pp. 75 to 77.

24 See, for example:
Daniel Gervais: "*Collective Management of Copyright: Theory and Practice in the Digital Age*" in Gervais, Third Edition ("ERS ['extended repertoire system' used as a synonym of extended collective management] is not a prohibited formality under Berne. It guarantees an orderly exploitation of the repertoire that will be licensed but offers authors the option of going back to Level 0 by sending a simple notice."), Chapter 1, p. 29;
Stef Van Gompel: "*Formalities in Copyright Law. An Analysis of their History, Rationales and Possible Future*", Wolters Kluwer, 2011 ("The question [is[whether the 'opt-out' procedure complies with the prohibition on formalities. It seems that it does. The possibility to 'opt-out' from the ECL scheme does not affect the 'enjoyment' or the 'exercise' of copyright. The right is exercised in any event either collectively as statutory default rule or individually if the author 'opts out'".), p. 209;
Séverine Dusollier – Caroline Colin: "Peer-to-Peer File Sharing and Copyright: What Could Be the Role of Collective Management?" in Columbia Journal of Law & the Arts, Vol. 34 No. 4 (2011), p. 862 ("Extended collective licensing does not prevent the exercise of an author's copyright, but rather enables it. Therefore, opting out is not so much a restoration of an author's right to exercise her ownership, but rather is a choice to exercise that right in a different way."), p. 862;
Desmond Osaretin Oriakhogba: "Collective Management of Copyright in Nigeria: Should it Remain Voluntary, may it Be Mandatory or Extended?"; see at https://papers.ssrn.com/sol3/papers.cfm?abstract_id=3498393 ("The opt-out option expressly provided for under extended collective management makes it unique compared to the mandatory model. The opt-out option also insulates the extended model from negatively impacting the right to property, freedom of association, the no formality rule, the three-step test and copyright exclusivity."), p. 23.

25 *See* Jane Ginsburg in "*Extended Collective Licenses in International Treaty Perspective: Issues and Statutory Implementation*" ("National rules providing for presumptions of transfer and establishing

However, she stresses that the fulfillment of the other above-mentioned requirements of an appropriate extended collective management scheme, in particular those regarding "opt-outs", is also needed to avoid formality implications[26]. She – with reference to *Soulier and Doke* – mentions the absence of adequate information available to the rightholders who have not explicitly authorized the CMO to manage their rights and the burdensome conditions prescribed in the French legislation judged in the case as those which may have the effect of formalities.[27] It seems to follow from this *a contrario* that, without such defective elements, the question of formalities is not supposed to arise. The judgment of the CJEU does reflect this position too, since, as discussed below, it follows from it that, in case of a combination of a duly presumable tacit consent of non-member rightholders with an adequate "opt-out" system, the issue of formalities does not emerge.

As regards the other question – whether or not an extended collective management may involve a limitation of rights – it is necessary to point out the difference between mandatory and extended forms of collective management. Those who are of the view that extended collective management may have the effect of a limitation do not take into account the basic difference between the two systems; namely that, in case of mandatory collective management – in contrast with extended collective management – the rightholders cannot "opt out". Thus, mandatory collective management, as clarified under the relevant title in this article above, beyond any doubts means a limitation where it is applied for the exercise of an exclusive right.[28] In

mechanisms to rebut those presumptions should similarly fall outside art. 5(2). Because the ECL extension effect operates like a presumption of transfer of rights to the CMO, and the opt-out provides the means for authors to withhold their rights from the CMO, that is, to rebut the presumption of transfer, an appropriately designed opt-out should fit comfortably within the declaratory measures that member states may impose respecting transfers of ownership, without running afoul of the prohibition on formalities."), available at https://papers.ssrn.com/sol3/papers.cfm?abstract_id=3068997, posted in 2017 (hereinafter: Ginsburg on extended collective management), p.4.

26 She points out: "It does not, however, follow, that an opt-out system never imposes a "formality." [...] The permissibility of the opt-out may also turn on ensuring that the author is in fact informed of the presumption of transfer, understands the consequences of exercising her right to opt-out, and is able effectively to exercise that right without incurring unreasonable burdens.", *ibid.*

27 *See ibid.*, pp. 6-7.

28 *See* for example, Alain Strowel's analysis in his article on „*The European 'Extended Collective Licensing' Modell": („*With an ECL [= extended collective license], exclusive rights are preserved, which indicates at first sight that an ECL should not be equated with an exception to copyright. However, at the same time, the author cannot exercise her rights; only the CMO can. The author cannot individually negotiate and the outsiders are affected in the absence of any express mandate. So, an ECL works in practice as an exception."),*Columbia Journal of Law & the Arts, Vol 34, No 4 (2011), p. 668)*

In the article of the author of this book in the Gervais-edited third edition of the book on collective management, added this comment to the text quoted above: "Strowel's description of extended collective management seems to correspond rather to mandatory collective management. This is so since he states that 'the author cannot exercise her rights; only the CMO can' which, in this way, is only applies for mandatory collective management. Extended collective management is an enabling system; it is based on the presumption of the legislators that the given right may only be exercised normally and efficiently through a CMO. It is an indispensable element of such a system that rightholders must be contrast, it follows from the analysis above that, where it may be presumed that the non-member rightholders tacitly agree to the management of their rights by a CMO (and such a presumption may be effective rebutted by an "opt-out")[29], it could hardly be characterized that there is a limitation of the right.[30] Johan Axhamn, expresses the same view in his article, after a thorough analysis of the differences between mandatory and extended forms of collective management: "[W]hereas provisions on mandatory collective management must probably be regarded as limitations to exclusive rights, this is not the case for provisions on ECL. This important feature makes the ECL model substantially different from mandatory collective licensing and thus more appealing as a policy alternative to pure exceptions and limitations (which are subject to the three-step test)."[31]

The view referred to at the end of the preceding paragraph is in accordance with the last sentence of point (14) of the Conclusions chapter of the second edition of the WIPO book on collective manegement in that, if the "opt-out" system does not fulfill the requirements of an adequate extended collective management scheme, the system may have an effect similar to limitation of exclusive rights by mandatory collective management; therefore, it is only applicable if it corresponds to all the three cumulative conditions of the three-step test. Jane Ginsburg, in her article mentioned above, offers a thorough analysis how the three-step test may be applied for mandatory collective management and for those schemes which, although, in principle, they are referred to as extended collective management, for the reasons mentioned above, turn to be a de facto limitation of the rights concerned with effects similar to mandatory collective management.[32]

The concept of extended collective management may also be misunderstood, misinterpreted and abused. In the course of on the transformation of the collective management systems of countries of centrally planned economies to the requirement of market economy, there were typical cases where such kinds of problems emerged

---

able to opt out (in a way, rebutting the legislators' presumption in their case). Due to this, in regard of a real 'ECL', it is not the case that 'the author cannot exercise her rights'; she can if she wants." (*Ficsor in Gervais, Third Edition*, Chapter 2, pp 74-75.)

29 It should also be seen that, where – for the exploitation of the given right – it is really indispensable or highly necessary to use the services of a CMO, they normally hardly wish to do so.

30 *See* also title 5.3 on "Why Extended Collective Management Does Not Result in an Exception or Limitation" in *Ficsor in Gervais, Third Edition*, Chapter 2, pp. 74 -75.

31 Johan Axhamn: "*Exceptions, limitations and collective management of rights as vehicles for access to information*", in Dana Beldiman: "Access to Information and Knowledge", Edward Elgar Publishing, 2013, p. 184.

32 Jane Ginsburg states this: "In the absence of those procedural safeguards [mentioned in the preceding sentence; namely that the author is in fact informed of the presumption of transfer, understands the consequences of exercising her right to opt-out, and is able effectively to exercise that right without incurring unreasonable burdens], extension of the license to an author who has not affirmatively consented to the CMO's representation should be treated like a limitation on the author's exercise of her rights whose consistency with international norms requires examination under the three-step test.", *Ginsburg on extended collective management*, p. 4. Later in the article, she analyzes how the three-step test should be applied for the limitations created by mandatory and inadequate "extended" collective management. *Ibid.*, pp. 7-8.

and it is outlined how they have been solved and certain "transition" problems (concerning the uncontrolled proliferation of CMOs to manage musical rights) have been settled through a duly regulated extended collective management model.

Extended Collective Management, a Nordic-origin System Applied Also in Other Countries

Extended collective management is referred to frequently as the Nordic extended collective management (ECL) system. This is certainly correct if this is a reference to the *origin* of the system. Tarja Koskinen and Vigdís Sigurdardóttir describe the birth and development of this system briefly as follows:

"Nordic legislators have paid much attention to easy access and legal security of users. A particular legal technique called 'extended collective license' (ECL) was introduced in the 1960s. This legislative support mechanism is based on exclusive rights of right holders and voluntary collective licensing with the aim of offering fully covering licenses to users who obtain a license. The first application area was primary broadcasting of musical and literary works in the 1960s, to be followed by reprography and re-transmission of broadcasts in the 1970s and 1980s.

"'In conjunction with the national implementations of the EU Copyright Directive [the Information Society Directive (Directive 2001/29/EC)], the Nordic countries added new ECL provisions to address digital uses, in particular in educational establishments, libraries, archives and museums. Since 2008, there has been a general possibility to conclude agreements with the support of an ECL in Denmark. Such a provision was introduced also in Sweden in 2013."[33]

In the meantime, also other countries have introduced extended collective management. In Hungary, for instance, where at least as many rights are managed in this way as in the Nordic countries. It seems to be worthwhile presenting it as an example to show what kinds of provisions have been found necessary to guarantee that its operation be in accordance with the international treaties and EU norms:

- The expression extended collective management is not defined separately in Article 3 of the Act on Collective Management (CM Act) implementing the EU's CM Directive in which, following the structure of the Directive, definitions are provided. The provisions on extended collective management are contained in Articles 17 and 18 of the CM Act which determine its basic aspects. The regulation is quite complex, because the relevant norms may be found in various provisions of the Copyright Law and the CM Act (the Copyright Law determines which rights are to be exercised through mandatory and extended collective management; the detailed rules are included in the CM Act). In the CM Act, for the regulation

[33] Tarja Koskinen and Vigdís Sigurdardóttir: "*Collective Management in the Nordic Countries*" in Gervais, Third Edition, Chapter 8, p. 244. It reflects the status at the time of the publication of the book, in 2016.

of extended collective management, also the expressions "prescribed collective management" and "representative collective management organization" are used, which, in contrast, are defined in Article 3 of the CM Act.

- Under Article 3, point 3 of the CM Act, "a case where prescribed collective management applies" is "that kind of use [of works or objects of related right] in connection with which, on the basis of the Copyright Law, the rightholders may only exercise their rights through a CMO as long as a notice opposing collective management made in accordance with Article 18(1) enters into force." The expression "prescribed collective management" might be misunderstood as to suggest that what is prescribed is that rightholders may only exercise their rights through collective management (which would mean mandatory collective management). However, this is not the case since rightholders may "opt out" from a prescribed collective management system in accordance with Article 18(1) of the Law (see below). In fact, "prescribed" collective management is extended collective management provided in the Copyright Law in those cases where collective management is a normal way of exercising rights, practically with a natural monopoly situation.
- In addition to the possibility of "opting out" from the collective management system, it is also generally recognized that extended collective management may only be regarded to be in accordance with the provisions on exclusive rights of authorization if it is applied where collective management is *necessary* to exercise the rights concerned and where the CMO is *duly representative both domestically and internationally* (and, if there are more than one CMO candidates, it is *the most representative*).
- These further conditions – in respect of "prescribed collective management" – are determined in the following way. Under Article 5(1) of the CM Act, not only mandatory collective management but also prescribed collective management may only be performed by "representative CMOs" (and the detailed norms on such organizations (see below) ensure that they are truly representative). Furthermore, Article 34(2) of the CM Act provides as follows: "In cases other than those where mandatory or extended collective management applies, authorization to perform collective management as a representative CMO may only be granted if the rightholders cannot exercise their rights efficiently on an individual basis." This provision confirms that "prescribed collective management" is a specific form of extended collective management for which the fulfillment of two of the above-mentioned conditions (the possibility of "opting out" and broad representativeness) is required, while the third condition (that the rights must be of a nature that they could not be exercised effectively on an individual basis), is fulfilled by the provisions of the Copyright Law which determine in an exclusive manner which rights may be exercised through "prescribed collective management".[34]

[34] The Copyright Law provides for such "prescribed collective management" in the following cases: public performance of musical works (other than dramatico-musical works) and literary works (other than scientific, technical and medical works and longer non-fiction works) (Article 25(1) and (3) of the Copyright Law);

- Under point 10 of Article 3 of the CM Act, a "representative collective management organization" is "a collective management organization which, in regard to the right under copyright or related rights managed by it, corresponds to the requirements determined in Article 34 and which for the said right has received authorization to function as a representative collective management." As it can be seen, this is not a substantive definition, since it only refers to Article 34 where the conditions to be fulfilled are truly determined.
- Article 17 of the CM Act includes provisions on the extension of the validity of licenses granted by representative CMOs to the rights of rightholders not covered by their repertoire and on the obligations of such CMOs in regard to the rights of such rightholders. Article 18 is on "opt-out" notices; they are supposed to cover all works or objects of related rights of the rightholders concerned, to be made in a written deed with full probative effect, and they enter into force on the first day after the end of the given financial year.

And this regulation does not include yet the provisions to implement Article 12 of the Digital Single Market Directive (Directive (EU) 2019/790) on extended collective management making the appropriate use of out-of-commerce works possible (the implementation of which was in process at the time of completion of the manuscript of this book). Those provisions and, the general EU regulation on extended collective management are discussed below.

Provisions in EU Directives on Extended Collective Management Before the Digital Single Market Directive

Although the Digital Single Market Directive now contains detailed norms on extended collective management, certain provisions were included also in other directives adopted before.

The first such provisions were adopted in the Satellite and Cable Directive. After that Article 2 stated that "Member States shall provide an exclusive right for the author to authorize the communication to the public by satellite of copyright works…" – and then Article 3.1 added that "Member States shall ensure that the authorization referred

satellite broadcasting of musical works (other than dramatico-musical works) and literary works (other than scientific, technical and medical works and longer non-fiction works) (Article 27(2) of the Copyright Law);
communication to the public in a way other than broadcasting of (non-dramatic) musical works and literary works (other than scientific, technical and medical works and longer non-fiction works), including (interactive) making available to the public provided in Article 26(8) of the Copyright Law (Article 27(3) of the Copyright Law);
making available performances (in an interactive manner) to the public, as provided in Article 73(1)(e) of the Copyright Act (Article 74(2) of the Copyright Law).

to in Article 2 may be acquired only by agreement" (that is, it must not be subject to a non-voluntary licensing system) – Article 3.2 outlined what may be regarded as an extended collective management system. It read as follows:

"A Member State may provide that a collective agreement between a collecting society and a broadcasting organization concerning a given category of works may be extended to rightholders of the same category who are not represented by the collecting society, provided that:

- the communication to the public by satellite simulcasts a terrestrial broadcast by the same broadcaster, and
- the unrepresented rightholder shall, at any time, have the possibility of excluding the extension of the collective agreement to his works and of exercising his rights either individually or collectively." [Emphasis added].

These provisions *allowed* to Member States the introduction of an extended collective licensing system (the "may" language clearly indicates this), which reflects the position that (i) such an authorization is needed; such a system cannot be applied in respect of any exclusive right; and (ii) where such a system is applied, there are certain conditions to be taken into account.

This was confirmed by Article 3.3 and 4 of the Directive which had been based on the recognition that extended collective management is only justified where it is indispensable or highly necessary, and where the rightholders usually do not intend to – or could hardly – exercise their exclusive rights on an individual basi*s*. Article 3.3 identified a category of works where this is not the case. It provided that "[p]aragraph 2 shall not apply to cinematographic works, including works created by a process analogous to cinematography," while Article 3.4 underlines the exceptional nature of extended collective management by introducing a specific notification procedure.[35]

The other directives before the adoption of the Digital Single Market Directive only confirmed the applicability of extended collective management without regulating it. Article (24) of the Orphan Works Directive is mentioned above, and before it the Information Society Directive and after it the CM Directive also contained such clarification. Recital (18) of the Information Society Directive simply stated: "This Directive is without prejudice to the arrangements in the Member States concerning the management of rights such as extended collective licenses." The reference to extended collective management was included in a more complex recital – recital (12) of the CM Directive:

"(12) *This Directive*, while applying to all collective management organisations, with the exception of Title III, which applies only to collective management organisations managing authors' rights in musical works for online use on a multi-territorial basis, *does not interfere with arrangements concerning the management of rights* in

[35] Article 3.4 provided as follows: "Where the law of a Member State provides for the extension of a collective agreement in accordance with the provisions of paragraph 2, that Member States shall inform the Commission which broadcasting organizations are entitled to avail themselves of that law. The Commission shall publish this information in the *Official Journal of the European Communities* (C series)."

the Member States such as individual management, the extended effect of an agreement between a representative collective management organisation and a user, i.e. *extended collective licensing, mandatory collective management, legal presumptions of representation* and transfer of rights to collective management organisations." [Emphasis added.]

It was a surprising aspect of the CM Directive that it included very detailed provisions on a number of aspects of the structure and operation of CMOs, in general, and it did not include any substantive norms on extended collective management (neither on mandatory and presumption-based agreement) except perhaps one; namely in the form of an implied requirement that the CMOs operating such systems are supposed to be "representative". This lacuna – at least as far as extended collective management is concerned – was only eliminated in the Digital Single Market Directive (in which the requirement of representativeness was also determined more in detail).

The Soulier and Doke Case

In France, in 2012, a new law was adopted which was an example of the enabling potential of extended collective management to serve efficiently the interest of the rightholders, the users and the general public.

Law No 2012-287 on the digital exploitation of out-of-print 20th century books added to Title III of Book One of the first part of the Intellectual Property Code, a Chapter IV, entitled „Special provisions relating to the digital exploitation of out-of-print books" comprising Articles L. 134-1 to L. 134-9 of the Code. (Some of those articles were subsequently amended or repealed by the Law No 2015-195.) The new legislation introduced an extended collective management which contained the following key elements:

- "Out-of-print book" was determined as a book published in France before 1 January 2001 which is no longer commercially distributed by a publisher and is not currently published in print or in a digital format.
- A public database indexing out-of-print books was to be created and made openly available through an online, public communication service.
- When a book had been registered in the database for more than six months, the right to authorize its reproduction and performance in digital format were to be exercised by a CMO approved for that purpose by the minister responsible for culture.
- The authors or the publishers of out-of-print books were able to oppose the exercise of their rights by the CMO in a notification no later than six months after a book in question had been registered in the database mentioned above.
- If, upon expiration of that term, the author or publisher had not given notice of opposition, the CMO was to offer authorization to reproduce and perform an out-of-print book in digital format to the publisher having the right to reproduce

that book in print. The authorization was to be issued on an exclusive basis for a 10-year period which was tacitly renewable.

- The authors of out-of-print books were able to decide at any time to withdraw from the collecting society referred to in Article L. 134-3 the right to authorize the reproduction and performance of books in digital format if they provided evidence that they alone held the rights laid down in L. 134-3.
- The author and publisher having the right of reproduction in print of an out-of-print book were able at any time jointly notify the CMO of their decision to withdraw the latter's right to authorize the reproduction and performance of that book in digital format.
- Publicity measures were provided which had to include an information campaign initiated by the minister responsible for culture, in conjunction with the CMO and the professional organizations in the book sector. The campaign had to include the presentation of the framework for an online public communication service, an online mailing operation, the publication of flyers in the national press and the distribution of banners on news websites.

Two authors – Marc Soulier and Sara Doke – initiated the annulment of the Law at the *Conseil d'État* which turned with a preliminary question to the CJEU. The CJEU adopted the following judgment in the case:

"Article 2(a) and Article 3(1) of Directive 2001/29/EC [Information Society Directive]... must be interpreted as precluding national legislation, such as that at issue in the main proceedings, that gives an approved collecting society the right to authorise the reproduction and communication to the public in digital form of 'out-of-print' books, namely, books published in France before 1 January 2001 which are no longer commercially distributed by a publisher and are not currently published in print or in digital form, while allowing the authors of those books, or their successors in title, to oppose or put an end to that practice, on the conditions that that legislation lays down."[36]

It should be noted that the Court has not ruled that extended collective management in general, or for the purpose of facilitating the use of out-of-commerce works in particular, would not be in accordance with the EU (and the international) norms, but only that it would be the case if it supposed to be done "on the conditions that that [the concrete French] legislation lays down." According to the judgment, there were two reasons for which the conditions laid down in the French legislation were in conflict with the EU law. First, although the Court recognized that, if the rightholders did not "opt out", it could have served as a basis to presume that they had implicitly authorized the CMO to license the use of their out-of-commerce works,[37] for this, they would have had to be duly informed about this possibility, which was not guaranteed by the French legislation.[38] Second, although an appropriate "opt-out" system might not qualify as a formality to exercise the exclusive rights concerned, under the French

[36] Case C-301/15.

[37] *See ibid.*, paras 35 and 42.

[38] *See ibid.*, paras, 39-40, 43.

legislation, the authors could have only "opted out" if they were able to prove that they are the only rightholders, there was no print right in force by others (normally to publishers) licensed by them, which would have been so difficult condition to fulfill that it might act as a formality.[39]

The Digital Single Market Directive has maintained the essential elements of the French system, but has provided the necessary publicity measures to make the rightholders aware of the possibility of "opting out" (included in Article 10 of the Directive). By this, the first reason for which the CJEU found the French law incompatible with the EU norms has been eliminated. The second feature of the French legislation that the Court found to cause conflict with the EU law has not emerged under the Directive because it does not contain the condition that for "opting out" from the extended collective management to authorize the use of out-of-commerce works,[40] rightholders would have to be proved that the rights involved have not been transferred to others. Article 8(4) of the Directive simply prescribes that "Member States shall provide that all rightholders may, at any time, easily and effectively, exclude their works or other subject matter from the licensing mechanism [...] either in general or in specific cases, including after the conclusion of a licence or after the beginning of the use concerned."

General Regulation of the Requirements of Extended Collective Management

The clarification of the requirements of the extended collective management for the use of out-of-commerce works offered the occasion to codify in general these requirements. It has taken place in Article 12 of the Digital Single Market Directive. The key provisions of the Article are these:

"1. Member States may provide [...] subject to the safeguards provided for in this Article, that where a collective management organization [...] in accordance with its mandates from rightholders, enters into a licensing agreement for the exploitation of works or other subject matter:

(a) such an agreement can be extended to apply to the rights of rightholders who have not authorised that collective management organisation to represent them by way of assignment, licence or any other contractual arrangement; or

(b) with respect to such an agreement, the organisation has a legal mandate or is presumed to represent rightholders who have not authorised the organisation accordingly.

[39] *See ibid.*, paras 49- 51.

[40] Article 8 defined out-of-commerce works in this way: "a work or other subject matter is to be deemed to be out of commerce when it can be presumed in good faith that the whole work or other subject matter is not available to the public through customary channels of commerce, after a reasonable effort has been made to determine whether it is available to the public."

"2. Member States shall ensure that the licensing mechanism referred to in paragraph 1 is only applied within well-defined areas of use, where obtaining authorisations from rightholders on an individual basis is typically onerous and impractical to a degree that makes the required licensing transaction unlikely, due to the nature of the use or of the types of works or other subject matter concerned, and shall ensure that such licensing mechanism safeguards the legitimate interests of rightholders.

"3. For the purposes of paragraph 1, Member States shall provide for the following safeguards:

(c) the collective management organisation is, on the basis of its mandates, sufficiently representative of rightholders in the relevant type of works or other subject matter and of the rights which are the subject of the licence, for the relevant Member State;

(d) all rightholders are guaranteed equal treatment, including in relation to the terms of the licence;

(e) rightholders who have not authorised the organisation granting the licence may at any time easily and effectively exclude their works or other subject matter from the licensing mechanism established in accordance with this Article; and

(f) appropriate publicity measures are taken, starting from a reasonable period before the works or other subject matter are used under the licence, to inform rightholders about the ability of the collective management organisation to license works or other subject matter, about the licensing taking place in accordance with this Article and about the options available to rightholders as referred to in point (c). Publicity measures shall be effective without the need to inform each rightholder individually."

Subparagraph (d) is important from the viewpoint of the applicability of extended collective management, in particular in those cases where it is newly introduced – like in the case of authorizing the use of out-of-commerce works. It is important because it has determined the information requirement of the procedure of "opt-out" in a reasonable way. It guarantees that the fulfillment of this requirement do not get into conflict with the objective and the very the raison d'être of such a system.

Recital (41) of the Digital Single Market Directive underlines the need for flexibility in this respect:

"[A]ppropriate publicity measures might need to be taken on a case-by-case basis in order to increase the awareness in that regard of the rightholders concerned, for example through the use of additional channels of communication to reach a wider public. *The necessity*, the nature and the geographic scope *of the additional publicity measures should depend on the characteristics of the relevant out-of-commerce works or other subject matter, the terms of the licences or the type of use under the exception or limitation, and the existing practices in Member States. Publicity measures should be effective without the need to inform each rightholder individually.*" [Emphasis added.]

It is submitted that the more fully the other requirements of an appropriate extended collective management system are fulfilled the less relevant the role of publicity may become. First of all, if such a system is only applied "where obtaining authorisations from rightholders on an individual basis is typically onerous and impractical to a degree that makes the required licensing transaction unlikely, due to the nature of the use or of the types of works or other subject matter concerned" (as provided in Article 12(1) of the Directive), the need for "opt-out" does not truly emerge. It may hardly does because the individual exercise of the right to be made possible by means of an "opt-out" would be "by definition" so impractical and onerous that it would be unlikely. Second, if the CMO fulfills the requirements of both Article 12 of the Digital Single Market Directive and of the provisions on good governance of the CM Directive, it guarantees that non-members enjoy equal treatment, that due efforts are taken (a kind of "diligent search") to identify and locate unknown and/or non-locatable rightholders, and that the remuneration due to the known and located rightholders are transferred to them. What kind of "publicity" could be more adequate on the (unattractive and, from the viewpoint of the genuine interests of the rightholders, undesirable) possibility of "opt-out" than the transfer of remuneration to such rightholders accompanied with a standard note drawing attention to the possibility of "opt-out" (as indicated on the website on the CMO)?

EXTENDED AND MANDATORY COLLECTIVE MANAGEMENT IN THEORY AND PRACTICE

Johan Axhamn*

1 Introduction

Throughout its history, the protection of copyright has been adapted to new technological challenges. This includes, for example, the advent of the radio, cinematography, the gramophone, satellite broadcasting, etc. The adjustment of copyright protection in relation to these technological advancements has often resulted in expansion of copyright, for example by a broadening of the scope of exclusive economic rights, and the introduction of neighboring or related[1] rights. Even the introduction of the three-step test in the Berne Convention at the Stockholm Conference for the revision of the Berne Convention in 1967 could be understood as an expression of safeguarding rightholders' interests: The three-step test served the purpose of providing limits on the possibility of Contracting Parties to introduce exceptions or limitations to the right of reproduction, which was introduced in the Convention for the first time at the Stockholm conference.

The expansion of copyright is reflected in the many revisions of the Berne Convention[2] and the establishment of conventions on the protection of neighboring rights, such as the Rome Convention[3]. The last, major, update to the international framework with the purpose of strengthening copyright was carried out in 1996 with the adoption of the WIPO Internet Treaties – the WIPO Copyright Treaty[4] and the WIPO Performances and Phonograms Treaty[5]. The treaties were adopted against the backdrop of the so called WIPO Digital Agenda, with the purpose of updating the international

* Senior Lecturer in Business Law, Department of Business Law, Lund University School of Economics and Management.

1 In the purpose of streamlining the language, this article will hereafter only refer to "neighboring" rights.

2 Berne Convention for the Protection of Literary and Artistic Works of September 9, 1886, completed at Paris on May 4, 1896; revised at Berlin on November 13, 1908; completed at Berne on March 20, 1914; revised at Rome on June 2, 1928; at Brussels on June 26, 1948; at Stockholm on July 14, 1967; and at Paris on July 24, 1971, and amended on September 28, 1979.

3 Rome Convention for the Protection of Performers, Producers of Phonograms and Broadcasting Organizations, done at Rome on October 26, 1961.

4 The WIPO Copyright Treaty (WCT), adopted in Geneva on December 20, 1996. The WCT is a special agreement under the Berne Convention which deals with the protection of works and the rights of their authors in the digital environment.

5 WIPO Performances and Phonograms Treaty (WPPT), adopted in Geneva on December 20, 1996. The WIPO Performances and Phonograms Treaty (WPPT) deals with the rights of two kinds of beneficiaries, particularly in the digital environment: (i) performers (actors, singers, musicians,

copyright framework to the development of the digital technology. It was not possible to reach global consensus on updates to the existing main international conventions in the field, the Berne Convention and the Rome Convention. Hence two adjacent conventions were introduced. In addition to this, the Beijing Treaty on Audiovisual Performances[6] was adopted in 2012.

There is however no doubt that the internet and online services has evolved in a different and encompassing direction than what was supposed when the WIPO Internet Treaties were adopted. Digital technology has established countless new ways to create, adapt and disseminate content, and new business models have emerged. Innovative services for the provision of, for example, music and film have surfaced. Traditional players such as newspapers are present also online, and novels are often made available also in e-book format and as audiobooks. In many instances, the online service or business has become the main or primary business, whereas the traditional (analogue) business model has become secondary.

At the same time, the technological developments have led to challenges with increased piracy in the online environment. Almost at the push of a button, it has become possible for individuals to share content with each other without permission or on the basis of an exception or limitation to copyright protection or other support in law. Examples include online filesharing or streaming services and social media were content is uploaded or shared with other internet users without the permission from rightholders.

The new possibilities and challenges for copyright, posed by the digital environment, has led to demands for further updates to the copyright framework. Put simply, the demands have been twofold and contradictory. On the one hand, representatives of rightholders have requested further expansion of the copyright framework, including clarifications on copyright liability and improved (or more “effective” and “dissuasive”[7]) enforcement measures and remedies. Conversely, representatives of internet users and online platforms and other intermediaries have argued that copyright needs to be adjusted to better consider the realities of the online environment. This adjustment, it is argued, should focus more attention to exceptions[8] and limitations to copyright.

Numerous copyright scholars have been active in these discussions on copyright policy. The increased political awareness of copyright protection is also reflected in the establishment of the Pirate Party which at present has a seat in the European Parliament.

In the view of this author, the discussions on copyright have been based on a somewhat binary (or simplified) perspective on alternative mechanisms for solving some

etc.); and (ii) producers of phonograms (persons or legal entities that take the initiative and have the responsibility for the fixation of sounds).

6 Beijing Treaty on Audiovisual Performances, adopted by the Diplomatic Conference on the Protection of Audiovisual Performances in Beijing, on June 24, 2012.

7 See Directive 2004/48/EC of the European Parliament and of the Council of 29 April 2004 on the enforcement of intellectual property rights, article 3(2).

8 In the purpose of streamlining the language, this article will hereafter only refer to “limitations”.

of the challenges to copyright indicated above. This contribution, which is based on the author's presentation at the 2019 ALAI Congress in Prague, is focused on an alternative mechanism, adjacent to limitations to copyright – namely collective management of rights. The purpose is to describe and analyze mechanisms of extended and mandatory collective management of copyright in theory and practice, with a focus on the online environment, and relate these mechanisms to limitations.

The article is structured as follows. Section 2 will provide a general overview of different legal bases for providing access to copyright protected content, including individual rights management, collective rights management and limitations. Section 3 will describe and analyse some relevant provisions in the EU directive on collective management of copyright (CRM Directive). Section 4 will focus on a case from the CJEU, the Soulier and Doke case, which gave rise to some concerns related to mechanisms on collective rights management on a national level. Section 5 describes and analyses two articles on collective management on the EU directive on copyright in the digital single market. Section 6 discusses whether and to what extent collective licensing supported by legislation could provide a solution to the licensing requirements set out in Article 17 of the DSM Directive. Section 7 includes a discussion with some final conclusions.

2 Legal bases for use of copyright protected content

The main rule in copyright is exclusivity, or in other words that copyright is a right of a preventive nature. This is expressed in international[9] and regional[10] instruments on copyright, as well as in national legislation. In addition, a starting point is that copyright is (in the main) to be managed or exercised individually.

In many situations it is possible for authors to manage their rights individually. This is, for example, the case when it comes to publishing agreements, i.e. a contract between a publisher and an author to publish original content by the author.[11] Individual management of rights is also common in the audiovisual (movie) sector. In these instances, the individual authors etc. enter into agreements covering transfers of rights to the publisher or the film producer, against payment of royalties and/or a lump sum.

Areas of copyright where individual management is prevalent is often referred to as primary markets or primary uses. For example, the primary market for a publishing agreement is to publish the book, and the primary market for a movie is often to screen the movie in theatres.

9 See, for example, article 9(1) of the Berne Convention, and article 8 WCT.

10 See, for example, articles 2 and 3 of Directive 2001/29/EC of the European Parliament and of the Council of 22 May 2001 on the harmonisation of certain aspects of copyright and related rights in the information society.

11 This may involve a single written work, or a series of works.

Other uses have traditionally been referred to as secondary markets or uses. This includes, for example, photocopying of a book or making a movie available via DVD for sale or rental. The secondary uses have some features in common. It is often difficult or even impossible for an author to manage his or her rights individually in relation to the users. The secondary uses often involve many works, i.e. secondary uses often comprise so called mass use situations. It is not always possible to know beforehand which works are going to be used, and the transaction costs for individual permissions between individual authors and the users would be unproportionate if not overwhelming.

The presence of secondary uses has led to the establishment of collective management and collective management organisations (CMOs). By acting as intermediators, these organisations attract individual authors and other right holders as members or represented rightholders and are thereby able to provide a license covering many authors and other rightholders in a specific area. For secondary uses, users often prefer to enter into an agreement with an organization that represents many authors in the relevant field, for example musical works. Thus, via one agreement, the user can use many works in the relevant field.[12]

In addition to granting of licences to users, collective management of rights include auditing of users, monitoring of the use of rights, enforcement of copyright and realted rights, collection of rights revenue derived from the exploitation of rights and the distribution of the amounts due to rightholders. Collective management organisations thus enable rightholders to be remunerated for uses which they would not be in a position to control or enforce themselves.[13] Thus, from an economic perspective, the CMOs solve a transaction cost problem. CMOs often enter into reciprocal representation agreements with similar organisations in other countries. Via such collaboration, the CMOs are able to represent not only the rights belonging to authors based on their own territory, but also rightholders based in other countries. In practice, the CMOs have developed beyond being mere economic intermediators to organisations that also provide services to their members and improve cultural diversity.

As not all rightholders are members or have signed up to a CMO, some countries have chosen to introduce legislative support for the inclusion of such "outsiders' rights"

12 See, for example, recital 45 to the DSM Directive. The recital holds that given the nature of some uses, together with the usually large amount of works or other subject matter involved, the transaction cost of individual rights clearance with every rightholder concerned is prohibitively high. As a result, it is unlikely that, without effective collective licensing mechanisms, all the transactions in the areas concerned that are required to enable the use of such works or other subject matter would take place. Extended collective licensing by collective management organisations and similar mechanisms can make it possible to conclude agreements in those areas where collective licensing based on an authorisation by rightholders does not provide an exhaustive solution for covering all works or other subject matter to be used. Such mechanisms complement collective management of rights based on individual authorisation by rightholders, by providing full legal certainty to users in certain cases. At the same time, they provide an opportunity to rightholders to benefit from the legitimate use of their works.

13 Recital 2 to the CRM Directive.

in the collective management. Examples of such support is the so called extended collective licensing (ECL) model, as developed in the Nordic countries from the 1960s and onwards.[14] Another example is so called mandatory collective management of rights.

A provision on ECL establishes that the effects of a freely negotiated collective agreement between a user of a work and a representative CMO pertaining to specific forms of exploitation of works is extended to right holders who are not members of the organization. The agreement which is given the "extended" effect is referred to as an ECL agreement. Once an ECL agreement has been concluded, the user may use the works covered by the agreement and does not run the risk of getting a claim, either legal or financial, from a non-represented right holder ("outsiders"). A user who enters into an ECL agreement with a representative organization is thus assured that the organization will meet all claims from those affected by the extension. To safeguard their interests, the non-represented right holders have a right to individual remuneration and in most cases, a right to opt out of the agreement. In addition the requirement of representativeness of the eligible CMO gives the model legitimacy as a means of managing outsider's right.

Mandatory collective management of rights means that a right cannot be managed individually, but only via a collective management organisation. This is the case with, for example, the cable retransmission right which in the European Union is subject to so-called mandatory collective management.

Arrangements on extended collective licensing has traditionally been deemed not to constitute limitations to copyright: the right as such is intact, it is only managed in a specific way. This view is also reflected in recital 18 to Directive 2001/29/EC, which holds that "[t]his Directive is without prejudice to the arrangements in the Member States concerning the management of rights such as extended collective licences." This recital has been deemed to be very important for the "safeguarding" of national arrangement on, for example, extended collective licensing, as article 5 of Directive 2001/29/EC includes a closed list of permitted limitations. Recital 18 was inserted into the preamble at the request of Sweden during the negotiations on the directive, and similar recitals have later on been set out also in other, subsequent directives.

Sometimes, provisions on collective management of rights are combined with a remuneration right or a compulsory license. Examples include for example, the resale right, the private copying levy and the right related to extended term of protection of performers' rights.

Over time, areas considered as secondary markets have increased. In addition to reprography and rental and lending, areas of secondary uses also include the market for radio broadcasting of music. Countries with a tradition of extended collective management of rights or mandatory collective management of rights have traditionally responded to the development of new markets for secondary uses by introducing new rules on extended or mandatory collective licensing.

[14] See, for example, Study on emerging issues on collective licensing practices in the digital environment, Final Report (2021). The author of this article contributed to the Study, as an expert for Sweden.

The advent of the internet gave rise to the question of whether the new technology would lead to increased individual or collective management. Some scholars argued that the technology would make it possible for authors to manage their rights individually to a greater extent. It was, for example, submitted that the right of making available (on demand) – which was introduced on the international level with the WIPO Internet Treaties – would pave the way for individual management of rights to a greater extent. The development and potential of technological protection measures and electronic rights information, also protected by the WIPO Internet Treaties,[15] were held to stimulate increased individual management of rights.

However, the market seems to have development in a different direction. The fact that individual authors are able to reach out to a wider audience via the internet, has in general not had the effect of increased individual management. It is still not practicable for authors to manage their rights individually, and in many instances the users – often large, commercial online platforms – prefer standardized and streamlined collective licenses provided by CMOs. Thus, the development of online services has in many instances had the effect that the demand for collective management of rights has increased for online uses.

It has been submitted that the lack of possibility to manage rights individually online, should lead to the introduction of more limitations to meet the demand of (legal) access to copyright protected content online. Examples of suggestions include replacing the exclusive rights with a broad limitation permitting individual users to share content with other internet users online.

However, and at the same time, it has been recognized that the three-step test, puts limits on the possibility to introduce such broad limitations to copyright. In short, it is not permissible in relation to the Berne Convention and the WCT to introduce such broad limitations.

Given that many types of uses on the internet are not possible to make "legal" on the basis of individual management of rights or the introduction of exceptions and limitations to such rights, the question has been raised whether it is possible to meet the demand by stimulating collective rights management. This is stressed, for example, in recital 46 to the recently adopted EU DSM Directive[16]:

"Given the increasing importance of the ability to offer flexible licensing schemes in the digital age, and the increasing use of such schemes, Member States should be able to provide for licensing mechanisms which permit collective management organisations to conclude licences, on a voluntary basis, irrespective of whether all rightholders have authorised the organisation concerned to do so. Member States should have the ability to maintain and introduce such mechanisms in accordance with their national traditions, practices or circumstances, subject to the safeguards

15 WCT, articles 11 and 12.

16 Directive (EU) 2019/790 of the European Parliament and of the Council of 17 April 2019 on copyright and related rights in the Digital Single Market and amending Directives 96/9/EC and 2001/29/EC, OJ L 130, 17.5.2019, p. 92–125.

provided for in this Directive and in compliance with Union law and the international obligations of the Union."

Increased dependence on collective rights management however requires that the CMOs are well functioning and meet high standards of good governance and transparency. Within the EU, a major step towards better collective management of rights was taken with the adoption of CRM Directive.[17]

3 EU Directive on collective management of copyright and related rights

A proposal for a directive on collective management was put forward by the European Commission in July 2012.[18] While some of the previous EU directives in the field of copyright contained references to the collective management of rights, none of them addressed the modus operandi of the organizations as such.[19] After negotiations in the Council and the Parliament, and after an agreement was reached between these institutions (and the European Commission), the final text of the CRM Directive was adopted in February 2014.

The Directive lays down requirements necessary to ensure the proper functioning of the management of copyright and related rights by collective management organisations. It also lays down requirements for multi-territorial licensing by collective management organisations of authors' rights in musical works for online use.[20] The Directive is fairly detailed; it contains 45 articles, supplemented by 58 recitals. The articles are separated into 5 titles: Title I on General provisions (articles 1-3), Title II on Collective management organisations (articles 4-22), and Title III on Multi-territorial licensing of online rights in musical works by collective management organisations (Articles 23-32), Title IV on Enforcement measures (articles 33-38), and Title V on Reporting and final provisions (articles 39-45). Title II includes the general provisions on good governance and transparency. It is divided into 5 chapters on Representation

17 OJ L 84, 20.3.2014, p. 72–98. The author represented (the Government of) Sweden in the negotiations on this Directive, in the Council Working Party on Copyright.

18 Proposal for a Directive of the European Parliament and of the Council on collective management of copyright and related rights and multi-territorial licensing of rights in musical works for online uses in the internal market, COM/2012/0372 final – 2012/0180 (COD).

19 In addition, Commission Recommendation 2005/737/EC on the collective cross-border management of copyright and related rights for legitimate online music services invited Member States to promote a regulatory environment suited to the management of copyright and related rights for the provision of legitimate online music services and to improve the governance and transparency standards of collecting societies. Being a Recommendation, it was non-binding and its voluntary implementation was deemed unsatisfactory. See section 1.3. in the Explanatory Memorandum in the Commission's Proposal for a CRM Directive. See also the CRM Directive, recital 6. The CRM Directive complements other relevant directives, such as Directive 2006/123/EC of 12 December 2006 on services in the internal market, OJ L 376, 27.12.2006, p. 36–68. CMOs are subject to Directive 2006/123/EC as providers of collective management services.

20 CRM Directive, Article 1.

of rightholders and membership and organisation of collective management organisations, Management of rights revenue, Management of rights on behalf of other collective management organisations, Relations with users, and Transparency and reporting.

However, while the CRM Directive sets out requirements on the activities of CMOs, it does not regulate the mechanisms under which a CMOs manages rights, i.e. whether it is a license or some other mechanism. This follows already from the definition of CMO in article 3(a) of the Directive:

"'Collective management organization' means any organization which is authorized by law or by way of assignment, licence or any other contractual arrangement to manage copyright or rights related to copyright on behalf of more than one rightholder, for the collective benefit of those rightholders, as its sole or main purpose, and which fulfils one or both of the following criteria: (i) it is owned or controlled by its members; (ii) it is organized on a not-for-profit basis."

Recitals in the preamble to the Directive also stress that CMOs may base their authorization on different mechanisms, either contractual or set out in legislation. One effect of this is that the directive, in line with previous directives on copyright, does not interfere with arrangements in the Member States concerning the management of rights, such as extended collective licences.[21] Another effect of this broad definition of CMO is that the CRM directive is applicable to all types of collective management of rights, irrespective of whether it relates to exclusive rights, compulsory licenses or rights of remuneration. At the same time, rightholders shall have the right to freely choose the collecting society for the management of their rights, provided the collecting society already manages such rights or categories of rights.[22]

That the CRM Directive was not supposed to have an impact on the ways in which CMOs base their authorization, either contractual or set out in legislation, was stressed by several Member States in connection with the implementation of the directive. During the implementation of the CRM Directive, it was also highlighted that the definition of CMO in article 3(a) does not cover all organizations that manage rights collectively. The reference in article 3(a) to "to manage copyright or rights related to copyright on behalf of more than one rightholder … *as its sole or main purpose*" (my emphasis) was deemed to exclude organisations that do not have "colletive management of rights" as its sole or main purpose. This could include, for example, labor unions and similar organizations that have other "main" activities than managing rights.[23]

Another aspect that was highlighted during the implementation of the CRM Directive was that in some cases, the activities of collective management – such as negotiating, licensing, collecting remuneration etc. – may be divided between different organizations. In some instances, some aspects of collective management are carried out by an organization that is partly or wholly owned or controlled by other

21 CRM Directive, recital 12.

22 CRM Directive, article 5 and recital 9.

23 See also Study on emerging issues on collective licensing practices in the digital environment, Final Report (2021). The author of this article contributed to the Study, as an expert for Sweden.

organizations. To some extent, this situation is taken care of by article 2(3) of the Directive which holds that

"The relevant provisions of this Directive apply to entities directly or indirectly owned or controlled, wholly or in part, by a collective management organization, provided that such entities carry out an activity which, if carried out by the collective management organization, would be subject to the provisions of this Directive."

However, there could still be situations where activities of collective management are carried out by an organization which in itself does not fulfill the requirements of being a collective management organization, and where article 2(3) does not become applicable as the organization is owned or controlled by organizations that do not fulfill the requirement of being CMOs either. It thus seems as if the CRM Directive, either by mistake or by purpose, has left some collective management of rights outside of its scope.

In summary, although the CRM Directive takes aim at collective management of copyright and related rights, the strict scope of the directive is activities of CMOs. In other words, the directive regulates specific activities of CMOs (and organizations owned or controlled by CMOs), but not collective management as such. To the extent that collective management is carried out by organizations that do not fulfill the conditions for being a CMO in article 3(a) of the directive, or by an organization owned or controlled by a CMO according to article 2(3), that collective management is not subject to the rules set out in the directive.

That the scope of the CRM Directive is limited in this way, was deemed advantageous by some Member States that rely on collective management of rights as a mechanism to allow supply to meet demand, and where some collective management is carried out by organizations that do not fulfill the requirement of being CMOs in article 3(a) of the CRM Directive. This was deemed beneficial especially in situations where the collective management was based on extended collective licensing.

New challenges for the ECL model however arose with a case before the CJEU – the Soulier and Doke case.

4 The Soulier and Doke case

In November 2016, the CJEU handed down its judgement in Case C-301/15, Soulier and Doke.[24] The case concerned a request for a preliminary ruling on the interpretation of Articles 2, 3 and 5 of Directive 2001/29/EC. The request was made in the course of proceedings between, on the one hand, Mr Marc Soulier and Ms Sara Doke and, on the other, the Prime Minister of France and the French Minister for Culture and Communication concerning the legality of a French legislation relating to the digital exploitation

[24] Case C-301/15, Soulier and Doke. ECLI:EU:C:2016:878.

of out-of-print 20th century books.[25] The French legislation created a presumption of representation for a CMO when entering into agreements covering the said use.

Before national courts, Mr Soulier and Ms Doke, who were both authors of literary works, had requested that the national legislation should be annulled. In support of their claim, the authors submitted that the legislation established an exception or a limitation to the exclusive reproduction right laid down in Article 2(a) of Directive 2001/29 and that that exception or limitation is not included among those listed exhaustively in Article 5 thereof.

The French legislation is based on a similar, however not identical, mechanism as arrangements on extended collective licensing. Depending on the outcome of the case, the judgment could thus have posed challenges to such arrangements.

In its judgement, the CJEU stressed that Article 2(a) and Article 3(a) of Directive 2001/29/EC must be interpreted as precluding national legislation, such as that at issue in the main proceedings, that gives an approved collecting society the right to authorize the reproduction and communication to the public in digital form of "out-of-print" books, while allowing the authors of those books, or their successors in title, to oppose or put an end to that practice, on the conditions that that legislation lays down. The court stressed that Article 2(a) and 3(a) of Directive 2001/29 protects both the enjoyment and exercise of the rights. They are rights of a preventive nature, requiring prior consent of the rightholder.

The Court stressed that Article 2(a) and Article 3(1) do not specify the way in which the prior consent of the author must be expressed: (i) No requirement of such consent to be expressed explicitly, (ii) those provisions also allow that consent to be expressed implicitly. However, according to the Court, the circumstances in which implicit consent can be admitted must be strictly defined in order not to deprive of effect the very principle of the authors prior consent. In particular, every author must actually be informed of the future use of his work by a third party and the means at his disposal to prohibit it if he so wishes.[26]

Failing any actual prior information relating to that future use, the author is unable to adopt a position on it and, therefore, to prohibit it, if necessary, so that the very existence of his implicit consent appears purely hypothetical in that regard. Consequently, without guarantees ensuring that authors are actually informed as to the envisaged use of their works and the means at their disposal to prohibit id, it is de facto impossible for them to adopt any position whatsoever as to such use.[27]

It does not follow from the decision to refer that that legislation offers a mechanism ensuring authors are actually and individually informed. Therefore, it is not inconceivable that some of the authors concerned are not, in reality, even aware of the envisaged use of their works and, therefore, that they are not able to adopt a position,

---

[25] Décret n° 2013-182, du 27 février 2013, portant application des articles L. 134-1 à L. 134-9 du code de la propriété intellectuelle et relatif à l'exploitation numérique des livres indisponibles du XXème siècle.

[26] Case C-301/15, Soulier and Doke, paras 37 and 38.

[27] Case C-301/15, Soulier and Doke, paras 39 and 40.

one way or the other, on it. In those circumstances, a mere lack of opposition on their part cannot be regarded as the expression of their implicit consent to that use.[28]

The Court also emphasized that Article 5 of Directive 2001/29/EC sets out an exhaustive list of permitted limitations. The French legislation did not fall within the list.

In summary, the CJEU held that Article 2(a) and Article 3(1) of Directive 2001/29/EC precludes national legislation, such as that at issue in the main proceedings, that gives an approved collecting society the right to authorise the reproduction and communication to the public in digital form of 'out-of-print' books, while allowing the authors of those books, or their successors in title, to oppose or put an end to that practice, on the conditions that that legislation lays down.

Although the Soulier and Doke case did not deal explicitly with arrangements on extended collective licensing, it was recognized in legal scholarship that the French legislation had similarities with the Nordic model, and that the outcome of the case thus posed challenges to the Nordic model. It was somewhat surprising that the recitals often put forward by the Nordic legislators as the "safeguard" of the ECL model – e.g. recital 18 to Directive 2001/29/EC – was not mentioned at all in the case. This was interpreted by some legal scholars and other commentators in two different ways. One interpretation was the French legislation at hand in the Soulier and Doke case was fundamentally different in nature from the Nordic ECL model. Another interpretation was that the Court implied that the recital, by not being part of the operative part of the directive, was not to be emphasized. Especially the second interpretation gave rise to some concerns, and this led to efforts to clarify the acceptance or compatibility of rules on extended collective licensing in relation to EU copyright norms. Negotiators from the Nordic countries made an effort to include such a clarification in the DSM Directive, which had been proposed by the European Commission just a few weeks before the judgment was handed down in the Soulier and Doke case.

5 Provisions on collective licensing with an extended effect in the DSM Directive

The adopted text of the DSM Directive includes two provisions that take aim at collective licensing with and extended effect: Article 8 on Use of out-of-commerce works and other subject matter by cultural heritage institutions, and Article 12 on Collective licensing with an extended effect. The proposal[29] by the European Commission however included only an article on the first matter (Article 7 in the Proposal). Article 12 of the Directive was brought forward by Sweden during the negotiations, together with some other Member States, as a response to the judgement in the Soulier and Doke case and the uncertainty it posed in relation to the Nordic ECL model.

28 Case C-301/15, Soulier and Doke, para 43.

29 Proposal for a Directive of the European Parliament and of the Council on copyright in the Digital Single Market, COM/2016/0593 final – 2016/0280 (COD).

5.1 Article 8 on use of out-of-commerce works and other subject matter by cultural heritage institutions

Article 8 sets out obligations on member states to provide for provisions on collective management of rights for use of out-of-commerce works and other subject matter by cultural heritage institutions. The Member States have flexibility in choosing the specific type of licensing mechanism, such as extended collective licensing or presumptions of representation, that they put in place.[30] The purpose of Article 8 is to provide cultural heritage institutions with a clear framework for the digitisation and dissemination of works or other subject matter that are considered to be out of commerce.[31]

The mechanism set out in article 8 is without prejudice to the use of such works or other subject matter under exceptions or limitations provided for in Union law, or under other licences with an extended effect, where such licensing is not based on the out-of-commerce status of the covered works or other subject matter.[32]

Article 8 is combined with some safeguards, such as the possibility to opt out and the right to obtain equitable remuneration.[33] In cases where there are no licenses available, Member States shall provide for the possibility to use the works on the basis of an exception or limitation.[34] There are also safeguards related to types of works and other subject matter; works that have their original outside of the EU are as a rule not covered by the provision.[35]

The licensing mechanism set out in Article 8 takes aim at licenses provided by "collective management organisations". The notion of "collective management organisation" is however not defined in the DSM directive, but in line with the CJEUs method of interpretation, this notion should be given the same meaning as article 3(a) of the CRM Directive (see above).[36] This is also implied in recital 34 to the Directive.[37]

Article 9 provides for a cross-border effect, Article 10 provides for publicity measures,[38] and Article 11 provides for a stakeholder dialogue.[39]

---

30 See DSM Directive, recital 33.

31 See DMS Directive, recital 30 and recital 31.

32 See DMS Directive, recital 43.

33 See also DSM Directive, recital 35.

34 See also DSM Directive, recital 32.

35 See also DSM Directive, recital 39.

36 On coherency and unity in EU intellectual property law, and the tendency of the court to establish "autonomous" concepts, see, for example, Striving for Coherence in EU Intellectual Property Law: A Question of Methodology, in Liber Amicorum Jan Rosén, eddy.se, 2016, p. 35-60.

37 According to recital 34 of the DSM Directive, "for the purpose of those licensing mechanisms" [as referred to in Article 8], "a rigorous and well-functioning collective management system is important. Directive 2014/26/EU provides for such a system and that system includes in particular rules on good governance, transparency and reporting, as well as the regular, diligent and accurate distribution and payment of amounts due to individual rightholders."

38 See also DSM Directive, recital 40 and recital 41.

39 See also DSM Directive, recital 42.

5.2 Article 12

Article 12 is more general than article 8. It is provided with the heading "Collective licensing with an extended effect" and the heading of the chapter in which the article (which is the only article in the chapter) is set out is "Measures to facilitate collective licensing". Whereas Article 8 is mandatory for the Member States, Article 12 is a voluntary ("may") provision.

As mentioned above, Article 12 was not included in the Commission's initial proposal. The article is the result of efforts by Sweden and some other Member States during the negotiations. The purpose of the article is to safeguard national mechanisms on extended collective licensing, inter alia against the backdrop of the judgement in the Soulier and Doke case.

It is stressed in recital 44 to the Directive that systems built on mechanisms such as extended collective licensing, legal mandates or presumptions of representation, are a well-established practice in several Member States and can be used in different areas. It is further held that a functioning copyright framework that works for all parties requires the availability of proportionate, legal mechanisms for the licensing of works or other subject matter. Against this backdrop, recital 44 holds that Member States therefore should be able to rely on solutions allowing collective management organisations to offer licences covering a potentially large number of works or other subject matter for certain types of use.

Article 12(1) holds that Member States may provide that where a CMO, in accordance with its mandates from rightholders, enters into a licensing agreement for the exploitation of works or other subject matter, such an agreement can be extended to apply to the rights of rightholders who have not authorised that CMO to represent them, or that the organisation has a legal mandate or is presumed to represent rightholders who have not authorised the organisation accordingly. In the following, I will refer only to "extended effect", although the use of this expression here is intended to also cover the other mechanisms referred to in article 12(1) – "legal mandate" and "presumption of representation".

A prerequisite for article 12 to apply is that the relevant organisation is a "collective management organisation" (CMO) that is subject to the national rules implementing the CRM Directive. As mentioned above, the definition of a CMO in article 3(a) does not include organisations that manage rights collectively but have another activity as their main purpose, such as (labour) union activities.

Another important prerequisite for the extended effect to come about according to article 12(1) is that the CMO is "representative". This requirement is explained in article 12(3)(a), where it is held that "the collective management organisation is, on the basis of its mandates, sufficiently representative of rightholders in the relevant type of works or other subject matter and of the rights which are the subject of the licence, for the relevant Member State." The requirement of representativeness is further elaborated on in recital 48 to the Directive, where it is held that Member

States should determine the requirements to be satisfied for those organisations to be considered sufficiently representative, taking into account the category of rights managed by the organisation, the ability of the organisation to manage the rights effectively, the creative sector in which it operates, and whether the organisation covers a significant number of rightholders in the relevant type of works or other subject matter who have given a mandate allowing the licensing of the relevant type of use, in accordance with the CRM Directive.

The requirement of representativeness in article 12 is similar to existing requirements on representativeness in Sweden and the other Nordic countries, where this requirement is deemed to bring legitimacy to the ECL model. The argument is that licensing conditions that are accepted and have been approved by the members or rightholders represented by the organisation, should as a starting point be acceptable also for rightholders whose rights are covered by the extended effect.

For the extended effect or legal presumption to apply, certain additional safeguards need to be in place. Rightholders whose rights are covered by the extended effect may at any time easily and effectively exclude their works or other subject matter from the licensing mechanism ("opt out") (article 12.3.c)[40] and all rightholders are to be treated equally, including in relation to the terms of the licence (article 12.3.b).[41]

In addition, Member States shall make sure that appropriate publicity measures are taken to inform rightholders about the ability of the CMO to license works or other subject matter, about the licensing taking place in accordance with article 12 and about the options available to rightholders to opt out.[42] Such publicity measures shall be effective without the need to inform each rightholder individually (article 12(3)(d)). It is further held in recital 48 to the Directive that publicity measures should be effective throughout the duration of the licence and should not involve imposing a disproportionate administrative burden on users, CMOs or rightholders. This obligation to inform builds on similar (but more far reaching) obligations to inform, following from the CJEU judgment in the Soulier and Doke case.

The possibility to introduce provisions in national legislation on extended effect based in article 12(1) is not unrestricted. An important requirement is set out in article 12(2), where it is held that Member States shall ensure that the licensing mechanism referred to in article 12(1) is only applied within well-defined areas of use, where obtaining authorisations from rightholders on an individual basis is typically onerous and impractical to a degree that makes the required licensing transaction unlikely, due to the nature of the use or of the types of works or other subject matter concerned.[43] It is also held that Member States shall ensure that such licensing mechanism safeguards the legitimate interests of rightholders. Article 12(2) thus limits the possibility for Member States to introduce provisions on ECL to situations where individual licensing or collective licensing based on individual authorisation (mandates) is impossible or almost

40 See also DSM Directive, recital 48.

41 See also DSM Directive, recital 47.

42 See also DSM Directive, recital 48.

43 See also DSM Directive, recital 49.

impossible. i.e. situations that can be described as market failure.[44] This requirement, together with the reference to the importance of safeguarding the legitimate interests of rightholders, can be understood as inexplicit references to the second ("do not conflict with a normal exploitation of the work") and third step ("do not unreasonably prejudice the legitimate interests of the right holder") of the three-step test.[45]

However, the fact that article 12(2) does not explicitly relate the mechanism of ECL to the three-step test, means that the DSM directive does not take a clear stance on an aspect that has been widely discussed in the literature: whether mechanisms of ECL are limitations to copyright protection, or whether they are (merely) "arrangements concerning the management of rights" (as indicated in recital 18 to directive 2001/29/EC). That article 12(2) does not provide a clear answer to this question is further complicated by the wording of article 12(4), where it is held that article 12 "does not affect the application of collective licensing mechanisms with an extended effect in accordance with other provisions of Union law, including provisions that allow exceptions or limitations". The references in article 12(4), combined with the fact that article 12(1) is a "may" provision, means that it is unclear to what extent article 12 harmonises existing regimes of ECL in the Member States (which I believe is the intention) or whether it provides an additional option for Member States (to introduce or shape such regimes).[46]

As mentioned above, it is common in some Member States, for example Sweden, that collective management is carried out by organisations that are not to be considered as "collective management organisations" and they would thus fall outside the scope of harmonisation set out in article 12.

6 Collective licensing – a potential solution to article 17 of the DSM Directive?

As further described in the introduction to this contribution, the challenges posed by the digital technology has led to contradictory demands on how to adjust, or update, the copyright framework. The most recent update to the copyright framework within the EU is the DSM Directive. In addition to the provisions mentioned above on collective licensing (articles 8 and 12), the directive includes provisions on, inter alia, limitations for text and data mining (articles 3-7), provisions on the protection of press publications concerning online uses (article 15) and provisions on fair remuneration in exploitation contracts of authors and performers (articles 18 to 23).

Maybe the most contentious provision in the directive is Article 17 on the use of protected content by online content-sharing service providers.[47] Simply put, the

44 See also DSM Directive, recitals 45 and 47.

45 See also DSM Directive, recital 47.

46 See also DSM Directive, recital 46.

47 Article 17 is based on article 13 in the Commission's proposal.

Article holds that when the services of an online content-sharing service provider, i.e. and online platform for social media or similar service, are used by internet users to upload images, sounds, videos and other material which infringes copyright, the intermediary may under certain conditions be considered (directly) liable for those infringements. This article has been extensively discussed by legal scholars, but simply put, these paragraphs hold that if intermediaries cannot (or do not) obtain licences for the legal provision of the material, they must take certain steps to ensure that infringing material is not made available.

A fundamental criticism directed against Article 17 concerns the obligation on the intermediary to enter into licensing agreements with rightholders to avoid liability for infringement. It has been submitted that, in practice, it can be difficult for the intermediary to obtain licenses that cover all the material that is made available via the platform. It is at the same time clear that the Directive highlights the need for flexible and broad licensing solutions for the material present on the platforms. The licensing mechanisms envisioned in Article 12 may provide effective and balanced solutions to some of the licensing challenges that Article 17 raises, which rightholders, intermediaries and the public (internet users) can benefit from. Collective management, supported by legislation on extended effect or similar mechanism, can thus strike a fair balance between the different interests involved as it makes it possible to move away from binary solutions based on limitations.

7 Conclusions

Copyright protection has expanded over time, both as regards the scope of exclusive rights but also the introduction of neighboring rights. For the increased protection to have immediate value for rightholders it must be possible for them to manage their rights also for exploitations in the new technological environment. In many situations it is difficult or even impossible for rightholders to manage their rights individually in the online environment, and similarly for users – for example online platforms – to obtain necessary permissions from rightholders. An example of this is the obligations, set out in article 17 in the DSM Directive, on online platforms to obtain permissions for use of content uploaded on their services by their users.

Some scholars have argued that (the only) solutions to the challenges to copyright in the online environment are to be found in the realm om limitations. At the same time, practice has shown that many challenges to copyright related to high transaction costs in mass use situations can be solved by collective management. To provide full legal certainty to the user, collective licensing is sometimes supported by legislation on extended effect of a collective agreement or mandatory collective management. However, the viability of such mechanisms has been questioned, for example in relation to international and EU norms on copyright, such as the three-step test and the closed list of permitted limitations in article 5 of Directive 2001/29/EC.

Article 12 of the DSM Directive makes clear that mechanisms on extended collective licensing are permitted according to EU copyright norms. National implementations of Article 12 in the Member States can provide an incentive for rightholders to organize themselves in representative organizations. This could, for example, provide a solution to some of the licensing challenges posed by article 17. In such a scenario, the new rules would fulfil their (copyright) purpose of providing remuneration to rightholders when their works, etc., are used online, while the public's (legitimate) interest and demand in getting access to copyright-protected material in the online environment would be met. The rules would thus also fulfil their basic (copyright) function: to give the public access to a wide range of films, music and other copyrighted material, while providing authors and other creators with a say in the use of their works and other protected works – and to stimulate future creativity and investments in such activities. With Article 12, the gate is thus now open for solutions based on collective management as a mechanism for making copyright work in mass-use situations in the online environment, including social media.

PART III REPORTS

IMPACT OF EU POLICY ON CULTURAL DIVERSITY AND SMALL COUNTRIES

CHALLENGES OF THE EU REGULATORY FRAMEWORK OF EXTENDED COLLECTIVE MANAGEMENT FOR THE SMALL CMOS

Gábor Faludi*

Collective Management in the EU Substantive Copyright Law

Where EU substantive copyright law provides for equitable remuneration, it either restricts the exercise of the remuneration right to mandatory collective management, e.g. 2006/115/EC on public lending and rental: equitable remuneration under Art. 4(3) and (4), or 2011/77/EU on the term of protection: the assertion of annual supplementary remuneration right of performing artists under Art 2/d., or offers it as an option (2001/84/EC on resale right, Art 6. 2.: Member States may provide for mandatory or optional collective management of the royalty). The cable remuneration right is the only exclusive right, where EU law prescribes mandatory collective management [93/83/EEC, Art 9, as applied and corroborated in the Uradex preliminary ruling, C-169/05, that holds that the CMO shall exercise that rightholder's exclusive right of licensing cable retransmission and the mandate is not limited to the management of the collection of remuneration)].The mandatory collective management is extended as per the choice of the Member States to licenses granted by CMOs to program (signal) distributors to transmit directly injected broadcast programs to the subscribers under Article 8 (2) of the Broadcasting Directive (2019/789/EU on the exercise of copyright and related rights applicable to certain online transmissions of broadcasting organisations and retransmissions of television and radio programmes, and amending Council Directive 93/83/EEC).

* Associated professor at the Eötvös Lorand University Law School in Budapest; attorney at law; external counsel for Artisjus.

The Collective Management Directive

The draft CM Directive prepared by the Commission did not provide for either the extended or the mandatory collective management. The Council and the European Parliament stressed that „(…) they (the CMOs) have an important social and cultural role as promoters of the diversity of cultural expressions by enabling the smallest and less popular repertoires to access the market".

As a compromise Art.167 of the TFEU (…) was included into the preamble (3) of the CM Directive. „CMOs have and should continue to have an important role as promoters of the diversity of cultural expression, both by enabling the smallest and less popular repertoires to access the market and by providing social, cultural and educational services for the benefit of their rightholders and the public". The CM Directive seems to acknowledge, that one of the most prominent functions of both the extended as well as the mandatory collective management is to ensure cultural diversity, and legal safety of commercial users, therefore preamble (12) lays down that Member States are not precluded from maintaining extended collective management, mandatory collective management, legal presumptions of representation and transfer of rights to CMOs. The CM Directive itself does not include uniform rules on extended or collective management, and its approach is fully based on voluntary collective management, and unrestricted choice of rightholders as reflected in Art 5. It is interesting to see how the right of choice of rightholders is evaluated by the legislator: under preamble 19 „Where a Member State, in compliance with Union law and the international obligations of the Union and its Member States, provides for mandatory collective management of rights, rightholders' choice would be limited to other collective management organisations." (CMOs operate in the EEA states usually as factual monopolies…).

CM in the Digital Single Market and the Broadcasting Directives

The DSM Directive (2019/790/EU on copyright and related rights in the Digital Single Market and amending Directives 96/9/EC and 2001/29/EC) did not have an original objective to provide for either the extended or the mandatory collective management. Neither the preceding communications nor the relevant EU strategy envisaged harmonized legal provisions on these topics (Towards a modern, more European copyright framework' COM/2015/0626 final), a Digital Single Market Strategy for Europe COM(2015) 192 final – both are silent on collective management).

Due to the efforts of the Council and the European Parliament the DSM Directive contains both substantive law provisions on the exercise of extended collective management and common rules on the introduction or maintenance of extended collective management in the Member States. As to the substantive law provisions are concerned, Art 5 (2) provides for the exceptions to digital and cross-border educational exceptions that cover licences for material that is primarily intended for the educational market or for sheet music. Here the DSM Directive envisages (offers) collective or extended collective management with a view to avoid educational establishments having to negotiate individually with rightholders. Art 8 deals with the licensing of use of out of commerce works and other protected subject matter by cultural heritage institutions. Here again extended collective management is preferred, and if there is no CMO to exercise extended collective management in the licensing of cultural heritage institutions, an exception applies for the benefit of the institutions. The license granted by the relevant CMOs may have legal effect in all Member States depending on the level of representativity of the given CMO. Here the question arises, whether the licensing of the communication to the public by online content sharing platforms – this is a per se multi-territorial use – can be made via extended collective management? Outside the scope of licensing of cultural heritage institutions the extended license may only have a domestic territorial scope.)

Under Art 12 and preambles 44-50 of the DSM Directive extended collective management can be introduced (maintained)

- in well-defined areas of use, where individual licensing is typically onerous and impractical to a degree that makes the required licensing transaction unlikely, due to the nature of the use or of the types of works or other subject matter concerned if,
- due safeguards of the legitimate interests of rightholders are ensured, and
- the extended license may authorize domestic use only.

The collective management is extended, if the license of the relevant CMO is extended to apply to the rights of rightholders who have not authorised the CMO in any transactional way or the CMO has a statutory mandate or is presumed to represent the said rightholders.

The most important safeguard is the right of withdrawal of the rightholder represented under the extension of the representation right. The withdrawal shall be easy and effective, the right may be exercised either before or after the conclusion of a license agreement concluded by the CMO or after the beginning of the use concerned, and either in general or in specific cases. In the event of the lawful exercise of the withdrawal right any ongoing uses licensed by the CMO are to be terminated within a reasonable period. All rightholders represented under the extended scheme shall be guaranteed equal treatment.

The chart below goes to show the comparison between the requirements of the exercise of the withdrawal right in the voluntary and the extended collective management:

Voluntary CM (under the CM Directive)	Extended CM (under the CDSM Directive)
– per category of rights / types of work – upon serving reasonable notice not exceeding six months. – the withdrawal may take effect at the end of the financial year.	– easy and effective – after the conclusion of a license or – after the beginning of the use concerned – either in general or in specific cases (per works/per usages) – any ongoing uses are terminated within a reasonable period... – (Soulier and Doke, C-301/15)

One can conclude that the withdrawal rules of the DSM Directive offer incentives to the rightholders to terminate the contractual affiliation with their CMO to facilitate their individual exercise of right. Was it a genuine purpose of the legislator? Hardly ever...

As to the easy and effective withdrawal is concerned issues may arise in practice.

Are the following rules/acts barriers of the easy and effective exercise of the withdrawal, right?

- the law requires the declaration of withdrawal to be made in a deed of full probative value,
- in the event of split copyright of a musical work with lyrics a previous warning given by the CMO to the composer, that the lyricist's and/or the publishers' license represented by the CMO are also required to grant a full and valid license to use the musical work?
- the requirement made by a CMO to certify the full title chain in the event an assignee (any derivative rightholder) wishes to exercise the right of withdrawal?
- the expression of the legal position of a CMO that it regards the withdrawal right as a right attached to the person of the rightholder, therefore no person other than the rightholder may exercise the withdrawal right.

One will hopefully find the answers to these questions in the prospective judicial practice. In the view of the speaker all these acts/rules are by far justified and may not be regarded as unfounded barriers of the exercise of the withdrawal right.

INDEPENDENT MANAGEMENT ENTITY ON THE EXAMPLE OF SOUNDREEF

Massimo Scialò*

Soundreef Ltd, an independent management body listed in the public register of the Intellectual Property Office of the United Kingdom, Greece, Spain and Portugal, manages the royalties of tens of thousands of authors and publishers worldwide. Soundreef is absolutely enthusiastic to be in a context like ALAI Congress, gathering CMOs defining themselves as sisters.

Soundreef's vision has not changed ever since the company started taking its first steps as a tech start-up: simplicity, speed, and transparency in the distribution as key and essential elements, so that the greatest possible level of protection can be guaranteed to authors, composers and publishers. These values are already widely shared and implemented by most of the CMOs, which have been acting in the best interest of right holders for much longer than Soundreef.

What makes Soundreef's path different is the choice to put technology at the service of its purposes, right from the very first steps of the business. This choice is reflected primarily in the composition of the professionals working at Soundreef. In fact, in Soundreef technical roles are pivotal, with internal and dedicated development teams. In this sector, engineers have the most important role, they are the key. Engineering is the first element to understand how to get money from a broadcaster to an author / publisher in the shortest time possible and as accurately as possible. The engineers, the tech part, must be at the core of the architecture.

Thanks to its tech team, Soundreef can implement an internal monitoring of radio, TV and online uses. Soundreef collects and processes the reports directly from its monitoring; then, it compares them with those sent by both DSPs and broadcasters, national and international. It is precisely this crossmatch between reports that guarantees greater transparency in the calculation and allows the company to proactively intervene in the event of a discrepancy. Additional advantages come from this kind of approach: authors and publishers, for example, can have access to detailed, and always free, statistics through their accounts – available in real time for radio and TV, and monthly for YouTube.

Also worth mentioning is the level of detail that Soundreef reporting is able to offer: for each reported radio / TV spin, authors and publishers can see the title of the track, the station on which it was used, the name of the show, the time (accurate to the minute) and the amount accrued.

* International Sales Director at Soundreef.

Going back to the topic of the use of technology and its related clear advantages, mention should be made of payment timings for authors and publishers receiving royalties they have accrued. Soundreef manages to guarantee a quarterly payment through its collection process, made easier by the technology used. Therefore, Soundreef aims to report the usage on a daily basis, in fact technology allows so and right holders deserve it. So, it is evident how embracing a natural technological evolution can positively impact an entire industry, raising the general quality of the services offered.

When describing the structure and composition of the company, it is also important to mention our customer service dedicated to rightholders, a department of great importance in all management societies. Being aware of the peculiarity and sensitivity of copyright topics, even for authors themselves, Soundreef has again chosen to streamline processes and make them more efficient, building a network of professionals who follow each case from start to finish, thus guaranteeing continuity in assistance.

Beyond the approach that Soundreef follows and continues to pursue, there are also central topics for the entire industry.

First and foremost the universe of online uses, which includes both streaming platforms (among the most well-known digital service providers: Spotify, YouTube, Apple Music) and video on demand platforms (Netflix, Amazon Prime, etc.).

The process of digitalization of the music, started with the advent of mp3 files and arrived at the numerous platforms available today, has brought a revolution in the way listeners engage with the music, a way which has undoubtedly become easier and more accessible. However, even though the online sector currently plays an economically predominant role within the entire recording chain, a clear regulation and a proper remuneration of the author's right by the DSPs still appear to be distant.

The issue is well known, and was also raised by famous international artists who have often expressed their dissent towards the applied remuneration policies. Still, some streaming giants demean the role of the author's right with unfair commercial practices and do not disclose publicly the methods and fees applied for the distribution, with insufficient and inadequate remunerations, especially considering the role that these platforms fulfil.

The discussion can also be referred to the "video on demand" platforms, which are globally widespread by now. Also in this case, the current conditions are absolutely disadvantageous for the authors, also with respect to the ability of these platforms to report the spins in a precise and analytical way. Some of these platforms are involved in the "buy out" practice thus depriving authors and composers of the songs of their copyright.

Once again, Soundreef believes that only from the dialogue and the cooperation between all the CMOs and the independent management entities, shared and effective solutions to face common problems might arise.

Another particularly important topic is that of the territorial usages, which reports too often arrive at the CMOs with altered, incomplete and uncertain data. Within these contexts, users often paid little attention and education to the topic, so authors and publishers' representatives have the task of pushing users to report usages efficiently and safely by treating these reports with the same diligence and caution that would be used in processing financial data between banks and insurance companies. At the same time it is important to propose continuous innovation aimed at the analytical recovery of all information about the usage from all market segments.

If today Soundreef's reporting allows authors, composers and publishers to know even the minute and the second in which their piece has been used, then it is clear that it is possible to take important steps forward with respect to the transparency and fairness of the royalties' distribution still respecting the analytical distribution criterion as much as possible. This event is a precious opportunity for all the CMOs, which herein have the chance to interact and build a dialogue with each other. Exactly with the aim of building a fruitful and uplifting dialogue, which allows a real communication between the parties, Soundreef wants to highlight how its role is to be considered anything but antagonistic.

In fact the evolution of our company has been possible only thanks to the work previously done by the other CMOs and to the experiences they gained over time. If Soundreef exists today – and exists in this specific form – it is because much has been done before its coming. Within this perspective, Soundreef is anything but an opponent: it is rather the result of a natural technological development to which, in part, all the entities here have contributed.

In Soundreef's vision, the exchange of ideas, insights and ideas about technology are the necessary lifeblood for the progress of an entire sector: looking at oneself, comparing oneself and improving oneself is certainly useful and effective. Most of the CMOs share the same mission: to set as the main objective of their activity the protection of the interests of Authors, Composers and Publishers. In this context, therefore, a closer collaboration between all the companies committed to managing and collecting the rights of their members becomes necessary.

Finally, looking at the future of the company, Soundreef aims to be welcomed soon into CISAC (International Confederation of Societies of Authors and Composers).[1]

1 Soundreef has been admitted in CISAC from the 17th of December 2020.

SPÉCIFICITÉS DES ARTS VISUELS DANS LA GESTION COLLECTIVE DES DROITS D'AUTEUR

Marie-Anne Ferry-Fall*

1 Les missions de l'ADAGP

L'ADAGP (organisme de gestion collective pour les arts visuels) a été créée en 1953, à l'initiative d'artistes et a rapidement accueilli dans ses rangs les plus grands créateurs de l'époque (Georges Braque, Bernard Buffet, Marc Chagall, Léonard Foujita, Pierre Soulages, Joan Miró, Zao Wou Ki, etc.). L'ADAGP est gérée par les artistes. Les adhérents (artistes, auteurs, ayants droit, cessionnaires) en contrôlent la gestion et élisent le conseil d'administration qui décide des orientations stratégiques de la société.

Grâce à la richesse de son répertoire et à son réseau mondial de 50 sociétés sœurs, l'ADAGP est la plus importante société d'auteurs des arts visuels au monde et représente aujourd'hui près de 200 000 artistes dans plus de 40 disciplines : affichistes, architectes, artistes d'art urbain, auteurs de bandes dessinées, calligraphes, céramistes, décorateurs, designers, dessinateurs, dinandiers, graffeurs, graveurs, illustrateurs jeunesse, mangakas, mosaïstes, orfèvres, peintres, photographes, plasticiens, sculpteurs, tapissiers, verriers, vidéastes...

La mission première de l'ADAGP est la perception et la répartition des droits d'auteur, c'est-à-dire collecter la rémunération des artistes et la leur reverser, que ce soit des droits primaires (droit de suite, droit de reproduction et droit de représentation) ou collectifs (rémunération pour copie privée, reprographie, etc.).

L'ADAGP encadre l'utilisation des œuvres pour tous les modes d'exploitation (éditions de livre, publications dans la presse papier ou en ligne, publicités, produits dérivés, expositions, ventes aux enchères et en galeries, diffusions à la télévision ou en vidéo à la demande, utilisations sur des sites Internet, etc.) et facture les montants correspondants. L'ADAGP a passé près de 200 conventions avec la plupart des musées, FRAC, centres d'art, de nombreux organes de presse (papier et internet), des contrats généraux avec 275 chaînes audiovisuelles, ainsi qu'avec des sites Internet afin de faciliter et fluidifier les relations avec ces utilisateurs réguliers d'œuvres des arts visuels.

---

* General Director ADAGP.

1.1 Présence dans les instances internationales

L'ADAGP déploie également ses compétences et son expertise au service de la défense du droit d'auteur et des arts visuels. Siégeant au sein de plusieurs institutions internationales de la propriété intellectuelle, tels que la CISAC (Confédération internationale des sociétés d'auteurs et compositeurs), le CNPAV (Conseil National des Professions des Arts Visuels), le CSPLA (Conseil Supérieur de la Propriété Littéraire et Artistique), EVA (European Visual Artists), le GESAC (Groupement Européen des Sociétés d'Auteurs et Compositeurs), l'OMPI (Organisation Mondiale de la Propriété Intellectuelle), elle intervient ainsi régulièrement en France et à l'étranger sur les enjeux actuels tels que le partage de la valeur sur internet, l'universalité du droit de suite ou le respect du droit d'exposition.

2 Spécificités des arts visuel

En matière de gestion de droits collectifs, les arts visuels regroupent un répertoire très spécifique. Cela tient à la fois à la nature des œuvres d'art visuel, à leurs usages, aux droits qui en découlent.

2.1 Spécificité lié à la nature des œuvres des arts visuels

En effet, le répertoire des arts visuels est immense : à titre d'exemple, un peintre produira tout au long de sa carrière une moyenne de 5 000 œuvres. Nombre de photographes produisent plus de 1 000 œuvres au cours d'un seul mois. On estime ainsi que le répertoire de l'ADAGP (200 000 auteurs) représente un corpus compris entre 500 millions et 1 milliard d'œuvres.

Autre spécificité due à la nature des œuvres d'arts visuels, ce répertoire est bien souvent mal documenté. Beaucoup d'artistes ne tiennent pas de documentation à jour de leurs créations, n'ont constitué aucunes archives, et une part non négligeable d'œuvres reste sans titre et non documentée.

Contrairement à d'autres secteurs de la création artistique (comme la musique, la production audiovisuelle, le livre), le secteur des arts visuels n'est pas structuré en industrie créative, où des opérateurs dans leurs domaines de diffusion agrègent les données des œuvres.

2.2 Spécificité des usages

Une autre spécificité des arts visuels réside dans ses usages : les photographies d'art sont littéralement partout : dans les livres, dans la presse, sur les sites internet culturels, sur les réseaux sociaux, sur les produits dérivés (vêtements, objets, accessoires de mode, merchandising divers, ...). Mais aussi dans la rue, dans l'espace public, dans les transports en commun, dans des films, dans des documentaires... Le terrain est immense.

D'autant plus que ces images d'art sont fréquemment incorporées à d'autres œuvres (livres, films, etc.). Cela rend l'identification des œuvres originelles compliquée et cela requiert une vigilance constante. De fait, cela peut provoquer des difficultés, c'est-à-dire le non-respect des droits d'auteur des artistes visuels, quand une législation ne prend pas en compte cette particularité dans la loi.

2.3 Spécificité des droits

La dernière spécificité notable est celle des droits liés aux œuvres des arts visuels. Le droit le plus spécifique pour les artistes d'arts visuels, et sans doute l'un des plus importants, est le *droit de suite*. Né en 1920 en France, le droit de suite est la rémunération dont bénéficient les auteurs d'œuvres originales graphiques et plastiques lors des reventes de leurs œuvres au cours desquelles intervient un professionnel du marché de l'art. C'est le seul droit optionnel dans la Convention de Berne pour la protection des œuvres littéraires et artistiques (1886).

Globalement, les arts visuels sont les créations les plus affectées par les exceptions aux droits d'auteur, leur exclusion de la protection ou tout simplement *l'inapplication de certains droits*, à l'instar du droit d'exposition, très peu respecté en France comme à l'étranger.

Le respect de l'œuvre est une notion fondamentale pour les artistes des arts visuels. Cela requiert un haut degré d'individualisation dans la gestion des droits de chaque artiste : le cas par cas est bien souvent la règle.

Enfin, les arts visuels ont un lien très étroit avec le marché de l'art, où le sujet des faux et de la contrefaçon oblige à une surveillance constante. Le marché de l'art a ainsi sa propre logique et ses propres spécificités de fonctionnement.

3 Points communs avec les autres secteurs

Au-delà de toutes les spécificités des arts visuels à prendre en compte pour la gestion des droits collectifs des artistes-auteurs, des points communs existent dans la gestion des droits collectifs.

Ainsi, l'ADAGP a conclu des contrats généraux regroupant l'ensemble des répertoires (musique, audiovisuel, image) avec chacun des diffuseurs, services VOD, plateformes de contenus générés par les utilisateurs (CGU), sites de musées, presse spécialisés, etc. La part attribuée aux auteurs d'images a été négociée dans ces accords.

En France, la loi a instauré la gestion collective de certains droits d'auteur (rémunération pour copie privée, reprographie, droit de prêt, etc.). Cette gestion collective est régie par des règles très précises de répartition et se fonde sur plusieurs paramètres de données tels que le volume de facturation des droits primaires et les déclarations des auteurs entre autres.

La gestion des droits collectifs s'appuie également sur des outils technologiques. L'un des meilleurs exemples est sans doute AIR (Automated Image Recognition). En partenariat avec la CISAC, l'ADAGP développe AIR depuis plusieurs années. Cet outil de traçabilité des œuvres dans l'environnement numérique utilise la technologie des empreintes numériques afin de reconnaitre, d'extraire et de filtrer les images recherchées sur les sites internet, la presse en ligne, les ouvrages en PDF et, à terme, dans les vidéos et sur les réseaux sociaux.

Plus de 900 000 images (en 2021) servent actuellement dans cette base de données.

4 Les «Règles de Rio»: un très haut niveau d'individualisation de la gestion des droits

Cette individualisation est inhérente au respect des «Règles de Rio» adoptées en 2011 par la CISAC sous l'égide du CIAGP, et précisées en 2017.

Ces règles stipulent ainsi que :

(a) The societies emphasise that they always respect the moral rights of their members. The societies confirm that they do not authorize any distortion, mutilation or other modification of the work likely to infringe the author's moral rights without the members' prior permission.

(b) Regarding uses of works predominantly focusing on one author, highly commercial uses of works, and unconventional uses of works, societies are required to duly seek prior permission from the member before licensing the rights in question, in particular for the uses listed below:
   i. monographic uses (including books, films, etc);
   ii. use of a large number of works by one author;
   iii. advertising uses;
   iv. merchandising uses;
   v. cover uses (including for books, magazines, CDs, DVDs, etc).

(c) It follows, that, the societies are entitled to grant licences based on applicable tariffs, without seeking the members' prior permission, in particular with regard to:
   i. cultural uses;
   ii. educational uses;

iii. non-monographic uses;
iv. press and television uses.

(d) To ensure that the system of reciprocal representation of collective societies is not undermined and to ensure that the system is applied in a uniform manner – in the interests of all rightsholders the following rules for dealing with members are to be observed:
   i. Direct licensing: Subject to relevant laws in particular regarding non-commercial uses, members shall not circumvent the collective societies by authorising users directly.
   ii. Retroactive waivers: Members shall not grant fee waivers in particular with retroactive effect where societies have already engaged with the user to negotiate a licence.
   iii. Notification requirement: In any case, members shall notify their collective society upon reasonable notice in circumstances where they decide to license uses directly and/or free of charge.

Le but de ces règles est d'harmoniser au niveau international le fonctionnement du réseau des organismes de gestion collective. Il s'agit de trouver le juste équilibre entre la gestion individuelle des droits avec validation des ayants-droits et les processus de gestion collective permettant aux utilisateurs de bénéficier d'une grande fluidité dans les authorisations d'exploitations.

5 Parmi les défis de l'ADAGP : Focus sur la directive européenne sur le droit d'auteur et son application en France (2019-2021)

La réforme du droit d'auteur en Europe a mobilisé les équipes et les artistes de l'ADAGP depuis 2015. Après plusieurs années d'engagement en faveur de la Directive Européenne sur les droits d'auteur, ces efforts ont porté leurs fruits avec l'adoption de la Directive en avril 2019 qui doit permettre de renforcer la protection et la rémunération des artistes-auteurs.

Les efforts de l'ADAGP ont ensuite porté sur la transposition de la Directive dans la loi française, un processus législatif et parlementaire long, complexe et essentiel pour respecter l'esprit de la directive européenne. En France, le projet de loi « relatif à la communication audiovisuelle et à la souveraineté culturelle à l'ère numérique » a transposé certaines dispositions de la directive européenne d'avril 2019. Initialement prévue pour être examinée en mars 2020 par les parlementaires, ce texte de loi a été débattu durant l'année 2021, et les décrets d'application, ne sont, à ce jour, pas encore parus.

L'article 17 de cette directive rend les plates formes de partage d'œuvres en ligne (Facebook, Instagram, Twitter, etc.) responsables des contenus postés par leurs utilisateurs et les oblige à respecter les droits des auteurs, soit en passant des contrats avec les organismes de gestion collective, soit en retirant les œuvres dont la diffusion n'est pas autorisée.

L'ADAGP demeure particulièrement vigilante concernant la transposition de cette directive dans chaque pays de l'Union, actuellement en cours. Cette transposition doit prendre en compte les caractéristiques spécifiques de chaque secteur du droit d'auteur.

L'article 15 de la directive, qui encadre les droits voisins des éditeurs et des agences de presse, a été l'objet d'une loi française très précoce entrée en application en octobre 2019. Elle prévoit que les services en ligne qui partagent des articles de presse, y compris partiellement, sont tenus de reverser aux éditeurs de presse une rémunération au titre d'un nouveau droit voisin, distinct du droit d'auteur. Une part de cette rémunération doit être partagée avec les auteurs des textes, des photographies et des autres catégories d'œuvres incorporées dans les publications de presse. La loi prévoit expressément que les auteurs d'œuvres figurant dans ces publications peuvent bénéficier d'une part de ces rémunérations.

L'ADAGP est attentive à ce que le droit voisin n'affecte par les droits des auteurs, et que les législations nationales en Europe assurent une juste rémunération aux artistes.

L'article 12 de la directive institue la possibilité de recourir à des licences collectives étendues. Ces dernières pourront être utilisées pour appréhender des utilisations massives d'œuvres (plateformes de partage, usages pédagogiques, illustrations contenues dans des articles de chercheurs, etc.).

L'ADAGP a démarré les discussions avec les acteurs technologiques concernés par ces textes pour conclure des accords aux fins de perception de droits d'auteur pour les utilisations des œuvres de son répertoire.

Par ailleurs, il faut signaler un accord de partenariat signé entre l'ADAGP, la SAIF et Google en juin 2021. D'une durée de 10 ans, cet accord est destiné à soutenir et à rémunérer les auteurs des arts visuels dans le contexte du numérique.

VOLUNTARY LICENSING OF TEXT BASED WORKS IN THE UNITED STATES: COPYRIGHT CLEARANCE CENTER

Frederic Haber*

1 Introduction – Making Copyright Work

Discussion of the collective management of copyrights usually focuses on the collective management of copyrights in musical works because of (i) the broad attraction, and very public performance, of music across the world, (ii) the frequency with which collective licenses for such uses are required – traditionally for live and broadcast performance and today for streaming as well – and (iii) the general decision that seems to have been made in that industry early in its history that, outside of a few high-profile circumstances, each musical work could be treated as equal in value to each other musical work before being multiplied by the number of copies or exposures for purposes of calculating royalties either collected from users or distributed to rightsholders. All of that makes a lot of the process of collective licensing more straightforward.

I do not presume to understand the music licensing industry and the many, many choices that rightsholders and users have made there. And I do not propose that my brief comments above take into account what I am sure is a substantial amount of nuance in the music licensing environment that is invisible to the outsider. Rather, they are the impressions of someone outside that industry but inside the world of collective management of copyrights.

The collective management of text reproduction rights – that is, the rights to use and share copyrighted text materials for the internal purposes of the user organization through e-mail, digital postings, certain other uses, and even the old standby of photocopying – proceeds from different sets of market facts and assumptions than those in music. And, while the worldwide collective licensing market for text rights is smaller than that for music performance rights, royalties from such collective licenses for text still exceed US$1 billion every year.

What are such collective licenses for? An ALAI conference room full of lawyers and other voracious readers, writers and users of copyrighted works makes these kinds of reproduction and sharing uses of research materials simply by dint of what

* Vice President and General Counsel of Copyright Clearance Center, Inc. (Danvers, Massachusetts, USA). CCC and its subsidiary RightsDirect B.V. (Amsterdam, NL) provide collective repertory and individualized pay-per-use copyright licensing services, as well as rights and content management and workflow services and technology tools, to copyright rightsholders and users.

we do for a living, and regardless of whether we work for a business organization or an academic institution or a government agency or even for ourselves in a group setting. There is a very wide variety of text-based materials that we need to use in our everyday business or research lives, many different ways in which we use and share those materials, and sometimes very large variations in "value" between individual works, whether determined by price or otherwise (reputation, "loss leaders" to sell something else, etc.). All of those variables bring a set of complications to collective management of text-based works that I posit are largely absent from the most prominent collective-licensing spaces for music.

Those ALAI attendees who need licenses for at least some portion of their reproduction and sharing of text works – and they know who they are – are, I'm sure, fully licensed, either directly or through their employers. Individual licenses for this kind of use are available from the copyright rightsholders or their representatives virtually everywhere in the world. Licenses are also available on a collective basis in many countries, whether through traditional CMOs – in the text-licensing world called Reproduction Rights Organizations or RROs (betraying their origins in photocopy licensing) – or through other kinds of collectives, whether the rights they administer are collected from rightsholders by agreement or are governed by some form of statutory license.

Copyright Clearance Center, the main RRO in the United States, is not a traditional RRO in the European sense but, rather, operates on an entirely voluntary basis solely through contracts with rightsholders or their representatives on one side and with user organizations on the other side. CCC is not alone in the world as an entirely-voluntary collective, but it is by far the largest at least in the text-rights space. And what CCC has learned in more than 40 years of operation is that the main principle underlying voluntary copyright licensing is that the licensing organization has to find ways to *make copyright work*; it has to work for all participants in the market, whether the holders of rights in copyrighted works or those who want to use the copyrighted works of others; and making copyright work is about saying *yes*. That is, saying *yes* to content users who want an easy way to share published information while respecting copyright... and also saying *yes* to copyright rightsholders who want to control how their works can be used and at what price... and, as CCC sought to grow its business over time, also saying *yes* to both copyright rightsholders and content users who ask for alternative models, or supplements, to the traditional collective license and who ask "can you help us help ourselves?"

2 Voluntary Collective Licensing Requires a Commercial Approach

At its essence, voluntary, opt-in, non-exclusive collective licensing is a concept built on understanding and compromise, and it is driven by the customers and "customers" means *both* the rightsholders *and* the users who participate in the licensing system. Voluntary licenses have to be marketed and actively *sold* to both rightsholders and users because they are not imposed by law, or even favored by the law, at least in the United States. This requires a more commercial approach, including adapting technology and service structures to attract the customers, and as necessary adding rights and types of uses to those covered by the license.

This more commercial approach requires at least two conditions that are not always natural to CMOs. In order to accomplish active participation by large numbers of both rightsholders and users, but while still occupying the legal role of licensing agent for rightsholders, CCC recognized at its founding that making copyright work requires *balance*. Balance means that in a market where rightsholders like authors, other creators and publishers co-exist with users of copyrighted content, all of them have to be satisfied – or at least satisfied *enough* – to participate and make collective licensing possible.

A second necessary condition to making copyright work in a voluntary collective licensing model is that the CMO must *understand*. That is, it is necessary for the CMO – in the text case, the RRO – to understand the limits of rightsholders' willingness to participate in a collective effort when they can perceive all kinds of benefits to going it alone in the marketplace, and to also understand the limits of users' willingness to pay for the privilege of respecting copyright in a context where the use is integral to the user's own business needs and almost none of the use is publicly visible (or publicly audible, as in most music performance).

But to accomplish that balance and to display understanding (and to continue delivering rights to users and royalties to rightsholders), it is necessary for a voluntary collective organization to regularly come up with new ideas, new products and new services to support the market, and to introduce those products and services to participants who might not have known they were interested in them until they heard about them. In short, to make copyright work, even for a not-for-profit organization like CCC (and maybe especially for a not-for-profit organization), a completely commercial approach is required. This approach supplements the basic case CCC makes to rightsholders and users all the time: that participating in collective licensing is a way of doing the right thing – on the one side, making your rights available for users to use your works and, on the other side, paying for the right to use others' copyrighted materials because that use benefits you – and then it seeks to extend the basic case by developing ways to keep all those participants within the system.

3 Unique Issues Facing Collective Licensing of Text in the U.S.

The text licensing environment for business markets presents a handful of relatively unique and difficult issues, particularly in the USA.

First, of course, is the uniquely complicated issue of fair use which faces copyright holders in the USA (and is too often considered for implementation in the law, out of all cultural context, in other countries as well). Despite what some would like to believe, a claim of fair use does not automatically grant a user free use in any individual circumstance; rather, evaluating that claim always requires application of the famous four-factor balancing test that attempts to take into consideration both the rightsholder's statutory rights and the reasonable activities and expectations of users in the American system. Hundreds of judges in copyright cases, and many, many thousands of lawyers and businesspeople, both in litigation and in making business decisions, try to apply that balancing test every year. A reasoned application of the balancing test means that similar-looking uses may result in different fair use assessments because of specific differences in the circumstances of each use. Application of this balancing test to uses of copyrighted text in the U.S. largely (though not entirely) replaces application of the much more common lists of limitations and exceptions that are found in the laws of most other countries (and, in a small way, in the laws of the U.S. as well).

Fair use presents a particular problem for text licensing because, unlike other copyrighted works, text is most frequently reused for reproduction and distribution *in portions*. So, in addition to the issues that might face practitioners assessing fair use in the music-performace licensing space, text almost always presents the issue of whether a particular reproduction or other use of a paragraph, or a page, or a chapter, is "too much" to qualify as a fair use and, again, what is "too much" must be evaluated in the particular circumstances.

A second difficult issue facing a collective license for use of text is finding and collecting the necessary rights for that license when it is clear that reproduction of text focuses not on the most popular books but primarily on relatively low-distribution science, technical and medical (STM) professional, and news content, because that is the content most likely to be reproduced and distributed within a research-and-development-oriented organization. Thus, because the STM and news publishing industries are focused on collective works and works in which the publisher routinely has the responsibility (subject to its own contractual obligations) to manage reproduction and distribution rights, those are the rightsholders with whom CCC deals most frequently. That said, CCC invites participation from any rightsholder – including an author or other creator – who holds the necessary rights to authorize CCC to do its licensing. Many authors (and their representatives, including agents and estates) have signed standard CCC contracts, participate in its systems as the equals of all other rightsholders, and receive royalties directly when usage-data collection indicates that their works have been used by licensees.

A third difficulty facing establishment of a collective licensing service in the United States for the reuse of text was the reality that, given the U.S. business environment, there was no, and still is no – and could be no – statutory support, or even favourable statutory treatment as exists in some other countries, for a license covering reproduction and distribution uses that would inevitably include some that might qualify as fair uses.

Fourth – unlike in the music field – both customer constituencies are relatively unconcentrated from an economic point of view and very widespread. That is, there are no users in the market for collective licensing of internal uses of text that are the equivalents of large broadcasters, cablecasters or streaming services, and there is no rightsholders in that market quite like the worldwide labels that dominate music distribution and management.

And finally, in the United States neither rightsholders nor users are organized around these issues. The trade associations which founded CCC represent even today only about 300 publishers and about 8000 authors out of the hundreds of thousands that exist in the United States. At the same time, there was, and is, no association representing users generally; instead, a few large users who cared about copyright contributed to CCC's founding and today even fewer are willing to advocate publicly for CCC's systems. And yet today CCC's completely voluntary business-market licenses include rights to reuse tens of millions of works from hundreds of thousands of rightsholders and are issued to companies representing more than 35 million employees in literally every industry.

4 Practical Responses to Those Unique Issues

In light of the above issues, since CCC's beginning it has been necessary (and it continues to be necessary today) to focus on practicality in order to accomplish successful entirely-voluntary licensing services that are attractive to all participants, at least for the text-based community in the United States. And CCC has done this step by step.

First, unlike virtually every other RRO in the world, CCC chose to start by focusing on the business market. Under fair use principles in the United States, the business market is where the law is most likely to insist that fair use is limited and that users must pay for most uses of copyrighted materials. And, in the United States (with a highly decentralized higher-education academic community that must raise its own funds and is perennially underfunded), the business market is, as they say, where the money is.

More importantly in CCC's experience, most business organizations that rely heavily on published scientific, technical, medical or business materials to drive their own research and development are prepared to pay for the privilege of using them, largely because their own businesses depend on the protection of intellectual property. They are therefore prepared to recognize their own obligation to respect others' intellectual property too. Finally, CCC discovered that, as a general matter, very many businesses are willing to pay for the privilege of using others' intellectual property if the process is not made too difficult. As a result, CCC has been selling licenses to businesses since 1978 in a marketplace where there are *no* requirements that either rightsholders *or* users must participate.

Licensing academic users on a similar annual basis – the bread-and-butter of virtually every other RRO in the world – came to CCC only later and has been less well-accepted not only by users in the U.S., as might be expected in light of fair use, but by some rightsholders as well.

Second, in order to serve the business market CCC recognized that the repertory provided had to be the one that business users use – science, technical and medical materials, trade press and general and business periodicals, and the general press. And the law in the United States provided no head start – without contracts from rightsholders, CCC had no rights to license-out. So, CCC spent years soliciting the participation of rightsholders, and then signing contracts with rightsholders, and then promoting, selling, signing and renewing licenses with users, a process that continues without cease every day.

Third, as noted above, the repertory license for businesses needed to be built on compromise and could not focus on the needs and desires of rightsholders to the exclusion of the needs and desires of users, even though CCC acts as the contracted licensing agent of those rightsholders. So CCC had to convince rightsholders to authorize certain uses they might not otherwise authorize – and then had to convince user companies to accept certain restrictions they would otherwise hope to avoid. That is, rightsholders had to agree to offer rights extending beyond any that might be considered fair use, and users had to acknowledge that those additional rights – beyond any reasonable conception of fair use – were worth paying for. This was a key compromise that allowed the license to be successful.

Fourth, based on close communicawtion with buyers, CCC has evolved the standard license over time to meet their needs with the participation and agreement of the rightsholders who receive the royalties. CCC's license is voluntary and non-exclusive, and virtually every rightsholder exercises his or her right to license individually in parallel to all of CCC's offerings. But, from the user's point of view, the CCC license contains a standard set of terms and conditions that helps to smooth out the variations in the thousands of individual licenses that are available from rightsholders by offering a collective floor of rights. Further, with the evolution of technology and the way in which users use copyrighted works, users made clear to CCC that they wanted more than the bare minimum; as a result, CCC has returned to the rightsholders to evolve the licenses to keep them attractive and sale-able to users prepared to buy. CCC has done that several times. For example, around the year 2000, the core business license was adapted to add digital uses to the original photocopy rights. As another example, around 2012, CCC went back to the rightsholders to obtain the authorization to include in that license a limited right to deliver individual copies outside the licensee to the licensee's customers.

As the license was sold to companies in the U.S., it was reaching more and more companies with employees outside the country. So CCC obtained the authorization to expand the license to cover these employees and, when companies headquartered outside the U.S. started contacting CCC for licenses of the breadth and depth they could not find elsewhere, CCC set out to meet that need too, offering licenses from its headquarters in the U.S. But it quickly became clear to CCC that those non-U.S. customers had different needs and wanted closer relationships with CCC. Thus, in the early 2010s, CCC established a sales subsidiary called RightsDirect with a tiny handful of sales staff located in Europe and Japan. Both user companies and rightsholders and their content were crossing oceans and borders, and so CCC and its licenses followed. That said, however, CCC's approach has been to collaborate with local partners wherever possible to create a license that would meet local market demand and so, for example in Germany, CCC formed a partnership with the local RRO, VG Wort. VG Wort and CCC combined their repertories of works and rights to jointly offer a digital copyright license to German companies and their global subsidiaries.

Fifth, by the time the basic license had been extended in these ways, both rightsholders and users were asking CCC to build on its skills and licenses to offer more. Its variety of pay-per-use and collective license services, all built with the cooperation of rightsholders and input from users, are flexible solutions that support the principles of copyright and simplify compliance. But CCC needed to do more to help preserve, protect and promote copyright as a concept, and to encourage users as well as rightsholders to continue to participate in licenses.

5 Recent Developments Support Voluntary Collective Licensing in New Ways

To that end, the company moved in several directions simultaneously: First, at the specific request of some large users, CCC partnered with rightsholder representatives in other media – specifically, television and motion pictures, and music – to offer its licensee base some additional rights that were desirable for internal uses. CCC also acquired from text rightsholders the rights to deliver content (in the form of copies of articles) to make the licensed rights more valuable. Finally, and in what has turned out to be the most valuable addition, CCC has developed technology, services and software (i) to facilitate direct online licensing by publishers (RightsLink for Permissions), (ii) to facilitate authors' submissions of articles to publishers to support the new Open Access publishing model for science and medicine (RightsLink for Scientific Communications), (iii) to make license and content management easier on the user side (the RightFind suite of services), and (iv) to build internal consulting skills and resources that can be offered to customers to help them derive the maximum benefit from CCC's software and services as well as from the content that forms the core of its licenses.

These technology developments benefit both of CCC's customer groups: participating rightsholders have obtained new ways to easily acquire, manage and convey rights both outside and inside CCC's traditional licenses, and interested users have obtained software and services that help them to more easily understand what licensed rights they possess to use content they have acquired and to search and manage that content as required by front-line researchers. And both groups of customers have received these benefits through software and facilities that fit within their daily workflows.

In short, CCC's experience has led its staff to develop new and sometimes unexpected technology solutions to problems that both sets of customers have in copyright management and compliance. And all of this is in service of the collective licenses. By providing its customers – both rightsholders and users – with more, and more varied, services and software that are built on top of the licenses, both sides have an interest in continuing to work with CCC. That is, on one side, rightsholders see a marketplace for their secondary rights organized and administered by CCC as a professional organization dedicated to the task, but without undermining their primary subscriptions and sales. And, on the other side, users are offered an efficient, effective and easy means for complying with copyright and, through CCC's offer of supplementary tools and services, they are encouraged to stay licensed (and pay royalties).

As a result, the technology helps *make copyright work* and helps all parties say *yes* to copyright in the entirely voluntary context in which the CCC operates.

6 Conclusion

Licensing is a powerful tool for ensuring that both copyright rightsholders and users of copyrighted material can say *yes* to copyright. And voluntary non-exclusive collective licensing can be especially powerful. It is – it must be – <u>driven</u> by the market, in the sense of simultaneously serving both rightsholders and users and providing a bridge between them. And, in the same manner, it is <u>regulated</u> by the market – that is, it is regulated by rightsholders' ability to choose whether or not to participate (and by their grant of non-exclusive mandates only), and by users' ability to evaluate the licenses on offer against alternative ways to comply with the law. It does not need special government regulation and receives no special government attention. Most importantly, it strengthens respect for, and voluntary compliance with, copyright as the mechanism most countries have created to ensure the growth of culture and knowledge through appropriate rewards to rightsholders for making their works available.

And part of the operation of the market is its dictate that a successful licensing system will foster innovation – both in ways to expand the license system itself and in ways to build on that system, which today means by supplementing it with technology-driven tools for all participants. Failure to do so will either invite alternatives (which may or may not support the concept of copyright in general) or lead to stasis or collapse. In the context of text-based licensing, that imperative means that both rightsholders and CCC have had to, and must continue to, innovate to remain relevant, and that voluntary licensing – saying *yes* to copyright – is fundamental to a future where licensing is embedded in the workflow of both users and rightsholders, is made more transparent through technology, continues to balance the needs of rightsholders and users, and strengthens copyright for the next generation to say *yes* too.

DEVELOPING THE COPYRIGHT INFRASTRUCTURE – METADATA AND BEYOND

Viveca Still*

1 Why Am I Here?

To present the IP priority "Developing the Copyright Infrastructure" of Finland's presidency to the Council of the European Union, which fits neatly with the topic of this congress and links closely to the ALAI questionnaire *"Online practises of identification of authors"* that was first launched in 2016 – relaunched now.

Thanks to Fabienne Brisson at the ALAI secretariat for offering the opportunity to speak here. Let me know present the topic "Developing the Copyright Infrastructure"

Finland has a few key priorities for our Presidency:

- First and foremost, sustainability should be the common denominator for all EU action. Thus our slogan: Sustainable Europe – Sustainable Future.
- In line with the new Strategic Agenda 2019-2024, one of our Presidency priorities is to make the EU more competitive and socially inclusive – an EU IP policy that is fit for the data economy is key to sustainable growth in the single market.

2 What Do We Mean When We Talk About the Copyright Infrastructure?

In a digital world the functioning of the licensing market and the recognition of copyright needs to be adapted to the digital environment.

One of the earliest questions arising was how the 1s and 0s representing works can be distinguished from all other 1s and 0s on the networks. Hence the need to develop unique identifiers for different types of works. Other important building blocks have been various registration systems, in particular the ones managed by CMOs and rights languages enabling machine-to-machine communication. A particularly important building block is the need for complete, accurate and up-to-date metadata on works and their rightholders.

When we talk about the copyright infrastructure, we have an inclusive approach in mind;

* Counsellor at the Ministry of Education and Culture, Finland.

- Coexistence of individual licensing + collective licensing
- No single technology to be favoured
- For both professionals and non-professionals

In our mind, digitalization of the copyright system itself would at best *recognize all the rights and rightholders* of *all kinds of works* in the digital environment *with the best possible legal certainty technology can offer.*

3 What is the Issue That We Attempt to Address?

3.1 The Challenge

The challenge of copyright has always been to transmit to the users the need to request for a licence. Users know in theory that works do not come out of nowhere but have required creative input from one or more individuals that need to be compensated. But *the copyright system has never been very user-friendly.* Often the relationship between users and rightholders is only about opposite interests. As technology evolves, the expectations to be able to access data about the rightholders increases. One of the most common reasons why the rightholder needs to be reachable, is to ask for permission. Users also need to know when a license is not required, for example if the work is no longer protected, if the rightholder has permitted the work to be used freely or under certain terms or standardized licenses such as Creative Commons, or if a limitation or exception to copyright applies. As creators themselves also more frequently use works of others in particular in the form of samples or clips, the potential obstacles in clearing of rights eats the growth potential of the industry itself. It is not us versus them anymore – we are all potential creators and users of protected content.

3.2 The Benefit

The benefit of developing the copyright infrastructure is making the licensing of works more efficient, reliable, and transparent – and it will bring more revenue to all rightholders. It will boost the application of creators' moral rights too, their right to be credited. This aspect of copyright has been neglected (almost vanished) in the past ten to twenty years while the music sector has been battling with unlawful use and piracy. The economic situation is finally better, revenue levels are up. Quality metadata could improve licensing of other creative content as well, such as images, audiovisual and literary works. Therefore, we believe that now is the time to make sure that the main justification of the copyright system, the *individual behind the creation, is lifted to the core of this development.* The creator does not deserve only credit for the creative input she/he has given to a work but is also entitled to receive revenues based on the exploitation of the work.

3.3 Some Questions to be Addressed in the Discussions

- How can *interoperability* be improved (Sector-specific and proprietary systems)?
- How can comprehensive, up-to-date and verified *metadata* be ensured?
  (a) How can we ensure access to relevant data? The aim should not be to replace any actors in the market but to share data while building on the data assets available to bring growth and win-win for all.
  (b) The commonly accepted fact is, that the best use of your data will *most likely be* invented by someone else. The sharing of data is essential and it applies both ways. An efficient infrastructure needs both usage data and data on works and rightholders in order to function in a transparent manner.
- Do we need new metadata or other *standards* to facilitate transactions and communication of copyright information?
- Is there a need to develop *voluntary registration systems*? We know from the practices of CMO's that voluntary registration in fact usually is key to exercise your rights in an efficient manner. It is up for discussion whether voluntary registering of works for identification purposes should be a normal part of the creative process, and a part of the education of young creators and makers of user-generated content.[1]
- *What other elements are needed to ensure a sufficient level of trust*, which is a prerequisite for a well-functioning marketplace and copyright system?

To sum, *how can we achieve a more efficient, inclusive and trustworthy digital marketplace*, that provides a win-win-win situation, i.e. *Increased access to works for the public, efficient and easy clearance for businesses and improved revenue streams and recognition of moral rights for authors (rightholders)?*

4 How Does This Theme Relate to the Data Economy?

Already back in 2001, the legislators of the European Union encouraged the rightholders to ensure access to copyright information. According to *Recital 55 of the InfoSoc directive*: "Technological development will facilitate the distribution of works, notably on networks, and this will entail the need *for rightholders* to identify better

[1] In this context I would also like to note an ongoing process at WIPO level. Member States of WIPO were encouraged to reply to a questionnaire about voluntary registrations systems in the field of copyright but also systems that register transfer of rights and also legal deposit systems.

the work or other subject-matter, the author or any other rightholder, and *to provide information about the terms and conditions* of use of the work *in order to render easier the management of rights attached to them*. Rightholders should be encouraged to use markings indicating, in addition to the information referred to above, inter alia their authorisation when putting works or other subject-matter on networks."

Later, in 2014, the Directive on collective management of copyright mandates collective management organisations to provide sufficient information on their repertoire.

It is important to recognise that the value of the copyright data increases through new ways of using it and innovations within and outside the traditional copyright sector. At the same time, the lack of appropriate and up-to-date copyright information reduces the operative efficiency of the copyright markets and easily leads to suboptimal use of copyright protected content or even outright piracy.

The *investment* of building a system with complete, continuously updated and verified data *needs first a fact-finding mission for each creative sector*. We should know what has already been done to this effect and evaluate whether the infrastructure works properly. The industries have had the opportunity to invest in electronic rights management information for 20 years or more. So the issue is not new. However, the complexity of the copyright system and the silos in each sector serve only the internal interests and leave the overall benefit limited. The industries seldom appreciate interference from the government level. Nonetheless, we believe this is what we should now start discussing. How to invest in the improved functioning and licensing of the EU's content markets.

The UKIPO published in June this year the study Music 2025: The Music Data Dilemma. It tackles issues facing the music industry in improving data management. While it only addresses the music industry, it concludes with recommendations that would be suitable for all creative fields.

These recommendations are:

(a) education and awareness – improving the standards of data input at all points to ensure correct attributions in the digital space;

(b) collaboration – opportunities to improve communication across a diverse and fractured sector;

(c) interoperability – all players are developing their own datasets and databases in isolation;

(d) governance – opportunities for the music industry to learn from the banking sector in terms of governance, to ensure adherence to data standards

Here are listed some projects that dealt with issues of work and rightholder data management. There are many projects and studies that have aimed to address these issues before. Our approach is to build on them and to encourage sharing lessons learned.

INTRODUCING AMRA AND ITS BUSINESS MODEL

Tomas Ericsson*

AMRA was created to enable collections from digital services to be more efficient and therefore bring more value to creators. AMRA licenses and collects royalties from the exploitation of digital rights from over 29 digital service providers (DSPs) in 212 territories. AMRA does not use any intermediary such as a local society to help with any aspect of the licensing, administration, data processing and money flow. AMRA's model allows for all the money and the usage data to flow from the DSP's directly to AMRA without anything being passed through a local society. This way, AMRA can receive all of the money from the DSPs for all territories and avoid the local society fees. Furthermore, AMRA also receives all of the usage data by territory. Using AMRA's state of the art technology to ingest, process and match the data, AMRA has the ability to bring more granular and transparent data back to its creators where each creators is able to see which music is used, where it is used, when it is used and what the value and streams it generated.

DSP's such as Spotify, Apple, YouTube and TikTok are global services that look identical in each territory. We want to provide an easy way for them to clear all the rights from AMRA in one place for all territories. This means that the DSPs can ensure AMRA's entire repertoire is cleared and licensed for all territories where the DSP operate. And all of this under one single agreement.

AMRA's transformational model provides a lower administration cost, better processing and matching capabilities which results in more money for creators.

* CEO at AMRA Music.

TECHNOLOGY DRIVEN CMOS: THE IMPORTANCE OF CMOS IN THE DIGITAL ERA

José-Luis Sevillano*

1 Introduction

SCAPR (Societies Council for the Collective Managem ent of Performers) is a not-for-profit organisation based in Brussels, Belgium. Operating as an international platform for the development of the practical cooperation between performers' CMOs, SCAPR was founded in 1986 and currently represents 57 CMO's from 43 countries.

The mission of SCAPR is to improve the efficiency of management of rights through the signing of reciprocal agreements.

SCAPR has developed and manages IPD and VRDB databases and other technical systems housing information on performers and their performances for a more efficient international distribution of the collected payments. SCAPR provides also assistance for the exchange of information between CMOs via administrative procedures, legal proceedings and arbitrations, collecting procedures, publication of tariffs and distribution schemes.

Traditionally, performers' CMOs have managed the remuneration rights for broadcasting and communication to the public (jointly with producers' CMOs). In the last 15 years, they have been managing other rights such as compensation for private copying, remuneration for communication of audiovisual recordings to the public, making available right or the EU's annual supplementary remuneration.

AIE (*Artistas Intérpretes o Ejecutantes*) is Spanish music performers' society that has more than 30,000 associates and collects performers' compensation from the exploitation of the related rights throughout the world for 800,000 artists through one hundred reciprocal agreements.

Spain is one of the countries with high level of protection of performers' rights, and AIE manages the remunerations of communication to the public and making available of phonograms and audiovisual recordings, the compensation for private copying and the annual supplementary remuneration.

AIE and our sister societies have the objective to defend the rights of music artists when their performances have been fixed in phonograms or audiovisual recordings.

* Chairman of the Board, SCAPR. General Manager, AIE.

2 The Reciprocity Management Challenge

From the traditional exchange, which has been complex and time-consuming existing reciprocity process between CMOs (SDEG protocol) which creates multiple exchanges between all CMOs, the performers' CMOs have created a simplified exchange process between the CMO and a centralised repository which provides more agile and reliable results based on a unique source of truth for the repertoire, available to all the CMOs and maintained on the basis of agreed rules. The solutions for such a great challenge are IPD and VRDB.

On the one hand, IPD is the International Performers Database. An international and centralized service to enable member Societies to accurately identify every member and their mandates to the different CMOs set up in 1997 with more than 1.000.000 unique performers rightsholders. It is a reference in the industry.

On the other hand, VRDB is an international and centralized service to enable member societies to accurately identify sound recordings and audiovisual works, to exchange the necessary information to simplify reciprocity processes, to achieve efficiencies and maximize the flow of royalties exchanged between member societies, for the ultimate distribution to the appropriate rights owners.

The technology is an essential tool for the protection and development of the performers' rights. There is no other organization managing these rights counting with more technological tools for the management than the performers' CMOs.

3 Artists' Remuneration in the Digital Era

3.1 Digital Music Business Models

The beginning of new online business models – firstly, the downloading and, secondly, the streaming – was the reaction to the illegal exploitation of music (peer to peer) and, since that moment, the industry tried to keep the analogical or physical business model, transforming its value chain to the digital environment, while maintaining its status and, in most cases, increasing its value share.

The first legal music services breaking into the market (2002) were limited to replacing the physical copy for the digital one; in other words, audios files (MP3) instead of CDs, vinyl records, DVDs or cassettes, which can be bought in the web pages, instead of CDs stores and shopping centres.

The business models of digital music sale were based on the right of making available to the public (article 8 of the WCT and articles 10 and 14 of the WPPT), in contrast with the right of distribution (article 6 of the WCT and article 8 of the WPPT) on which the physical sales were based.

In 2008, new digital music services through streaming were launched. This business models allow the user to access a vast catalogue of albums and songs (30-40 million songs), without being necessary to obtain a digital copy in our devices.

In the streaming music models, users do not acquire a product – tangible or intangible – but access a service which allows them to enjoy the music for certain period.

3.2 The Effects of the New Business Models for Performers

In 2015, the income from the digital market overcame the income arising from the physical sales, this tendency has been consolidated in the next years. In fact, in 2019 the income from digital market is 12.9 USD billions and, especially, 11.4 USD billions from streaming services (almost the 90% of digital income).

Regarding the music production and its commercialization in the new streaming digital market, the value chain has changed undoubtedly since digital technology has introduced many changes in the music production and commercialization, in particular, the disintermediation of the value chain of physical production provided that the traditional agents disappear (production, logistic, physical store...). This digitalisation process in the industry has allowed the recording companies to extend their presence in respect of almost all the value chain, controlling all the production process and increasing their weight in the value chain.

Despite of this change in the way music consumption by part of the users of these platforms and the business model change, the recording companies try to keep the economical and legal scheme related to the analogical business; they keep the licensing system, the royalties system and the agreements signed up to 50 years ago to settle the performers' rights, even with the same deductions system related to the physical environment, such as packaging, manufacturing, etc.

This model is a drama for artists since even those who have accepted royalties based on sales in their agreements see how the ratio of payment per stream/download is tiny and, despite of having a great volume of reproductions, they do not obtain a remuneration according to the real use of their music.

The delimitation of the rights and modalities of exploitation in the digital environment is seriously harming authors and performers, provided that the translation of the traditional-analogous model to the new uses is being carried out on the base of the physical sale, while the streaming music models are closer to the rental model: "access to a repertoire of phonograms in certain conditions".

Streaming music services are not a "business model based on distribution through sale" in the sense that providers do not transfer ownership of the music file (neither a physical medium, obviously). The commercial model of music streaming services is based on access to a repertoire for a limited time and conditions: when the service ends, the user cannot access any music file or maintain any ownership on it. In other words, it would be the digital equivalent to the rental of tangible media related to the modality of distribution right, Article 9 of the WPPT, which establishes the exclusive right of authorizing the commercial rental to the public of the original and copies of their performances fixed in phonograms, and in addition, it includes the possibility for contracting parties to recognize a system of equitable remuneration for performers for the rental of copies of their fixed performances in phonograms. In fact, within the scope of the European Union, the Rental and Lending Directive (92/100/EEC) foresees this remuneration right.

However, the legal scheme which fits in the producer's view is the one based on exclusive rights, which allows it to "agglutinate" rights to negotiate licenses including the biggest number of rights (making available, communication to the public, reproduction...) and the biggest number of rightsholders (the producers themselves, performers, authors...). This way they enjoy a strong bargaining power when negotiating the terms with the digital services. However, this view does not fit in relation to performers and authors.

4 The Role of the CMOs in Digital Music Business

Performers' CMOs have shown the capacity to adapt their performance to any situation, critical or evolutional.

Performers' CMOs have proven capacity and experience to successfully manage digital rights and the fair interaction with platforms to properly manage artists rights. Performers' CMOs are creating and managing powerful databases with all recordings and complete line ups.

Since 2014, the EU acquis provides a legal framework for the whole activity of CMOs: membership, collection, distribution, accounting, transparency, etc. The Directive 2014/26/EU is the framework that provides security and acknowledgement about the collective management to rightsholders, users, others CMOs and general public.

The aim of the Directive "*is to lay down requirements applicable to collective management organisations, in order to ensure a high standard of governance, financial management, transparency and reporting*" and, currently, these requirements have been implemented by all member States of the European Union and therefore the CMOs are the unique organization that guarantee a high level of management and transparency to the rightsholder, in the case of Performers' CMOs, the music artists.

Performers' CMOs defend artists remuneration rights in digital music at international level to find the fair remuneration and proportional distribution for *all* artists. Performers' CMOs are the sole organizations that in fact represent and defend all artists: session musicians and featured performers.

5 The Spanish Model Exclusive and Remuneration Rights

There are several countries that foresaw a solution to this problem when they implemented this right. As an example, Spain (and we can show off about this) granted an unwaivable remuneration right in favour of performers once the exclusive right is transferred to producers. Croatia, Hungary, Slovenia, Czechia and, in a different way, Portugal, have taken similar solutions.

Literally, the right of making available to the public for performers is regulated in Spanish Copyright Act in following way:

Art. 108.1: "The performer shall have the exclusive right to authorize the communication to the public: (...) b) In any case, of the fixations of his performances, by means of making available to the public (...)."

This is the exclusive right that is recognized in Art. 10 WPPT. As an exclusive right, artists transfer it to the producer in the contract, and the producer licenses to the digital platform. If the artist records his performance without a record label, the artist will assign the management of his rights to the collecting society. Since this is unlikely to happen, Art. 108.3 of the Spanish Copyright Act provides: *"If the performer has assigned or transferred to a phonogram or audiovisual recordings producer his right of making available to the public to which § 1.b) refers with reference to a phonogram or an original or a copy of an audiovisual recording, he shall preserve his unwaivable right an equitable remuneration to be received by whom makes it available to the public."* And Art. 108.6: *"The right to the remuneration referred to in § (...) 3 shall be exercised though the collective management organization."*

In Spain, AIE manages this performers' remuneration right to obtain an equitable remuneration for the making available of phonograms.

Artists all around Europe and America believe that remuneration right is the most effective mechanism to assure a fair remuneration for artists in digital environment.

The digital music services have modalities called "radios" (not only the ones offering this modality exclusively such as Last.fm, Rdio or Pandora, but those combining "music on demand" such as, again, Spotify or Apple Music). These acts clearly involve a public communication of phonograms since these modalities do not allow accessing specific performances/phonograms or do not allow choosing the time to access. In this case, we are speaking about the right granted to performers and producers of phonograms: the right to obtain an equitable remuneration for the communication to the public of phonograms.

Despite this legal and conceptual difference, collective management societies in charge of performers' rights are seeing how, in practice, the license granted by producer covers all performers' rights (although they do not have legitimacy to do so). To this end, producers try to assimilate all modalities run by music services, driving them to the making available right. In this scenario, producers have an almost all-powerful dominion, condemning performers to make their creativity available to big companies without obtaining a fair remuneration.

DEALING WITH TERRITORIALITY IN EU COPYRIGHT

Peter Bernt Hugenholtz*

Despite thirty years of copyright harmonization, the law of copyright in the EU has remained essentially national and territorial. The exclusivity that a copyright confers upon its owner is, in principle, limited to the territorial boundaries of the Member State where the right has been granted. In its *Lagardère* ruling[1] the CJEU expressly confirmed the territorial nature of copyright and related rights, notwithstanding extensive harmonisation.

The territorial nature of copyright has various consequences. One is that copyrights can, and often will be fragmented along territorially defined lines. This is especially prevalent in the music business and the audio-visual realm, where CMOs and film distributors traditionally hold on to national or regional grants of rights.

Another consequence is that cross-border transmissions of copyright works inevitably have spill-over effects in other jurisdictions. This follows from the *Hejduk* decision,[2] where the CJEU considered that a website containing unauthorized content infringes copyright in every Member State from where the work is accessible.

As a result, any online content provider wishing to reach out to the entire EU market needs to acquire licenses for all member states – often from many different, nationally operating right holders and CMOs. Obviously, this requirement is difficult to square with the European ideal of a *Digital Single Market*.

Yet, the tension between territorially defined rights and the freedoms of the Internal Market are by no means new. Over time, the European legislature and its institutions have responded to the challenges of copyright territoriality, by mitigating its consequences in various manners. These responses, however, have been uneven and remain incomplete, particularly with regard to making works available online.

1 EU-wide Exhaustion

The CJEU recognized early on that the territorial exercise of rights of intellectual property negatively affects the free circulation of goods, which is a core

* Professor, University of Amsterdam; Visiting Professor, Charles University, Prague

1 ECJ 14 July 2005, case C-192/04 (Lagardère Active Broadcast).

2 CJEU 22 January 2015, case C-441/13 (Hejduk).

characteristic of the internal market. In a series of decisions preceding the harmonization of copyright and related rights, the Court held that the right to control the distribution of copyright protected goods is exhausted following the initial marketing of these goods inside the European Community with the right holder's consent.[3] This rule of 'Community exhaustion' was later codified in article 4(2) of the Information Society Directive and in various other directives. As a consequence, markets for copyright protected goods can no longer be partitioned along national borders.

However, save for a narrow exception in respect of computer software,[4] exhaustion does not occur online, as follows clearly from article 3 of the Information Society Directive. The CJEU has confirmed this in its *Tom Kabinet* decision.[5]

2 The 'SatCab' Approach

An entirely different legislative solution to the problem of market fragmentation by territorial rights can be found in the Satellite and Cable ('SatCab') Directive of 1993. According to article 1(2)(b) of the directive, a satellite broadcast will amount to communication to the public only in the country of origin of the signal, i.e., where the 'injection' of the program-carrying signal can be localized. Thus, the directive departed from the so-called 'Bogsch theory', which held that a satellite broadcast requires licenses from all right holders in all countries of reception (i.e. within the footprint of the satellite). Since the transposition of the directive, only a license in the country of origin of the satellite broadcast is needed.

The 2019 Online Broadcasting Directive (2019/789), which amended the SatCab Directive, extends the SatCab Directive's country of origin rule to certain radio and television broadcasts offered over the Internet. The scope of the new directive is, however, extremely limited. First, it only applies to Internet broadcasts that are 'simulcast' with terrestrial broadcasts, including so-called 'catch-up' services. Second, its remits is restricted to television news and current affairs programming, and (other) content produced and financed by the broadcasters themselves.

3 Collective Rights Management Directive

Yet another approach towards territoriality can be found in the EU Collective Rights Management (CRM) Directive, which introduced a legal mechanism aimed at enhancing multi-territorial licensing of online uses of musical works. If a collective

3 See e.g. ECJ June 1971, Case 78/70 (Deutsche Grammophon v Metro SB).

4 CJEU 3 July 2012, Case C-128/11 (UsedSoft).

5 CJEU 19 December 2019, Case C-263/18 (Nederlands Uitgeversverbond and Groep Algemene Uitgevers).

management organization is unwilling or incapable of offering online licenses for multiple states in the EU, either directly or through an affiliated society, right holders may withdraw their online rights from the society, and either entrust these rights to another society, or manage the rights themselves.

The CRM Directive has fostered the establishment of supranational licensing hubs offering multi-territorial online licenses across Europe. Nevertheless, the scope of the CRM Directive remains necessarily narrow. It applies online to musical works made available online.

4 EU Competition Law

Less structural, but occasionally effective nonetheless, are the remedies found in EU competition law, notably articles 101 and 102 of the Treaty on the Functioning of the European Union (TFEU). The CJEU has produced extensive case law on the anti-competitive exercise of IP rights along national borders that result in the unjustified partitioning of the internal market. For example, in *Coditel II* the Court held that a contract providing for an exclusive right to exhibit a film for a specified time in the territory of any member state may well be in violation of that provision if it has as its object or effect the restriction of film distribution or the distortion of competition on the cinematographic market.[6]

In *Premier League*, the CJEU held that an exclusive pay television licence agreement that obliges the broadcaster not to supply decoding devices to users outside the territory covered by that licence infringes article 101 TFEU.[7] The decision is in line with general principles of EU competition law that distinguish between "active" and "passive" sales to consumers in Member States not covered by a territorial licence. Whereas EU competition law does allow a licensor to oblige a licensee not to actively seek customers outside the licensed territory, a licensee may not be prevented from "passively" selling to such consumers. In other words, a territorial broadcasting licence will never be absolute.

5 Conclusion

In conclusion, while EU law has tackled the issue of territorial copyrights in distinct areas, in other areas the problem remains unresolved. In the online realm, in particular, territoriality still largely rules. This is a counter-intuitive conclusion, given the maxim that the Internet, almost by definition, "knows no national borders".[8]

6 ECJ 6 October 1982, Case 262-81 (Coditel v Ciné Vog Films).

7 CJEU 4 October 2011, joined cases C403/08 and C429/08 (Football Association Premier League Ltd a.o. v. QC Leisure a.o.; Karen Murphy v Media Protection Services Ltd).

8 Quote attributed to Alan Dershowitz.

With the advent of new Internet-related rights, such as the right to make works available on content-sharing platforms (art. 17(1) of the DSM Directive) and the neighbouring right for news publishers (art. 15 DSM Directive), the need for trans-European solutions will undoubtedly become more urgent

COLLECTIVE MANAGEMENT IN CYBERSPACE

Adriana Moscoso*

Buenas tardes, queridos colegas, es un placer estar aquí con todos vosotros. Muchas gracias a ALAI y en particular a Rudolf Leška por la invitación, por la excelente organización de este congreso y por la oportunidad de venir a Praga y reencontrarme con tantos amigos.

He pensado que lo más interesante de mi aportación sería sin duda compartir con todos vosotros el estado de los trabajos en el marco de la transposición de las directivas 2019/789 "sat/cab" y 2019/790 de mercado único digital, *desde la perspectiva de un Estado miembro.*

Como sabéis, el plazo límite de transposición es el 7 de junio de 2021 y en ese margen de tiempo debemos de trabajar.

Me centraré principalmente en la *directive 2019/790 del mercado único digital* ya que es en ésta donde se ha Avanzado más desde su adopción el pasado 17 de abril.

En relación con ésta:

1 Nuestra idea de transposición en Gral

- Estamos trabajando ya en un borrador de proyecto de ley que trasponga ambas directivas en un único texto (idea inicial que puede variar).
- Transmitido al MAEC el plan de transposición de la Directiva. Nuestra idea era tener un texto listo para remitir al Congreso de los Diputados a finales de mayo.
- Teniendo en cuenta las próximas elecciones generales en España, el 10 de noviembre, de aquí a entonces vamos a poder únicamente iniciar la consulta pública sin texto y probablemente el calendario inicialmente previsto se retrase.
- Hemos empezado a trabajar ya en los artículos más relevantes de la directiva MUD. Algunos ejemplos:
  (a) Editores de prensa: artículo 15 vs. artículo 32.2 TRLPI: derecho remuneración, gestión colectiva obligatoria, sin límite de tiempo (régimen general). Directiva establece una duración de dos años. Tendremos que recortar nuestro actual sistema.
  (b) Artículo 17: Transposición lo más ajustada a la literalidad de la Directiva posible.

* Director of Cultural Industries and Cooperation, Ministry of Culture of the Kingdom of Spain.

(c) Excepciones y limitaciones:
  i. ¿Incorporar concepto de excepción en la LPI (sólo hay una categoría general de "limitaciones")
  ii. ¿Regular *exnovo* todas las excepciones y limitaciones incorporadas? Probablemente.
  iii. Incorporar art 16 (reprobel) en excepción por copia privada.

2 Triangulo de transparencia. Arts. 18-20. Transponer con literalidad, no problemas específicos.

2.1 En qué punto estamos en law reunions, tendencias de los países, sobre la directive mud

Dos reuniones del Comité de Contacto celebradas a estas alturas, una en junio y otra el lunes de esta semana.

La próxima reunión será en enero, tras el diálogo de la COM con las partes interesadas y previamente a que la COM dicte orientaciones sobre el artículo 17.

Por el momento se visualizan dos grupos de países:

- Uno que defiende una transposición lo más próxima posible al texto de la Directiva y que defiende un alto nivel de protección de los derechos de autor en el mercado único digital, donde se encuentra España, entre otros.
- Otro de países "menos entusiastas" con la Directiva. Aquí cabe destacar el paso dado por Polonia, al recurrir ante el TJUE la anulación de dos apartados del artículo 17. Yo al menos *nunca había visto una situación igual* a ésta, en la que un Estado Miembro recurra una Directiva recién aprobada, lo que muestra que el *acalorado debate* que acompañó todo el proceso de aprobación de esta Directiva sigue de alguna modo vivo y probablemente no se apague hasta que entre en vigor la directiva, comience a aplicarse y se vea que el mercado único digital europeo no sólo no colapsa, sino que se robustece gracias a que las industrias culturales y creativas europeas y sus creadores van a encontrar un retorno a su inversión y a su trabajo (pero también los usuarios y todos un marco jurídico más claro; y los equilibrios entre los derechos fundamentales de expresión y propiedad intelectual se mantienen bajo estándares de absoluta corrección.
- En cuanto a los *procesos internos de transposición*, algunos países ya han finalizado la fase de consulta pública, como Países Bajos o Rumanía, incluso con un texto de borrador de transposición, como es el caso de Francia.

3 Recurso Polonia

Interpuesto ante el TJUE el 24 de mayo de 2019 (DOUE 12 agosto 2019) solicitando anulación de dos incisos del artículo 17, en concreto los apartados b) y c) del apartado 4 que establece la obligación para las plataformas de hacer los mayores esfuerzos por evitar la disponibilidad de contenidos conforme a las normas sectoriales estrictas de diligencia profesional y actuar de forma expeditiva para retirar contenidos y evitar que se carguen en el futuro.

Polonia considera que estos apartados exigen una verificación automática previa (filtro) por parte de las plataformas y por consiguiente una vulneración del derecho a la libertad de expresión y de información (art. 11 Carta Dchos Fundamentales UE).

Con carácter subsidiario, Polonia pide la anulación de todo el artículo 17 de la Directiva.

España: Demanda de intervención en apoyo del PE y del Consejo (12 de septiembre 2019) alegando que:

- Directiva sí garantiza el equilibrio entre derechos fundamentales en juego, sobre la base de la extensa jurisprudencia del TJUE al respecto.
- Texto fruto de un amplio debate político y de un cuidadoso equilibrio de los diferentes intereses en juego.

4 Sobre la directive sat/cab

Por el momento, el debate de la Directiva MUD acapara todo el tiempo en las reuniones del grupo de contacto. Tampoco a nivel nacional hemos comenzado a abordar este texto, pero lo haremos en este otoño.

ASIAN IP OFFICES' POLICIES ON COLLECTIVE MANAGEMENT

Satoshi Watanabe*

1 Introduction

How is collective management of music copyrights conducted in the Asia-Pacific region? There are 19 CISAC member music societies in the Asia-Pacific region. These sister societies administer performing rights and mechanical rights of each other under reciprocal representation agreements on a respective territorial basis in most of the cases.

In the global collection of CISAC societies, the share of the Asia-Pacific region was 14.2 % of the total in 2018. In view of the economic growth of the region, this share may grow in the future. Collections from "digital use" represent 24.4 %, the second largest share, following a 32.4 % share for "broadcasts." Digital use is a rapidly growing area among all types of music usages.

2 Direct licensing of digital services

Direct licensing or multi-territorial licensing of digital services in Europe and North America have extended to cover other territories in the world. While certain societies mandated by major publishers are making direct licensing deals with global DSPs, they are proposing Asian societies to change their reciprocal representation contracts from an exclusive basis to a non-exclusive basis, and thus, those direct licensor societies may also include Asian territories in their direct licensing.

3 Asian IP Offices' Policies

Intellectual property authorities China, Taiwan, Indonesia, Korea, Malaysia, and the Philippines express their views that due to laws and regulations, only a locally registered CMO can conduct collective copyright licensing in its own territory.

* Senior Administrator of JASRAC, Chair of CISAC Asia-Pacific Regional Committee.

3.1 China

The laws of mainland China prohibit foreign CMOs from directly engaging in collective management business in mainland China. Specific provisions are provided in Articles 6 and 22 of China's regulations on Collective Copyright Administration. Foreign CMOs can only sign reciprocal agreements with similar CMOs in mainland China which then exercise the copyright on their behalf.

3.2 Chinese Taipei

TIPO (Taiwan Intellectual Property Office) states that only domestically approved CMOs can engage in collective licensing.

According to Art.3.1.1 of the Copyright Collective Management Organization Act in the Republic of China, copyright collective management services refer to "services for the management of economic rights on behalf of multiple economic rights holders, in which uniform royalty rates and methods for distribution of royalties are adopted as the basis for collection and distribution of royalties, and in which license agreements with users are established in the name of those providing the management." Also, in Article 10 of the same Act, "A person not organized and approved for establishment as a CMO in accordance with this Act shall not conduct collective management services or perform any other juristic act in the name of a CMO. Where any party violates the preceding paragraph, any individual or blanket license agreement executed by it shall become null and void[...]."

3.3 Indonesia

It is stipulated in Article 88 paragraph (3) of the Copyright Act that a CMO with no operational permit from the minister of culture is prohibited to obtain, collect and distribute royalties. CMOs with no operational permit which engage in royalty collecting activities shall be subject to a maximum imprisonment of (4) years, and/or a maximum fine of Rp. 1,000,000,000.

A foreign CMO with no operational permit from the minister is prohibited to obtain, collect and distribute royalties accruing from economic rights in Indonesia on behalf of the author or copyright holder or the related rights holder.

LMKN, the national CMO, was established in 2014. It represents all rights of copyright and related rights societies. All licenses need to be issued under the name of LMKN.

3.4 Korea

According to the Article 105(1) of the Copyright Act of Korea, any person who intends to engage in a copyright trust service shall obtain permission from the minister of culture, sports and tourism as prescribed by a presidential decree.

Under Article 105(3)4 of the Copyright Act, any person who has no domicile in the Republic of Korea shall not be eligible to obtain a license to engage in a copyright trust service or copyright agency or brokerage service.

3.5 Malaysia

Under Article 27A of the Copyright Act 1987, CMOs wishing to carry out licensing activities in Malaysia need to satisfy the governmental requirements before they are declared as official "Licensing Bodies".

3.6 Philippines

Section 183 the Intellectual Property Code requires CMOs to seek the accreditation of the Intellectual Property Office of the Philippines: "The Owner of copyright and related rights or their heirs may designate a society of artists, writers, composers and other rightholders to collectively manage their economic or moral rights on their behalf. For the said societies to enforce the rights of their members, they shall first secure the necessary accreditation from the Intellectual Property Office."

4 Conclusion

Expansion of cross-border digital licensing triggered by EU legislation has generated friction with territory-based societies' administration, and also with the Asian IP offices' policies. There are several issues which need to be addressed for the healthy development of the collective management system, ensuring fair remuneration for creators and fostering a sound digital service market in the Asian region:

- Traditional copyright legislative regime vs Local IP offices' policies
- Domestic collective licensing regime vs Cross-border digital licensing
- Risk of under- and over-claiming of rights
- Correct identification of interested parties and their shares
- Transparency of distribution
- Applicability of local regulations to a foreign entity
- Tax liability of a foreign entity

Without doubt, multi-territorial licenses must comply with the local laws and regulations of a given country. It should be also noted that the collective management system in any country has grown through concentration of domestic rights and foreign rights and has contributed to cultural diversity by remunerating all creators on an equal basis. The issues mentioned above are not specific to the Asian region but could apply to any region of the world.

THE EQUITABLE REMUNERATION OF AUDIOVISUAL AUTHORS: A PROPOSAL OF UNWAIVABLE REMUNERATION RIGHTS UNDER COLLECTIVE MANAGEMENT

Raquel Xalabarder*

Authors of audiovisual works are granted exclusive rights to exploit their works. However, they rarely obtain equitable remuneration for the whole exploitation. This is especially true regarding new (and rapidly growing) markets for online exploitation: they do not generate additional remuneration for audiovisual authors. Granting audiovisual authors exclusive rights of exploitation in their works but, in practice, denying them the possibility to obtain an equitable remuneration for it – beyond the initial fee, usually a flat fee, agreed in the production contract –, is as much as granting them no rights at all. What is the benefit of exclusive rights -secured by national laws and international treaties – if audiovisual authors cannot, in practice, obtain equitable remuneration for the exploitation of their works?

The remuneration of audiovisual authors depends largely on the contracts signed with the producer and these contracts fail to secure an equitable remuneration for the whole exploitation of their works. Production contracts, signed before the audiovisual work is created, tend to convey a full transfer of exploitation rights in favour of the producer, usually in exchange for a buy-out (a lump-sum). Follow up payments, along the exploitation of the work, are rarely agreed in the production contract, thus ultimately depriving audiovisual authors of an equitable remuneration for the overall exploitation of their works.

Several reasons might explain (never justify) this less than optimal scenario.

Determination of authorship and initial ownership in audiovisual works is a complex issue that receives different solutions in different countries. Some countries allocate co-authorship in the main creative contributors (together with a statutory presumption of transfer of the exploitation rights in favour of the producer), while others prefer to allocate authorship and, at least, ownership *ab origine* in the producer

* Chair of Intellectual Property, Universitat Oberta de Catalunya (UOC), Barcelona. Based on the *International legal study on the implementation of an unwaivable right of audiovisual authors to obtain equitable remuneration for the exploitation of their works* commissioned by CISAC. Cf. *The remuneration of authors and performers*, Revue Internationale du Droit d'Auteur (RIDA), vol. 264 (2020), p. 129-162.

(for instance, under "work made for hire" or "*cessio legis*" provisions). At the end, the producer owns all copyright in the audiovisual work, controlling the long and intricate chain of exploitation of the audiovisual work/recording and channelling all revenues from it.

Most national laws impose specific restrictions on the transfer of authors' exclusive rights to the producer as well as requirements of (and even professional) equitable remuneration for authors; but these measures alone are proving to be insufficient to protect the economic interests of audiovisual authors, because they are easily trumped by the specific terms agreed in the production contract.

Collective negotiation of production contracts may also help secure remuneration of authors, but this is only a reality in a handful of countries, which are equipped with powerful labour union representing authors (such as the guilds in the USA) capable of negotiating contractual payments (*residuals*) in production contracts.

Collective management of rights has also proven to be a major source of revenues for audiovisual authors. On a voluntary basis, its success largely depends on a combination of external factors, such as the specific economic and market conditions of each country, including the development of collective management schemes, the strength of CMOs to obtain a mandate of rights and, at the end, a statutory design of rights to facilitate collective management.

CMOs may always be entrusted by audiovisual authors to manage, on their behalf, the licensing and remuneration for the exploitation of their works. To do so, authors must contractually reserve (or "carve out," as it is sometimes referred to) the right in the production contract, to entrust its management to a CMO. This requires collective bargaining power, which only exists in some countries (such as France) and only a few audiovisual authors (such as music composers). Furthermore, even when successful, it has limited effects (for new/future audiovisual productions) and fails to benefit already existing audiovisual productions (subject to the terms of previously signed production contracts).

Instead, statutory remuneration under collective management rights have proven to be an efficient option to secure "secondary" revenues for audiovisual authors via CMOs, especially when these remuneration rights are unwaivable, inalienable and subject to mandatory collective management. Remuneration rights are well-known in international instruments as well as in national laws (notably -but not only- in Europe).

For all these reasons, in countries where audiovisual production contracts fail to secure equitable remuneration to authors for the whole exploitation of their works, the author proposes the introduction of a statutory provision securing for audiovisual authors an unwaivable and inalienable right to obtain equitable remuneration for any acts of exploitation of their works, in exchange for the transfer of the exploitation rights to the producer; the remuneration will be subject to collective management (administered by CMOs) and paid directly by the licensees.

The remuneration right, as proposed, neither grants a new exclusive right, nor turns any exclusive right into a remuneration right. It is a "residual" remuneration right granted to audiovisual authors to secure remuneration – via CMOs- once they have exercised their exploitation rights by transferring them to the audiovisual producer.

The proposal is in full compliance with the obligations acquired under international instruments for the protection of copyright, namely the Berne Convention, the WIPO Copyright Treaty and the TRIPs Agreement, as well as with the EU *acquis*.

The remuneration right proposed would equally benefit authors and producers by ensuring a constant flow of equitable remuneration to authors, directly from the users (as licensed by producer) via CMOs; safeguarding any transfer of exploitation rights to the producer and any payments agreed in the production contracts (allowing the producer to retain all ownership of the exploitation rights and to control of the licensing process); alleviating constant pressure on producers (and production contracts) to secure fair remuneration and reducing management costs, via CMOs. The unwaivable and inalienable nature of the remuneration right, and its collective management, are necessary measures to overcome the unbalanced bargaining position of authors in front of producers, and to maximize the efficient negotiation and implementation of the remuneration via CMOs. The remuneration right would ultimately benefit both licensed operators and consumers, by fostering the development of lawful channels of exploitation of audiovisual works and facilitating wider access to repertoires while securing further creative production.

The remuneration right proposed would neither upset any regimes currently in place to efficiently secure equitable remuneration for audiovisual authors, such as *residuals* agreements (i.e., by US Guilds), ECL mechanisms (i.e., in the Nordic countries) or any schemes of voluntary collective management already in place in some countries (i.e., for music composers), nor any other remuneration rights already provided for in national laws. In fact, the proposal would reinforce these national regimes and mechanisms, enlarging their scope, making them more efficient (subject, when necessary, to mandatory collective management) and expanding their application in countries which currently offer none.

In Europe, remuneration rights are unwaivable, – inherently – inalienable and tend to be subject to collective management. The unwaivable nature of remuneration rights of any kind (be it compensation for E&L, be it residual remuneration rights or non-voluntary licensing) is uniform in EU *acquis* as well as in EU laws. The CJEU, in *Luksan,* confirmed that remuneration rights that compensate for E&L are unwaivable, as well as inalienable. The same unwaivable and inalienable nature is shared by *residual* remuneration rights "retained" by authors upon the transfer of an exclusive right to the producer. Its unwaivable nature results from complying with the principle that authors must be fairly remunerated for the exploitation of their works; in fact, Art.5 Rental & Lending Directive already set the rental remuneration right as unwaivable. Furthermore, this inalienable and unwaivable nature is confirmed by the fact that, in practice, most remuneration rights are subject to mandatory collective management.

The audiovisual market is a global one; any legal mechanisms to secure equitable remuneration for audiovisual creators will be most effective when implemented at international level – especially if set as mandatory (for member states)- and subsequently regulated at national level, considering the specific circumstances and needs of different national markets and revenue streams, as well as different national legal structures. A national or supra-national implementation (such as, at EU level) would also have some benefits, at a regional scale. Yet, every bit counts.

Over the past years, unwaivable/inalienable remuneration rights, for all means of exploitation – including online –, paid by licensees and managed by CMOs, have proven to be the best solution to secure equitable remuneration for audiovisual authors. The mechanism has been endorsed by a few national legislators, stakeholders as well as by academic experts.

Remuneration rights and CMOs are best placed to secure remuneration in long, complex markets, worldwide, such as the audiovisual one. All it takes is a little help from legislators. An invitation has already been extended by Art.18 Directive on Copyright in the Digital Single Market when reminding national legislators of the "different existing or newly introduced mechanisms" available to secure that Authors and Performers receive appropriate and proportionate remuneration.

PART IV
CONCLUSION

RAPPORT GÉNÉRAL: GESTION COLLECTIVE DES DROITS

Romana Matanovac Vučković*

Les réponses au questionnaire préparé par le groupe tchèque de l'ALAI - ont été fournies par les groupes nationaux suivants de l'ALAI: Allemagne, Argentine, Belgique, Canada, Colombie, Corée, Croatie, Espagne, France, Grèce, Hongrie, Israël, Italie, Japon, Nouvelle-Zélande, Pays-Bas, Portugal, République tchèque, Suisse et États-Unis. Les résultats ont été présentés au congrès sur le droit d'auteur ALAI 2019 à Prague le 18 septembre 2019. Ce texte reflète donc l'état des lieux de septembre 2019 concernant la situation législative et pratique dans lesdits pays, en s'appuyant sur les réponses fournies par les groupes nationaux de l'ALAI.

Le questionnaire était divisé en trois parties. La première partie faisait référence à un aperçu général de la gestion collective. La seconde était consacrée à la relation entre les organisations de gestion collective (CMO), les auteurs et les autres titulaires de droits. Enfin, la troisième partie a examiné la relation entre les CMO et les utilisateurs. Les réponses seront comprises plus loin.

1 Aperçu général de la gestion collective

1.1 Organismes de gestion collective : monopoles naturels ou légaux

Tout au long de l'histoire, les organisations de gestion collective ont souvent été perçues comme des sociétés ayant une position de monopole sur le marché. Cependant, leur position de monopole était en même temps remise en cause, notamment par les règles de concurrence. Certains pays ont décidé de répondre à ce défi en réglementant leur position de monopole dans la loi. Certains les considèrent comme des monopoles naturels. Certains se sont tournés vers la concurrence sur le marché, notamment sur Internet.

Peu de pays ont décidé de réglementer les organisations de gestion collective comme des monopoles légaux. L'Argentine, où toutes les CMO ont un monopole légal, en est un. La Croatie et la République tchèque réglementent également expressément le monopole des CMO dans leurs lois sur le droit d'auteur. Il s'agit

* Professor, University of Zagreb, Faculty of Law.

essentiellement de catégories de titulaires de droits et de catégories de droits, ce qui signifie qu'une catégorie de titulaires de droits peut créer une CMO par catégorie de droits. Une implication pratique est cependant qu'il y a une CMO par catégorie de titulaires de droits sur leurs marchés, réglementant toutes les catégories de droits. L'exception au monopole légal est constituée par les CMO des auteurs de musique pour la concession de licences transfrontalières de musique sur Internet. La Corée réglemente également de manière générale le monopole légal des CMO, sauf pour les auteurs de musique.

Dans la plupart des pays, tels qu'Israël, le Canada, la Colombie, la France, la Grèce, l'Allemagne, la Nouvelle-Zélande, le Portugal, l'Espagne et la Suisse, les CMO sont des monopoles naturels. Cela signifie que leur position de monopole n'est pas régie par les lois sur le droit d'auteur des pays respectifs, mais qu'elle est la conséquence du comportement du marché. Bien que la loi ne prévoie pas qu'il n'y ait qu'une seule CMO pour une catégorie de titulaires de droits et une catégorie de droits, le marché n'a développé qu'une seule CMO en position de monopole par rapport auxdits critères en question.

Plusieurs pays connaissent une combinaison de monopoles légaux, de monopoles naturels et parfois aussi de CMO concurrentes. Par exemple, en Belgique, les CMO sont des monopoles naturels pour les utilisations traditionnelles de matières protégées. Toutefois, en ce qui concerne les droits à rémunération, la retransmission par câble et les CMO d'injection directe sont des monopoles légaux prévus par la loi sur le droit d'auteur pertinente. En même temps, il n'y a pas de monopole du tout pour les droits en ligne. En outre, la loi hongroise sur le droit d'auteur ne prévoit de monopole légal que dans les cas où la gestion collective des droits est obligatoire. Dans les autres cas, il n'y a pas de monopole légal et la concurrence est possible, bien que dans la pratique les CMO soient souvent des monopoles naturels.

Par exemple, il n'existe pas de monopole pour les droits exclusifs au Japon, mais un monopole légal est prévu pour les droits à rémunération. Ce groupe inclut la copie privée et la rémunération statutaire pour l'exécution publique de phonogrammes commerciaux. Aux Pays-Bas, certaines CMO sont légalement désignées comme des monopoles, par exemple dans le cas de la copie privée, du prêt public et des droits voisins. D'autre part, certaines CMO, comme celles qui sont compétentes pour la gestion collective des droits de reproduction, sont des monopoles naturels. Enfin, il existe des CMO concurrentes dans le même domaine et la même catégorie de droits, essentiellement sur Internet.

Aux États-Unis, en raison de la taille du territoire et du marché, de raisons historiques et de circonstances nationales spécifiques, il y a souvent plus d'une CMO par catégorie de droits et par catégorie de titulaires de droits. Par exemple, il existe plusieurs CMO pour les auteurs de musique pour l'exécution publique, comme ASCAP, BMI, SESAC et GMA. L'autorité de la concurrence reconnaît cependant les CMO comme des monopoles naturels.

1.2 Gestion collective volontaire, étendue et obligatoire

La question posée dans l'enquête était de savoir si le système du droit d'auteur fait la différence entre la gestion collective volontaire, étendue et obligatoire et quels droits sont gérés sous quel régime. La Belgique, le Canada, la Croatie, la République tchèque, la France, l'Allemagne, la Grèce, la Hongrie, Israël, le Japon, la Corée, les Pays-Bas, la Nouvelle-Zélande, le Portugal, l'Espagne, la Suisse et les États-Unis ont répondu que leurs lois sur le droit d'auteur prévoient la gestion collective volontaire dans la plupart des cas. Cela signifie que le titulaire du droit peut choisir de gérer son droit d'auteur individuellement ou par le biais d'un système de gestion collective. Par exemple, dans le système de gestion collective volontaire, même si une CMO a été créée pour une certaine catégorie de droits, le titulaire du droit peut décider de ne pas administrer cette catégorie de ses droits par le biais de la CMO.

La Colombie est un exemple rare où tous les droits ne peuvent être administrés que de manière volontaire et collective. La gestion collective n'est jamais obligatoire car le tribunal constitutionnel a décidé que la gestion collective obligatoire est contraire à la constitution et donc interdite comme modèle de gestion des droits d'auteur. En revanche, l'Argentine ne pratique la gestion volontaire des droits d'auteur que dans certains cas. Dans la plupart des cas dans ce pays, les droits, tels que l'exécution publique et la reproduction, sont gérés de manière obligatoire et collective par le biais des CMO.

En Belgique, une gestion collective obligatoire est prévue pour les droits de rémunération, la retransmission par câble et l'injection directe. Au Canada, seuls les droits de rémunération et les recouvrements sont gérés collectivement de manière obligatoire. La liste des droits exclusifs obligatoirement gérés collectivement en Croatie est inhabituelle par rapport aux autres pays de l'Union européenne. Là, les droits de radiodiffusion doivent être gérés collectivement, à côté de la retransmission par câble, des autres types de retransmission et de l'injection directe. En outre, les droits à rémunération et la copie privée sont également gérés obligatoirement de manière collective. En République tchèque, la gestion collective obligatoire est réglementée pour les rémunérations des phonogrammes commerciaux, de la copie privée et des autres droits à rémunération. En France, la retransmission par câble, la copie privée et les autres droits de rémunération seront également obligatoirement gérés collectivement. La loi allemande sur le droit d'auteur prévoit une gestion collective obligatoire pour les droits de retransmission par câble et les rémunérations statutaires. En Grèce, la copie privée, la rémunération pour l'exécution publique de phonogrammes commerciaux, les autres droits de rémunération et la retransmission par câble à droits exclusifs sont également gérés de manière obligatoire et collective. Comme en Croatie, en Hongrie, la radiodiffusion d'œuvres musicales, la retransmission par câble, le droit de reproduction, la copie privée et les autres droits de rémunération seront soumis au régime de la gestion collective obligatoire. Israël prévoit la gestion collective obligatoire pour la copie privée et la rémunération des prestations audiovisuelles. Le Japon réglemente la gestion collective obligatoire pour la copie privée et les droits à rémunération statutaire pour l'exécution publique de phonogrammes commerciaux. La Corée réserve la gestion collective obligatoire uniquement aux droits de rémunération. Aux Pays-Bas, la liste des droits qui doivent obligatoirement être gérés collectivement est plus longue. La liste comprend la retransmission par câble, la communication au public d'œuvres cinématographiques, la copie privée, le prêt et la compensation équitable pour les phonogrammes commerciaux. En Nouvelle-Zélande, la gestion collective obligatoire n'est réglementée qu'en cas de nécessité et non dans la loi sur le droit d'auteur.

La loi portugaise sur le droit d'auteur réglemente la gestion collective obligatoire pour les redevances de copie privée, la rémunération pour la communication au public de phonogrammes commerciaux, les rémunérations pour les droits connexes et la retransmission par câble en tant que droit exclusif. En Espagne, seuls les droits de rémunération et la retransmission par câble sont obligatoirement gérés collectivement. La Suisse a la même réglementation. Enfin, les États-Unis n'ont une gestion collective obligatoire que dans quelques cas, comme les licences statutaires et les licences obligatoires.

La gestion collective élargie implique que le contrat signé entre la CMO et l'utilisateur concerne tous les titulaires de droits de la même catégorie, même si tous n'ont pas accepté d'être représentés par la CMO respective. Cela signifie que le contrat a un effet prolongé. Cependant, dans certains pays, ce résultat ne sera pas atteint avec l'effet prolongé du contrat. Il sera plutôt obtenu par la présomption de représentation de tous les titulaires de droits dans la même catégorie. Par exemple, au Canada, une gestion collective étendue est prévue pour les droits de rémunération lorsque la gestion collective est obligatoire. En Croatie, il existe une présomption de représentation prévue pour tous les droits exclusifs et tous les droits à rémunération. Cela signifie que la CMO sera réputée représenter tous les titulaires de droits de la même catégorie, à l'exception de ceux qui se sont retirés dans une déclaration écrite adressée à la CMO concernée. En République tchèque, la gestion collective étendue s'applique à l'exécution publique d'œuvres musicales, à la diffusion et à divers droits à rémunération. En France, elle s'applique à la gestion des droits sur les livres considérés comme hors commerce, en Allemagne pour la retransmission par câble en tant que droit exclusif, et en Grèce pour la rémunération pour copie privée et la rémunération pour communication au public de phonogrammes commerciaux. En Hongrie, la gestion collective élargie s'applique dans toutes les situations où il existe un monopole naturel et où la gestion collective est obligatoire, par exemple, dans l'exécution publique d'œuvres musicales, y compris la radiodiffusion. Aux Pays-Bas, la gestion collective étendue s'applique aux droits relevant d'un régime de gestion collective obligatoire. En Nouvelle-Zélande, elle n'est appliquée que pour l'utilisation par nécessité et au Portugal pour les droits d'auteur dans la radiodiffusion par satellite, sauf pour les œuvres audiovisuelles. Néanmoins, la gestion collective élargie concerne ici tous les utilisateurs qui participent à la négociation collective.

1.3 La concurrence entre CMO

La question a également été posée dans l'enquête, à savoir si la concurrence entre les organisations de gestion collective est autorisée dans les juridictions concernées. Dans quelles circonstances, à quelle fréquence et dans quels domaines la concurrence peut-elle avoir lieu ?

Ce n'est que dans certains pays, comme l'Argentine, la Croatie, la République tchèque et la Corée, que la concurrence entre CMO n'est généralement pas autorisée. Néanmoins, en Croatie, une exception est prévue pour les CMO qui gèrent les droits d'auteur en ligne sur les œuvres musicales et la Corée pour tous les auteurs de musique. Dans tous les autres pays, la concurrence est autorisée mais n'est pas partout en application pratique. Par exemple, elle est autorisée et existe en Belgique. Bien qu'elle soit autorisée, sauf pour la copie privée et les droits de rémunération, la concurrence n'existe pas en pratique au Canada. La même situation se présente en Colombie, où la concurrence entre les CMO est autorisée mais n'existe pas dans la pratique. En France, elle est autorisée, soutenue et suggérée. En Allemagne, la concurrence existe dans la gestion des droits d'auteur de la musique en ligne, où le répertoire est fragmenté. Dans toutes les autres situations, bien qu'elle soit autorisée, la concurrence n'existe pas dans la pratique.

En Grèce, la concurrence n'est pas interdite, et elle existait en pratique pour le répertoire musical, mais l'une des CMO musicales s'est effondrée. Depuis lors, il n'y a pas eu de concurrence dans l'application pratique. En Hongrie, la concurrence entre les CMO est généralement autorisée, sauf dans les cas où la gestion collective est obligatoire ou lorsque la gestion collective étendue s'applique. Malgré la possibilité légale de concurrence, toutes les CMO sont des monopoles naturels en Hongrie. En Israël, le paysage des CMO est fragmenté. Au Japon, il existe plusieurs CMO pour les droits musicaux, suite à la possibilité de concurrence. Dans ce cas, la concurrence n'est pas autorisée, sauf pour les droits de rémunération statutaires. La loi néerlandaise sur le droit d'auteur autorise également la concurrence entre les CMO, et elle est appliquée dans plusieurs situations. Bien qu'elle soit autorisée par la loi, la concurrence n'existe pas en pratique entre les CMO au Portugal. En Espagne, en revanche, elle est autorisée et existe dans certains cas, comme pour le répertoire audiovisuel. En Suisse, la concurrence existe pour les droits en ligne et dans d'autres situations, elle n'est pas appliquée bien qu'autorisée par la loi. La loi nord-américaine sur le droit d'auteur autorise et encourage la concurrence entre les CMO. Toutefois, en ce qui concerne les droits d'auteur sur la musique, un mandat exclusif n'est absolument pas autorisé.

Les entités de gestion indépendantes, qui sont des concurrents des CMO, sont réglementées par la directive 2014/26/UE sur la gestion collective du droit d'auteur. C'est la raison pour laquelle les lois nationales des États membres de l'Union européenne, tels que la Croatie, la République tchèque, l'Allemagne, la Grèce, les Pays-Bas et l'Espagne, les mentionnent dans leurs rapports concernant la concurrence. Cependant, le problème des entités de gestion indépendantes et de leur réglementation dans ladite directive et dans les lois nationales est l'incohérence concernant la transparence de leurs activités et, par conséquent, l'inégalité de traitement dans la gestion collective du droit d'auteur.

1.4 Forme des organismes de gestion collective

Selon les rapports, la plupart des pays prévoient dans leurs lois respectives que les CMO doivent être organisées comme des organisations à but non lucratif. Il s'agit, par exemple, de l'Allemagne, de l'Argentine, de la Croatie, de la Corée, de la France, d'Israël, des Pays-Bas, du Portugal, de la République tchèque et de la Suisse. Selon la législation belge et espagnole, les CMO nationales doivent être constituées en organisations à but non lucratif. Toutefois, les CMO étrangères des autres États membres de l'Union européenne, qui effectuent des licences transfrontalières en ligne, peuvent également être établies en tant qu'associations ou sociétés à but lucratif. Au Canada, les CMO sont généralement constitués en organisations à but non lucratif, mais il est également possible d'avoir une société ou d'autres organisations à but lucratif opérant en tant que CMO. Bien que la loi colombienne prévoie que les CMO soient constituées en tant qu'organisations à but non lucratif, les titulaires de droits peuvent toujours gérer leurs droits par le biais d'autres formes d'associations. Il est également possible d'avoir des sociétés à but lucratif qui gèrent des entreprises de gestion collective en Grèce. Toutefois, une particularité de la législation grecque permet à l'agence d'État d'agir en tant qu'CMO dans des cas exceptionnels. C'est ce qui s'est passé dans la réalité avec CMO, qui opère sous l'AEPI, mais qui s'est effondré en 2018. En pratique, en Hongrie, les CMO sont des organisations à but non lucratif, bien qu'il soit possible de constituer une CMO en tant que société à but lucratif. Au Japon, où la rémunération statutaire est administrée collectivement de manière obligatoire, il est réglementé que cette CMO doit être établie en tant qu'organisme à but non lucratif. Il en va de même pour tous les autres cas où la gestion collective est obligatoire. En Nouvelle-Zélande et aux États-Unis, il est possible, mais pas obligatoire, de constituer les CMO en organisations à but non lucratif. Pourtant, aux États-Unis, plusieurs CMO existent en tant que sociétés à but lucratif.

1.5 Contribution des organisations de gestion collective au développement culturel et social de la société

À l'exception des États-Unis, où les CMO ne déduisent traditionnellement pas à des fins culturelles et sociales et où les lois ne soutiennent pas leur participation au développement culturel et social de la société, ni volontairement, tous les autres pays ont des activités visant à sensibiliser les CMO à agir dans ce sens. Par exemple, les CMO argentines créent souvent des fonds culturels et sociaux sur une base volontaire. En Belgique, les CMO peuvent affecter jusqu'à 30% de la rémunération pour copie privée et jusqu'à 10% des autres rémunérations à des fins culturelles et sociales. En Croatie, des pourcentages similaires sont réglementés dans la législation sur le droit d'auteur, autorisant les CMO à déduire les coûts à des fins culturelles, sociales et éducatives. Au-delà, la CMO peut déduire jusqu'à 3 % du revenu total pour des programmes de sensibilisation et de lutte contre le piratage. Au Canada, les CMO accordent souvent des subventions et soutiennent financièrement des prix pour des réalisations culturelles et artistiques. De même, les programmes culturels et éducatifs peuvent être partiellement financés par les rémunérations perçues par les CMO. Les CMO colombiennes déduisent volontairement jusqu'à 10 % à des fins culturelles et sociales.

En République tchèque, les CMO peuvent créer des fonds à des fins culturelles, sociales et éducatives, tandis qu'en France, les fonds culturels sont également appliqués sur une base volontaire. Toutefois, il est prévu que 25% de la rémunération pour copie privée soit reversée au fonds culturel ainsi que des montants non distribuables. Il n'y a pas de limitations spéciales pour les déductions culturelles et sociales en Allemagne, à l'exception des règlements qui doivent être basés sur des critères équitables et des règles fixes et transparentes. En Grèce, les montants non distribuables sont affectés aux fonds culturels, sociaux et éducatifs des CMO. En Hongrie, ces montants sont alloués au Fonds culturel national dans le même but. En outre, 25 % des rémunérations pour copie privée sont également versées au Fonds national et culturel. Israël a peu d'allocations à des fins culturelles et sociales sur une base volontaire. Ces CMO attribuent des prix et récompenses culturels et artistiques et sont autorisées à créer des fonds pour les créateurs dans le besoin et à des fins similaires. Au Japon, les CMO peuvent soutenir les conférences et les universités liées à la culture, aux arts et aux concerts. Ils peuvent déduire jusqu'à 20% des rémunérations pour copie privée pour les activités de sensibilisation et les fonds culturels. Lorsque la gestion collective est obligatoire, les CMO peuvent affecter des montants non distribuables à des activités d'intérêt public en Corée.

Aux Pays-Bas, les déductions à des fins culturelles et sociales sont traditionnellement appliquées dans la pratique. Cependant, depuis que l'autorité de surveillance a publié de nouvelles règles, elle est devenue réticente aux déductions, et n'est plus la bienvenue. Certaines CMO appliquent volontairement des fonds culturels en Nouvelle-Zélande. En Suisse, la plupart des CMO allouent souvent des fonds à des fins culturelles et sociales. La loi portugaise sur le droit d'auteur stipule qu'au moins 5% des rémunérations perçues doivent être allouées à des fonds culturels, sociaux et de sensibilisation. En outre, au moins 20 % de la rémunération pour copie privée doivent être affectés à des activités culturelles. Enfin, la législation espagnole impose aux CMO de promouvoir des activités culturelles et des actions de sensibilisation.

2 Relations entre les organismes de gestion collective et les titulaires de droits

2.1 Les titulaires de droits ont-ils le droit d'être représentés ?

La question a été posée de savoir si les auteurs et autres titulaires de droits ont le droit d'être représentés par une CMO. La plupart des pays, notamment les membres de l'Union européenne, disposent d'un tel droit, comme la Belgique, le Canada, Israël, le Japon et les Pays-Bas. Pourtant, l'Allemagne, l'Argentine, la Croatie, l'Espagne, la France, la Grèce, la Hongrie, la République tchèque et la Suisse font une distinction entre les membres et les auteurs représentés. Cela signifie que tous les auteurs et titulaires de droits n'ont pas le droit de devenir membres de la CMO, mais qu'ils ont tous le droit d'être représentés. Comme beaucoup d'autres pays européens, une procédure spéciale de plainte interne est établie pour résoudre les conflits liés au droit d'être représenté au Portugal. En outre, plusieurs CMO recommandent des procédures alternatives de résolution des litiges pour les conflits liés au droit d'être représenté et certains tribunaux ordinaires.

En revanche, en Colombie, en Corée, en Nouvelle-Zélande et aux États-Unis, le droit d'être représenté n'existe pas, ni dans la législation ni dans l'application pratique.

2.2 Résolution des conflits entre titulaires de droits pour «double revendication»

Les conflits de «double revendication» concernent les situations où deux ou plusieurs titulaires de droits affirment détenir des droits contradictoires sur le même objet. Par exemple, deux auteurs prétendent détenir un droit d'auteur sur la même chanson en tant qu'auteurs individuels. Il s'agit d'une situation conflictuelle car chaque demande exclut la demande de la partie adverse. Les CMO ont souvent des dispositions dans leurs actes internes sur la manière de procéder lorsqu'une «double réclamation» apparaît.

L'Argentine, par exemple, réglemente des systèmes facultatifs de règlement interne des litiges, alors que les tribunaux ordinaires sont également à la disposition des parties en conflit. En Belgique, au Canada, en France, au Japon, aux Pays-Bas et en Suisse, les titulaires de droits sont invités à régler le différend pendant que les paiements pour les objets de protection contestés sont suspendus. En Colombie, en Croatie, en République tchèque, en Allemagne, en Grèce, en Hongrie, en Espagne et aux États-Unis, il existe un mécanisme alternatif de règlement des litiges réglementé par les lois sur le droit d'auteur pour les litiges relatifs à la «double réclamation», qui constitue une issue possible. Néanmoins, les parties devraient avoir à leur disposition des mécanismes de plainte spéciaux au sein des CMO et, bien sûr, des tribunaux ordinaires. Pendant que le litige est en cours, les paiements liés aux objets de protection contestés sont suspendus. La plupart des CMO disposent de modes alternatifs de résolution des conflits en Israël, alors que certaines CMO prévoient un arbitrage obligatoire sur la question litigieuse. En Corée, les parties adverses choisissent entre le tribunal ordinaire et les mécanismes alternatifs de résolution des conflits. Le droit portugais réglemente les mécanismes de résolution des plaintes et des litiges au sein des CMO et les mécanismes alternatifs de règlement des litiges, en outre. En Nouvelle-Zélande, il n'existe pas de procédure spécifique pour les «doubles réclamations».

2.3 Participation des auteurs aux conseils d'administration des organismes de gestion collective

La participation des auteurs aux conseils d'administration des organismes de gestion collective est généralement réglementée par les CMO qui, dans la plupart des cas, prescrivent certaines conditions préalables à la candidature pour participer en tant que membres des conseils d'administration ou de surveillance au sein des CMO. C'est le cas en Allemagne, en Argentine, en Belgique, en Croatie, en Corée, en Colombie, en Espagne, en France, en Grèce, en Hongrie, en Nouvelle-Zélande, aux Pays-Bas, au Portugal, en République tchèque et en Suisse. Les conditions préalables établies sont, en général, la durée de l'adhésion aux CMO respectives et le revenu minimum perçu au titre des redevances. En outre, la composition des conseils d'administration doit refléter la structure des différentes catégories de titulaires de droits représentés. Cela signifie qu'un équilibre doit être atteint entre les membres de différents secteurs, c'est-à-dire différentes catégories de titulaires de droits, dans la plupart des cas. Un exemple en est le CMO canadien opérant sous le nom de ReSound.

L'ancienneté peut également jouer un rôle en tant que critère de participation aux conseils d'administration et de surveillance. En outre, en Israël, certaines CMO comptent plusieurs administrateurs (un tiers) qui n'ont aucun intérêt personnel dans la CMO, ce qui signifie qu'ils ne sont pas détenteurs de droits mais élus sur proposition en tant qu'»administrateurs publics». En outre, l'IFPI en Israël a réservé plusieurs postes au conseil d'administration aux membres fondateurs. Aux États-Unis, la composition des conseils d'administration est souvent prévue par les CMO respectifs. Néanmoins, dans certains cas, il existe des conditions préalables réglementées par la loi.

2.4 Répartition des revenus

Les CMO réglementent généralement les règles de distribution et la politique de distribution en tant que politique générale de l'organisation. Ainsi, les CMO argentine, croate, belge, canadienne, colombienne, croate, tchèque, française, allemande, grecque, hongroise, israélienne, japonaise, coréenne, néerlandaise, néo-zélandaise, portugaise, espagnole, suisse et américaine réglementent les règles de distribution en leur sein. Exceptionnellement, dans certains cas, les lois sur le droit d'auteur réglementent également les systèmes de distribution pour répartir les revenus entre les différentes catégories de titulaires de droits s'ils perçoivent les revenus ensemble. Cela peut être le cas, par exemple, pour les recettes perçues pour la communication au public de phonogrammes commerciaux, où les recettes doivent être réparties entre les interprètes et les producteurs de phonogrammes. On peut également trouver des exemples d'intervention juridique dans les recettes perçues conjointement pour différentes catégories de titulaires de droits dans le cadre de la rémunération pour copie privée.

2.5 Autonomie de la volonté d'accorder des licences individuelles directes

La question a été posée de savoir comment la loi ou la pratique juridique reflète la volonté de l'auteur d'accorder des licences individuelles et s'il est permis à l'utilisateur d'obtenir la licence directement de l'auteur représenté. La possibilité de l'»autonomie de la volonté» d'accorder des licences directes individuelles peut être réglementée dans les contrats entre les CMO et les titulaires de droits en Nouvelle-Zélande et en Colombie. Or, ces contrats interdisent souvent l'»autonomie de la volonté». En Israël, l'»autonomie de la volonté» est autorisée, mais le double paiement est interdit, ce qui signifie que si le titulaire du droit délivre une licence à l'utilisateur, la CMO ne peut pas facturer l'utilisateur. L'Argentine, le Canada, la Grèce, le Japon, l'Espagne et les États-Unis connaissent une situation où l'»autonomie de la volonté» d'accorder des licences individuelles est possible, bien que le titulaire du droit ait déjà autorisé la CMO concernée à gérer son droit.

En revanche, si le mandat de représentation a déjà été donné à la CMO, la concession de licences individuelles n'est pas autorisé en Allemagne, en Belgique, en Croatie, en Corée, en France, en Hongrie, en République tchèque et en Suisse. En outre, l'»autonomie de la volonté» n'est pas possible dans la gestion collective obligatoire en Argentine, au Canada, en Grèce, au Japon, en Espagne et aux États-Unis. Toutefois, dans lesdits pays, elle peut se produire dans d'autres situations où la gestion collective est volontaire. Enfin, au Portugal et aux Pays-Bas, l'»autonomie de la volonté» n'est pas autorisée, même si elle apparaît parfois dans la pratique.

2.6 Possibilité de licences non commerciales

L'»autonomie de la volonté» doit être distinguée de la situation de délivrance d'une licence directe non commerciale par un titulaire de droits individuel qui a déjà mandaté la CMO pour représenter ses droits. Cela signifie, par exemple, que la CMO représentera l'auteur, mais que, dans le même temps, il conservera le droit de céder son œuvre sous la licence *creative commons* .

Si les mandats étaient déjà confiés aux CMO, les titulaires de droits ne seraient pas autorisés à accorder en même temps des licences individuelles non commerciales en Argentine. Au Canada et en Allemagne, la gestion collective obligatoire n'est pas possible. Au Japon, la possibilité de licences non commerciales est exclue dans certains cas. En Colombie et en Nouvelle-Zélande, la possibilité de licences non commerciales est réglementée dans un contrat entre la CMO et le titulaire du droit. En revanche, la possibilité de licences individuelles non commerciales, bien que le mandat ait déjà été donné à la CMO, est garantie en Belgique, en Croatie, en République tchèque, en France, en Allemagne, en Grèce, en Hongrie, en Israël, au Japon, en Corée, aux Pays-Bas, au Portugal, en Espagne, en Suisse et aux États-Unis.

3 Relations entre les organismes de gestion collective et les utilisateurs

3.1 Rémunération pour copie privée

La rémunération pour copie privée est réglementée dans la plupart des pays participant à cette enquête, comme la Belgique, le Canada, la Croatie, la République tchèque, la France, l'Allemagne, la Grèce, la Hongrie, Israël, le Japon, les Pays-Bas, la Nouvelle-Zélande, le Portugal, l'Espagne et la Suisse. Toutefois, en Argentine, en Colombie, en Corée et aux États-Unis, la rémunération des droits d'auteur privés n'est pas réglementée par la loi ni appliquée dans la pratique.

Dans certains pays, le principe général de la liberté contractuelle est également respecté pour la fixation du tarif de la rémunération pour copie privée. Dans ces pays, un tarif pour la rémunération pour copie privée est donc négocié entre les CMO et les associations d'utilisateurs. Par exemple, en Allemagne et en Nouvelle-Zélande, il n'y a pas d'interventions légales à la liberté contractuelle lors de la fixation des tarifs pour la copie privée.

En revanche, en Hongrie, l'approbation du ministère de la justice est nécessaire pour un tel tarif. Au Japon, l'approbation d'un organe administratif est nécessaire, et en Suisse, l'approbation de la Commission spéciale est requise.

En outre, en Suisse, en l'absence d'accord sur le tarif de la rémunération pour copie privée, la Commission sera autorisée à fixer le tarif après avoir obtenu un avis préalable non contraignant du Surveillant des prix.

En Croatie, un arbitrage volontaire est possible s'il n'y a pas d'accord sur le tarif entre les CMO et les associations d'utilisateurs. Toutefois, si les parties ne se mettent pas d'accord sur l'arbitrage, la CMO se référera au Conseil d'experts pour un avis non contraignant sur le tarif proposé par les CMO respectives.

Aux Pays-Bas et en France, une commission composée de parties intéressées fixe le tarif de la rémunération pour copie privée. Au Canada, le tarif sera fixé par une Commission du droit d'auteur.

Un acte législatif fixera le tarif de la rémunération pour copie privée dans plusieurs pays, comme la République tchèque, la Grèce, Israël et le Portugal.

En Belgique, le tarif est fixé par un arrêté royal après avis non contraignant de la Commission composée des représentants des parties intéressées.

Enfin, en Espagne, avant que le tarif de la rémunération pour copie privée ne soit fixé dans un acte législatif, il convient de discuter avec les parties intéressées et d'obtenir des rapports consultatifs du Conseil des consommateurs et une médiation ou un arbitrage indépendant.

Étant donné que la majeure partie de l'utilisation se fait sur l'internet, la question s'est posée de savoir s'il y avait eu des tentatives d'introduire des rémunérations ou des taxes pour copie privée pour l'utilisation d'objets protégés sur l'internet, que ce soit sous la forme d'un «forfait» ou d'une taxe spéciale. Seuls deux pays ont fait état de tentatives infructueuses. Au Portugal, il y a eu une tentative en 2016, et en Belgique, plusieurs tentatives ont été rejetées avec l'explication que les FAI ne réalisent pas de communication au public. En France, une rémunération spéciale pour les services de NPVR a été introduite. Dans tous les autres pays, aucune tentative n'a été signalée. Il s'agit de l'Argentine, du Canada, de la Croatie, de la République tchèque, de la Colombie, de l'Allemagne, de la Grèce, de la Hongrie, d'Israël, du Japon, de la Corée, des Pays-Bas, de la Nouvelle-Zélande, de l'Espagne, de la Suisse et des États-Unis.

3.2 Procédures de fixation des tarifs

En fonction de la tradition juridique et des circonstances nationales spécifiques, il existe généralement cinq façons de fixer les tarifs, qui peuvent être appliquées individuellement ou en combinaison. Il s'agit des négociations, du système d'approbation d'un organisme gouvernemental ou d'un comité indépendant, de l'avis non contraignant ou contraignant d'un organisme expert, de la procédure d'arbitrage, de médiation et/ou de conciliation et de l'examen par un tribunal.

Le premier moyen, et le plus souhaitable, de fixer les tarifs est la négociation entre les CMO et les utilisateurs et leurs associations. Les négociations sur les tarifs se déroulent généralement de telle sorte que la CMO propose un tarif. Ensuite, il est négocié avec l'association d'utilisateurs ou certains utilisateurs individuels s'il n'y a pas d'association, par exemple, en radiodiffusion. Dans les États membres de l'Union européenne, tels que la Belgique, la Croatie, la République tchèque, la France, l'Allemagne, la Grèce, la Hongrie, les Pays-Bas, le Portugal et l'Espagne, les tarifs sont proposés par la CMO. Cette proposition est ensuite négociée et éventuellement amendée et modifiée au cours des négociations. Il en va de même en Suisse, en Colombie et en Nouvelle-Zélande.

Au Japon, en revanche, des consultations avec les associations d'utilisateurs auront lieu avant l'établissement du tarif par la CMO. Enfin, dans certains pays, comme l'Argentine, le Canada et Israël, les tarifs peuvent être fixés uniquement par les CMO, sans négociations préalables avec les utilisateurs ou leurs associations. En Israël, au même moment, les tarifs de la radiodiffusion sont généralement négociés. Aux États-Unis, les tarifs des représentations publiques et des services numériques interactifs sont généralement fixés par les CMO. Dans ces pays, la loi ne réglemente pas les négociations.

L'approbation d'un organe gouvernemental ou d'un comité indépendant fait partie des systèmes permettant d'établir des tarifs. C'est le cas en République tchèque, en Hongrie, aux Pays-Bas et en Corée dans certaines situations. Par exemple, en République tchèque, une approbation est nécessaire si le tarif augmente plus que le taux d'inflation. Si tel est le cas, le ministère de la culture est invité à approuver le tarif. En Hongrie, après la fin des négociations entre les CMO et les associations d'usagers, le tarif sera approuvé par le ministère de la justice sans possibilité d'intervention sur les prix. Le rôle du ministère de la justice n'est ici que de supervision. Aux Pays-Bas, l'autorité de surveillance du droit d'auteur analysera le caractère excessif de l'augmentation des tarifs et l'approuvera. En Corée, un ministre compétent approuve le tarif proposé par la CMO après avoir recueilli les avis des parties intéressées et l'avis de la commission spéciale. Contrairement à la République tchèque, à la Hongrie et aux Pays-Bas, où les négociations sur les tarifs proposés ont lieu avant l'approbation d'un organe gouvernemental ou d'un comité indépendant, le processus de négociation est modifié en Corée. Dans ce cas, l'organe gouvernemental joue un rôle actif et décisif dans l'approbation du tarif. Dans le même temps, le processus de négociation est remplacé par le processus de remise d'avis au ministre compétent.

Enfin, aux États-Unis, le Copyright Royalty Board, en tant que comité d'experts indépendants, fixe les tarifs pour certaines utilisations, telles que la retransmission, l'exécution de phonogrammes via des services non interactifs, les licences globales obligatoires pour les utilisations numériques et quelques autres.

Dans certains pays, il existe une possibilité ou une obligation, réglementée par les lois respectives sur le droit d'auteur, pour la partie intéressée de demander l'avis d'un organisme expert. Cet avis est souvent non contraignant. Par exemple, en Croatie, en l'absence d'accord sur le tarif et d'accord sur l'arbitrage pour la fixation du tarif, la CMO est obligée de demander un avis non contraignant du Conseil d'experts. Le contenu de l'avis est également prévu par la loi et se réfère à la question de savoir si les principes établis pour la fixation du tarif ont été suivis lors de la création du tarif en question. En Belgique, en revanche, les utilisateurs peuvent demander l'avis du Service de contrôle ou de l'Autorité de la concurrence pour examiner si la CMO a abusé de sa position dominante. Cet avis de l'organisme expert compétent sera contraignant.

En outre, par exemple, supposons qu'il n'y ait pas d'accord sur le tarif au Japon. Dans ce cas, les parties peuvent soumettre la demande à l'Agence pour les affaires culturelles, qui consultera préalablement le Conseil de la culture et émettra ensuite un avis non contraignant sur le tarif. En Corée, à la demande du ministre compétent dans le processus d'approbation du tarif, la Commission émettra un avis non contraignant sur le tarif proposé.

Les lois respectives sur le droit d'auteur de nombreux pays réglementent la procédure d'arbitrage, de médiation ou de conciliation pour la fixation des tarifs. Ceci est systématisé ici comme la quatrième façon possible de fixer le tarif.

La procédure d'arbitrage est généralement similaire à la procédure judiciaire, mais sans formalités et basée sur des critères d'équité. Alors que le résultat de la procédure d'arbitrage est généralement contraignant pour les deux parties à un processus, la médiation est plus souple. Il est demandé au médiateur d'aider les parties à parvenir à un accord et il est donc invité à soumettre des propositions de règlement. Le médiateur doit proposer le tarif en fonction des suggestions des parties. Si les parties ne s'opposent pas en temps voulu à la proposition des médiateurs, celle-ci doit être considérée comme un tarif contraignant. Dans les Etats membres de l'Union européenne, la procédure de médiation est réglementée dans la fixation des tarifs de retransmission par câble. Il s'agit d'une procédure harmonisée au niveau européen. Enfin, dans une procédure de conciliation, le rôle du conciliateur est encore plus souple, et ses suggestions ne seront acceptées que sur une base volontaire.

Dans le même ordre d'idées, en Croatie et en Grèce, la procédure d'arbitrage sur les tarifs est possible si les parties conviennent de l'arbitrage, et dans ce cas, la décision de l'arbitre est définitive. Une solution similaire est appliquée au Portugal, où les parties peuvent se référer au Comité d'experts pour un arbitrage sur le tarif. En Suisse, un tarif établi par la CMO peut être contesté devant la Commission d'arbitrage. Aux Pays-Bas, le Tariff Tribunal examinera le caractère raisonnable du tarif, comme en Nouvelle-Zélande.

La commission d'arbitrage propose le règlement en Allemagne, bien que cette proposition ne soit pas contraignante. Bien qu'il s'agisse d'un arbitrage, il s'agit donc en fait d'une médiation par le contenu. En Hongrie, la médiation est possible dans le processus de fixation des tarifs avant l'approbation du Ministère de la Justice.

Une procédure de conciliation est possible lors des négociations sur les tarifs en République tchèque, la proposition du conciliateur étant non contraignante.

Il existe plusieurs procédures extrajudiciaires possibles en Espagne, où l'organisme expert en droit d'auteur compétent exerce des fonctions de médiation, d'arbitrage, de détermination et de contrôle des tarifs.

Si les parties l'invitent, le secrétaire chargé des médias de communication peut participer à une procédure de fixation des tarifs en Argentine. Au Canada, bien que les CMO aient le droit de fixer des tarifs sans procédure particulière, elles ont ensuite l'obligation de les soumettre à la Commission du droit d'auteur, qui peut intervenir si elle le juge nécessaire. Au Japon, où il n'existe pas d'accord sur le tarif de la rémunération des artistes-interprètes et des producteurs de phonogrammes, c'est l'Agence pour les affaires culturelles qui le fixe. En Corée, les parties peuvent faire appel à une procédure de médiation ou de conciliation, qui est non contraignante.

L'examen par le tribunal est généralement la dernière étape de la procédure de fixation des tarifs. C'est la cinquième façon d'établir le tarif. En Belgique et en Grèce, les utilisateurs peuvent soumettre le tarif au tribunal général si les négociations n'aboutissent pas. Selon les règles générales appliquées aux procédures d'arbitrage, il existe une possibilité limitée de contester la décision contraignante de la commission d'arbitrage sur le tarif devant un tribunal compétent en Croatie. En République tchèque, le tribunal peut être invité à statuer sur le dossier tarifaire en l'absence d'accord. Les tarifs peuvent être contestés devant les tribunaux allemands si les parties n'acceptent pas la proposition de la commission d'arbitrage. Le contrôle judiciaire est également possible en Hongrie, après la procédure d'approbation devant le ministère de la justice. Aux Pays-Bas, le dossier tarifaire peut être soumis au tribunal administratif après l'approbation de l'organe de surveillance. De même, le tarif peut être soumis au tribunal général après la décision du tribunal tarifaire sur son caractère raisonnable. Le tarif peut être contesté devant un tribunal compétent immédiatement après sa délivrance en Espagne. En Suisse, la décision de la Commission d'arbitrage peut être révisée par le tribunal. Après l'intervention de la Commission du droit d'auteur au Canada, le tarif peut faire l'objet d'une révision judiciaire. En Nouvelle-Zélande, la décision du Copyright Tribunal peut faire l'objet d'un appel devant le tribunal. Enfin, aux États-Unis, dans les cas où la CMO fixe le tarif, celui-ci peut être contesté devant le tribunal fédéral.

3.3 Critères de fixation des tarifs

Différents critères sont appliqués pour fixer les tarifs. La plupart des pays européens réglementent ces critères dans leurs lois respectives sur le droit d'auteur, en essayant d'atteindre un certain niveau d'harmonisation. Cependant, dans d'autres parties du monde, les critères de fixation des tarifs ne sont pas harmonisés dans les lois sur le droit d'auteur, bien qu'il n'y ait pas beaucoup de différences dans l'application pratique.

Par exemple, en Belgique, les critères de fixation des tarifs doivent être objectifs et non discriminatoires. En outre, la rémunération doit être raisonnable au regard, entre autres, de la valeur économique de l'utilisation des droits, de la nature et de l'étendue de l'utilisation et des services et de la valeur économique du service fourni par la CMO.

Des critères similaires s'appliquent en Croatie, alors que certains sont définis de manière plus détaillée. Dans ce cas, les tarifs doivent être raisonnables par rapport, entre autres, à la valeur économique de l'utilisation des droits sur le marché, compte tenu de la nature et de la portée de l'utilisation des objets protégés, de la valeur économique du service fourni par la CMO concernée et, par conséquent, des tarifs applicables dans d'autres États membres de l'Union européenne. En outre, comme en Allemagne, les besoins religieux, sociaux et culturels des utilisateurs qui appartiennent aux groupes sociaux sensibles des retraités, des enfants et des personnes handicapées seront pris en compte dans une mesure appropriée.

Selon la loi tchèque sur le droit d'auteur, les tarifs seront basés sur des critères objectifs et non discriminatoires et sur des critères de proportionnalité. Le but, la manière, la portée et les circonstances de l'utilisation seront donc pris en compte, ainsi que les critères de savoir si les œuvres protégées par le droit d'auteur sont utilisées dans le cadre de l'activité professionnelle et si l'utilisation a un caractère économique direct. En outre, il convient également de tenir compte de la spécificité du lieu où l'utilisation des œuvres protégées par le droit d'auteur a eu lieu, de la fréquence de l'utilisation dans les lieux d'hébergement où les œuvres sont utilisées, du nombre de titulaires de droits pour lesquels la CMO effectue une gestion collective ou du nombre de personnes auxquelles l'œuvre a été notifiée.

En France, comme dans tous les autres pays européens, il est stipulé que les tarifs seront basés sur des critères transparents, objectifs et non discriminatoires. En outre, ils doivent être raisonnables et établir des rémunérations appropriées pour les détenteurs de droits. En particulier, lors de la fixation des tarifs, la valeur économique du droit donné sera prise en compte, ainsi que des critères supplémentaires, à savoir si la licence fait référence au droit exclusif ou au droit à rémunération, la nature et l'étendue de l'utilisation du contenu protégé, les droits donnés et la valeur économique du service fourni par la CMO.

La loi allemande sur le droit d'auteur stipule qu'en général, un pourcentage du revenu de l'utilisateur est pris en compte pour fixer le tarif et que d'autres méthodes peuvent être appliquées. En outre, il convient de prendre en compte la part du répertoire sous licence dans l'ensemble du répertoire et la valeur économique des services fournis par la CMO. Les préoccupations religieuses, culturelles et sociales des usagers et celles des services de la jeunesse sont également des critères de fixation des tarifs.

En Grèce, les critères de fixation des tarifs doivent être objectifs. Par conséquent, la valeur économique de l'utilisation des droits dans le commerce ainsi que la nature et la portée de l'utilisation concernant la valeur économique des services fournis par la CMO seront prises en compte lors de la fixation des tarifs.

En Hongrie, toutes les circonstances pertinentes doivent être prises en compte lors de la fixation des tarifs. Le principe de l'égalité de traitement est appliqué.

Dans la loi néerlandaise sur le droit d'auteur, l'augmentation d'un tarif ne doit pas être excessive. Elle doit être justifiée, et les intérêts des utilisateurs doivent être pris en compte. Des catégories comparables d'utilisateurs doivent être traitées de la même manière. En outre, il est prévu que les tarifs doivent être raisonnables et fondés sur des critères objectifs et non discriminatoires. Le caractère raisonnable doit être atteint par rapport à la valeur économique de l'utilisation des droits commerciaux, en tenant compte de la nature et de la portée de l'utilisation du répertoire et de la valeur des services de la CMO.

La loi portugaise sur le droit d'auteur régit également les mêmes critères. Il s'agit de la non-discrimination, du caractère raisonnable et proportionnel, de la valeur économique des droits, du résultat d'une négociation sur le marché réel, du résultat d'une négociation sur le marché réel et de la valeur économique de l'utilisation du répertoire.

En Espagne, les tarifs sont établis dans des conditions raisonnables, en tenant compte de la valeur économique de l'utilisation des droits et en essayant de trouver un juste équilibre entre les parties. A cette fin, l'on tient compte au moins des critères suivants : le degré d'utilisation effective du répertoire dans le cadre de l'activité de l'utilisateur dans son ensemble, l'intensité et la pertinence de l'utilisation du répertoire dans le cadre de l'activité de l'utilisateur dans son ensemble, l'étendue du répertoire de l'entité de gestion, le revenu économique obtenu par l'utilisateur pour l'exploitation commerciale du répertoire, la valeur économique du service fourni par l'entité de gestion pour assurer l'application des tarifs, les taux établis par la CMO avec d'autres utilisateurs pour le même type d'utilisation, les taux établis par des CMO similaires dans d'autres Etats membres de l'Union européenne, à condition qu'il existe une base de comparaison homogène.

L'équité, le revenu de l'utilisateur, le répertoire utilisé, la relation entre les œuvres protégées et non protégées seront considérés comme des critères de fixation du tarif, parmi d'autres critères, en Suisse. En général, il faut prendre jusqu'à 10% du revenu pour les droits d'auteur et 3% pour les droits voisins.

Contrairement aux autres, le rapport argentin ne mentionne pas de critères spécifiques pour la fixation du tarif.

Les critères canadiens de fixation des tarifs mentionnent des acheteurs et des vendeurs consentants agissant dans un marché concurrentiel avec toutes les informations pertinentes. Outre ces critères de base, les intérêts publics doivent être pris en compte lors de la fixation des tarifs, parallèlement aux réglementations et autres critères appropriés.

La proportionnalité, le revenu de l'utilisateur, la catégorie de l'utilisateur, la capacité technologique, la capacité du lieu, la modalité et l'intensité de l'utilisation dans la commercialisation d'un bien ou d'un service et tout autre critère pertinent sont mentionnés dans le rapport colombien.

Les critères déclarés par Israël sont le pourcentage de recettes , la taille du public, la capacité, la superficie et d'autres méthodes.

Au Japon, les CMO respectives élaboreront des critères pour les différents types d'œuvres et d'exploitations. Entre autres, les critères suivants seront pris en compte : le type d'utilisateur, la capacité du public, la taille du lieu, la durée d'utilisation, le type de contrat.

Les CMO de Corée élaborent différents critères, tels que le type d'utilisateur, la capacité publique, la taille du lieu, la durée d'utilisation, le type de contrat, et diverses méthodologies, comme le pourcentage du revenu.

En Nouvelle-Zélande, il n'existe pas de critères statutaires pour la fixation des tarifs. Au lieu de cela, les CMO élaborent les critères, qui comprennent la comparaison avec d'autres tarifs, le caractère raisonnable et la non-discrimination.

Aux États-Unis, les critères de fixation des tarifs sont généralement élaborés sur le marché et non établis par la loi. Pour les spectacles publics et les utilisations similaires, les critères utilisés sont, par exemple, le type d'utilisateurs, la taille de la salle, etc. En revanche, les critères pour les services non interactifs sont prévus par la loi. Il s'agit notamment de la quantité et de la nature de l'utilisation, du soutien des services de promotion et des critères d'acheteur et de vendeur consentants. Tous les tarifs sont basés sur des informations économiques, concurrentielles et de programmation. Les tarifs tiendront compte des types d'utilisation comparables.

3.4 Transparence des tarifs

Selon la grande majorité des rapports nationaux, leur publication assure la transparence des tarifs. Les tarifs sont régulièrement publiés en Allemagne, Argentine, Belgique, Canada, Corée, Croatie, Espagne, Colombie, France, Grèce, Hongrie, Pays-Bas, Portugal, République tchèque, Suisse et Etats-Unis. En Israël, les tarifs sont aussi généralement publiés. Néanmoins, celles négociées ou fixées par l'arbitrage peuvent être inédites.

Au Japon, en revanche, les CMO ne sont pas obligées de publier les tarifs. Au lieu de cela, ils publient des données sur la collecte. Le rapport souligne toutefois que la transparence des tarifs est assurée par l'obligation faite aux CMO de donner aux utilisateurs 30 jours pour se préparer à l'application des nouveaux tarifs.

En Nouvelle-Zélande, les licences sont considérées comme des arrangements privés. Aucune règle de transparence statutaire ne leur sera donc appliquée.

3.5 Questions de concurrence

En Argentine, en Belgique, au Canada, en Colombie, en Croatie, en République tchèque, en France, en Allemagne, en Grèce, en Hongrie, en Israël, au Japon, en Corée, aux Pays-Bas, en Nouvelle-Zélande, au Portugal, en Espagne, en Suisse et aux États-Unis, les lois sur la concurrence reconnaissent la possibilité d'un abus de position dominante des CMO. Alors que la Hongrie, Israël, la Suisse et la Nouvelle-Zélande n'ont pas fait état d'exemples où l'autorité de la concurrence a décidé d'un abus de position dominante de la part des CMO, d'autres pays ont signalé quelques cas.

Par exemple, la Croatie a fait état de décisions des autorités de la concurrence dans lesquelles des remises différentes en fonction de la quantité de supports vendus pour la copie privée ont été qualifiées d'abus de position dominante de HDS ZAMP. Cette CMO a donc été condamnée à une amende pécuniaire et sommée de modifier ses pratiques. De même, en Espagne, il y a eu un cas d'abus de position dominante de la part de SGAE en raison de rabais non transparents pour la diffusion de musique et de rabais discriminatoires et non transparents pour les restaurants (mariages et occasions similaires). Selon une autre décision de l'autorité espagnole de la concurrence, l'AISGE a augmenté de manière unilatérale et injustifiée le taux général, d'une part, et a appliqué des taux et des primes différents à différents cinémas de manière discriminatoire, d'autre part. Dans d'autres cas soulevés contre AGEDI en Espagne, il a été décidé qu'il n'y avait pas d'abus de position dominante (cas Radio et cas AFEC-CEDRO).

La République tchèque a fait état d'une affaire de la CJUE, OSA, C-351/12, dans laquelle l'abus de position dominante consistait à imposer des frais élevés injustifiés à la CMO en situation de monopole. La SGAE en Espagne a également reçu une amende en raison de redevances injustes et excessives pour les concerts. En Grèce, l'imposition de frais de gestion excessifs et l'absence de transparence des informations à l'égard des utilisateurs et des membres ont été qualifiées d'abus de position dominante par une CMO.

D'autre part, une affaire contre la JASRAC au Japon a montré qu'une perception globale des redevances sur la base des revenus des radiodiffuseurs constitue une «monopolisation privée», mais avant la décision de l'autorité de concurrence respective, l'affaire a été rejetée parce que l'action en justice contre la JASRAC a été retirée. En même temps, en Colombie, en France, en Allemagne et en Corée, les procédures engagées contre les CMO pour abus de position dominante dans la fixation des tarifs n'ont révélé aucun abus. En outre, en Belgique, l'autorité de la concurrence a décidé que le tarif n'est pas abusif lorsqu'il est établi en pourcentage des recettes publicitaires ou lorsqu'il établit des minima garantis.

Par ailleurs, l'application du même tarif à un organisateur du festival qui prétend que son festival est différent des autres ne constitue pas un abus de position dominante.

Par ailleurs, l'affaire portugaise s'est terminée devant la Cour de justice des Communautés européennes (MEO, C-525/16). Il a donc été décidé que toutes les circonstances pertinentes doivent être prises en compte lors de l'évaluation des cas individuels. Les différences entre les tarifs applicables à deux utilisateurs similaires ne sont donc pas susceptibles de fausser la concurrence car elles n'ont pas été suffisantes pour provoquer la distorsion sur le marché.

En Colombie, il a été décidé que l'abus de position dominante est une pratique de la CMO qui ne permet pas à ses membres de limiter le mandat donné et d'obtenir une licence directement pour les droits de diffusion. Une affaire contre BUMA / STEMRA aux Pays-Bas a montré l'abus de position dominante d'une CMO envers ses membres. Il a donc été recommandé de faire preuve de plus de souplesse à l'égard des mandats des membres. Les «Consent decrees» (c'est-à-dire les injonctions utilisées comme moyen de réguler les industries monopolistiques) contre l'ASCAP et le BMI aux États-Unis ont abouti à des accords de représentation non exclusive pour les droits de représentation publique avec leurs membres.

Plusieurs affaires en cours ont également été signalées. Par exemple, en Argentine, l'association hôtelière soutient que la SADAIC a abusé de sa position dominante. L'affaire contre la SABAM est pendante devant la Cour d'appel de Bruxelles. L'on a affirmé que la SABAM abuse de sa position dominante en raison d'une augmentation excessive des tarifs d'une année à l'autre, de l'absence de déductions suffisantes, d'une prise en compte insuffisante du répertoire représenté, et de redevances minimales imposées trop élevées. Enfin, BUMA / STEMRA ont été poursuivis aux Pays-Bas en raison de leurs tarifs prétendument discriminatoires pour la musique de fond. Les décisions devraient être rendues sous peu.

GENERAL REPORT: COLLECTIVE MANAGEMENT OF RIGHTS

Romana Matanovac Vučković*

The answers to the questionnaire prepared by the Czech group of ALAI were provided by the following ALAI national groups: Argentina, Belgium, Canada, Columbia, Croatia, Czechia, France, Germany, Greece, Hungary, Israel, Italy, Japan, Korea, Netherlands, New Zealand, Portugal, Spain, Switzerland and the USA. The results were presented at ALAI 2019 Copyright Congress in Prague. Therefore, this text reflects the state of play from September 2019 regarding the legislative and practical situation in the said countries, relying on the answers provided by the national ALAI groups.

The questionnaire was divided into three parts. The first part referred to a general overview of collective management. The second was dedicated to the relationship between CMOs, authors, and other right holders. Finally, the third part examined the relationship between CMOs and users. The answers will be comprehended hereafter.

1 General overview of collective management

1.1 Collective management organisations: natural or legal monopolies

Throughout history, CMOs were regularly perceived as societies with a monopoly position on the market. However, their monopoly position was at the same time challenged, particularly by competition rules. Some countries decided to answer this challenge by regulating their monopoly position in the law. Some let them as natural monopolies. Some turned their path towards competition in the market, especially on the internet.

Not many countries decided to regulate collective management organisations as legal monopolies. Among them is Argentina, where all CMOs have a legal monopoly. Croatia and Czechia also expressly regulate that CMOs have a monopoly in their copyright laws. This refers basically to categories of rights holders and categories of rights, which means that one category of right holders may establish one CMO per category of rights. Nevertheless, a practical implication is that there is one CMO per category of right holders in their markets, regulating all categories of rights. The

* Professor, University of Zagreb, Faculty of Law.

exception from legal monopoly is the CMOs for music authors for cross-border licensing of music on the internet. Korea also generally regulates the legal monopoly of CMOs, except for music authors.

In most countries, such as Israel, Canada, Columbia, France, Greece, Germany, New Zealand, Portugal, Spain and Switzerland, CMOs are natural monopolies. This means that their monopoly position is not regulated in copyright laws of the respective countries but the consequence of the market behaviour. Although the law does not prescribe that there should be only one CMO for a category of right holders and a category of rights, the market developed only one CMO with a monopoly position with respect to said criteria.

Several countries have a combination of legal monopolies, natural monopolies and sometimes also competing CMOs. For example, in Belgium, CMOs are natural monopolies for traditional uses of protected subject matters. Still, for remuneration rights, cable retransmission and direct injection CMOs are legal monopolies prescribed by the relevant copyright act. At the same time, there is no monopoly at all for online rights. Also, Hungarian copyright law prescribes legal monopoly only in cases where collective management of rights is compulsory. There is no legal monopoly in other cases, and competition is possible, although CMOs are regularly natural monopolies in practice.

For example, there is no monopoly for exclusive rights in Japan, but a legal monopoly is prescribed for remuneration rights. In this group fall private copying and statutory remuneration for the public performance of commercial phonograms. In the Netherlands, some CMOs are legally appointed as monopolies, for example, in the case of private copy, public lending and neighbouring rights. On the other hand, some CMOs, such as those competent for collective management of reproduction rights, are natural monopolies. Finally, there are competing CMOs in the same field and category of rights, basically on the internet.

In the USA, due to the size of the territory and market, historical reasons and specific national circumstances, there are regularly more than one CMOs per category of rights and category of right owners. For example, there are several CMOs for music authors for public performance, such as ASCAP, BMI, SESAC and GMA. Nevertheless, competition authority recognises CMOs as natural monopolies.

1.2 Voluntary, extended and mandatory collective management

The question in the survey was posed, whether the copyright system differentiates between voluntary, extended and mandatory collective management and which rights are managed under which regime. Belgium, Canada, Croatia, Czechia, France, Germany, Greece, Hungary, Israel, Japan, Korea, Netherlands, New Zealand, Portugal, Spain, Switzerland, and the USA answered that their copyright laws provide voluntary collective management for most cases. This means that the right owner may choose to administer his copyright individually or through a collective management system. For example, in the system of voluntary collective management, even if a CMO was established for some category of rights, the right owner might decide not to administer this category of his rights through CMO.

Columbia is a rare example where all rights may be only voluntary administered collectively. Collective management is never mandatory because the constitutional court decided that mandatory collective management is contrary to the constitution and therefore forbidden as the model for copyright management. On the other hand, Argentina has voluntary management of copyright only in a few cases. In most cases in this country, rights, such as public performance and reproduction, are administered mandatory collectively through CMOs.

In Belgium, mandatory collective management is provided for remuneration rights, cable retransmission, and direct injection. In Canada, only remuneration rights and levies are administered mandatory collectively. The list of exclusive rights mandatorily administered collectively in Croatia is unusual compared to other European Union countries. There, broadcasting rights must be administered collectively, alongside cable retransmission, other types of retransmission and direct injection. In addition, remuneration rights and private copying are also administered mandatorily collectively. In the Czech Republic, mandatory collective management is regulated for remunerations for commercial phonograms, private copying and other remuneration rights. Cable retransmission, private copying and other remuneration rights will also be mandatory collectively administered in France. German copyright law provides mandatory collective management for cable retransmission rights and statutory remunerations. In Greece, private copying, remuneration for the public performance of commercial phonograms, other remuneration rights, and cable retransmission of exclusive rights are also administered mandatory collectively. Similar to Croatia, in Hungary, broadcasting of musical works, cable retransmission, reproduction right, private copying, and other remuneration rights will be in the regime of mandatory collective management. Israel prescribes mandatory collective management for private copying and remuneration for audiovisual performances. Japan regulates mandatory collective management for private copying and statutory remuneration rights for the public performance of commercial phonograms. Korea reserves mandatory collective management only for remuneration rights. In the Netherlands, the list of rights that mandatorily need to be administered collectively is longer. The list includes cable retransmission, communication to the public of film works, private copying, lending and fair compensation for commercial phonograms. In New Zealand, mandatory collective management is regulated only when necessary and not in copyright law.

Portuguese copyright law regulates mandatory collective management for private copy levies, remuneration for communication to the public of commercial phonograms, remunerations for related rights, and cable retransmission as an exclusive right. In Spain, only remuneration rights and cable retransmission are mandatorily administered collectively. Switzerland has the same regulation, and, finally, the USA has mandatory collective management only in a few cases, such as statutory licences and compulsory licences.

Extended collective management implies that the contract signed between the CMO and the user shall affect all right owners in the same category, although not all of them agreed to be represented by the respective CMO. This means that the contract has extended effect. However, in some countries, this result will not be achieved through the extended effect of the contract. Instead, it will be achieved through the presumption of representation of all right owners in the same category. For example, in Canada, extended collective management is provided for remuneration rights when collective management is mandatory. In Croatia, there is a presumption of representation provided for all exclusive rights and all rights of remuneration. This means the CMO will be deemed to represent all right owners in the same category, except those who opted out in a written statement directed towards the respective CMO. In the Czech Republic, extended collective management applies to the public performance of musical works, for broadcasting and several rights to remuneration. In France, it is applied to the administration of rights in books considered to be out-of-commerce, in Germany for cable retransmission as the exclusive right, and in Greece for private copy remuneration and remuneration for communication to the public of commercial phonograms. In Hungary, extended collective management shall occur in all situations where there is a natural monopoly and where collective management is mandatory, for example, in public performance, including broadcasting, of musical works. In the Netherlands, extended collective management applies for rights under a mandatory collective management regime. In New Zealand, it is applied only for use-through-necessity and in Portugal for authors' rights in satellite broadcasting except for audiovisual works. Nevertheless, here extended collective management relates to all users who participate in collective bargaining.

1.3 Competition among CMOs

The question was also posed in the survey, whether competition among collective management organisations is permitted in the relevant jurisdictions. Under which circumstances, how often and in which fields the competition may occur?

Only in several countries, such as Argentina, Croatia, the Czech Republic and Korea, the competition among CMOs is generally not allowed. Nevertheless, in Croatia, an exception is provided for CMOs that administer online copyright in musical works and Korea for all music authors. In all other countries, competition is allowed but not everywhere is in practical application. For example, it is allowed and exists in Belgium. Although allowed except for private copying and remuneration rights, there is no competition in practice in Canada. The same situation is in Columbia, where competition between CMOs is allowed but does not exist in practice. In France, it is allowed, supported and suggested. In Germany, competition exists in online music copyright management, where the repertoire is fragmented. In all other situations, although allowed, competition is not existing in practice.

In Greece, competition is not forbidden, and it existed in practice for music repertoire, but then one of the music CMOs collapsed. Since then, there has been no competition in practical application. In Hungary, competition of CMOs is generally allowed, except in cases where collective management is mandatory or where extended collective management applies. Despite the legal possibility of competition, all CMOs are natural monopolies in Hungary. In Israel, the landscape for CMOs is fragmented. In Japan, there are multiple CMOs for music rights, following the possibility of competition. There, only for statutory remuneration rights competition is not allowed. Netherlandian copyright law also allows competition among CMOs, and it is applied in several situations. Although permitted by the law, competition does not exist in practice among CMOs in Portugal. In Spain, on the other hand, it is allowed and exists in some cases, such as for audiovisual repertoire. In Switzerland, competition exists for online rights and in other situations is not applied although permitted by the law. USA copyright law allows and encourages competition between CMOs. However, regarding music copyright, an exclusive mandate is not allowed at all.

Independent management entities, which are competitors to CMOs, are regulated in Directive 2014/26/EU on collective management of copyright. Therefore, national laws of the European Union's member states, such as Croatia, the Czech Republic, Germany, Greece, the Netherlands, and Spain, mention them in their reports regarding the competition. However, the problem with independent management entities and their regulation in the said Directive and national laws is the inconsistency regarding transparency of their activities and, therefore, unequal treatment in collective management of copyright.

1.4 Form of collective management organisations

According to the reports, most countries in their respective laws regulate that CMOs should be organised as not-for-profit organisations. Those are, for example, Argentina, Croatia, Czech Republic, France, Germany, Israel, Korea, the Netherlands, Portugal and Switzerland. According to the law in Belgium and Spain, national CMOs should be formed as not-for-profit organisations. Still, foreign CMOs, originating from the other Member States of the European Union, which perform online cross-border licensing, may also be established as for-profit associations or companies. In Canada, CMOs are usually formed as not-for-profit organisations, but it is possible to have also company or other for-profit organisations operating as CMO. Although in Columbia it is provided for in the law that CMOs would be formed as not-for-profit organisations, right holders still can manage rights through other forms of associations. It is also possible to have for-profit companies that operate collective management businesses in Greece. Still, one peculiarity in Greek law enables the state agency to operate as

CMO in exceptional cases. This was the case in real life with CMO, which operates under AEPI, but collapsed in 2018. In practice in Hungary, CMOs are not-for-profit organisations, although there is a possibility to form CMO as a for-profit company. In Japan, where statutory remuneration is administered mandatory collectively, it is regulated that this CMO needs to be established as a not-for-profit. The same applies to all other cases where collective management is mandatory. In New Zealand and the USA, it is possible, but not mandatory, to form CMOs as not-for-profit organisations. Still, in the USA, several CMOs exist as for-profit companies.

1.5 Contribution of collective management organisations to the cultural and social development of the society

Apart from the USA, where CMOs traditionally do not deduct for cultural and social purposes and where the laws do not support their participation in society's cultural and social development, neither voluntarily, all other countries have some activities directed towards sensitisation of CMOs to act with this respect. For example, Argentinian CMOs regularly establish cultural and social fonds on a voluntary basis. In Belgium, CMOs can allocate up to 30% from private copying remunerations and up to 10% from other remunerations for cultural and social purposes. In Croatia, similar percentages are regulated in copyright legislation, allowing CMOs to deduct for cultural, social and educational purposes. Above that, up to 3% of the total income CMO may deduct for raising awareness and anti-piracy programs. In Canada, CMOs regularly give grants and financially support awards for cultural and artistic achievements. Similarly, cultural and educational programs may be partly financed from remunerations collected by CMOs. Columbian CMOs voluntarily deduct up to 10% for cultural and social purposes.

In the Czech Republic, CMOs may establish fonds for cultural, social and educational purposes, while in France, cultural fonds are also applied voluntarily. Still, it is regulated that 25% from private copying remunerations goes to cultural fond and non-distributable amounts also. There are no special limitations for cultural and social deductions in Germany, except the regulations that need to be based on fair criteria and fixed and transparent rules. In Greece, non-distributable amounts are allocated to the cultural, social and educational fonds of CMOs. In Hungary, those amounts are allocated to the National Cultural Fond with the same purpose. In addition, 25% of the private copying remunerations also go to the National and Cultural Fond. Israel has few allocations for cultural and social purposes on a voluntary basis. Those CMOs allocate for cultural and artistic prizes and awards and are allowed to establish fonds for creators in need and similar purposes. CMOs may support Japan's lectures and universities connected with culture, arts, and concerts. They can deduct up to 20% from private copying remunerations for raising awareness activities and cultural fonds. Where collective management is mandatory, CMOs may allocate non-distributable amounts for public interest activities in Korea.

In the Netherlands, deductions for cultural and social purposes are traditionally applied in practice. Still, since Supervision Authority issued new rules, it became reluctant to deductions, no longer welcomed. Some CMOs apply cultural fonds voluntarily in New Zealand. In Switzerland, most of CMOs regularly allocate for cultural and social purposes. Portuguese copyright law regulates that no less than 5% of collected remunerations shall be allocated to cultural, social, and raising awareness fond. Furthermore, no less than 20% from private copying remuneration shall be earmarked for cultural activities. And finally, Spanish law requires CMOs to promote cultural activities and raise awareness activities.

2 Relations between collective management organisations and right owners

2.1 Do right holders have a right to be represented?

The question was posed whether the authors and other right owners have a right to be represented by a CMO. Most countries, particularly Members of the European Union, have such a right as Belgium, Canada, Israel, Japan, and the Netherlands. Still, Argentina, Croatia, the Czech Republic, France, Germany, Greece, Hungary, Spain and Switzerland distinguish between members and represented authors. This means that not all authors and right holders have the right to become members of the CMO, but they all have the right to be represented. Like many other European countries, a special internal complaint procedure is established to resolve conflicts related to the right to be represented in Portugal. In addition, several CMOs recommend alternative dispute resolution procedures for conflicts related to the right to be represented and some regular courts.

On the other hand, in Columbia, Korea, New Zealand and the USA, there is no right to be represented, neither in legislation nor in practical application.

2.2 Resolution of conflicts between rights holders for "double claim"

"Double claim" conflicts relate to situations where two or more rights holders claim that they own conflicting rights in the same object. For example, two authors claim they own a copyright in the same song as individual authors. This is a conflicting situation because each claim excludes the opposing party's claim. CMOs regularly have some provisions in their internal acts on proceeding when a "double claim" appears.

Argentina, for example, regulates optional internal dispute resolution systems, while ordinary courts are also at the disposal of conflicting parties. In Belgium, Canada, France, Japan, the Netherlands and Switzerland, rights holders are invited to settle the dispute while the payments for disputed objects of protection are suspended. In Columbia, Croatia, the Czech Republic, Germany, Greece, Hungary, Spain and USA, there is an alternative dispute mechanism regulated in copyright laws for "double claim" disputes as a possible way out. Still, parties should have at their disposal special complaint mechanisms within CMOs and, of course, the regular courts. While the dispute is pending, payments related to the disputed objects of protection are suspended. Most CMOs have alternative dispute resolution at disposal in Israel, while some CMOs provide for compulsory arbitration on the disputed issue. In Korea, opposing parties choose between the regular court and alternative dispute resolution mechanisms. Portuguese law regulates complaint and dispute resolution mechanisms within CMOs and alternative dispute mechanisms, in addition. In New Zealand, there is no specific procedure for "double claims".

2.3 Participation of authors in boards of collective management organisations

Participation of authors in boards of collective management organisations is usually regulated by CMOs which in most cases prescribe some preconditions for candidacy to participate as members of administrative or supervisory boards within CMOs. This is the situation in Argentina, Belgium, Croatia, Czech Republic, Columbia, France, Germany, Greece, Hungary, Korea, Netherlands, New Zealand, Portugal, Spain and Switzerland. The prescribed preconditions are, in general, duration of membership within the respective CMOs and minimum income received from royalties. In addition, the composition of the boards should reflect the structure of different categories of rights holders represented. This means that balance should be achieved among members from different sectors, *i.e.* different categories of rightsholders, in most cases. An example of this is the Canadian CMO operating under the name ReSound.

Seniority may also play a role as a criterion for participation in administrative and supervisory boards. Also, in Israel, some CMOs have several directors (one third) with no personal interest in CMO, which means they are not right holders but elected on the proposal as "public directors". In addition, IFPI in Israel reserved several board positions for founding members. In the USA, membership in boards is regularly prescribed by respective CMOs. Still, in some cases, there are preconditions regulated by the law.

2.4 Distribution of revenues

CMOs usually regulate distribution rules and distribution policy as a general policy of the organisation. So, Argentinian, Croatian, Belgian, Canadian, Columbian, Croatian, Czech, French, German, Greek, Hungarian, Israeli, Japanese, Korean, Netherlandian, New Zealandian, Portuguese, Spanish, Swiss and American CMOs regulate distribution rules within themselves. Exceptionally, in some cases, copyright laws also regulate distribution schemes for splitting the revenues between different categories of the right holders if they collect the revenues together. For example, this may be the case for revenues collected for communication to the public of commercial phonograms, where revenues must be distributed between performers and phonogram producers. Also, examples of legal intervention may be found in revenues collected jointly for different categories of right holders in private copying remuneration.

2.5 Autonomy of will to grant individual direct licences

The question was posed on how the law or legal practice reflects the author's will to grant licences individually and whether it is allowed for the user to obtain the licence directly from the represented author. The possibility of the "autonomy of will" to grant individual direct licences may be regulated in contracts between CMOs and right owners in New Zealand and Columbia. However, those contracts regularly forbid the "autonomy of will". In Israel, "autonomy of will" is permitted, but double payment is forbidden, which means that if the right owner issues a licence to the user, the CMO may not charge the user. A situation where "autonomy of will" to grant individual licences is possible, although the right owner already authorised the respective CMO to manage his right, occurs in Argentina, Canada, Greece, Japan, Spain and USA.

On the other hand, if the mandate for the representation was already given to CMO, the grant of individual licences is not permitted in Belgium, Croatia, Czech Republic, France, Germany, Hungary, Korea and Switzerland. Furthermore, the "autonomy of will" shall not be possible in mandatory collective management in Argentina, Canada, Greece, Japan, Spain and USA. However, in said countries, it may occur in other situations where collective management is voluntary. And finally, in Portugal and the Netherland, "autonomy of will" is not permitted, although it sometimes appears in practical application.

2.6 Possibility of non-commercial licences

"Autonomy of will" should be distinguished from the situation of issuing direct non-commercial licence by an individual right owner who already mandated CMO to represent his rights. This means, for example, that CMO will represent the author, but at the same time, he will remain entitled to licence his work under the *creative commons* licence.

If the mandates were already given to CMOs, the right owners would not be allowed at the same time to grant individual non-commercial licences in Argentina. In Canada and Germany, it is not possible for mandatory collective management. In Japan, the possibility of non-commercial licences is excluded in some cases. In Columbia and New Zealand, the possibility of non-commercial licences shall be regulated in a contract between CMO and the right owner. On the other hand, the possibility of individual non-commercial licences, although the mandate was already given to CMO, is guaranteed in Belgium, Croatia, the Czech Republic, France, Germany, Greece, Hungary, Israel, Japan, Korea, the Netherlands, Portugal, Spain, Switzerland and USA.

3 Relations between collective management organisations and users

3.1 Private copying remuneration

Private copying remuneration is regulated in most of the countries participating in this survey, such as Belgium, Canada, Croatia, the Czech Republic, France, Germany, Greece, Hungary, Israel, Japan, the Netherlands, New Zealand, Portugal, Spain and Switzerland. However, in Argentina, Columbia, Korea and USA, private copyright remuneration is not regulated in the law nor applied in practice.

In some countries, the general principle of contractual freedom is also respected regarding setting the tariff for private copying remuneration. Therefore, in those countries, a tariff for private copying remuneration shall be negotiated between CMOs and associations of users. For example, in Germany and New Zealand, there are no legal interventions to the contractual freedom while setting tariffs for private copying.

On the other hand, in Hungary, the approval of the Ministry of Justice is needed for such a tariff. In Japan, approval of an administrative body is needed, and in Switzerland, approval of the special Commission is required.

Moreover, in Switzerland, if there is no agreement on tariff for private copying remuneration, the Commission will be authorised to set the tariff after getting a prior non-binding opinion of the Price Supervisor.

In Croatia, voluntary arbitration is possible if there is no agreement on tariff between CMOs and associations of users. However, if the parties do not agree on arbitration, CMO will refer to the Council of Experts for a non-binding opinion on the tariff proposed by the respective CMOs.

In the Netherlands and France, a commission consisting of interested parties will set the tariff for private copying remuneration. In Canada, the tariff will be set by a Copyright Board.

A legislative act will set the tariff for private copying remuneration in several countries, such as the Czech Republic, Greece, Israel, and Portugal.

In Belgium, the tariff shall be set by a Royal Decree after acquiring a non-binding opinion of the Commission consisting of the representatives of the interested parties.

And finally, in Spain, before the tariff for private copying remuneration is set in a legislative act, the discussion of interested parties should be conducted, and advisory reports from Consumers Council and independent mediation or arbitration should be acquired.

Since the major use occurs on the internet, there was a question of whether there have been attempts to introduce private copying remunerations or levies for the use of protected subject matters on the internet, either in the form of a "flat fee" or a special tax. Only two countries reported on unsuccessful attempts. In Portugal, there was an attempt in 2016, and in Belgium, several attempts were rejected with the explanation that the ISPs do not perform communication to the public. In France, there is a special remuneration for NPVR services introduced. In all other countries, no attempts were reported. Those are Argentina, Canada, Croatia, the Czech Republic, Columbia, Germany, Greece, Hungary, Israel, Japan, Korea, the Netherlands, New Zealand, Spain, Switzerland and USA.

3.2 Tariff setting procedures

Depending on the legal tradition and national specific circumstances, there are generally five ways of setting tariffs, which may be applied individually or in a combination. Those are negotiations; a system of approval of a governmental body or independent committee; non-binding or binding opinion of an expert body; arbitration, mediation and/or conciliation procedure and a court review.

The first and the most desirable way of setting the tariffs are through negotiations between CMOs and users and their associations. Negotiations on tariffs usually occur in a way that CMO proposes a tariff. Then it is negotiated with the association of users or some individual users in case there is no association, for example, in broadcasting. In the European Union's Member States, such as Belgium, Croatia, the Czech Republic, France, Germany, Greece, Hungary, the Netherlands, Portugal and Spain, tariffs are proposed by the CMO. Then this proposal is negotiated and possibly amended and changed in the course of negotiations. The same is also applied in Switzerland, Columbia and New Zealand.

In Japan, on the other hand, consultations with users' associations will occur before the establishment of the tariff by the CMO. Finally, in some countries, such as Argentina, Canada and Israel, tariffs may be set solely by CMOs, without prior negotiations with users or their associations. In Israel, at the same time, tariffs for broadcasting are usually negotiated. In the USA, tariffs for public performance and interactive digital services are usually set by CMOs. In those countries, the law does not regulate negotiations.

Among other systems of how tariffs may be established is the approval of a governmental body or independent committee. This shall be the case in the Czech Republic, Hungary, the Netherlands, and Korea in some situations. For example, in the Czech Republic, approval is needed if the tariff is increased more than the inflation rate. If this is the case, the Ministry of Culture is invited to approve the tariff. In Hungary, after negotiations between CMOs and users' associations are completed, the tariff will be approved by the Ministry of Justice without the possibility of intervention in prices. The role of the Ministry of Justice is here only supervisory. In the Netherlands, the Copyright Supervisory Authority will analyse the excessiveness of the tariff increase and approve it. In Korea, a competent minister shall approve the CMO's proposed tariff after collecting opinions from interested parties and the opinion of the special Commission. Unlike the Czech Republic, Hungary and the Netherlands, where negotiations on proposed tariffs will take place before the approval of a governmental body or independent committee, the negotiation process is modified in Korea. There, the governmental body has an active and decisive role in approving the tariff. At the same time, the process of negotiations is replaced by the process of giving opinions to the competent minister.

And finally, in the USA, Copyright Royalty Board, as an independent expert committee, sets tariffs for some uses, such as retransmission, the performance of phonograms via non-interactive services, compulsory blanket licences for digital uses and some others.

In some countries, there is a possibility or obligation regulated in the respective copyright laws for the interested party to request an opinion of an expert body. Such opinion is regularly non-binding. For example, in Croatia, if there is no agreement on tariff and no agreement on arbitration for setting the tariff, CMO is obliged to ask for a non-binding opinion of the Council of Experts. The content of the opinion is also prescribed in the law and refers to whether the principles provided for setting the tariff were followed in creating the tariff in question. In Belgium, on the other hand, users may ask for an opinion from the Control Service or Competition Authority to examine whether CMO abused its dominant position. This opinion of the competent expert body will be binding.

Furthermore, for example, suppose there is no agreement on the tariff in Japan. In that case, the parties may submit the request to the Agency for Cultural Affairs, which will previously consult the Culture Council and then issue a non-binding opinion on the tariff. In Korea, upon request of the competent minister in the process of approval of the tariff, the Commission will issue a non-binding opinion on the proposed tariff.

Respective copyright laws in many countries regulate arbitration, mediation, or conciliation procedure for setting tariffs. This is systematised here as the fourth possible way how the tariff may be set.

The arbitration procedure is usually similar to the court procedure, only without formalities and based on the fairness criteria. While the result of the arbitration procedure is usually binding for both parties in a process, mediation is more flexible. The mediator is requested to assist the parties to achieve an agreement and therefore is invited to submit proposals of the settlement. The mediator should suggest the tariff based on the parties' suggestions. If the parties do not timely object to the mediators' proposal, it should be considered a binding tariff. In European Union member states, the mediation procedure is regulated in setting the tariffs for cable retransmission. This is a harmonised procedure on the European level. And finally, in a conciliation procedure, the role of the conciliator is even more flexible, and his suggestions will be accepted only voluntarily.

Continuing on this, in Croatia and Greece, the arbitration procedure on tariff is possible if the parties agree on arbitration, and in this case, the arbitrator's decision is final. A similar solution is applied in Portugal, where the parties may refer to the Committee of Experts for arbitration on tariff. In Switzerland, a tariff established by CMO may be challenged before the Arbitration Commission. In the Netherlands, the Tariff Tribunal will examine the reasonableness of the tariff, same as in New Zealand.

The Arbitration Board proposes the settlement in Germany, notwithstanding this proposal is not binding. Therefore, although named as arbitration, this is, in fact, mediation by the content. In Hungary, mediation is possible in the process of tariff setting before the Ministry of Justice's approval.

A conciliation procedure is possible during the negotiations on tariffs in the Czech Republic, whereby the conciliator's proposal is non-binding.

There are several possible extrajudicial procedures in Spain, where the relevant expert copyright body has mediation, arbitration, tariff determination and tariff control functions.

If invited by parties, the Communication Media Secretary may participate in a tariff setting procedure in Argentina. In Canada, although CMOs are entitled to set tariffs without any particular procedure, they are afterwards obliged to submit them to the Copyright Board, which may intervene if found necessary. In Japan, where there is no agreement on tariff for performers and phonogram producers' remuneration, the Agency for Cultural Affairs will fix it. In Korea, parties may call upon mediation or conciliation procedure, which is non-binding.

The court review is usually the final step in the tariff setting procedure. This is the fifth way on how the tariff may be established. In Belgium and Greece, users may submit the tariff to the general court if negotiations are unsuccessful. According to the general rules applied to arbitration procedures, there is a limited possibility to challenge the binding decision of the Arbitration Board on the tariff before a competent court in Croatia. In the Czech Republic, the court may be invited to rule on the tariff case if there is no agreement. Tariffs may be contested before the German courts if the parties do not accept the proposal of the Arbitration Board. Court review is possible also in Hungary, after the approval procedure before the Ministry of Justice. In the Netherlands, the tariff case may be submitted to the administrative court after the approval of the Supervisory Body. Similarly, the tariff may be submitted to the general court after the decision of the Tariff Tribunal on its reasonableness. The tariff may be challenged before a competent court immediately after being issued in Spain. In Switzerland, the decision of the Arbitration Commission may be reviewed by the court. After the intervention of the Copyright Board in Canada, the tariff may be subject to judicial review. In New Zealand, the decision of the Copyright Tribunal may be subject to the appeal in the court. And finally, in the USA, in cases where CMO sets the tariff, it may be disputed before the federal court.

3.3 Criteria for setting tariffs

Many different criteria are applied in setting the tariffs. Most European countries regulate these criteria in their respective copyright laws, trying to achieve a certain level of harmonisation. However, in other parts of the world, criteria for tariff setting are not harmonised in copyright laws, although there are not many differences in the practical application.

For example, in Belgium, the criteria for setting the tariffs must be objective and non-discriminatory. In addition, the remuneration must be reasonable concerning, among other things, the economic value of the use of the rights, nature and extent of the use and services and economic value of the service provided by the CMO.

Similar criteria will apply in Croatia, while some are defined in more detail. Here, tariffs must be reasonable in relation to, among other things, the economic value of the use of the rights on the market, taking into account the nature and scope of the use of the subject matters of protection, the economic value of the service provided by respective CMO and accordingly the tariffs applicable in other European Union member states. In addition to the said, same as in Germany, religious, social and cultural needs of users who belong to sensitive social groups of pensioners, children and people with disabilities will be taken into account to an appropriate extent.

According to Czech copyright law, tariffs will be based on objective and non-discriminatory criteria and criteria of proportionality. Therefore, the purpose, manner, scope, and circumstances of the use will be considered, alongside the criteria of whether the copyrighted works are used in the course of business and whether the use is of a direct economic character. Furthermore, it should also be taken into account the specificity of the place where the use of copyrighted works occurred, frequency of the use in the accommodation places where the works are used, number of rights holders for which CMO carries out collective management or the number of persons to whom the work has been notified.

In France, same as in all other European countries, it is stipulated that tariffs will be based on transparent, objective and non-discriminatory criteria. Furthermore, they should be reasonable and establish appropriate remunerations for the right holders. Particularly, while setting tariffs, the economic value of the given right will be taken into consideration, alongside additional criteria whether the licence refers to the exclusive right or right to remuneration, the nature and extent of the use of protected content, the given rights, and the economic value of the service provided by the CMO.

German copyright law regulates that generally, a percentage from the user's income will be considered while setting the tariff and that other method may apply. In addition, the share of the licensed repertoire in the entire repertoire and the economic value of the services given by the CMO should be considered. The users' religious, cultural and social concerns and the youth services' concerns are also criteria for setting the tariffs.

In Greece, criteria for setting the tariffs need to be objective. Therefore, the economic value of the use of the rights in trade and the nature and scope of the use concerning the economic value of the services provided by the CMO will be considered when setting tariffs.

In Hungary, all relevant circumstances shall be considered when setting tariffs. The principle of equal treatment shall be applied.

In Netherland copyright law, an increase of a tariff may not be excessive. However, it should be justified, and the users' interests should be considered. Comparable categories of users need to be treated equally. In addition, it is regulated that tariffs need to be reasonable and based on objective and non-discriminatory criteria. Reasonableness should be achieved in relation to the economic value of the use of the rights in trade, taking into account the nature and scope of the use of the repertoire and the value of the services of the CMO.

Portuguese copyright law also regulates the same criteria. These are non-discrimination, reasonableness and proportionality, the economic value of the rights, the result of a real market negotiation, the result of a real market negotiation, and the economic value of the use of the repertoire.

In Spain, tariffs will be established under reasonable conditions, considering the economic value of the use of rights and trying to achieve the right balance between parties. To this end, at least the following criteria shall be taken into account: the degree of effective use of the repertoire within the user's activity as a whole, the intensity and relevance of the use of the repertoire within the user's activity as a whole, the breadth of the repertoire of the management entity, the economic income obtained by the user for the commercial exploitation of the repertoire, the economic value of the service provided by the management entity to enforce the application of tariffs, the rates established by the CMO with other users for the same type of use, the rates established by similar CMOs in other European Union Member States, provided there is a homogeneous basis of comparison.

Fairness, user's income, used repertoire, the relationship between protected and unprotected works will be considered as criteria for setting the tariff, among other criteria, in Switzerland. Generally, up to 10% of the income should be taken for copyright and 3% for related rights.

Unlike others, the Argentinian report did not mention specific criteria for setting the tariff.

Canadian criteria for setting tariffs mention willing buyers and willing sellers acting in a competitive market with all relevant information. In addition to these basic criteria, public interests should be considered while setting tariffs alongside regulations and other appropriate criteria.

Proportionality, the income of the user, category of the user, technological capacity, the capacity of the venue, modality and intensity of the use in the commercialisation of a good or service and any other relevant criteria are mentioned in the Columbian report.

Israel's reported criteria are the revenue percentage, audience size, capacity, area, and other methods. In Japan, respective CMOs will develop criteria for different types of works and exploitations. Among others, the following criteria will be considered: type of user, the capacity of the public, size of the venue, duration of use, contract type.

CMOs in Korea develop different criteria, such as type of user, public capacity, venue size, duration of use, contract type, and various methodologies, such as percentage of the income.

In New Zealand, there are no statutory criteria for setting tariffs. Instead, CMOs develop the criteria, which include comparison with other tariffs, reasonability and non-discrimination.

In the USA, criteria for setting the tariffs are usually developed in the market and not prescribed by the law. For public performance and similar uses, the criteria used are, for example, the type of users, venue size and alike. On the other hand, criteria for non-interactive services are prescribed in the law. They include quantity and nature of the use, promotive service support, and willing buyer / willing seller criteria. All tariffs are based on economic, competitive and programming information. The tariffs will consider comparable types of uses.

3.4 Transparency of tariffs

According to the vast majority of the country reports, their publication ensures the transparency of tariffs. The tariffs are regularly published in Argentina, Belgium, Canada, Croatia, the Czech Republic, Columbia, Korea, France, Germany, Greece, Hungary, the Netherlands, Portugal, Spain, Switzerland and USA. In Israel, the tariffs are also usually published. Nevertheless, the ones negotiated or set by the arbitration may be unpublished.

In Japan, on the other hand, CMOs are not obliged to publish the tariffs. Instead, they publish data on collection. However, the report points out that transparency of tariffs is ensured by an obligation of CMOs to give the users 30 days to prepare for the application of new tariffs.

In New Zealand, licences are considered private arrangements. Therefore, no statutory transparency rules will apply to them.

3.5 Competition issues

In Argentina, Belgium, Canada, Columbia, Croatia, the Czech Republic, France, Germany, Greece, Hungary, Israel, Japan, Korea, the Netherlands, New Zealand, Portugal, Spain, Switzerland and USA, the competition laws do recognise the possibility of abuse of a dominant position of CMOs. While Hungary, Israel, Switzerland and New Zealand did not report on examples where the competition authority decided on the abuse of a dominant position by CMOs, other countries reported some cases.

For example, Croatia reported on decisions of the competition authorities where different discounts depending on the quantity of the media sold for private copying was characterised as the abuse of the dominant position of HDS ZAMP. As a result, this CMO was condemned to a monetary fine and directed to change its practices. Similarly, in Spain, there was a case on the abuse of a dominant position by SGAE because of non-transparent discounts for music broadcasting and discounts in a discriminatory and non-transparent manner for restaurants (weddings and similar occasions). According to another Spanish competition authority's decision, AISGE unilaterally and unjustifiably increased the general rate, on the one hand, and applied different rates and bonuses to different cinemas in a discriminatory manner on the other. In some other cases raised against AGEDI in Spain, it was decided that there were no abuses of dominant position (Radio case and AFEC-CEDRO case).

The Czech Republic reported on a CJEU case OSA, C-351/12, where the abuse of a dominant position was the imposing of unjustified high fees of the CMO with the monopoly position. SGAE in Spain was also fined because of unfair and excessive fees for concerts. In Greece, imposing excessive management fees and no transparency on information towards users and members was characterised as an abuse of a dominant position by a CMO.

On the other hand, a case against JASRAC in Japan showed that a comprehensive collection of royalties based on the broadcasters' revenues constitute „private monopolisation", but before the decision of the respective competition authority, the case was dismissed because the lawsuit against JASRAC was withdrawn. At the same time, in Columbia, France, Germany and Korea, cases raised against CMOs for abuse of their dominant position in setting tariffs showed no abuse. Moreover, in Belgium, the competition authority decided that the tariff is not abusive when built as a percentage of advertising revenues or when it establishes guaranteed minimums.

Furthermore, applying the same tariff to an organiser of the festival who claimed that his festival is different from the others does not constitute an abuse of a dominant position.

Also, the Portuguese case ended at the European Court of Justice (MEO, C-525/16). As a result, it was decided that all relevant circumstances need to be considered when assessing individual cases. Therefore, differences in applicable tariffs for two similar users are not likely to distort competition because they were not enough to cause the distortion on the market.

In Columbia, it was decided that the abuse of a dominant position is a practice of CMO not allowing its members to limit the given mandate and licence directly for broadcasting rights. A case against BUMA / STEMRA in Netherland showed the abuse of a dominant position of a CMO towards its members. As a result, it was recommended more flexibility towards members' mandates. „Consent decrees" (i.e. injunctions used as a way to regulate monopolistic industries) against ASCAP and BMI in the USA ended in non-exclusive representation agreements for public performance rights with their members.

Several pending cases were also reported. For example, in Argentina, the hotel association argues that SADAIC abused its dominant position. Before the Brussels Court of Appeal, the case against SABAM is pending. It was claimed that SABAM abuses its dominant position because of an excessive increase of tariffs from one year to another, not providing enough deductions, not sufficiently taking into account the repertoire represented, and because minimum fees imposed were too high. And finally, BUMA / STEMRA in the Netherlands were sued because of their allegedly discriminatory tariffs for background music. The decisions are expected to be issued in the meanwhile.

INFORME GENERAL: GESTIÓN COLECTIVA DE DERECHOS

Romana Matanovac Vučković*

Las respuestas al cuestionario preparado por ALAI - Grupo Checo fueron proporcionadas por los siguientes grupos nacionales de ALAI: Alemania, Argentina, Bélgica, Canadá, Colombia, Croacia, Corea, España, EE.UU., Francia, Grecia, Hungría, Israel, Italia, Japón, Nueva Zelanda, Países Bajos y Portugal. Los resultados se presentaron en el Congreso de Derechos de Autor ALAI 2019 en Praga el 18 de septiembre de 2019. Así pues, este texto refleja el estado de la cuestión a partir de septiembre de 2019 en cuanto a la situación legislativa y práctica en dichos países, contando con las respuestas proporcionadas por los grupos nacionales de ALAI.

El cuestionario se dividía en tres partes. La primera parte se refería a una visión general de la gestión colectiva. La segunda se dedicaba a la relación entre las organizaciones de gestión colectiva (OCM), los autores y otros titulares de derechos. Por último, la tercera parte examinaba la relación entre las OCMs y los usuarios. Las respuestas se presentarán más adelante.

1 Visión general de la gestión colectiva

1.1 Organizaciones de gestión colectiva: monopolios naturales o legales

A lo largo de la historia, las organizaciones de gestión colectiva fueron habitualmente percibidas como sociedades con una posición de monopolio en el mercado. Sin embargo, al mismo tiempo, se cuestionaba su posición de monopolio, especialmente por las normas de competencia. Algunos países decidieron responder a este desafío regulando su posición de monopolio en la ley. Algunos los dejaron como monopolios naturales. Algunos se orientaron hacia la competencia en el mercado, especialmente en Internet.

No son muchos los países que han decidido regular las organizaciones de gestión colectiva como monopolios legales. Entre ellos está Argentina, donde todas las OCMs tienen un monopolio legal. Croacia y la República Checa también regulan expresamente que las OCMs tienen el monopolio en sus leyes de derechos de autor. Esto

* Professor, University of Zagreb, Faculty of Law.

se refiere básicamente a las categorías de titulares de derechos y a las categorías de derechos, lo que significa que una categoría de titulares de derechos puede establecer una OCM por categoría de derechos. Sin embargo, una implicación práctica es que hay una OCM por categoría de titulares de derechos en sus mercados, regulando todas las categorías de derechos. La excepción al monopolio legal son las OCMs de los autores musicales para la concesión de licencias transfronterizas de música en Internet. Corea también establece de forma general el monopolio legal de las OCM, excepto para los autores de música.

En la mayoría de los países, como Israel, Canadá, Colombia, Francia, Grecia, Alemania, Nueva Zelanda, Portugal, España y Suiza, las OCMs son monopolios naturales. Esto significa que su posición de monopolio no está regulada en las leyes de derechos de autor de los respectivos países, sino que es consecuencia del comportamiento del mercado. Aunque la ley no establece que deba haber una sola OCM para una categoría de titulares de derechos y una categoría de derechos, el mercado ha desarrollado una sola OCM con una posición de monopolio con respecto a dichos criterios.

Varios países tienen una combinación de monopolios legales, monopolios naturales y, a veces, también OCMs competidoras. Por ejemplo, en Bélgica, las OCMs son monopolios naturales para los usos tradicionales de materias protegidas. Aun así, en lo que respecta a los derechos de remuneración, la retransmisión por cable y las OCMs de inyección directa son monopolios legales establecidos por la ley de derechos de autor correspondiente. Al mismo tiempo, no existe ningún monopolio de derechos en línea. Además, la ley húngara de derechos de autor establece el monopolio legal sólo en los casos en que la gestión colectiva de derechos es obligatoria. En los demás casos no hay monopolio legal y la competencia es posible, aunque en la práctica las OCMs suelen ser monopolios naturales.

Por ejemplo, en Japón no existe un monopolio para los derechos exclusivos, pero se establece un monopolio legal para los derechos de remuneración. En este grupo se encuentran la copia privada y la remuneración legal por la ejecución pública de fonogramas comerciales. En los Países Bajos, algunas OCMs son designadas legalmente como monopolios, por ejemplo, en el caso de la copia privada, el préstamo público y los derechos de vecindad. Por otra parte, algunas OCM, como las competentes para la gestión colectiva de los derechos de reproducción, son monopolios naturales. Por último, hay competidores de las OCMs en el mismo campo y categoría de derechos, básicamente en Internet.

En EE.UU., debido al tamaño del territorio y del mercado, a razones históricas y a circunstancias nacionales específicas, suele haber más de una OCM por categoría de derechos y categoría de titulares de derechos. Por ejemplo, hay varias OCMs para autores de música para la interpretación pública, como ASCAP, BMI, SESAC y GMA. Sin embargo, la autoridad de la competencia reconoce a las OCMs como monopolios naturales.

1.2 Gestión colectiva voluntaria, ampliada y obligatoria

En la encuesta se planteó la cuestión de si el sistema de derechos de autor distingue entre la gestión colectiva voluntaria, ampliada y obligatoria, y qué derechos se gestionan en cada régimen. Alemania, Bélgica, Canadá, Corea, Croacia, España, EE.UU., Francia, Grecia, Hungría, Israel, Japón, Nueva Zelanda, Países Bajos, Portugal y República Checa respondieron que sus leyes de derechos de autor contemplan la gestión colectiva voluntaria en la mayoría de los casos. Esto significa que el titular de los derechos puede optar por administrar sus derechos de autor individualmente o a través de un sistema de gestión colectiva. Por ejemplo, en el sistema de gestión colectiva voluntaria, aunque se establezca una OCM para alguna categoría de derechos, el titular del derecho puede decidir no administrar esta categoría de sus derechos a través de la OCM.

Colombia es un raro ejemplo en el que todos los derechos sólo pueden ser administrados voluntariamente de forma colectiva. La gestión colectiva nunca es obligatoria porque el Tribunal Constitucional decidió que la gestión colectiva obligatoria es contraria a la Constitución y, por tanto, está prohibida como modelo de gestión de los derechos de autor. Por otro lado, en Argentina la gestión voluntaria de los derechos de autor sólo se da en algunos casos. En la mayoría de los casos en este país, los derechos, como los de ejecución pública y reproducción, se administran obligatoriamente de forma colectiva a través de las OCM.

En Bélgica, la gestión colectiva obligatoria está prevista para los derechos de remuneración, la retransmisión por cable y la inyección directa. En Canadá, sólo los derechos de remuneración y los gravámenes se administran obligatoriamente de forma colectiva. La lista de derechos exclusivos administrados obligatoriamente de forma colectiva en Croacia es inusual en comparación con otros países de la Unión Europea. Allí, los derechos de radiodifusión deben administrarse colectivamente, junto con la retransmisión por cable, otros tipos de retransmisión y la inyección directa. Además, los derechos de remuneración y la copia privada también se administran obligatoriamente de forma colectiva. En la República Checa, la gestión colectiva obligatoria está regulada para las remuneraciones de los fonogramas comerciales, la copia privada y otros derechos de remuneración. Los derechos de retransmisión por cable, de copia privada y otros derechos de remuneración también serán de administración colectiva obligatoria en Francia. La ley alemana de derechos de autor establece una gestión colectiva obligatoria para los derechos de retransmisión por cable y las remuneraciones legales. En Grecia, la copia privada, la remuneración por la ejecución pública de los fonogramas comerciales, otros derechos de remuneración y la retransmisión por cable de los derechos exclusivos también se administran obligatoriamente de forma colectiva. Al igual que en Croacia, en Hungría, la difusión de obras musicales, la retransmisión por cable, el derecho de reproducción, la copia privada y otros derechos de remuneración estarán en el régimen de gestión colectiva obligatoria. Israel establece la gestión colectiva obligatoria para la copia privada y la remuneración de las actuaciones audiovisuales. Japón establece la gestión colectiva obligatoria para la copia privada y los derechos de remuneración legales para la ejecución pública de fonogramas comerciales. Corea reserva la gestión colectiva obligatoria sólo para los derechos de remuneración. En los Países Bajos, la lista de derechos que deben administrarse obligatoriamente de forma colectiva es más larga. La lista incluye la retransmisión por cable, la comunicación al público de obras cinematográficas, la copia privada, el préstamo y la compensación equitativa por fonogramas comerciales. En Nueva Zelanda, la gestión colectiva obligatoria se establece sólo cuando es necesario y no en la ley de derechos de autor.

La ley portuguesa de derechos de autor establece la gestión colectiva obligatoria de los cánones por copia privada, la remuneración por comunicación al público de fonogramas comerciales, las remuneraciones por derechos conexos y la retransmisión por cable como derecho exclusivo. En España, sólo los derechos de remuneración y las retransmisiones por cable se administran obligatoriamente de forma colectiva. Suiza tiene la misma regulación y, por último, en EE.UU. la gestión colectiva es obligatoria sólo en algunos casos, como las licencias legales y las obligatorias.

La gestión colectiva ampliada implica que el contrato firmado entre la OCM y el usuario afectará a todos los titulares de derechos de la misma categoría, aunque no todos hayan aceptado ser representados por la OCM respectiva. Esto significa que el contrato tiene un efecto ampliado. Sin embargo, en algunos países, este resultado no se conseguirá mediante el efecto ampliado del contrato. En cambio, se logrará mediante la presunción de representación de todos los titulares de derechos en la misma categoría. Por ejemplo, en Canadá se prevé una gestión colectiva ampliada para los derechos de remuneración cuando la gestión colectiva es obligatoria. En Croacia, existe una presunción de representación prevista para todos los derechos exclusivos y todos los derechos de remuneración. Esto significa que se considerará que la OCM representa a todos los titulares de derechos de la misma categoría, excepto a aquellos que hayan optado por no participar con una declaración escrita dirigida a la OCM respectiva. En la República Checa, la gestión colectiva ampliada se aplica a la interpretación pública de obras musicales, a la radiodifusión y a varios derechos de remuneración. En Francia se aplica a la gestión de los derechos sobre los libros considerados fuera de comercio, en Alemania a la retransmisión por cable como derecho exclusivo y en Grecia a la remuneración por copia privada y a la remuneración por comunicación al público de fonogramas comerciales. En Hungría, la gestión colectiva ampliada tendrá lugar en todas las situaciones en las que exista un monopolio natural y en las que la gestión colectiva sea obligatoria, por ejemplo, en la interpretación pública, incluida la radiodifusión, de obras musicales. En los Países Bajos, la gestión colectiva ampliada se aplica a los derechos de un régimen de gestión colectiva obligatoria. En Nueva Zelanda, sólo se aplica para el uso por necesidad y en Portugal para los derechos de los autores en la radiodifusión por satélite, excepto para las obras audiovisuales. Sin embargo, aquí la gestión colectiva ampliada se refiere a todos los usuarios que participan en la negociación colectiva.

1.3 Competencia entre OCMs

En la encuesta también se planteó la cuestión de si la competencia entre organizaciones de gestión colectiva está permitida en las jurisdicciones pertinentes. ¿En qué circunstancias, con qué frecuencia y en qué ámbitos puede producirse la competencia?

Sólo en varios países, como Argentina, Croacia, la República Checa y Corea, la competencia entre las OCMs no suele estar permitida. No obstante, en Croacia se prevé una excepción para las OCMs que administran los derechos de autor en línea de obras musicales y en Corea para todos los autores de música. En todos los demás países, la competencia está permitida, pero no en todas partes es de aplicación práctica. Por ejemplo, está permitido y existe en Bélgica. Aunque está permitida, salvo para los derechos de copia privada y de remuneración, en la práctica no hay competencia en Canadá. La misma situación se da en Colombia, donde la competencia entre OCMs está permitida pero no existe en la práctica. En Francia, está permitido, apoyado y sugerido. En Alemania existe competencia en la gestión de los derechos de autor de la música en línea, donde el repertorio está fragmentado. En todas las demás situaciones, aunque se permite, la competencia no existe en la práctica.

En Grecia, la competencia no está prohibida, y existía en la práctica para el repertorio musical, pero entonces una de las OCMs de música colapsó. Desde entonces, no ha habido competencia en la aplicación práctica. En Hungría, la competencia de las OCMs está generalmente permitida, excepto en los casos en los que la gestión colectiva es obligatoria o cuando se aplica la gestión colectiva ampliada. A pesar de la posibilidad legal de competencia, todas las OCMs son monopolios naturales en Hungría. En Israel, el panorama de las OCMs está fragmentado. En Japón, existen múltiples OCMs para los derechos musicales, tras la posibilidad de competencia. Allí, sólo para los derechos de remuneración legales no se permite la competencia. La legislación neerlandesa sobre derechos de autor también permite la competencia entre las OCM, y se aplica en varias situaciones. Aunque la ley lo permite, en la práctica no existe competencia entre las OCMs en Portugal. En España, en cambio, está permitido y existe en algunos casos, como el del repertorio audiovisual. En Suiza, la competencia existe para los derechos en línea y en otras situaciones no se aplica aunque lo permita la ley. La ley de derechos de autor de EE.UU. permite y fomenta la competencia entre las OCM. Sin embargo, en lo que respecta a los derechos de autor de la música, no se permite en absoluto un mandato exclusivo.

Las entidades de gestión independientes, competidoras de las OCM, están reguladas en la Directiva 2014/26/UE sobre gestión colectiva de derechos de autor. Por ello, las legislaciones nacionales de los Estados miembros de la Unión Europea, como Croacia, la República Checa, Alemania, Grecia, los Países Bajos y España, las mencionan en sus informes sobre la competencia. Sin embargo, el problema de las entidades de gestión independientes y su regulación en dicha Directiva y en las legislaciones nacionales es la incoherencia en cuanto a la transparencia de sus actividades y, por tanto, la desigualdad de trato en la gestión colectiva de los derechos de autor.

1.4 Forma de las organizaciones de gestión colectiva

Según los informes, la mayoría de los países regulan en sus respectivas legislaciones que las OCMs deben organizarse como organizaciones sin ánimo de lucro. Son, por ejemplo, Alemania, Argentina, Croacia, Corea, Francia, Israel, Países Bajos, Portugal, República Checa y Suiza. Según la legislación de Bélgica y España, las OCMs nacionales deben constituirse como organizaciones sin ánimo de lucro. Aun así, las OCMs extranjeras, procedentes de los demás Estados miembros de la Unión Europea, que realizan licencias transfronterizas en línea, también pueden establecerse como asociaciones o empresas con ánimo de lucro. En Canadá, las OCMs suelen constituirse como organizaciones sin ánimo de lucro, pero también es posible que una empresa u otras organizaciones con ánimo de lucro operen como OCM. Aunque en Colombia está previsto en la ley que las OCMs se constituyan como organizaciones sin ánimo de lucro, los titulares de derechos pueden seguir gestionándolos a través de otras formas de asociación. También es posible tener empresas con ánimo de lucro que exploten negocios de gestión colectiva en Grecia. Sin embargo, una peculiaridad de la legislación griega permite a la agencia estatal actuar como OCM en casos excepcionales. Así ocurrió en la vida real con la OCM, que opera bajo la AEPI, pero que colapsó en 2018. En la práctica, en Hungría las OCMs son organizaciones sin ánimo de lucro, aunque existe la posibilidad de constituirlas como empresas con ánimo de lucro. En Japón, donde la remuneración estatutaria se administra obligatoriamente de forma colectiva, está regulado que esta OCM debe constituirse como una organización sin ánimo de lucro. Lo mismo ocurre con todos los demás casos en los que la gestión colectiva es obligatoria. En Nueva Zelanda y EE.UU. es posible, aunque no obligatorio, constituir las OCMs como organizaciones sin ánimo de lucro. Sin embargo, en EE.UU. existen varias OCMs como empresas con ánimo de lucro.

1.5 Contribución de las organizaciones de gestión colectiva al desarrollo cultural y social de la sociedad

Aparte de los EE.UU., donde las OCMs tradicionalmente no deducen para fines culturales y sociales y donde las leyes no apoyan su participación en el desarrollo cultural y social de la sociedad, ni voluntariamente, todos los demás países tienen algunas actividades dirigidas a la sensibilización de las OCMs para actuar en este sentido. Por ejemplo, las OCMs argentinas crean regularmente fondos culturales y sociales de forma voluntaria. En Bélgica, las OCMs pueden destinar hasta un 30% de las remuneraciones por copia privada y hasta un 10% de otras remuneraciones a fines culturales y sociales. En Croacia, la legislación sobre derechos de autor establece porcentajes similares, permitiendo a las organizaciones de gestión colectiva deducir para fines culturales, sociales y educativos. Por encima de eso, hasta el 3% de los ingresos totales de la OCM puede deducirse para programas de concienciación y antipiratería. En Canadá, las OCMs conceden regularmente subvenciones y apoyan económicamente los premios a los logros culturales y artísticos. Del mismo modo, los programas culturales y educativos pueden financiarse en parte con las remuneraciones recaudadas por las OCMs. Las OCMs colombianas deducen voluntariamente hasta un 10% para fines culturales y sociales.

En la República Checa, las OCMs pueden crear fondos con fines culturales, sociales y educativos, mientras que en Francia los fondos culturales también se aplican de forma voluntaria. No obstante, está regulado que el 25% de las remuneraciones por copia privada se destine a fondos culturales y también a cantidades no distribuibles. En Alemania no hay limitaciones especiales para las deducciones culturales y sociales, salvo las regulaciones que deben basarse en criterios justos y reglas fijas y transparentes. En Grecia, las cantidades no distribuibles se destinan a los fondos culturales, sociales y educativos de las OCM. En Hungría, esas cantidades se asignan al Fondo Cultural Nacional con la misma finalidad. Además, el 25% de las remuneraciones por copia privada también se destinan al Fondo Nacional y Cultural. Israel tiene pocas asignaciones voluntarias para fines culturales y sociales. Estas OCMs financian premios y galardones culturales y artísticos y pueden crear fondos para creadores necesitados y fines similares. Las OCMs pueden apoyar las conferencias y universidades japonesas relacionadas con la cultura, las artes y los conciertos. Pueden deducir hasta un 20% de las remuneraciones por copia privada para actividades de sensibilización y fondos culturales. Cuando la gestión colectiva es obligatoria, las OCMs pueden destinar cantidades no distribuibles a actividades de interés público de Corea.

En los Países Bajos, las deducciones por motivos culturales y sociales se aplican tradicionalmente en la práctica. Sin embargo, desde que la Autoridad de Supervisión emitió nuevas normas, se volvió reticente a las deducciones, que ya no son bienvenidas. Algunas OCMs aplican voluntariamente los fondos culturales en Nueva Zelanda. En Suiza, la mayoría de las OCMs se asignan regularmente a fines culturales y sociales. La ley portuguesa de derechos de autor establece que no menos del 5% de las remuneraciones recaudadas se destinen a fondos culturales, sociales y de sensibilización. Además, no menos del 20% de la remuneración por copia privada se destinará a actividades culturales. Y, por último, la legislación española obliga a las OCMs a promover actividades culturales y de sensibilización.

2 Relaciones entre las organizaciones de gestión colectiva y los titulares de derechos

2.1 ¿Tienen los titulares de derechos derecho a ser representados?

Se planteó la cuestión de si los autores y otros titulares de derechos tienen derecho a ser representados por una OCM. La mayoría de los países, especialmente los miembros de la Unión Europea, tienen este derecho, como Bélgica, Canadá, Israel, Japón y los Países Bajos. Sin embargo, Alemania, Argentina, Croacia, España, Francia, Grecia, Hungría, República Checa y Suiza distinguen entre miembros y autores representados. Esto significa que no todos los autores y titulares de derechos tienen derecho a ser miembros de la OCM, pero todos tienen derecho a estar representados. Como en muchos otros países europeos, se ha establecido un procedimiento especial de reclamación interna para resolver los litigios relacionados con el derecho a ser representado en Portugal. Además, varias OCMs recomiendan procedimientos alternativos de resolución de litigios relacionados con el derecho a ser representado y algunos tribunales ordinarios.

En cambio, en Colombia, Corea, Nueva Zelanda y EE.UU., no existe el derecho a ser representado, ni en la legislación ni en la aplicación práctica.

2.2 Resolución de litigios entre titulares de derechos por "doble reivindicación"

Los litigios de "doble reivindicación" se refieren a situaciones en las que dos o más titulares de derechos afirman poseer derechos contradictorios sobre el mismo objeto. Por ejemplo, dos autores reclaman la propiedad de los derechos de autor de una misma canción como autores individuales. Se trata de una situación conflictiva porque cada reivindicación excluye la de la parte contraria. Las OCMs suelen tener algunas disposiciones en sus actos internos sobre cómo proceder cuando aparece una "doble reivindicación".

Argentina, por ejemplo, establece sistemas opcionales de resolución de litigios internos, a la vez que los tribunales ordinarios también están a disposición de las partes en litigio. En Bélgica, Canadá, Francia, Japón, Países Bajos y Suiza, se invita a los titulares de los derechos a resolver el litigio mientras se suspenden los pagos por los objetos de protección objeto de litigio. En Alemania, Colombia, Croacia, España, EE.UU., Grecia, Hungría y la República Checa, existe un mecanismo alternativo de resolución de litigios regulado en las leyes de derechos de autor para los litigios por "doble reivindicación" como posible salida. Aun así, las partes tienen a su disposición mecanismos especiales de reclamación dentro de las OCMs y, por supuesto, los tribunales ordinarios. Mientras el litigio está pendiente, se suspenden los pagos relacionados con los objetos de protección en litigio. En Israel, la mayoría de las OCMs disponen de medios alternativos de resolución de litigios, mientras que algunas OCMs prevén un arbitraje obligatorio sobre la cuestión en litigio. En Corea, las partes enfrentadas eligen entre el tribunal ordinario y los mecanismos alternativos de resolución de litigios. La legislación portuguesa regula, además, los mecanismos de reclamación y resolución de litigios en el seno de las OCMs y los mecanismos alternativos de resolución de litigios. En Nueva Zelanda no existe un procedimiento específico para las "dobles reivindicaciones".

2.3 Participación de los autores en los consejos de administración de las organizaciones de gestión colectiva

La participación de los autores en los consejos de administración de las organizaciones de gestión colectiva suele estar regulada por las OCMs que, en la mayoría de los casos, establecen algunas condiciones previas a la candidatura para participar como miembros de los consejos de administración o de supervisión dentro de las OCM. Esta es la situación en Alemania, Argentina, Bélgica, Croacia, Corea, España, Francia, Grecia, Hungría, Nueva Zelanda, Países Bajos, Portugal, República Checa y Suiza. Las condiciones previas establecidas son, en general, la duración de la pertenencia a la respectiva OCM y los ingresos mínimos percibidos por los derechos. Además, la composición de los consejos debe reflejar la estructura de las diferentes categorías de titulares de derechos representados. Esto significa que debe lograrse un equilibrio entre los miembros de diferentes sectores, *es decir,* diferentes categorías de titulares de derechos, en la mayoría de los casos. Un ejemplo de ello es la OCM canadiense que opera bajo el nombre de ReSound.

La antigüedad también puede desempeñar un papel como criterio de participación en los consejos de administración y de supervisión. En Israel, además, algunas OCMs tienen varios directores (un tercio) sin intereses personales en la OCM, lo que significa que no son titulares de derechos sino que son elegidos a propuesta como "directores públicos". Además, la IFPI de Israel tiene reservados varios puestos en el consejo de administración para los miembros fundadores. En EE.UU., la pertenencia a los consejos de administración es establecida regularmente por las respectivas OCM. Aun así, en algunos casos, existen condiciones previas reguladas por la ley.

2.4 Distribución de los ingresos

Las OCMs suelen regular las normas y la política de distribución como política general de la organización. Así, las OCMs argentinas, croatas, belgas, canadienses, colombianas, checas, francesas, alemanas, griegas, húngaras, israelíes, japonesas, neerlandesas, neozelandesas, portuguesas, españolas y estadounidenses regulan las normas de distribución en su seno. Excepcionalmente, en algunos casos, las leyes de derechos de autor también regulan los esquemas de distribución para dividir los ingresos entre las diferentes categorías de los titulares de los derechos, si estos recaudan los ingresos conjuntamente. Por ejemplo, este puede ser el caso de los ingresos recaudados por la comunicación al público de fonogramas comerciales, donde los ingresos deben distribuirse entre los artistas intérpretes o ejecutantes y los productores de fonogramas. También se pueden encontrar ejemplos de intervención legal en los ingresos recaudados conjuntamente para diferentes categorías de titulares de derechos en la remuneración por copia privada.

2.5 Autonomía de la voluntad para conceder licencias directas individuales

Se planteó la cuestión de cómo la ley o la práctica jurídica refleja la voluntad del autor de conceder licencias individualmente y si se permite que el usuario obtenga la licencia directamente del autor representado. La posibilidad de la "autonomía de la voluntad" para conceder licencias directas individuales puede estar regulada en los contratos entre las OCMs y los titulares de derechos en Nueva Zelanda y Colombia. Sin embargo, esos contratos suelen prohibir la "autonomía de la voluntad". En Israel, se permite la "autonomía de la voluntad", pero está prohibido el doble pago, lo que significa que si el propietario del derecho expide una licencia al usuario, la OCM no puede cobrarle. Se da una situación en la que es posible la "autonomía de la voluntad" para conceder licencias individuales, aunque el titular del derecho ya haya autorizado a la respectiva OCM a gestionar su derecho, en Argentina, Canadá, Grecia, Japón, España y EE.UU..

Por otro lado, si el mandato de representación ya se ha otorgado a la OCM, la concesión de licencias individuales no está permitida en Alemania, Bélgica, Croacia, Corea, Francia, Hungría, República Checa y Suiza. Además, la "autonomía de la voluntad" no será posible en la gestión colectiva obligatoria en Argentina, Canadá, Grecia, Japón, España y EE.UU.. Sin embargo, en dichos países, puede darse en otras situaciones en las que la gestión colectiva es voluntaria. Y, por último, en Portugal y los Países Bajos, no se permite la "autonomía de la voluntad", aunque aparece a veces en la aplicación práctica.

2.6 Posibilidad de licencias no comerciales

La "autonomía de la voluntad" debe distinguirse de la situación de expedición de una licencia no comercial directa por parte de un titular de derechos individual que ya ha encargado a la OCM la representación de sus derechos. Esto significa, por ejemplo, que la OCM representará al autor, pero al mismo tiempo seguirá teniendo derecho a licenciar su obra bajo la licencia *bienes comunes de la creación*.

Si los mandatos ya se han otorgado a las OCM, los titulares de los derechos no podrán conceder al mismo tiempo licencias individuales no comerciales en Argentina. En Canadá y Alemania no es posible la gestión colectiva obligatoria. En Japón, la posibilidad de licencias no comerciales está excluida en algunos casos. En Colombia y Nueva Zelanda, la posibilidad de conceder licencias no comerciales se regulará en un contrato entre la OCM y el propietario del derecho. Por otro lado, la posibilidad de obtener licencias individuales no comerciales, aunque el mandato ya se haya otorgado a la OCM, está garantizada en Alemania, Bélgica, Croacia, Corea, España, EE.UU., Francia, Grecia, Hungría, Israel, Japón, Países Bajos, Portugal y República Checa.

3 Relaciones entre las organizaciones de gestión colectiva y los usuarios

3.1 Remuneración por copia privada

La remuneración de la copia privada está regulada en la mayoría de los países que participan en esta encuesta, como Alemania, Bélgica, Canadá, Croacia, España, Francia, Grecia, Hungría, Israel, Japón, Nueva Zelanda, Países Bajos, Portugal, República Checa y Suiza. Sin embargo, en Argentina, Colombia, Corea y EE.UU., la remuneración de los derechos de autor privados no está regulada en la ley ni se aplica en la práctica.

En algunos países también se respeta el principio general de libertad contractual en lo que respecta a la fijación de la tarifa de la remuneración por copia privada. Por lo tanto, en esos países, se negociará una tarifa para la remuneración de la copia privada entre las OCMs y las asociaciones de usuarios. Por ejemplo, en Alemania y Nueva Zelanda no hay intervención legal a la libertad contractual a la hora de fijar las tarifas de la copia privada.

En cambio, en Hungría, se necesita la aprobación del Ministerio de Justicia para dicha tarifa. En Japón, se necesita la aprobación de un organismo administrativo, y en Suiza, la aprobación de la Comisión especial.

Además, en Suiza, si no hay acuerdo sobre la tarifa de la remuneración por copia privada, la Comisión estará autorizada a fijar la tarifa tras obtener un dictamen previo no vinculante por parte del Supervisor de Precios.

En Croacia, el arbitraje voluntario es posible si no hay acuerdo sobre las tarifas entre las OCMs y las asociaciones de usuarios. No obstante, si las partes no se ponen de acuerdo sobre el arbitraje, la OCM se remitirá al Consejo de Expertos para que emita un dictamen no vinculante sobre la tarifa propuesta por las respectivas OCM.

En los Países Bajos y Francia, una comisión formada por las partes interesadas fijará la tarifa de la remuneración por copia privada. En Canadá, la tarifa la fijará una Junta de Derechos de Autor.

Un acto legislativo fijará la tarifa de la remuneración de las copias privadas en varios países, como la República Checa, Grecia, Israel y Portugal.

En Bélgica, la tarifa se fijará mediante un Real Decreto tras recabar un dictamen no vinculante de la Comisión formada por los representantes de las partes interesadas.

Y, por último, en España, antes de fijar la tarifa de la remuneración por copia privada en un acto legislativo, deberían debatir las partes interesadas, y adquirirse los informes consultivos del Consejo de Consumidores y la mediación o el arbitraje independientes.

Dado que el mayor uso se produce en Internet, se planteó la cuestión de si se ha intentado introducir remuneraciones por copia privada o gravámenes por el uso de materias protegidas en Internet, ya sea en forma de "tarifa plana" o de impuesto especial. Sólo dos países informaron de intentos fallidos. En Portugal, hubo un intento en 2016, y en Bélgica, varios intentos fueron rechazados con la explicación de que los ISP no realizan comunicación al público. En Francia se ha introducido una remuneración especial para los servicios de NPVR. En todos los demás países, no se registraron intentos. Se trata de Alemania, Argentina, Canadá, Corea, Croacia, España, EE.UU., Grecia, Hungría, Israel, Japón, Nueva Zelanda, República Checa y Suiza.

3.2 Procedimientos de fijación de tarifas

Dependiendo de la tradición jurídica y de las circunstancias específicas de cada país, existen generalmente cinco formas de fijar las tarifas, que pueden aplicarse individualmente o de forma combinada. Se trata de negociaciones; un sistema de aprobación de un organismo gubernamental o un comité independiente; un dictamen no vinculante o vinculante de un organismo de expertos; un procedimiento de arbitraje, mediación y/o conciliación y una revisión judicial.

La primera forma, y la más deseable, de fijar las tarifas es mediante negociaciones entre las OCMs y los usuarios y sus asociaciones. Las negociaciones sobre las tarifas suelen producirse de manera que la OCM propone una tarifa. Luego se negocia con la asociación de usuarios o con algunos usuarios individuales en caso de que no haya asociación, por ejemplo, en la difusión. En los Estados miembros de la Unión Europea, como Alemania, Bélgica, Croacia, España, Francia, Grecia, Hungría, Países Bajos y Portugal, las tarifas son propuestas por la OCM. A continuación, esta propuesta se negocia y, posiblemente, se modifica y cambia en el transcurso de las negociaciones. Lo mismo ocurre en Suiza, Colombia y Nueva Zelanda.

En Japón, en cambio, se consultará a las asociaciones de usuarios antes de que la OCM establezca la tarifa. Por último, en algunos países, como Argentina, Canadá e Israel, las tarifas pueden ser fijadas únicamente por las OCM, sin negociaciones previas con los usuarios o sus asociaciones. En Israel, al mismo tiempo, se suelen negociar las tarifas para la radiodifusión. En EE.UU., las tarifas de los servicios digitales interactivos y de espectáculos públicos suelen ser fijadas por las OCM. En esos países, la ley no establece las negociaciones.

Entre otros sistemas de cómo pueden establecerse las tarifas está la aprobación de un organismo gubernamental o un comité independiente. Este será el caso de la República Checa, Hungría, los Países Bajos y Corea en algunas situaciones. Por ejemplo, en la República Checa, es necesaria la aprobación si la tarifa se incrementa más que la tasa de inflación. En ese caso, se invita al Ministerio de Cultura a aprobar la tarifa. En Hungría, una vez concluidas las negociaciones entre las OCMs y las asociaciones de usuarios, la tarifa será aprobada por el Ministerio de Justicia sin posibilidad de intervenir en los precios. El papel del Ministerio de Justicia es aquí sólo de supervisión. En los Países Bajos, la Autoridad de Supervisión de los Derechos de Autor analizará el carácter excesivo del aumento de las tarifas y lo aprobará. En Corea, un ministro competente aprobará la tarifa propuesta por la OCM tras recabar las opiniones de las partes interesadas y el dictamen de la Comisión especial. A diferencia de la República Checa, Hungría y los Países Bajos, donde las negociaciones sobre las tarifas propuestos tendrán lugar antes de la aprobación de un organismo gubernamental o un comité independiente, el proceso de negociación se modifica en Corea. Allí, el organismo gubernamental tiene un papel activo y decisivo en la aprobación de la tarifa. Al mismo tiempo, el proceso de negociación se sustituye por el proceso de emisión de dictámenes al ministro competente.

Y, por último, en EE.UU., el Copyright Royalty Board, como comité de expertos independientes, fija las tarifas para algunos usos, como la retransmisión, la interpretación de fonogramas a través de servicios no interactivos, las licencias globales obligatorias para usos digitales y algunos otros.

En algunos países, existe la posibilidad o la obligación regulada en las respectivas leyes de derechos de autor de que la parte interesada solicite el dictamen de un organismo de expertos. Dicho dictamen no es regularmente vinculante. Por ejemplo, en Croacia, si no hay acuerdo sobre la tarifa y no hay acuerdo sobre el arbitraje para fijarla, la OCM está obligada a pedir un dictamen no vinculante del Consejo de Expertos. El contenido del dictamen también está establecido en la ley y se refiere a si se han seguido los principios previstos para la fijación de la tarifa al crear la tarifa en cuestión. En Bélgica, en cambio, los usuarios pueden solicitar un dictamen al Servicio de Control o a la Autoridad de la Competencia para examinar si la OCM ha abusado de su posición dominante. Este dictamen del organismo de expertos competente será vinculante.

Además, por ejemplo, supongamos que no hay acuerdo sobre la tarifa en Japón. En ese caso, las partes pueden presentar la solicitud a la Agencia de Asuntos Culturales, que consultará previamente al Consejo de Cultura y emitirá posteriormente un dictamen no vinculante sobre la tarifa. En Corea, a petición del ministro competente en el proceso de aprobación de la tarifa, la Comisión emitirá un dictamen no vinculante sobre la tarifa propuesta.

Las leyes de derechos de autor de muchos países regulan el procedimiento de arbitraje, mediación o conciliación para fijar las tarifas. Esto se sistematiza aquí como la cuarta forma posible de fijar la tarifa.

El procedimiento de arbitraje suele ser similar al procedimiento judicial, sólo que sin formalidades y basado en criterios de equidad. Mientras que el resultado del procedimiento de arbitraje suele ser vinculante para ambas partes en proceso, la mediación es más flexible. Se pide al mediador que ayude a las partes a alcanzar un acuerdo y, por tanto, se le invita a presentar propuestas de acuerdo. El mediador debe sugerir la tarifa basándose en las sugerencias de las partes. Si las partes no se oponen en su momento a la propuesta de los mediadores, debe considerarse que se trata de una tarifa vinculante. En los Estados miembros de la Unión Europea, el procedimiento de mediación está regulado en la fijación de las tarifas de retransmisión por cable. Se trata de un procedimiento armonizado a nivel europeo. Y, por último, en un procedimiento de conciliación, el papel del conciliador es aún más flexible, y sus sugerencias sólo se aceptarán voluntariamente.

Siguiendo con esto, en Croacia y Grecia, el procedimiento de arbitraje sobre la tarifa es posible si las partes están de acuerdo con el arbitraje, y en este caso, la decisión del árbitro es definitiva. Una solución similar se aplica en Portugal, donde las partes pueden recurrir al Comité de Expertos para el arbitraje sobre la tarifa. En Suiza, una tarifa establecida por la OCM puede ser impugnada ante la Comisión de Arbitraje. En los Países Bajos, el Tribunal de Tarifas examinará el carácter razonable de la tarifa, al igual que en Nueva Zelanda.

La Junta Arbitral propone el acuerdo en Alemania, aunque esta propuesta no es vinculante. Por tanto, aunque se denomine arbitraje, se trata en realidad de una mediación por el contenido. En Hungría, la mediación es posible en el proceso de fijación de tarifas antes de la aprobación del Ministerio de Justicia.

Durante las negociaciones sobre las tarifas en la República Checa puede haber un procedimiento de conciliación, en el que la propuesta del conciliador no es vinculante.

En España existen varios procedimientos extrajudiciales posibles, en los que la entidad experta en derechos de autor correspondiente tiene funciones de mediación, arbitraje, determinación y control de tarifas.

Si es invitado por las partes, el Secretario de Medios de Comunicación puede participar en un procedimiento de fijación de tarifas en Argentina. En Canadá, aunque las OCMs tienen derecho a fijar las tarifas sin ningún procedimiento particular, posteriormente están obligadas a presentarlas al Consejo de Derechos de Autor, que puede intervenir si lo considera necesario. En Japón, donde no hay acuerdo sobre la tarifa de remuneración de los artistas y productores de fonogramas, la Agencia de Asuntos Culturales la fijará. En Corea, las partes pueden recurrir al procedimiento de mediación o conciliación, que no es vinculante.

La revisión judicial suele ser el último paso del procedimiento de fijación de tarifas. Esta es la quinta forma de establecer la tarifa. En Bélgica y Grecia, los usuarios pueden presentar la tarifa ante el tribunal general si las negociaciones no tienen éxito. Según las normas generales aplicadas a los procedimientos de arbitraje, existe una posibilidad limitada de impugnar la decisión vinculante de la Junta Arbitral sobre la tarifa ante un tribunal competente en Croacia. En la República Checa, se puede invitar al tribunal a pronunciarse sobre el caso de las tarifas si no hay acuerdo. Las tarifas pueden ser impugnadas ante los tribunales alemanes si las partes no aceptan la propuesta de la Junta Arbitral. También puede haber revisión judicial en Hungría, tras el procedimiento de aprobación ante el Ministerio de Justicia. En los Países Bajos, el caso de las tarifas puede someterse al tribunal administrativo tras la aprobación del Órgano de Supervisión. Asimismo, la tarifa puede someterse al tribunal general tras la decisión del Tribunal de Tarifas sobre su razonabilidad. La tarifa puede ser impugnada ante un tribunal competente inmediatamente después de ser emitida en España. En Suiza, la decisión de la Comisión de Arbitraje puede ser revisada por el tribunal. En Canadá, tras la intervención del Consejo de Derechos de Autor, la tarifa puede ser objeto de revisión judicial. En Nueva Zelanda, la decisión del Tribunal de Derechos de Autor puede ser objeto de recurso en los tribunales. Y, por último, en EE.UU., en los casos en que la OCM fija la tarifa, ésta puede ser impugnada ante el tribunal federal.

3.3 Criterios para fijar las tarifas

Se aplican muchos criterios diferentes para fijar las tarifas. La mayoría de los países europeos regulan estos criterios en sus respectivas leyes de derechos de autor, intentando alcanzar un cierto nivel de armonización. Sin embargo, en otras partes del mundo, los criterios para la fijación de tarifas no están armonizados en las leyes de derechos de autor, aunque no hay muchas diferencias en la aplicación práctica.

Por ejemplo, en Bélgica, los criterios para fijar las tarifas deben ser objetivos y no discriminatorios. Además, la remuneración debe ser razonable en relación, entre otras cosas, con el valor económico de la utilización de los derechos, la naturaleza y el alcance de la utilización y los servicios y el valor económico del servicio prestado por la OCM.

En Croacia se aplicarán criterios similares, aunque algunos se definen con más detalle. En este caso, las tarifas deben ser razonables en relación, entre otras cosas, con el valor económico de la utilización de los derechos en el mercado, teniendo en cuenta la naturaleza y el alcance de la utilización de las materias objeto de protección, el valor económico del servicio prestado por la respectiva OCM y, en consecuencia, las tarifas aplicables en otros Estados miembros de la Unión Europea. Además, al igual que en Alemania, se tendrán debidamente en cuenta las necesidades religiosas, sociales y culturales de los usuarios pertenecientes a grupos sociales sensibles como los pensionistas, los niños y las personas con discapacidad.

Según la ley checa de derechos de autor, las tarifas se basarán en criterios objetivos y no discriminatorios y en criterios de proporcionalidad. Por lo tanto, se tendrán en cuenta la finalidad, el modo, el alcance y las circunstancias del uso, junto con los criterios de si las obras protegidas por derechos de autor se utilizan en el curso de la actividad empresarial y si el uso tiene un carácter económico directo. Además, también debe tenerse en cuenta la especificidad del lugar donde se ha producido la utilización de las obras protegidas por derechos de autor, la frecuencia de la utilización en los lugares de alojamiento donde se utilizan las obras, el número de titulares de derechos para los que el organismo de gestión colectiva lleva a cabo la gestión colectiva o el número de personas a las que se ha notificado la obra.

En Francia, al igual que en todos los demás países europeos, se estipula que las tarifas se basarán en criterios transparentes, objetivos y no discriminatorios. Además, deben ser razonables y establecer remuneraciones adecuadas para los titulares de los derechos. En particular, a la hora de fijar las tarifas, se tendrá en cuenta el valor económico del derecho concedido, junto con otros criterios adicionales, como si la licencia se refiere al derecho exclusivo o al derecho de remuneración, la naturaleza y el alcance del uso de los contenidos protegidos, los derechos concedidos y el valor económico del servicio prestado por la OCM.

La ley alemana de derechos de autor establece que, por lo general, se tendrá en cuenta un porcentaje de los ingresos del usuario a la hora de fijar la tarifa y que puede aplicarse otro método. Además, hay que tener en cuenta la proporción del repertorio autorizado en el conjunto del repertorio y el valor económico de los servicios prestados por la OCM. Las preocupaciones religiosas, culturales y sociales de los usuarios, así como las de los servicios para jóvenes, son también criterios para fijar las tarifas.

En Grecia, los criterios para fijar las tarifas deben ser objetivos. Por lo tanto, a la hora de fijar las tarifas se tendrá en cuenta el valor económico de la utilización de los derechos en el comercio y la naturaleza y el alcance de la utilización en relación con el valor económico de los servicios prestados por la OCM.

En Hungría, se tendrán en cuenta todas las circunstancias pertinentes a la hora de fijar las tarifas. Se aplicará el principio de igualdad de trato.

En la legislación neerlandesa sobre derechos de autor, el aumento de una tarifa no puede ser excesivo. Sin embargo, debe estar justificado y se deben tener en cuenta los intereses de los usuarios. Las categorías comparables de usuarios deben recibir el mismo trato. Además, se establece que las tarifas deben ser razonables y basarse en criterios objetivos y no discriminatorios. El carácter razonable debe lograrse en relación con el valor económico de la utilización de los derechos en el comercio, teniendo en cuenta la naturaleza y el alcance de la utilización del repertorio y el valor de los servicios de la OCM.

La ley portuguesa de derechos de autor también establece los mismos criterios. Se trata de la no discriminación, la razonabilidad y la proporcionalidad, el valor económico de los derechos, el resultado de una negociación en el mercado real, el resultado de una negociación en el mercado y el valor económico de la utilización del repertorio.

En España, las tarifas se establecerán en condiciones razonables, teniendo en cuenta el valor económico del uso de los derechos y tratando de lograr el justo equilibrio entre las partes. Para ello, se tendrán en cuenta al menos los siguientes criterios: el grado de utilización efectiva del repertorio en el conjunto de la actividad del usuario, la intensidad y relevancia de la utilización del repertorio en el conjunto de la actividad del usuario, la amplitud del repertorio de la entidad de gestión, los ingresos económicos obtenidos por el usuario a raíz de la explotación comercial del repertorio, el valor económico del servicio prestado por la entidad de gestión para hacer efectiva la aplicación de las tarifas, las tarifas establecidas por la OCM con otros usuarios para el mismo tipo de uso, las tarifas establecidas por OCMs similares en otros Estados miembros de la Unión Europea, siempre que exista una base homogénea de comparación.

En Suiza, la equidad, los ingresos de los usuarios, el repertorio utilizado, la relación entre las obras protegidas y las no protegidas serán considerados como criterios para fijar la tarifa, entre otros. Por lo general, se debe tomar hasta un 10% de los ingresos para los derechos de autor y un 3% para los derechos conexos.

A diferencia de otros, el informe argentino no menciona criterios específicos para fijar la tarifa.

Los criterios canadienses para fijar las tarifas mencionan a los compradores y vendedores dispuestos que actúan en un mercado competitivo con toda la información pertinente. Además de estos criterios básicos, debe tenerse en cuenta el interés público a la hora de fijar las tarifas junto con la normativa y otros criterios adecuados.

La proporcionalidad, los ingresos y la categoría del usuario, la capacidad tecnológica, la capacidad del local, la modalidad e intensidad del uso en la comercialización de un bien o servicio y cualquier otro criterio relevante se mencionan en el informe de Colombia.

Los criterios indicados por Israel son el porcentaje de ingresos, el tamaño de la audiencia, la capacidad, la superficie y otros métodos.

En Japón, las respectivas OCMs elaborarán criterios para los distintos tipos de obras y explotaciones. Entre otros, se tendrán en cuenta los siguientes criterios: tipo de usuario, capacidad de público, tamaño del local, duración del uso, tipo de contrato.

Las OCMs de Corea desarrollan diferentes criterios, como el tipo de usuario, el aforo público, el tamaño del local, la duración del uso, el tipo de contrato y diversas metodologías, como el porcentaje de los ingresos.

En Nueva Zelanda no hay criterios legales para fijar las tarifas. En cambio, las OCMs elaboran los criterios, que incluyen la comparación con otras tarifas, la razonabilidad y la no discriminación.

En EE.UU., los criterios para fijar las tarifas suelen desarrollarse en el mercado y no están establecidos por la ley. En el caso de los espectáculos públicos y usos similares, los criterios utilizados son, por ejemplo, el tipo de usuarios, el tamaño del local y otros similares. Por otro lado, los criterios para los servicios no interactivos están establecidos en la ley. Entre ellos se encuentran la cantidad y la naturaleza del uso, el apoyo de los servicios de promoción y los criterios de comprador dispuesto/vendedor dispuesto. Todas las tarifas se basan en información económica, competitiva y de programación. Las tarifas considerarán tipos de usos comparables.

3.4 Transparencia de las tarifas

Según la gran mayoría de los informes de los países, su publicación garantiza la transparencia de las tarifas. Las tarifas se publican regularmente en Alemania, Argentina, Bélgica, Canadá, Croacia, Corea, España, EE.UU., Francia, Grecia, Hungría, Países Bajos, Portugal y República Checa. En Israel, las tarifas también suelen publicarse. No obstante, las negociadas o fijadas por el arbitraje pueden ser inéditas.

En Japón, en cambio, las OCMs no están obligadas a publicar las tarifas. En cambio, publican los datos de la recaudación. Sin embargo, el informe señala que la transparencia de las tarifas está garantizada por la obligación de las OCMs de dar a los usuarios 30 días para preparar la aplicación de las nuevas tarifas.

En Nueva Zelanda, las licencias se consideran acuerdos privados. Por lo tanto, no se les aplica ninguna norma de transparencia legal.

3.5 Problemas de competencia

En Alemania, Argentina, Bélgica, Canadá, Colombia, Croacia, Corea, España, EE.UU., Francia, Grecia, Hungría, Israel, Japón, Nueva Zelanda, Países Bajos, Portugal y República Checa, las leyes de competencia reconocen la posibilidad de abuso de posición dominante de las OCM. Mientras que Hungría, Israel, Suiza y Nueva Zelanda no informaron de ejemplos en los que la autoridad de la competencia decidiera sobre el abuso de una posición dominante por parte de las OCM, otros países informaron de algunos casos.

Por ejemplo, Croacia informó sobre las decisiones de las autoridades de competencia en las que se calificaron como abuso de posición dominante de HDS ZAMP los diferentes descuentos en función de la cantidad de soportes vendidos para copia privada. Como resultado, esta OCM fue condenada a una multa monetaria y se le ordenó cambiar sus prácticas. Asimismo, en España, hubo un caso sobre el abuso de posición dominante por parte de la SGAE debido a los descuentos no transparentes para la difusión de música y los descuentos de forma discriminatoria y no transparente para los restaurantes (bodas y ocasiones similares). Según otra decisión de la autoridad de competencia española, AISGE incrementó de forma unilateral e injustificada la tarifa general, por un lado, a la vez que aplicó diferentes tarifas y bonificaciones a diferentes cines de forma discriminatoria. En algunos otros casos planteados contra AGEDI en España, se decidió que no existían abusos de posición dominante (caso Radio y caso AFEC-CEDRO).

La República Checa informó sobre el caso TJUE OSA, C-351/12, en el que el abuso de posición dominante era la imposición de tasas elevadas e injustificadas de la OCM con posición de monopolio. La SGAE en España también fue multada por las tarifas injustas y excesivas de los conciertos. En Grecia, la imposición de tasas de gestión excesivas y la falta de transparencia en la información hacia los usuarios y miembros se calificó como un abuso de posición dominante por parte de una OCM.

Por otra parte, un caso contra JASRAC en Japón demostró que el cobro global de cánones basado en los ingresos de las emisoras constituye una "monopolización privada", pero antes de la decisión de la autoridad de competencia respectiva, el caso fue desestimado porque se retiró la demanda contra JASRAC. Al mismo tiempo, en Colombia, Francia, Alemania y Corea, los casos planteados contra las OCMs por abuso de su posición dominante en la fijación de tarifas no mostraron ningún abuso. Además, en Bélgica, la autoridad de competencia decidió que la tarifa no es abusiva cuando se construye como un porcentaje de los ingresos publicitarios o cuando establece mínimos garantizados.

Además, la aplicación de la misma tarifa a un organizador del festival que alegó que su festival es diferente de los demás no constituye un abuso de posición dominante.

El caso portugués terminó en el Tribunal de Justicia Europeo (MEO, C-525/16). Por ello, se ha decidido que hay que tener en cuenta todas las circunstancias pertinentes a la hora de evaluar los casos individuales. Por lo tanto, no es probable que las diferencias en las tarifas aplicables a dos usuarios similares distorsionen la competencia porque no fueron suficientes para causar la distorsión en el mercado.

En Colombia, se decidió que el abuso de posición dominante es una práctica de la OCM que no permite a sus miembros limitar el mandato dado y la licencia directamente para los derechos de difusión. Un caso contra BUMA / STEMRA en los Países Bajos demostró el abuso de posición dominante de una OCM hacia sus miembros. Por ello, se recomendó una mayor flexibilidad hacia los mandatos de los miembros. Los "decretos de consentimiento" (es decir, las medidas cautelares utilizadas como forma de regular las industrias monopolísticas) contra ASCAP y BMI en los EE.UU. terminaron en acuerdos de representación no exclusiva de los derechos de ejecución pública con sus miembros.

También se informó de varios casos pendientes. Por ejemplo, en Argentina, la asociación hotelera sostiene que SADAIC abusó de su posición dominante. El Tribunal de Apelación de Bruselas tiene pendiente el caso contra SABAM. Se alegó que SABAM abusa de su posición dominante por un aumento excesivo de las tarifas de un año a otro, por no prever suficientes deducciones, por no tener suficientemente en cuenta el repertorio representado y porque las tarifas mínimas impuestas eran demasiado elevadas. Y, por último, se demandó a BUMA / STEMRA en los Países Bajos por sus tarifas supuestamente discriminatorias para la música de fondo. Se espera que las decisiones se emitan mientras tanto.

INDIVIDUAL AND COLLECTIVE MANAGEMENT RIGHTS: A THREE-DIMENSIONAL SNAPSHOT BY WAY OF CONCLUDING REMARKS

Paul Torremans*

1 Introduction

Allow me, by way of conclusion of these study days, to summarise matters in two words: Complexity and Technology or, in Spanish, 'complejidad y tecnología', or, in French, 'une situation complexe pour laquelle existe une solution technologique'. But let us get into a little bit more detail.

2 Continuity and Complexity

What has become clear in the opening moments of this conference is that individual management of rights, whilst it has always been difficult from an historical point of view, remains an option. Technology now opens new options, but these are not accessible for all players in this area. In other words, collective management of rights is still required and it will remain required, and even the norm, for the future.

There is still an imbalance of power that is to be redressed and collective management of rights is the main tool to do so. Here we find a main element of continuity. But if one looks at the other side of the coin there is also constant change. There is a transformation as a result of the never-ending technological change, or should one say the never-ending technological challenge. But against this background one still needs a collective management organisation as a tool to control the power of the intermediaries and to make sure that there is a fair remuneration for authors and creators. That became abundantly clear on the first day of this conference. However, that task has become a particularly complex one in the digital world, as there are increasing amounts of data that are to be treated, and, frankly, only a CMO with a certain power and with a certain form of financing can do that.

* Professor of Intellectual Property Law, School of Law, University of Nottingham, United Kingdom.

3 Private International Law with an Additional Layer of Complexity

The relationship between users and CMOs attracted a lot of attention in the very rich national reports that were drafted in preparation for this conference. In reality that very relationship stood out as the main point that attracted attention. However, this is where an additional element of complexity comes in. Let me try to explain. If we assume that copyright is at least approximatively a property right or a private right, if, secondly, a collective management organisation then takes often an assignment of such a right and if, thirdly, foreign authors are able to join CMOs, then one has an element of private international law.[1] We saw for example in the national reports that in relation to private copying tariff setting often ends with a court review in a fair number of national systems. Private international law will then tell you that there is a choice of law element involved and there is also a choice of jurisdiction or of court. in practical terms, at least in the European Union, the Brussels I Regulation[2] may them provide the answers. We will need to determine which court has jurisdiction to carry out such a review and when carrying out a review the private international law rules of that court and its national system of law will then determine which will be the law applicable to the review. One can run the same exercise for the criteria for tariff setting and yet again we see that these are very varied. In other words, depending on the applicable law the approach and the outcome may be radically different. Again, courts are asked to control these matters and in a trans-border world the question then arises which court will have the power to do so, which court will have jurisdiction in this respect. Luckily for us in this example the answer to the question which criteria such a competent court will use, that matter may on this point be a bit easier. It is, after all, fairly likely that the court will apply its own domestic rules in a domestic situation, taking account of copyright's territorial approach.

We also saw that in a number of countries administrative control is the solution, rather than control by the court. It has to be said that this is probably the easier solution here, or should we say the less complex option. At least, it is fairly clear in these cases that local administrations will apply their local law to deal with the matter. There is in other words no real choice of court or choice of applicable law problem here.

1 See J.J. Fawcett and Paul L.C. Torremans, *Intellectual Property and Private international Law*, Oxford University Press (2nd ed, 2011).

2 Regulation (EU) No 1215/2012 of the European Parliament and of the Council of 12 December 2012 on jurisdiction and the recognition and enforcement of judgments in civil and commercial matters [2012] OJ L 351/1.

4 Competition

Having dealt with this additional layer of complexity in terms of private international law by looking at these national reports the conference then turned to the issue of competition. It needs to be said straight away that there are two aspects to this. On the one hand there is competition on its own or as such and on the other hand there is competition law. In respect to the latter our president Frank Gotzen said in his opening words that copyright should not be subjected to pure competition law or at least CMO governance should not be submitted to pure competition law on the basis that CMOs also have cultural, social and trade union functions. In other words, they are more than mere undertakings.

It is fair to say that competition law cases in the European Union have over the years taken account of the essential function and the specific subject matter of copyright.[3] On that basis there is a certain balance that is struck, but there is more to it. It is indeed no longer sufficient to merely look at these historical cases and to say that competition law does take, to an extent, account of the specificities of copyright. Competition law does after all merely work as an external control mechanism on certain uses of copyright and the exclusive rights it is made up of. If one looks at the recent CMO directive[4] as a basis for copyright[5] then there is clearly a need that emerges for copyright to strike such a balance internally. That is even more the case if one looks at the decisions of the Court of Justice of the European Union of 29 July 2019, more specifically the judgments of the Grand Chamber in *Spiegel Online GmbH v Volker Beck*[6] and *Funke Medien NRW GmbH v Bundesrepublik Deutschland*[7]. In these seminal judgments the court clearly articulated the idea that the balance with fundamental rights needs to be struck inside copyright. There is no room for outside limitations and exceptions to be imposed by outside tools such as human rights. The balance needs to be struck internally in the area of intellectual property. In other words, one needs to interpret limitations and exceptions in the light of the interest of other fundamental rights. The same kind of principles can obviously also be applied when it comes to the application of competition law. Maybe, or rather probably, the answer is that copyright has the opportunity to deal with matters internally, to deal with the competition concerns on an internal basis. That would in turn reduce the need to use competition law and that is rather a positive idea after all, as competition law, as we were told, is a sector

3 Paul Torremans, *Holyoak and Torremans Intellectual Property Law*, Oxford University Press (9th ed, 2019), Ch. 18.

4 Directive 2014/26/EU of the European Parliament and of the Council of 26 February 2014 on collective management of copyright and related rights and multi-territorial licensing of rights in musical works for online use in the internal market [2014] OJ L 84/72.

5 Irini Stamatoudi and Paul Torremans (eds), *EU Copyright Law: A Commentary*, Edward Elgar Publishing (2014), Ch. 14.

6 Case C-516/17 *Spiegel Online GmbH v Volker Beck* ECLI:EU:C:2019:625.

7 Case C-469/17 *Funke Medien NRW GmbH v Bundesrepublik Deutschland* ECLI:EU:C:2019:623.

neutral tool that really can take no account of all the particularities of copyright. Despite certain flexibilities it remains a rather blunt tool. If one adds to that that we no longer have any block exemptions and nor do we have any ex ante notification option, that means that it is hard to predict the outcome in advance. There is no ex ante control and parties need to have a guess all by themselves. On that basis it is far better to internalise matters and keep competition law as the ultimate tool. The ultimate tool that for example could control excessive royalty rates at the very last moment. A further developed set of tools inside copyright would be far more specific, far more aware of the detailed characteristics of copyright and, above all, far more predictable.

That answer remains true and valid even if one accepts that the reality of the experience over the years shows that overall competition law played a rather positive role, rather than a negative role in relation to copyright and collective management.

But let us leave competition law to one side. In more general terms there is also competition, rather than competition law. What this conference showed us is that in this respect there are very different models around in the United States and the European Union, to name just these two, in terms of how we organise competition in the collective management field. Each of these models strikes a careful balance to enable and enhance competition and that careful balance comes as a package. In the US competition is focussed on services, services that can be delivered on top of the tariffs, for which there is no competition. Collective management on the other hand is seen rather as a necessary evil. By contrast, in the European Union the whole system is directed towards the opening up of markets and making multi-territorial licensing a possibility or a reality. That shows indeed clearly that the models are different and, on that basis, it is not a very sound idea to try and cherry pick one element in one model and try to incorporate it in the other model.

5 The 2019 Copyright Directives

Maybe the 2019 copyright directives[8] fit in here too, in this context of the internalisation of matters by copyright. These directives do after all develop the European copyright system further in a significant way and thereby enable that system to deal with ever more matters internally.[9] From that perspective the focus shifts to compe-

[8] Directive (EU) 2019/790 of the European Parliament and of the Council of 17 April 2019 on copyright and related rights in the Digital Single Market and amending Directives 96/9/EC and 2001/29/EC [2019] OJ L 130/92 and Directive (EU) 2019/789 of the European Parliament and of the Council of 17 April 2019 laying down rules on the exercise of copyright and related rights applicable to certain online transmissions of broadcasting organisations and retransmissions of television and radio programmes, and amending Council Directive 93/83/EEC [2019] OJ L 130/82.

[9] See Irini Stamatoudi and Paul Torremans (eds), *EU Copyright Law: A Commentary*, Edward Elgar Publishing (2nd ed, 2020), (forthcoming at the time of writing).

tition that is to be stimulated and organised internally, rather than to competition law that is needed as an external tool to handle certain situations and problems.

We heard on the other hand that exclusivity remains an essential element for collective management organisations. But that does not stand necessarily in the way of competition, as the author can split his or her works up over the various collective management organisations on the basis of the type of work, as he or she can change between collective management organisations on an annual basis and as he or she can join foreign collective management organisations. On this basis it is likely that the copyright system can address its issues of competition and competitiveness whilst holding on to exclusivity.

6 Setting and Litigating Tariffs

A further point that was discussed during this conference was the idea of setting and litigating tariffs. Yet again it became clear that there are many different models around. Each of these models has, however, its own issues. None of them is perfect. All of them come with certain issues. What is clear, is that there remains a rule for blanket licencing. Picking and choosing may well be an attractive idea in theory, especially for some of the larger players in the industry, but it comes with many disadvantages for other players. The key element here is that there is a massive need for transparency and on that point, there is still a lot of work to be done. Once more, this is work that has to be done inside copyright. We have to make the system of setting and litigating tariffs transparent.

7 The Current European Landscape

What also became clear during the conference is that we no longer solely have the traditional collective management organisations operating in this field. They have been complemented by IMEs and individual labels also administer a number of their own rights. What became clear from the presentations is that this has become a rather complex picture. There is a vast number of players, each of which has a slightly different task, administers a slightly different repertoire and these differences are also reproduced in a slightly different configuration on a cross border basis. In other words, on top of all that, in different countries and in different member states of the European Union the division of repertoire is not necessarily the same. The complete picture is therefore not simple. On the contrary, the picture is complex, or maybe one could be provocative by saying the system resembles a mess.

The question can indeed be asked whether the picture has not become too complex, specifically for the majority of small players, individual users and individual authors. We also see that kind of complexity in relation to the right of withdrawal. The detailed implications of that right of withdrawal are not yet clear and the picture is indeed rather messy. Once more, some form of simplification seems to be imposing itself if the system is to improve and if its efficiency and transparency are to be enhanced.

8 The Three Dimensions

I hope that along these concluding remarks it has become clear where these three dimensions that I referred to in my title come from. In a first dimension, there is a strong need for collective management organisations to engage in what I could call operational streamlining. An operational streamlining that also allows a detailed set of rules of copyright in the light of the 2019 directives to deal with matters internally. Internal copyright regulation is a stimulation of competition and it is clearly the best way forward. And that conclusion, be it at first glance a purely European one, can be replicated in the United States and in other territories around the world.

The second dimension is clearly that in terms of multi-territorial licensing one does open the door for problems of private international law. These issues cannot be ignored and need to be dealt with. Copyright is in that respect not free standing and there are private international law rules around that also apply to copyright. These are in most jurisdictions standard rules that apply across the board and to which we are also subjected. A further and third dimension is that of competition, competition that we all need, that we need to encourage, but that we need in a simplified and streamlined copyright landscape. And, of course, finally there is competition law as the ultimate external control for the system of collective rights management.

9 Conclusion

By way of conclusion, I would merely like to say that we have a very complex system in front of us. We are operating in an increasingly complex reality due to the introduction of forms of competition and multi-territorial licences. That complexity needs to be addressed. We need to simplify matters somewhat. We need, for example, to make sure that the endless overlaps, the kind of conflicting repertoires, etc. are addressed. That needs to be done by copyright and by the copyright community, inside our copyright home. The main message I would like to take away from this conference is that what we need is further harmonisation. That means further internal rules that put our house in order. We can deal with matters internally. We can do this as a copyright community and if successful that would be a very positive result. On the other hand, there is also a need to do this as the current system is not necessarily working for all parties involved. In other words, simplification and streamlining are not a luxury that we can do at a time when it becomes convenient. It is a necessity that we need to address in the years to come, rather than in the decades to come.

PART V
ANNEXES

ALAI 2019 CONGRESS PROGRAMME

Thursday, 19th September, 2019

Opening Session

Welcome Speeches

- Christian Archambeau, Executive Director of the European Union Intellectual Property Office
- Frank Gotzen, president of ALAI
- Rudolf Leška, president of ALAI Czech Republic

Keynote Speech

- Gadi Oron, CISAC, Director General: "Collective Management of Rights in a Transforming Market"

General Report

- Romana Matanovac Vučković, University of Zagreb, Faculty of Law: Collective Management of Rights

Competition and Collective Management of Copyright

Chair:

- Uma Suthersanen, Queen Mary University of London

Speakers:

- Daniel J. Gervais, Vanderbilt University Law School: Is Competition Among Collectives Leading to Positive Changes in Collective Management?
- Josef Drexl, Max Planck Institute for Innovation and Competition: The Contributions and Limitations of Competition Law to Regulate Collective Rights Management in the EU
- Sylvie Nérisson, Université de Bordeaux: Competition and Collective Management of Copyright
- Caroline Bonin, SACEM, Legal Department Director: Competition and collective management – practical experience

Setting and Litigating the Tariffs

Chair:

- Mina Kianfar, UNVERZAGT VON HAVE, Partner

Panellists:

- Jeannette Dietrich, Netflix, Director Global Music: Authors' and performers' rights: the challenges of global production and distribution
- Andrea Kokonis, SOCAN, Associate General Counsel: Practice of the Copyright Board
- Delia Lipszyc, University of Buenos Aires, Faculty of Law: Argentinian experience with competition and tariff setting

Five Years with the European Union Directive on Collective Management of Copyright

Chair:

- Jacqueline Seignette, Höcker Advocaten, Partner

Panellists:

- Véronique Delforge, European Commission, Directorate General CONNECT, Legal Officer – Copyright: EU Directive on Collective Right Management
- Maria Mercedes Frabboni, University of Sussex: Current UK perspectives and the developments of the expected withdrawal from the EU
- Tobias Holzmüller, GEMA, General Counsel: Five years with the EU Directive on collective management
- Gábor Faludi, Szecskay Attorneys at Law, Of Counsel, external counsel for Artisjus: Impact of EU policy on cultural diversity and small countries
- Massimo Scialò, Soundreef: Independent Management Entity on the Example of Soundreef

Friday, 20th September, 2019

Opening Speech

- Sylvie Forbin, WIPO, Deputy Director General of Copyright and Creative Industries

Technology Driven Copyright Management

Chair:
- Ysolde Gendreau, University of Montreal, Faculty of Law (CAN)

Panellists:
- Viveca Still, counsellor at the Ministry of Education and Culture:, Developing the Copyright infrastructure – metadata and beyond
- Tomas Ericsson, AMRA: Introducing AMRA and its business model
- Jose Luis Sevillano, AIE, Managing Director; SCAPR, member of the Board and President of Databases Committee: Technology Driven CMOs: The Importance od CMOs in the Digital Era
- Charlotte Aïdan, SACEM, Head of International Legal Affairs: uRights Project
- Jörn Radloff, Bytedance London, Head Counsel Music Licensing, EMEA: TikTok digital content licensing

Collective Management of Non-Music Repertoire

Chair:
- Silke von Lewinski, Max Planck Institute for Innovation and Competition

Panellists:
- Marie Anne Ferry-Fall, ADAGP, General Director: Spécificités des arts visuels dans la gestion collective des droits d'auteur
- Frederic Haber, Copyright Clearance Center, General Counsel: Voluntary Licensing of Text Based Works in the United States: Copyright Clearance Center
- Hubert Tilliet, SACD, Legal Department Director: Collective management in the audiovisual field

Managing Copyright in Cyberspace and Across the Borders

Chair:
- Markéta Trimble, University of Nevada, Las Vegas, William S. Boyd School of Law (USA)

Panellists:

- Bernt Hugenholtz, University of Amsterdam, Institute for Information Law, Faculty of Law: Territoriality from EU perspective
- Eleni-Tatiani Synodinou, University of Cyprus, Faculty of Law: Geoblocking in EU Copyright Law
- Pavel Koukal, Masaryk University, Faculty of Law: Digital Content Portability and its Relation to Conformity with the Contract
- Adriana Moscoso, Ministry of Culture of the Kingdom of Spain, Director of Cultural Industries and Cooperation: Collective Management in Cyberspace
- Satoshi Watanabe, Chairman of CISAC Asia-Pacific Regional Committee on Asian IP offices' policies on collective management: Asian IP Offices' Policies on Collective Management

Mandatory and Extended Collective Management – a Panacea or Limitation?

Chair:

- Jukka Liedes, Chairman, Finnish Copyright Society

Panellists:

- Mihály Ficsor, Chairman, Central and Eastern European Copyright Alliance (CEECA): EU acquis with regard to the extended and mandatory collective management
- Raquel Xalabarder, Open University of Catalonia, Faculty of Law and Political Science: he Equitable Remuneration of Audiovisual Authors: A Proposal of Unwaivable Remuneration Rights Under Collective Management
- Regan A. Smith, U.S. Copyright Office, General Counsel and Associate Register of Copyrights: New U.S. legislation on collective management of music
- Johan Axhamn, Special Government Adviser at the Swedish Ministry of Justice: Extended and Mandatory Collective Management in theory and practice

Closing Speech

- Paul Torremans, University of Nottingham, Faculty of Social Sciences: Individual and Collective Management of Rights: A Three-Dimensional Snapshot by Way of Concluding Remarks

ALAI General Assembly

www.ingramcontent.com/pod-product-compliance
Lightning Source LLC
Chambersburg PA
CBHW071431230926
51846CB00001B/188
9789403507576